A Vietnamese Family Chronicle

三代祖阮貴公字福寧　姓阮貴氏號貞深流落失傳本族招魂墓

在塘馬龍寺外边為此祖姓忌日及墳墓一皆失記

四代祖阮貴公字福善　姓阮貴氏號美行

五代祖阮貴公字光疇　姓黎氏號慈在

六代祖阮貴公字慶善　姓阮貴氏號慈全

公生下二支甲支德医公字廷銓祀在甲支長堂　奉祀伯庸　乙支阮貴公

號純謹祀在乙支長堂　奉祀嗣西甲支德医公生三男長男故蒭

鄉貢嘉興府知府阮貴公諱悠字廷鉡號福永諱和靖先生

次男延遂　奉祀次次男延禰　奉祀乙支純謹公生二男長男福壽詩　奉祀次男

福卣公延遂　自第六代以前其有園池田地以供忌腸歷代事迹以書時

其傳遺中間被刼徒焼盡祠堂及譜記維有其后筆記蹤遺來

A Vietnamese Family Chronicle

Twelve Generations on the
Banks of the Hat River

by
Nguyen Trieu Dan

McFarland & Company, Inc., Publishers
Jefferson, North Carolina, and London

This book on our village
and ancestry is dedicated to my parents.

It is written for my children
Huynh Chau, Trieu Minh, Trieu Quang and Hoang Anh,
who have grown up far away from their homeland.

My wife has been a constant source of strength.
She and the whole family have been wonderfully supportive.
This book owes much to them.

Frontispiece: A page of the chronicle written in the scholarly—or Chinese—script by my grandfather, circa 1910. Written on absorbent rice paper, with a writing brush made of rabbit hair, the page measures 14.5cms by 29.5cms. The characters should be read from top down and right to left. The photo shows part of one page and the whole of the following page.

British Library Cataloguing-in-Publication data are available

Library of Congress Cataloguing-in-Publication Data

Nguyen, Trieu Dan, 1930–
    A Vietnamese family chronicle : twelve generations on the banks of
the Hat River / by Nguyen Trieu Dan.
    p. cm.
    ISBN 0-89950-592-9 (lib. bdg. : 50# alk. paper) ∞
    1. Nguyên family. 2. Kim Bài (Vietnam)—Genealogy. 3. Vietnam—
Genealogy. I. Title.
DS559.93.K56N48   1991
929'.2'09597—dc20
                                       90-53513
                                          CIP

Manufactured in the United States of America

McFarland & Company, Inc., Publishers
Box 611, Jefferson, North Carolina 28640

Contents

Prologue

"Stone wears out with time.
But my heart will not forget."

The family chronicle, which we have managed to preserve through decades of war and the tragedy of exile, was compiled at the beginning of this century by my grandfather. It is being kept on the ancestors' altar in our Melbourne home, in a red and black lacquer box. Written in Chinese script, the traditional way of writing for scholars at that time, it opens with the following sentences:

> A tree has countless branches and a dense canopy of leaves, because its roots grow deep into the soil.
> The water flows out in a multitude of streams and currents, for it has its source a long way back in the mountains.
> He who inherits the merit acquired by his ancestors for many generations, has children and grandchildren in abundance.

The origins of a family are found not only in its lineage going back to the earliest ancestors in memory. They are also to be found in the land which has seen the generations succeed one another, has nourished them, and to whose fold all of us wish to return at the end of our lives. Attachment to our native land is as strong as to our kin. This is especially so for the Vietnamese who, for thousands of years, have lived in the delta of the Red River. The village and its rice fields, the river winding its way, the mountains on the horizon, have formed the setting of our lives since times immemorial. They have become part of our very soul.

This attachment to the land has been tinged with sorrow and sadness because, now as before, it has been the lot of many Vietnamese to spend their lives far from the villages where they were born.

They may have been soldiers sent to the borders, either to safeguard the country against aggression, or to take part in military campaigns to extend the national territory. They may have had to leave the overpopulated delta of the north and go south in search of new means of livelihood. It may have been, also, that the changing fortunes of war and the rise and fall of dynasties have forced those on the losing side into exile. Vietnam has had a tumultuous and violent history. During times of upheaval, which have been frequent, its people's fate has been at the mercy of the tide of events, just as in the rainy season, the pieces of wood floating in the Red River are at the mercy of its angry current.

In the old days, to leave one's village at all meant in most instances never to return. Few soldiers who went to the borders ever came back. If not killed in battle, they rarely survived the deadly climate of those areas. Eleven generations ago, our forebears were uprooted from their village and became refugees after the dynasty they served was overthrown. They stayed away for ten years or more, before some of them were able to go back. Many of our kinsmen migrated to the south during the eighteenth and nineteenth centuries and all contact with them was lost. One of our ancestors visited the south as a trader, but there he died. Yet, separation from home only increased the age-old sense of belonging. The smaller the hope of return, the more desperate the yearning to do so. Homesickness has been one of the main themes of Vietnamese poetry, from folk poems communicated orally to the *Story of Kieu*, a long romance in verse considered as the brightest jewel of our literature. All children were taught the following folk poem in their first years of school. Impossible to translate faithfully, it nonetheless runs like this:

> Last night I stood by the side of the pond.
> The fish had gone deep under the water,
> And the stars in the sky were dim.
> Sadly I watched a spider spinning its web,
> Was it waiting for a soul to befriend?
> And was the Morning Star so pale,
> Because of the loved one it missed?
>
> Night after night, I dreamed of the Milky Way,
> And the Polar Star of my own firmament.
> Three full years have gone by.
> Stone wears out with time, but my heart will not forget.
> The Tao River still flows, and will ever be there.

When I learned the poem I did not quite understand the last verse, although like many other children I could recite it by heart, because the rhyme is so melodious and easy to remember. As a young man, I went abroad for my university studies. On summer nights in France when the air was warm and filled with the sounds of insects just as it was at home, I often watched the sky to look for the familiar sights of my childhood: the cloudy Milky Way which in Vietnam we call Ngan Ha or Silvery River, the stars which form the image of Emperor Than Nong, the God of Agriculture, who at harvest time would change his posture and bend over to cut the rice plants, and the bright full moon on which one could clearly see the banyan tree of the legend with Master Cuoi sleeping in its shade instead of minding his water buffaloes. But the sky in Europe was different. Stars were not at their appointed places and the moon had no banyan tree. It was only then that I understood the anonymous poet. He had to dream of his familiar sky because, where he was living at the time, it could not be seen. He was an exile crying out his love and yearning for the land of his birth.

Today, hundreds of thousands of Vietnamese are in exile. Their country is under a regime which tramples on human rights and keeps itself in power using a ruthless apparatus of oppression. In a foreign land, they struggle and toil to make a living. But the source which had nourished their spirits and their hopes is missing and the night skies of Australia, Europe and America, beautiful though they may be, are not the companions of their dreams. The English poet Coleridge wrote:

> Work without hope draws nectar in a sieve,
> And hope without an object cannot live.

Was he thinking of exiles like us, I wonder. For which Vietnamese has not, when evening falls on his place of refuge, felt the years slipping by him like spring water through his fingers and the waste and uselessness of his life? Yet, it is not true to say that our country—the object of our hope—has been lost. We have been separated from it, but like the Tao River in the folk poem, Vietnam is still there and it will ever be. We do not know when history will begin another chapter, but we must have faith. As in the words of the poem, let our hearts not forget. Let them not waver.

I / The Land of My Forebears

1. Legends and History

The home of my family is in north Vietnam. My forebears came from a village in the northwestern corner of the Red River delta, not far from the hilly region covering the provinces of Phu Tho, Vinh Yen and Son Tay. That region is thought to be the cradle of the Viet race. The Viet people in all probability came down from there to settle in the plains next to the foothills, millenniums ago. They cultivated the land, set up villages. Gradually, they spread out on both sides of the Red River towards the Eastern Sea, the name by which we call the South China Sea. The country's first dynasty, the Hong Bang (2879 to 258 B.C.), established their capital at Phong Chau, a few dozen kilometers northwest of our village.

Among Vietnamese legends, some are believed to relate to events occuring under the first dynasty. The oldest is the legend of the Heavenly Prince of Phu Dong. In the reign of Hung Vuong VI, the country was attacked by the An people from China. The army was unable to contain the aggressors. The worried king sent messengers to all the provinces to look for warriors capable of saving the situation. In the village of Phu Dong, north of Hanoi, lived a four-year-old boy who was healthier and stronger than other boys of his age and whose handsome features bore the sign of precocious intelligence. But since birth, he had never uttered a sound, nor proffered a smile. Upon the arrival of the royal messenger, he suddenly burst into speech and asked his parents to take him to the visitor. The boy talked to the messenger like a grown man. He said that should the king give him an iron horse and a gold sword, he would pacify the An. The messenger brought the boy to the capital and duly made his report. King Hung Vuong, intrigued, called for the boy to be brought before him. He was impressed by his appearance and ordered the horse and sword to be cast. When these were ready and brought before him, the boy got up and, stretching his body, at once grew into a ten-foot-tall warrior of imposing presence. The warrior leapt onto the back of the iron horse, which thereupon was transformed into a splendid white steed. Brandishing his gleaming sword, the warrior hero fought the aggressors at the head of the army. Wherever he went the enemy ranks crumbled and before long peace and security returned to the country. But the warrior did not. His mission accomplished, he flew away on his steed into the sky and disappeared. The grateful king bestowed on the warrior the title of Heavenly Prince of Phu Dong and ordered that a temple be built in the village where he was born to honor his memory. Every year since that time, a festival is held at Phu Dong on the ninth day of the fourth lunar month to commemorate Anniversary Day, the day when the miracle-working warrior returned to the heavens.

My grandmother liked to tell me the legend of the Heavenly Prince. To the above version given in most of our history books, she usually added a number of details which belonged to the story as told by the people of Phu Dong. For Phu Dong was her village. Thus, she said that the Prince was of supernatural origins. His mother became pregnant after meeting with a spirit one night. Before he rode out on his steed to fight the aggressors, villagers of Phu Dong offered him food but, in view of his enormous size, did not know what would be a sufficient amount of rice to cook. "What is the largest pot you have?" asked the warrior. "We have a pot which can contain enough rice to feed thirty grown men," the villagers answered. "Then, cook enough rice for thirty people!" ordered the warrior. After the rice was cooked, the warrior seized the huge pot and swallowed in one gulp its contents of steaming rice. My grandmother did not always recall all the details, so that each time she told me the story, there was something new. "When the horse jumped high in the sky," she said, "it began to spit out fire. Many of the An bandits were turned into ashes." The warrior fought so hard that his gold sword broke. He directed his steed to a nearby village and uprooted a clump of tall bamboo to use as a weapon. Unfortunately for that village, his steed continued to spit out fire and the village was burnt out. Later on, it was rebuilt and given the name of Lang Chay, or Burned Village. The Heavenly Prince did not forget the harm done by his steed. Soon a new type of bamboo grew in the village. It had a black and yellow variegated trunk making it look as if it had been scorched. The bamboo was particularly straight and strong. Villagers of Lang Chay used it to make household utensils which became much sought after and gave them a good income.

Next to the great mass of China, Vietnam is a small country. It has survived because, like the Prince of the legend, its people have been able to rise above themselves in times of need to defeat the aggressors. The Prince has been a guardian spirit shielding them from despair and urging them to continue with the struggle, even when the odds were stacked against them and all seemed lost. When the country was still at peace, my grandmother used to take me and my uncle—her youngest son who is of the same age as I—to the celebrations of Anniversary Day. Phu Dong is about fifty kilometers from our village, on the other side of the Red River. As a boy, I never went there without a certain feeling of awe, for the sacred land of our Heavenly Prince was also rooted deep in Buddhist tradition. In the ninth century, the Chinese Zen master Vo Ngon Thong came to Phu Dong and asked to be admitted to one of its temples, called the Kien So. There, he spent the next six years practicing the "face to the wall meditation." Before he died, he passed the "seal-of-mind" to the Vietnamese head priest of the temple. That was the beginning of a famous Zen school which bore his name. In the eleventh century, Princess Dieu Nhan of the Ly dynasty became a nun in the village's Huong Hai Convent. She was the only bhiksuni—or nun—ever to receive the "seal-of-mind" in the Zen patriarchal tradition. She belonged to the seventeenth generation of the Ty-Ni-Da-Luu-Chi School, founded in the sixth century by the Indian priest Vinitaruci and the oldest Zen school in Vietnam.

We used to spend the eve of the festival in Phu Dong, in the ancestral home of the Dang Tran, my grandmother's family. I could never recognize all my uncles, aunts and cousins there. At festival time, the ancestral home overflowed with people and we hardly slept amidst all the noise and movement. My grandmother greatly enjoyed her visits to Phu Dong. She rarely missed a festival, not only because that was the only time during the year that she could meet with her family but also, as she told me one day, because it was on the festival grounds that she first saw my grandfather, many years ago. But I do not recall him accompanying us, except in the year when he was the governor of the province of Bac Ninh, where the village of Phu Dong was. The next morning, we would rise early and go to the temple dedicated to the Heavenly Prince, before the crowd of festival-goers arrived from Hanoi and the neighboring towns. The large temple was built in the eleventh century by King Ly Thai To, the founder of the Ly dynasty. Before he became king, Ly Thai To was a mandarin under the Le. He stayed for some time in the Kien So Pagoda and often came to the old temple to pray to the Heavenly Prince for guidance, for the country was in a desperate situation with an evil and bloodthirsty Le king, who led such a dissolute life that he could not even rise from his bed for Court audiences and was therefore nicknamed "The Reclining King." It was said that the Heavenly Prince appeared to Ly Thai To in his dream and revealed to him his royal destiny. After ascending the throne, Ly Thai To ordered that, in place of the old temple, a new and larger one be built.

The festivities started later in the day. They took place on a grassy hill outside the village. In the fourth lunar month, the heat was already upon us and the pretty faces of the village girls were hidden under wide conical hats. In the afternoon, a battle reenacted the crushing of the An bandits. The Vietnamese forces were played by well-built young men, dressed only in black loincloths, under the command of officers wearing ancient style military uniforms and shaded by parasols. The commander of the forces held an orange banner, said to be the color chosen by the Heavenly Prince for his campaign against the aggressors. Much of the attention of the crowd was directed to the "enemy," who were dressed much more elaborately in rich combinations of colors. They were young girls, looking like actresses on stage with their heavy makeup. That they were chosen to play the enemy was not intended as a slight to the fair sex, only to show that in a battle, they were no match for the young men, just as the An aggressors were no match for the Heavenly Prince. After a session of ancient music, songs and dances to strengthen the fighting spirit of the men, the battle was joined. The Vietnamese attacked, the enemy withdrew, then counterattacked, but they were beaten and captured. There was no show of fighting, just a series of slow moves back and forth. At the end, the girls remained as fresh and beautiful as when they started, and still attracted the better part of the crowd.

About forty kilometers as the crow flies from my village stands Mount Tan Vien. At 1300 meters, it dominates the region and on clear days can be seen behind the rampart of green foothills. Legend has it that King Hung Vuong XVIII had a very beautiful daughter, Princess Mi Nuong. When she reached marriageable age, proposals were numerous, but the king said, "My daughter is descended from the immortals, so mere human beings will not be considered." One day, two parties came to ask for the princess' hand, the Spirit of the Mountain and the Spirit of the River. Being supernatural, they both held great power. They were handsome too. The king was at a loss to know which of them to choose. Finally, he came to a decision. He said that whoever arrived first the next morning with the requisite betrothal gifts would be accepted. At dawn next day the Spirit of the Mountain arrived, bringing gold, silver, precious stones, as well as the rarest birds and animals of the forest. True to his word, the king gave him Mi Nuong in marriage and the Spirit of the Mountain took his wife home to Mount Tan Vien. Later in the day, the Spirit of the River arrived, but by then it was too late. Furious, he at once pursued the newlywed couple. He called up driving rain and a frightening storm and raised the waters to attack Tan Vien. But, as the waters rose, the Spirit of the Mountain raised the dikes around the mountain. Firstly, a frontal attack was launched from the Red River, the largest in the north; it was repulsed. Then, the angry suitor mobilized the waves of the Hat River, which flowed through our home region. Further up north, he joined their forces with those of the Da River and came up against Tan Vien from the rear; that second attack also failed. The Spirit of the River lost those battles, but he did not accept defeat. According to the legend, he came back every year for revenge. And that is the reason why, every year, our people have to build up the dikes to prevent swollen rivers from bursting their banks and flooding the rice fields.

The Hung Vuong kings were legendary rulers. The two stories above are legends, not history. But their settings were villages, mountains and rivers of our home region, which show that from the earliest times, the Viet people have settled there. They grew crops, built dikes, had an established social structure and even had an apparatus of state.

My village lies on the banks of the Hat River which, two thousand years ago, became inscribed in the hearts of all Vietnamese with the epic revolt of the Trung Sisters. Since the legendary Hung Vuong, our people had been masters in their country. In 111 B.C. however, China invaded Vietnam and imposed a domination which lasted over ten centuries. The Trung Sisters belonged to a noble Viet family living in Phong Chau, the ancient capital of the first dynasty. Trung Trac, the elder sister, was married to Thi Sach who was also from a family of feudal lords whose territory covered both sides of the Hat River and therefore included our own village. The Chinese governor of Giao Chi, as Vietnam was then called, was a man named Su Ding. His rule was tyrannical and deeply resented by the people. Thi Sach and the Trung sisters led the resistance against Chinese rule. In A.D. 40, they launched the war for independence. At the start of the campaign, Thi Sach was captured by Su Ding and executed. The two sisters vowed to avenge his death and save the country from tyranny. Refusing to wear the white color of mourning so as not to affect the morale of their troops, they went into battle on elephant back, wearing armor painted in gold, the color of royalty, and being shaded by parasols of the same color. The Vietnamese defeated the Han army of occupation and Su Ding was forced to flee. Other provinces rose up in support of the Trung Sisters. Among Vietnamese commanders of that time were found men as well as women, the most famous of the latter was a princess named Thanh Thien, who won many battles against the Han. Near our own village, people still recall the legend of a man called *Ong Cai* (The Commander) who had his troops dressed up as women; this piece of psychological warfare had the Chinese running, so scared were they of our women warriors. In a short time, the Trung Sisters captured sixty-five fortified towns and liberated the country. Trung Trac ascended the throne, assuming the title of Queen Trung. To reconquer Giao Chi, the Han Court in Northern China assembled a large expeditionary force. As commander, it appointed its most famous and experienced general, Ma Yuan, who was then an old man of over seventy. The war was violent and short. The young Viet army met the invaders head on and was defeated. The sisters retreated until they reached our Hat River. There, they leapt into the water to their death.

In a dark millennium of our national history, the Trung revolt was a shining light. For the first time, the mighty Han Empire was beaten. We were independent and sovereign again, not for long it is true, for the Chinese yoke was reimposed after only three years. But the way had been shown and the flame of revolt would never be extinguished. For this reason, the Trung will always be remembered with reverence and gratitude by our people. That they were women and that several of their military commanders were women is remarkable, indicating that in those early times there was some fundamental equality between the sexes in our society. Although victorious, old Ma Yuan sullied his reputation by a spiteful act: before returning to China, he put a curse on the Viet people. He erected a bronze post at the border and said: "When this bronze post breaks, the Giao Chi people will cease to exist." The answer of our people took the form of a custom by which each person passing by the post threw a stone at it; it was not long before no post remained to be seen, only a mound of stones. But the waters of the Hat River have kept on flowing and will for ever flow in our nation's memory.

Kim Bai

The name of my village is Kim Bai. I spent a great deal of time there during my youth and knew its folklore and traditions well. I cannot recall exactly how I learned them and from whom: my grandparents, parents or village elders. I just knew them and after I left Kim Bai in 1948, they remained tucked away in one corner of my memory. When I started writing this book, I asked my parents, who are now in their eighties and living in France, for information and guidance. They wrote to me, and each of their letters drew from that corner of my memory the legends and stories which for so long had lain there, seemingly forgotten. Of recent generations, the person best acquainted with our village's history was my grandfather. He was born and grew up there. Having passed the civil service examinations, he went away to serve as mandarin in various parts of the country, but his life and activities remained closely tied to his birthplace. He was the last *Tien Chi* or Head Dignitary of Kim Bai, holding that position until 1945, when the age-old system of village administration was dismantled by the communists. Much to my regret now, I never asked him about Kim Bai's history and the origins of sayings and prophecies which form part of its folklore. He died when I was seventeen. I had plenty of occasions to ask questions, for he was my teacher of Chinese script and the classics, but I was then too young to look back to the past. As for him, he was a man of few words, except when teaching or commenting on a text. He rarely told us stories of olden times. He kept in his library a large number of papers which could give precious information about our native place. Unfortunately, they were all lost in the war which broke out in 1946. Old village documents were kept in the Communal Hall. I do not know what happened to them after the communists took over in 1945, but it is unlikely that many could have survived the combined effects of war and revolution.

Being close to the very birthplace of the Viet people, Kim Bai must have been established in the most distant past. Its origins are lost in time. In the turbulent history of our country, it was not unusual for villages to be destroyed or abandoned because of natural disasters like flood and drought, or because of man-made tragedies such as war and banditry. Villages belonging to the losing side in a civil war could be levelled to the ground, or punished by having their names changed. Kim Bai was spared such traumatic events. It had its share of ups and downs. At the end of the sixteenth century, it suffered persecution following a change of dynasty, but escaped widespread destruction. Often, it was subjected to attacks by rebels and bandits. In the eighteenth century, insecurity became so bad that it was virtually abandoned for many years, but then the people came back and the village survived. In the chronicle of our family, which traces our line back to the fifteenth century, Kim Bai is mentioned several times. These references give a clear impression that, by that date, it was a stable and well-established place. Old records of the last century showed that Kim Bai was not just one village, but an agglomeration of three *thon*, or small villages bearing the names of Vuc, Nhuyen and Thuong-Lam-Tram. The nearest village to us, Kim Lam, was formerly part of Kim Bai itself but had become separate, because Kim Bai had grown too large.

The name Kim Bai means Golden Plaque. Plaque was the insignia of mandarins in ancient Vietnam. Made of ivory and worn on the chest, it indicated the rank and function of the mandarin. Kim Bai are words of our scholarly language, which differs from the colloquial language used in everyday life. Many villages in the Red River delta have two names, an original colloquial name and a scholarly name adopted at a later date. Ours has only a scholarly name. I believe that, in the past, it must have had also a colloquial name. But Kim Bai developed a strong tradition of scholarship and learning and, as a result, the scholarly name gained preference over the colloquial one, which dropped out of use. This must have happened very long ago, for today no one at all remembers the colloquial name.

Why the name Kim Bai? Elders said that, since early times, many of our people had been successful at the civil service examinations and became plaque-wearing mandarins. Some reached very high positions; that was the reason why our village carries the imposing name of Golden Plaque. It is not remembered when our village acquired its name. I think it rather unlikely that the villagers themselves would have chosen such a high-sounding name, modesty being a quality highly valued in our culture. The name Kim Bai was, more probably, conferred by the Court on our village as a mark of appreciation for the accomplishments of its citizens.

Did the name perhaps originate with two famous sons of our village, the Nguyen brothers, who were born at the end of the fifteenth century? Nguyen Tue and Nguyen Huyen both graduated as doctors and reached the high ranks of the mandarinate. Their successful careers might indeed

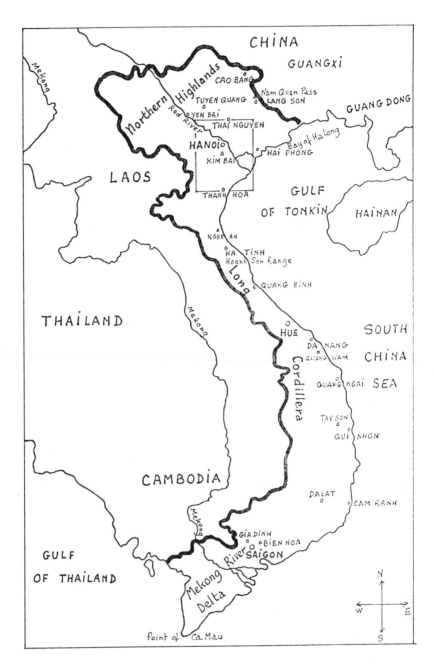

A general map of Indochina showing the regions, towns, rivers, mountains and places in Vietnam referenced in the narrative.

have been the reason for the present name. However, ancient examination records mentioned that they were "natives of the village of Kim Bai" and, thus, the name had been in existence before them. I had thought that the name might go back to the Ly dynasty (1010–1225) or the Tran dynasty (1225–1400). These dynasties were periods of great national development, in which native sons of our village may have played a part. But, as I would find later, the origins of the name Kim Bai are more ancient.

Among the earliest writings to have been preserved in Vietnam was a poem by a Buddhist monk who lived between 1020 and 1088. Dam Khi was, according to an anthology of Zen poetry compiled in the fourteenth century, "a native of the village of Kim Bai and a scholar of the Chinese classics, although he was also well versed in the Pali script." At nineteen, Dam Khi entered priesthood, taking the religious name of Ngo An. He became a Zen master of great fame. Disciples in his mountain temple included Vietnamese and Cham priests, the latter coming from the far south to receive his teachings. Ngo An belonged to the ninth generation of the Face-to-the-Wall school established by Vo Ngon Thong in Phu Dong two centuries before. Only one of his poems appeared in the anthology, the one he composed just before he died. Buddhist priests usually summed up in one last poem what they considered to be the essence of their life and their faith, to pass on to their disciples. Ngo An's was a four-line poem, written in the old scholarly script. The first two lines touch on the concepts of emptiness and enlightenment, and I cannot adequately translate them. But here are the last two, in which the Zen master used well-known Buddhist images to express the strength of his faith:

> Under the burning mountain sun, the precious stone does not lose
>   its shine,
> In a fiery furnace, the lotus blooms, still damp with the morning dew.

Although the anthology of Zen poetry dated from the fourteenth century, one can assume that our village was already called Kim Bai in Dam Khi's time. The name, therefore, existed prior to the eleventh century and the Ly dynasty. Only three Vietnamese dynasties preceded that of the Ly, and each only ruled for a short period: the Ngo (939–965), the Dinh (968–980) and the Earlier Le (980–1009). If our village did not acquire its name under one of the those dynasties, we would have to look back further, into the millennium of Chinese domination.

Whatever the case, I still believe that there was a time when sons of our village gained outstanding honors and brought fame to their birthplace, earning it a new name. Although the names of those sons, and their achievements, are lost to memory, the name Kim Bai remains to bear testimony that such a time did exist.

The Mountain of the Twins

Generations of villagers of Kim Bai have handed down this saying:

In Kim Bai stands the Mountain of the Twins,
One gate opens the way to its peaks.

When I was younger, I looked for the mountain in this old saying. I could not find it. Like all other villages in our region, ours was built on an elevation of no more than a few meters. All around were flat rice fields with a few grassy knolls here and there. Higher than these was the dike which overlooked the countryside, but this was only about ten meters high. The village certainly had no mountain. So what does the saying mean?

I learned that the Mountain of the Twins was no ordinary mountain but a geomantic feature, and the saying was a prophecy made about Kim Bai, a long time ago. In ancient Vietnam, as in other countries influenced by Chinese civilization, people believed in the art of foretelling the future by means of signs hidden in the contours of the earth. Each country had distinct geomantic features which were believed to condition the fate of its people. The story was told that near the end of the Chinese domination, which lasted from 111 B.C. to A.D. 939, Gao Pin was sent to our country as a governor. Well versed in geomancy, he was taken aback at observing so many auspicious signs. He foresaw that great leaders would emerge and that the country would certainly not remain a part of China. Gao Pin spent a good deal of time travelling all over the country, perched on a giant kite—a precursor of today's glider?—from where he could better observe the land from an elevated position. He tried his best to destroy those auspicious features with his geomantic powers. However, he did not succeed in preventing the inevitable.

Regions and villages also had their own geomantic characteristics, which served to explain why some had had more than their share of great men, warriors and scholars, while others never rated a mention in history books. Before building a house, Vietnamese usually consulted a geomancer to see whether the land was suitable for such a purpose and, if so, exactly where the house should be built and what orientation it should have. When a person died, the position of his or her grave would also depend on the advice of a geomancer.

The geomancer who discovered the Mountain of the Twins and made the prophecy about Kim Bai was probably Chinese. Since the art of geomancy came from China, the most sought after practitioners in Vietnam were Chinese, although there were also famous Vietnamese masters, such as Ta Ao who lived in the fifteenth century under the Le dynasty. Our own family tradition recalls that over the centuries, though our ancestral home has remained in the same plot, it has been rebuilt many times on the advice of Chinese geomancers to obtain the most auspicious orientation.

Prophecies are usually veiled in mystery and their meaning is never quite clear. Much depends on interpretation. The distinctive feature of a piece of land is given in geomancy a name, for instance Dragon, Tortoise or Mountain. The presence of a mountain is considered a good sign, although not for everyone concerned. It is good for those who can reach the summit and, from there, dominate the surrounding countryside. But the mountain becomes a barrier to those unable to climb it. "One gate opens the way to its peaks," here the prophecy means that the land of Kim Bai offers great promise of success and fulfillment, but only to a select few. Although there might be several gates, only one would lead to the top. Thus, not everyone with the ability to climb the mountain would succeed. To do so, a person also needs luck. To our people, luck means not just what may happen to someone by chance, but rather a combination of favorable circumstances which help a deserving person reach his goal. As we used to say, when a man acts according to the natural law of Heaven and with due regard to the feelings of his fellow men, the wind blows his way and rain comes when he needs it.

The prophecy was expressed in scholarly language. Translated into colloquial language, it can acquire another meaning and the second line would read: "One family succeeds at the highest examination," which means the doctorate examination. Over the centuries, many scholars in our village had met with success at the examinations. Most of them, however, were lower graduates holding bachelor or licentiate degrees. In the sixteenth century, one family produced a succession of *Tien Si* graduates, or doctors. That family was our own. Indeed, one cannot fail to link the twin peaks of the Mountain with the two Nguyen brothers, ancestors of ours. The brothers managed the rare feat of graduating at the same doctorate session, in 1511. This, I believe, is how the story of the prophecy may be told. Before the sixteenth century, a geomancer gave an opinion favorable to the land of Kim Bai. He must have enjoyed a good reputation for the opinion he expressed left a mark on the minds of the villagers. In due course, the Nguyen brothers both obtained the doctorate, the highest degree in the land, and had eminently successful public careers. Their twin success vindicated the prophecy, which then became a part of Kim Bai's folklore. The brothers' lives and careers constituted the high watermark in the history of our village and we shall come to another saying about them later.

The Mountain of the Twins has held a particular appeal to my family. My great-grandfather was a Taoist scholar known as Song Son Dat Dan, a pseudonym meaning Hermit of the Mountain of the Twins. In the 1930s, when my grandfather built a new house in our ancestral compound, he must have had the Mountain in mind because the two-storey brick building had a rectangular shape with three rooms on the ground floor, each next to the other, but on the upper floor, only two rooms separated by an open terrace, where our family went in the evening to wait for the southern breeze. The two upper rooms, each covered by a tiled roof, stood out and in this way the house called to mind the Mountain of the Twins in the prophecy.

I remember coming across the geomancer's prophecy for the first time in an old document which village officials brought in for my grandfather to read. I was then learning the scholarly script and could not understand the document, but I picked up the prophecy. I found it again in other documents and its repeated occurrence made a strong impression on me. It was usually put right at the beginning of the documents, as if its authors wanted to impress on the readers the unique character of the land of Kim Bai, before coming to the matters at hand. My imagination was captured by the mysterious features which ordinary eyes could not see. The Mountain of the Twins came to represent the place where the teachings of ancient masters would lead us and where Truth might be found. I might never reach or even come close to that place, which lay far away in the distant future. But I knew that, as said in the prophecy, it was there and a path could be found leading to it.

2. My Village

In the old administrative setup, the basic unit was the village. Above it was the canton, grouping a number of villages, then the prefecture, grouping a number of cantons and, finally, the province. My village Kim Bai belonged to the canton of Phuong Trung, the prefecture of Thanh Oai and the province of Ha Dong. Kim Bai lies on the banks of the Hat River, which started as a branch of the Red River, then flowed south through most of the province of Ha Dong, skirting Kim Bai to the west. For most of the year, it was a small and peaceful river. But came the monsoon season, and it became an expanse of water at places up to a hundred meters wide, with a strong current making it very difficult to cross.

Kim Bai lay about twenty-five kilometers from the ancient capital Hanoi, to the southwest. Since early times and under different names, Hanoi had been the seat of power in Vietnam. Being close to it, our home region had often been linked with events which shaped the nation's destiny. The territory of Thanh Oai was part of Hanoi's outer defenses and the Hat River constituted a natural barrier on the approaches to the capital. Both the Hat River and Thanh Oai prefecture were mentioned many times in history books. Many decisive battles were fought there. Since the traditional threat to our country came from China, one would have thought that such battles would take place north of the capital. It was not always the case. When the Mongols invaded Vietnam in the thirteenth century, their troops quickly occupied the capital, then called Thang Long. Vietnamese counterattacks came from the south and the famous victories of Ham Tu, Chuong Duong and Tay Ket in 1285, which defeated the invasion, all occurred southeast of Hanoi. In the fifteenth century Vietnam fell under Chinese domination for thirteen years (1414–1427). From the southern province of Thanh Hoa, Le Loi raised the banner of national revolt and in a ten-year struggle succeeded in recovering independence for our country. In 1426, Vietnamese forces moved from the south towards the old capital. The Ming Court sent a 50,000-strong army under the command of Wang Tong to reinforce the Chinese garrison. They set up a front of several miles long to defend the southwestern approach of Thang Long. This time, our region of Thanh Oai became the main battlefield. History books described the scene thus:

15

The enemy built fortified positions one following another for several miles, their flags and banners covering the fields, their lances and swords shining under the sun, confident that they could defeat the Vietnamese in one big battle.

This battle was fought over three days, first in Thanh Oai itself, then further south as the Vietnamese withdrew to lure the Chinese into a marshy area. The result was the victory of Tuy Dong and, eventually, the end of Chinese domination. Wang Tong retreated into Thang Long and barricaded himself behind the walls of the capital to emerge only a year later (1427), after having obtained a guarantee of safe passage for his troops from the Vietnamese. It was the last time that China was to rule Vietnam.

From the sixteenth century, our country was embroiled in internal conflicts and partitioned. This sorry state of affairs lasted for nearly three hundred years. Firstly, it was the Mac in the north against the Le in the south (1540–1592), then, the Trinh in the north against the Nguyen in the south (1627–1774), then, the Tay Son in the north against the same Nguyen (1789–1802). Our home region witnessed some major battles between rival dynasties. In 1592 for instance, the Hat River in Thanh Oai was the scene of a last-ditch action fought by the Mac before their downfall. In 1788, taking advantage of the civil war in Vietnam, Chinese troops moved in and occupied Thang Long. Emperor Quang Trung of the Tay Son led his army north to repulse the invaders. While the bulk of his troops operated in the east, the left wing of his army composed of elephant-born and cavalry troops moved up along the Western Mountains and through our region. The epic battle of Dong Da in the southwestern outskirt of Thang Long, in which Quang Trung defeated the Chinese army, stands out as one of the most glorious events in our military history. Dong Da was only twenty kilometers from our village.

To travel from Hanoi to Kim Bai in the early 1940s, one could take a rickshaw, which was the most widely used means of passenger transport in Vietnam as in other parts of Southeast Asia. Or one could take the tram from Hanoi to Ha Dong and change there to rickshaw. A private bus, with a very flexible timetable, ran from Ha Dong past our village to other localities further south. But the best and quickest way to travel was by bicycle. I still remember jumping on mine in the cool morning and pedaling along the silent tree-lined avenues of Hanoi. To own a bicycle was my dream as a young boy. Riding it gave me an exhilarating sense of speed and freedom which riding a motor car later in life never did. We youngsters liked to call a bicycle an "iron horse" on which we could be "moving as fast as if we were flying."

My family lived in Hanoi, not far from the old citadel. In days gone by a place where palaces stood, the citadel had become a group of barracks housing French and colonial troops. I cycled past it. Behind sturdy walls made of red stone, it seemed lifeless. At the time of the French conquest in the nineteenth century, Hanoi fell twice to the aggressors. Each time, the defeated Vietnamese commander wiped out his dishonor and "paid his debt to the country" by killing himself in the citadel. Perhaps for that reason, the citadel had always appeared to me more like a tomb for those heroes than a fortress.

Leaving the citadel behind, I soon reached the Temple of Literature, at the edge of the ancient city. For centuries, the Temple was a center for learning, where the cult of Confucius was celebrated and scholars studied for the highest civil service examination. Some of my ancestors who graduated as doctors had their names carved on stone stelae erected in the grounds of the Temple. But under the French, the place only remained as a relic of the past, lying under the shade of age-old trees. My route met with the tram lines going to the town of Ha Dong. I went through the dusty and noisy suburbs. The land was absolutely flat, but then on my right side a solitary hillock rose abruptly, with a temple on its top. That was Dong Da, the place where in 1789, Emperor Quang Trung vanquished the Chinese and tens of thousands of the invaders were killed. The hillock was their common grave.

The road continued past green orchards and vegetable gardens. After less than an hour I was in Ha Dong, a small and tranquil town, very provincial in appearance in spite of its proximity to the capital. Its streets were lined with trees, many of them flame-trees which exploded in masses of brilliant red flowers in the middle of summer. Back in the twenties and thirties, my grandfather served as a mandarin in Ha Dong. The bungalow he stayed in could still be seen in the official quarter of the town. Following her marriage, my mother went to live there with her in-laws and it was there that my elder brother, myself and a younger sister were born.

A few kilometers past Ha Dong the bitumen road divided into two branches, one going west towards the green hills of Hoa Binh, the other south to my village. The Japanese army had at that time a large base in Hoa Binh and one often met with columns of military lorries moving in the direction of Hanoi. The lorries were driven at high speed. Bullock carts, rickshaws, bicycles, pedestrians, all had to stop and move to the edge of the narrow road to let them pass. The soldiers in the lorries wore an impassive look, as if they did not see us. For several years, they had been in our country, yet no links seemed to exist between them and us. They remained total strangers. When Japanese forces came into the country in 1940, the Vietnamese thought that French rule would quickly end. They had heard much from Tokyo about Asia for the Asians and about a sphere of co-prosperity in Asia. They admired the way Japan had modernized and become a world power. I remember what strong impression the Japanese troops made on the schoolboy that I was. Their uniform, their guns, the vehicles they rode in, all had a battle-hardened and conquering look. How different they were from the antiquated French military! Surely, the Japanese could do away with the French whenever they wanted. Yet, for reasons of their own, they left in place the French colonial administration. Instead of playing the role of liberators, they settled in as an occupation force. Soon, they gained a reputation for harshness and brutality.

I took the branch of the road going south, and the countryside at once presented a familiar and welcoming appearance. Kim Bai was still more than ten kilometers away, but to me that fork on the road was where my home territory started. The hustle and bustle of the city was behind me. Among gentle rice fields, crisscrossed by small watercourses, I was going back to the place of my roots. As is well known, there is a Vietnamese fondness for snacks between meals, and as a consequence there were numerous tea stalls scattered along the road. These consisted of small huts with thatched roofs and earthen walls, where different brews of very strong teas were served with the food. Many places could boast a special delicacy for travellers. Next to a small bridge called Cau Khau, the tea stalls offered *banh dan,* or balls of dough with a filling of sweet bean paste and dotted with sesame seeds all over their surface. When deep-fried, they became a brownish red and expanded to the size of an orange. The hot cake jumped between my fingers and burnt my palate, so impatient was I to eat it. Then, I came to a village named Xom which produced *banh mat,* a cake made of rice flour and molasses wrapped in banana leaves. Just to look at the newly-cooked cakes and take in their light-brown, steaming sweetness was a delight. Everyone in our family had a particular fondness for that cake and we never failed to break our journey, go into Xom for a drink, eat some cakes and buy some more for the family. The village of Xom dated from ancient times and carried the distinction of having been visited twice by King Ly Thai Ton in the eleventh century. History books recorded that in the year of the Snake (1041), the king went to the Western Mountains to capture elephants and on the way back to the capital, he stayed the night in Kha Lam, the scholarly name for Xom. He liked the place and in the following year of the Horse, returned there for the springtime rite of tilling the fields and planting the young rice stalks. That manual task was performed once every year by the king to celebrate the cult of Emperor Than Nong, the God of Agriculture, who was worshipped as the ancestor of the Viet people and their provider.

Villages in our region were traditionally Buddhist, except for one that was converted to Catholicism at the beginning of this century. For most people in the vicinity, the church bells were their only means of knowing the "western" time, because they struck at midday every day. Otherwise, daily village activities still used traditional time measurements, based on the movements of the sun, moon and stars. I wonder under what circumstances that village adopted its new faith, as the introduction of Catholicism into Vietnam was the source of violent conflicts. By the 1940s however, that Catholic group, isolated in the midst of a Buddhist population, had been peacefully and completely accepted. The highway passed right through the village; a quite unusual occurence, for it meant that the village's bamboo enclosure could not be closed at night. For travellers, the attraction was a big statue on the side of the highway of Saint George plunging his lance into a dragon and crushing it under his foot. The statue was in stone which was rare in the countryside; more noticeably, it was sculpted in such a realistic manner that it appeared quite frightening, with blood spurting from the unfortunate dragon and the muscles of its body being torn apart by the blade of the lance. As children, we looked at that scene with apprehension and disbelief, for far from being an evil animal, the dragon was one of four supernatural and benevolent creatures in our mythology. It represented power and nobility and was in former times chosen as a kingly emblem. Often, we referred to the statue to frighten one another in the evening before going to sleep.

Riding past that Catholic village, I soon came to the township of Thanh Oai prefecture. This was just a small place, with the office and residence of the prefect in the middle of a cluster of brick houses. The main street had about a dozen or so shops and tearooms. At the end of it, I was out in the open fields again and the bamboo wall of my village could already be seen in the distance.

From the highway, Kim Bai looked like any one of the thousands of villages in north Vietnam, tucked behind its wall of bamboo. Our bamboo had quite a big trunk and and could be over ten meters high. It grew in thick clumps with long, hard thorns thrusting out in all directions. As a barrier, it was impossible to pass. The village could not be entered except through the gates. At evening, these were shut and barred. Strangers wishing to come in had to call at the gate and wait for a guard to open. For villagers who had to go in and out during the night, the bamboo thicket did have a few places where they could slip through, which only they knew and which the guards kept an eye on. The bamboo was truly a rampart protecting the village and its inhabitants. In times of old, when insecurity in our countryside was chronic, bandits attacking Kim Bai always did so at the gates, as they knew they could not force their way through the bamboo.

Our village was divided into hamlets, either five or six, as I remember. The main one was the "central hamlet" in which stood the Communal Hall. Another was called the "pagoda hamlet," where the Buddhist pagoda was to be found. The "market hamlet" had the old market, and so on. Each hamlet had its own gate to the outside world. The whole village therefore had five or six gates. The main gate belonging to the central hamlet looked out on the highway and was built in solid brick, while the other gates were made of bamboo. The main gate was not just a gate, but actually a small tower, constructed on the model of ancient citadel towers with a curved, tiled roof, very thick brick walls and a guardroom on top. It was wide enough for cars to pass under. The front bore the name Kim Bai in two big Chinese characters. The two gate wings were made of thick panels of ironwood, one of the hardest timbers found in Vietnam. The presence of a tower gate usually indicated that the village was the home of a high official. Entrances to other villages in the region were more modestly built. Even Phuong Trung, the seat of our canton and a much larger village than ours, did not have that sort of construction. Four centuries ago, Kim Bai produced a succession of high mandarins and holders of titles of nobility. It was said that it had then a tower gate of imposing size which served as a ceremonial gate to greet royal messengers when they came to bestow royal honors on the mandarins. That gate was destroyed long ago, either after the fall of the Mac dynasty or by bandits who were so often the scourge of our region. My mother recalls that at her wedding in 1926, the main gate was simply made of bamboo. The present tower gate was built by my grandfather some years later, in time for the reception of imperial decrees granting posthumous honors to his ancestors.

The main gate was called the Si Gate. *Si* is a tree similar to the banyan, with roots even longer than those of the banyan and hanging down from high branches. Next to the old gate, there used to be a large and very old *si* tree, hence its name. That tree was haunted. It had since disappeared, but villagers continued to see the Si Gate as a meeting place for the "lost souls" of those who had committed suicide or met with violent death. Many of these dead were buried in the graveyard, a small plot hidden in one corner of the village, where tumuli were placed in a chaotic manner facing in all directions. The graves there were called "without owners," as no relatives or descendants looked after them. To be buried there was an indication of a wretched condition, because country custom called for the dead to rest in their family land, out in the open fields instead of being confined in graveyards. A small shrine stood among the graves. No one was ever seen in that forsaken place. Yet, every time I passed by it, I could smell the smoke of incense and see the flickering light of an oil lamp in the shrine. It was an eerie feeling. As if the light and the smoke had been put there, not by any human being, but by the ghosts of the dead. Villagers believed that the tormented ghosts, instead of staying in their burial ground, crossed the village every day at nightfall to congregate at the Si Gate. There, they frightened passersby with strange happenings, such as crying and screaming in the wind or swinging on the roots or the long gone *si* tree and making a creaky noise. They made a nuisance of themselves and one might think that the villagers would look for a way to get rid of them. But it was not so. The ghosts also had their uses, for by staying near the main gate they prevented evil spirits on the outside from entering the village. Therefore, in their own way, they acted as guards and Kim Bai villagers were content to let them stay. Still, anyone who had to use the main gate in the evening would, consciously or not, hasten to get past it so as not to be caught or possessed by the ghosts. Stories of possession were not a figment of the imagination. They did happen as I was once a witness.

One evening, a commotion occurred in the hamlet. A crowd gathered near the Si Gate around a sixteen-year-old girl who, her hair let down and her eyes wide, was sitting in the middle of the path. She was a maidservant in our household but, in that state, was barely recognizable. She was being possessed by a ghost who, in a deep manly voice, was telling its story: how it had been the victim of an injustice, how it had died and become a lost soul. Relatives used mulberry branches dipped in urine, a well-established way of getting rid of ghosts, to whip the girl quite hard all over her body. Two persons took turns to use the whip, but she continued to be possessed and rambled on. Having watched a while, I left the scene to return home. My grandmother was not pleased. "You must not listen to those ghost talks," she said. A cousin of mine joked that I could have been possessed by the ghost myself. He was immediately silenced by her glare. "It would not have dared!" she muttered angrily. The commotion continued and intensified outside. It only stopped when the girl was carried into our compound, sound asleep. I was told that after I left, the ghost got up and started walking about in the hamlet. As it passed in front of houses, it uttered predictions about the future of people living there. Villagers were naturally superstitious and ready to believe in fortune telling, so the crowd which followed the girl grew in size. At one point, the ghost said that the Nguyen Dinh (our family) had held leadership position but the coming period would see our village placed under the authority of other people, so saying it pointed towards some thatched houses belonging to poor farmers. The crowd fell into a hush. Darkness had descended and the atmosphere grew scary. Those who beat the girl with mulberry branches had stopped doing so. The ghost continued its walk, foretelling the rise and fall of various families, until it came to the gate of our compound. There it stopped and remained silent. The crowd waited. Finally, in a tired and almost choked voice, the ghost said that the Nguyen Dinh had reached the top thanks to the auspicious feature of their ancestral land, but their way there had not been easy; they had not been spared difficulties and would have to face new ones. Then the girl sunk into a deep sleep. Strangely enough, the next morning she remembered nothing of what happened. Even more strangely, all the whipping she had received left absolutely no mark on her body. People said it was not she but the ghost which had been whipped.

In 1943 when that ghost incident took place, the Second World War was raging around Vietnam but our country had not yet been subjected to any upheaval. My grandfather was a retired mandarin and the Head Dignitary of his village. The status of our family seemed totally secure. Nobody could have foreseen that after only a few years, the communists would seize power and some poor farmers would indeed be put in charge of Kim Bai's affairs.

Each village had a Communal Hall located in its central part. The village deities and spirits were worshipped there; at the same time the Hall was also the seat of village government. It was therefore both a temple and the main public building. Our Communal Hall was a large building sitting majestically on a raised platform eight or nine steps high. The roof in traditional curving style was decorated with mortar sculptures of flying dragons among clouds. The Hall pillars consisted of big trunks of shining dark brown ironwood, so big that a fully grown man could not put his arms around them and join his hands. They divided the building into three sections. In the middle were the altars of deities and spirits. Our village worshipped in the first instance the deities who presided over the land of Kim Bai and the waters of the Hat. Next came the spirits of great men and heroes in our national history. On either side of the altars were rows of wooden platforms, where citizens met and had meals after the traditional ceremonies, some desks and chairs for village council meetings, and cabinets to keep official documents. Down the stairs in front of the Hall lay a large courtyard paved in red square bricks which led to a lotus pond. On one side of the yard was a small park shaded by several big trees. On the other side stood the entrance constituted by four tall brick pillars ornamented with sculptures of dragons and bicornes. Left and right of the entrance ran a brick wall carrying bas-reliefs of battle scenes with warriors, elephants and horses, all painted in bright colors. It is to be noted that the entrance was built, not in front of the Communal Hall, but on the left side, so that after passing through it, one had to make a right turn to face the Hall.

On top of the stairs, under the eaves of the Hall, was placed a big drum. The beat of the drum called villagers to attend ceremonies and festivals and announced meetings of the council. If the drum sounded suddenly, it was to warn the people of some danger or emergency, such as fire, flood or attack by bandits. On hearing it, it was the duty of all to go at once to the Hall—be it day or night—in case their services were required. Every citizen with an urgent problem to submit to the Council could at any time beat the drum and call the authorities. This was a traditional democratic right recognized in all villages. When I was thirteen years old, our soccer team was practicing one day when the ball landed in a private garden. The owner refused to throw it back, or let us in to get it. One word followed another and a shouting match ensued. Without a ball, we were unable to resume our practice, so we decided to go to the Communal Hall to call the authorities. It was early afternoon, siesta time. I beat the drum, not fast and continuously as in an emergency, but slowly and just a few times. After a while, some people turned up to see what was the matter. Then a village notable arrived. He was a former mayor who still held a position of influence. A relative of our family, he belonged to my grandfather's generation, so I addressed him as "Great-uncle Mayor." He settled the dispute swiftly. The owner was asked to return the ball. Our team was warned to be more careful with it in the future and, if the same thing happened again, to try and settle the matter amicably, instead of disturbing village officials. Notice that, although we were all teenagers, he did not say that we had no right to beat the drum. A full village citizen was a man who had reached maturity and had gone through an admission ceremony. However, anyone with a diploma was admitted, even when still under age. I was then a holder of the "end of primary school diploma," and thus had full civic rights, including that of beating the drum at siesta time to summon village notables. Normally, the front doors of the Communal Hall were kept locked. They were fully opened only for important ceremonies. At meetings of the village council, only one or two of the doors were opened, letting enough light in for the representatives to work while the rest of the Hall remained in the dark. As Head Dignitary, my grandfather presided over such meetings. I usually accompanied him, to carry his writing brushes and water pipe and to be there, in case I should be needed. Summer days in the north could be unbearably hot and the red brick courtyard in front of the Hall glowed under the sun. But once across the threshold and inside the Hall, coolness pervaded everything and my eyes felt the relief of shade. With a faint scent of fragrant wood and incense, the atmosphere was extraordinarily calm and restful. Often, when the council members were deliberating, I walked into the inner part of the Hall and sat upon the cool surface of the wooden platforms. There, just letting myself bask in the calm and restfulness, I felt wonderfully secure and happy. The Communal Hall was like the bamboo enclosure protecting our village; each represented all that was stable and permanent. Other things might change or disappear, I thought, but they would always be there.

On one side of Kim Bai was the highway. On the other side, a dike ran along the Hat River. It was a solidly built earthen wall up to ten meters high. The top was wide and flat, about five meters wide and all kinds of vehicles, cars too, could use it. In summer, we often went up there in the evening for a walk. "We" were then a group of boys and girls, home in Kim Bai for the summer vacation. After the sun had set, the far mountains were clothed in dark purple. Everything became quiet and peaceful. A gentle breeze blew past and from down in the village came the sound of the pagoda bell. It floated in the cool air of the evening and seemed to linger for a long time around us, over fields, orchards and hamlets before spreading towards the mountains in the distance where, so we believed, was to be found the cradle of our race. I have known other pagoda bells in Vietnam, visited many Buddhist temples in India and Japan, heard church bells in Europe. Nowhere have I found a sound so clear and blending in so well with its environment. The story was told that, after the pagoda was built, the first bell cast was "dumb." No sound came from it. A bad omen. The Kim Bai people believed they must have done something terribly wrong. They redoubled their efforts in prayer, searched for a better qualified person to cast the bell, but again it failed. One day a stranger came to the village. When told about the pagoda bell, he suggested that, as the word Kim in the name Kim Bai meant gold and gold was the geomantic sign of the village, a larger quantity of gold should be added to the bronze to make the bell ring. "With the right amount of gold," he said, "the bell will toll with a sound which comes from the very soul of your village." Villagers invited him to stay and cast the bell himself, but he would not accept. Following his suggestion, however, a great communal effort was made to contribute more gold. And the sound which was finally produced came up to our people's highest expectations.

Our dike had a distinguishing feature. Standing on top of it, one could see no river, only fields and orchards. The Hat River was several hundred meters away. As a child, I had often wondered why the dike was built so far from the river that, even during the flood season, water never came up to it. What was it for then? Later on, I found out. When it was built a long time ago, the Hat was flowing quite close to our village. But, like many rivers in the delta, it did not stay in one place. Every year as rainwater poured down from the mountains, it broke its banks and moved its bed. It happened that the movement was always in one direction, and thus every year the Hat wandered a little further away from our village. In the 1930s, a dam was built upstream at Day, in Son Tay province. It prevented annual flooding and, since then, the course of the river had stabilized.

After the Hat stopped breaking its banks, the space between our village and the river came permanently under cultivation. Villagers called it *Bai*, or the Field. On its alluvium-covered soil, anything could be grown: rice, maize, potatoes, beans, sugarcane, green vegetables, and a lot of fruit trees. Three sides of the Field were bordered by the Hat which made a wide bend there. During autumn and winter, mist rising from the river covered the place most mornings and evenings. Fruit which ripened in the mist acquired a delicate flavor, bananas in particular. A great variety of bananas grew there, such as the "moorhen banana" which, when ripe, had spots like those of moorhen eggs and the "skin banana," of which both the flesh and the inner part of the skin could be eaten. But what stood out most in the Field were lichee trees, so many in fact that it was also known as *Bai Vai,* or Lichee Field. One of the fondest memories of my youth was the lichee season. The trees were of a beautiful round shape, their neat and tidy branches were full of dark green leaves. Bunches and bunches of red fruit hung down. In our scholarly language, the lichee is known poetically as "the tear drop from the branch." Harvest time was in summer. The tree canopy offered its shade. The sandy soil underfoot was fresh and clear of grass and weeds. With trees neatly aligned in rows, a lichee grove conveyed an idyllic image, as if it belonged to golden ages long past. Every family in our village owned a few trees. Our own family had about twenty and we all knew where they were. When the fruit ripened we, the boys, would go to the Lichee Field early in the morning before the pickers came to take them for the market. Having chosen the best trees, we climbed up. This was easy, as lichee trees are of medium size with plenty of lateral branches. Once up, we took the ripest fruit; their flesh and juice were deliciously cool and tasted as only lichee eaten straight after being picked could. Sitting on a branch, I idly looked down on the river bending its way around the grove. The season was still dry and the water flowed indolently, untroubled by anything except the occasional small boat. When the sun was high, we went down the bank to wash our fingers sticky with the juice of lichee and, if the day was hot, to have a dip before going home.

The population of Kim Bai was over one thousand strong. Most dwellings were thatched cottages, but an indication of the prosperity that the village enjoyed was the presence of some thirty brick houses. The main lanes were laid with red bricks, which made the place look nice and tidy. From the highway a brick path, wide enough for cars to use, led up to the village center. The 1930s were, for Kim Bai, a period of growth. A proverb said that "when a man became a mandarin, the whole family could get assistance from him." In fact, his entire village could get assistance. My grandfather was a mandarin and he greatly contributed to the welfare of his village. Whereas markets in neighboring villages consisted of a few thatched huts, our own market had two large brick buildings under tiled roof. It was built in 1936 off the highway, outside our village's enclosure. I was only six at the time but could well recall the excitement on the day when the market was opened. High officials came from Ha Dong for the inauguration, bringing with them soldiers and military music. Products from everywhere in the region were displayed, especially delicate and shiny textiles made of raw silk for which our province of Ha Dong was famous. For the crowd of villagers, the occasion was a big festival of games and competitions which lasted all day. There was wrestling, fighting with wooden staves and, a great favorite with villagers, climbing a greasy pole to take the prize tied to the top, which was a live duck making a deafening noise. In the evening, a theatre group performed a traditional opera. Concluding the festivities was a display of fireworks, something people in the countryside could perhaps see only once in a lifetime.

The new market boosted the village economy. After a few years, it developed into a small shopping center. Though market day in Kim Bai was once every five days, villagers started to set up tea stalls which remained open all day every day for travellers on the highway. Then the bus began to make regular stops there. Finally, a sure sign of business opportunities, Chinese traders came to set up shops. There was a chemist selling herbal medicines, a bicycle repair shop and a small bazaar selling all sorts of things, from haberdashery to the sweets and dried salted fruits which we children were very fond of.

A state primary school was established in the early 1940s. In the old days, when Chinese script was used for teaching, Kim Bai was a local center of learning, with several private schools catering to students from the whole region. After the turn of the century, when the new Roman mode of writing was officially adopted, private schools teaching Chinese script died out, and for "modern" schooling, families had to send their children to the town of Ha Dong or even the capital Hanoi. The presence of a state school was a source of pride to village elders, who saw in it a return to the scholarly eminence that Kim Bai had held in the past. But the school was modest. It had a single classroom, built in solid brick and painted cream, with a red tiled roof. The floor was compacted earth. Tuition was free. Only one teacher had charge of the whole primary cycle, which covered six years. Still, there were very few villages which could boast of having a state school like ours.

Our village even had a soccer field next to the market. Unfortunately, lack of maintenance soon made it a great hazard to play on. Time and again I hurt my ankle by stepping into potholes. Water buffaloes grazed there, so that dung was an added risk to players. Next to the soccer field was a "swimming pool," which was in reality the place where clay was dug out to make bricks for the market. Rainwater filled it and youths used the brown water for swimming on hot afternoons while their buffaloes also took a dip.

Kim Bai enjoyed a relatively good standard of living, derived not only from agriculture, but also from industry and commerce. Farming was based on rice and a number of secondary crops such as maize, sweet potatoes, beans and manioc. The land yielded two crops of rice per year, the main one harvested in the tenth lunar month and a smaller one in the fifth month. A major cottage industry, traditional to our province, was silk. The soft and smooth raw silk of Ha Dong was highly prized by city women, who used it to make long dresses. That thin and delicate material was ideal for hot weather and light enough to flutter at the slightest breeze or movement. Dyed in soft pastel colors, the long flowing silk dresses added charm to our Vietnamese streets and many a poet has sung their praise. Fine silk of this kind was not made in our village, which produced only the rough cloth worn by country people. The yellowish cloth was dyed dark brown and sold in local markets. Down south in the Mekong delta, villagers all wore black pajamas but here in the Red River delta, the customary color was brown. The men had brown pajamas while the women wore brown blouses and skirts. Many families in Kim Bai had weaving looms. On both sides of the dike were found numerous mulberry fields.

Other occupations in Kim Bai included raising honey bees and manufacturing incense sticks, the latter quite a significant activity, as in every house stood an altar for ancestor worship on which incense was lit daily, or at least on the two holy days of the month, the first and the fifteenth. To travellers, the tea stalls in our marketplace offered a variety of food, of which mention should be made of soya bean curd. The white bean curd made in Kim Bai was not the soft and jelly-like kind usually found nowadays in oriental groceries, but a firm and compact variety. Heated up over steam or grilled and dipped in *tuong,* or thick bean sauce, it was a simple and popular dish of delicate taste which could be eaten with rice, or just by itself as a snack. Making thick bean sauce, which is different from the liquid Chinese soya sauce, was a specialty of my grandmother. Every year she produced it in numerous big jars, both for the family and to give away as presents. Her bright-red sauce had a flavor and consistency which earned her a high reputation among gourmet friends. In Vietnamese food, soya bean sauce is, with the *nuoc mam* or fish sauce, the most commonly used condiment. Making bean sauce requires precision because any slight variation can spoil the result. My grandmother's sauce was made from soya beans and glutinous rice. The beans were first roasted, then steamed, after which they were put in earthenware jars with water and left to soak for five days. The glutinous rice was steamed until cooked, then thinly spread on large flat baskets, covered with banana leaves and stored in a cool place to ferment. After about five days, it became covered with greenish mould and smelled strongly. The secret was to know exactly when to stop the fermentation by spreading salt over the mixture. If that was not done at the right time, the flavor and color of the sauce might be spoiled, or it might even go bad. When my grandmother was making bean sauce and the critical moment approached, the whole household had to stand ready. The atmosphere of crisis was heightened by the fact that this always occurred in the middle of the night. My grandmother would not go to bed at all. She kept a watchful eye on the jars of beans and kept smelling them, to judge the right moment. When it arrived, she woke everyone up. Under the light of small kerosense lamps, we quickly mixed salt with the rice and beans, then poured the contents of the baskets into the jars. After that, there was nothing more to do, except to wait until the sauce matured.

According to our custom, a good meal would start with hosts and guests enjoying a glass of rice brandy while savoring tidbits of meat such as pork tripes or chicken giblets. Normally, meat was served as an appetizer, not fish or vegetable. But it was said that fine gourmets would gladly have eaten with the brandy bean curd of the quality produced in Kim Bai, dipped in a good bean sauce like the one made by my grandmother. Bean curd can be fried instead of steamed, or marinated in thick bean sauce and cooked *à la casserole* with pork meat. Since a child, I have been particularly fond of that dish. My mother said that as a four- or five-year-old, I would at times wake up in the middle of the night crying and crying for some bean curd casserole. Bean curd and bean sauce have to go together to bring out their best. To eat bean curd with fish sauce, for instance, would be a waste of both.

Additional sources of income for the women of Kim Bai included weaving cloth, turning paddy into polished rice and selling their produce at the market. Many were also engaged in the petty trade of haberdashery, dyes, paper, pens and anything else that country people might need. Mornings would see them setting out for the market, young and graceful figures in groups of two or three, their working capital contained in two wooden counters nicely balanced at the ends of their bamboo pole. Women had traditionally played an important role in the economic life of our village. They were often praised for their diligence and resourcefulness, as well as their beauty. "A fortunate family is one whose son marries a girl from Kim Bai," older people used to say. A folk poem put it this way:

> Pretty girls in Kim Bai,
> Are as many as flowers of the *thien ly*.
> Young men from here and there,
> From everywhere,
> Who want to find a wife,
> All come and look.

The *thien ly* is a vine with heart-shaped leaves which grows in the countryside. Its purple flowers are grouped in bunches. When Vietnamese think of their village, they usually see in their imagination a group of thatched roofs shining in the morning sun with, next to each roof, an arbor of *thien ly*, whose flowers represent the simple and unpretentious beauty of country girls.

A folk-saying known throughout our region went simply like this:

> Girls of Kim Bai,
> Boys of Nga Vac.

It meant that the girls and boys of these two villages were the very best. The girls of Kim Bai seldom had to toil in the fields. They spent much of their time indoors working at their looms. Thus, they kept a slender figure and fair complexion. With their market activities, they provided an additional income for the family. Being used to buying and selling in the marketplace, they were not shy and knew how to strike a conversation. Pretty girls in the village were many and, in my youth, two relations stood out. One was my Aunt Quyen and the other my sister Trang. Everyone said they were beautiful but not without adding that Aunt Quyen was a shade too tall and sister Trang's complexion was a shade too dark. Such was the way the Kim Bai people appreciated beauty. In their eyes, beauty could never be perfect or absolute. Moreover, they believed that too much beauty was a bad omen.

Why the girls of Kim Bai were praised in the folk-saying was easy to understand. But why the boys of Nga Vac, a village not far from ours, were put on the same pedestal as the Kim Bai girls, I do not know. Nor do I understand why the boys of Kim Bai, a place known for having produced many bright young graduates, were not celebrated in any folk-saying.

3. Our Ancestral Home

My father worked as a civil servant in Hanoi. Our family belonged to the upper middle class, but after the Second World War spread to Asia, life for us became more and more difficult. The lot of civil servants was not bad before the war. We used to go to a seaside resort every summer. Then came the hostilities, inflation and rationing. Salaries did not keep up with rising prices. With a large family of seven, it must have been hard for my parents to make ends meet. I remember that they tried their hands at various business activities without much success. Once they went into a mining venture as shareholders; it proved to be a total failure.

My grandparents owned some land in Hanoi and Ha Dong, as well as rice fields in Kim Bai. They were moderately wealthy, although with several underaged children—the youngest being my age—their financial burden was still heavy and, by the 1940s, my grandfather had already retired. They helped us to some extent. Whenever my grandmother came to visit us from the village, she always brought with her provisions of rice and other produce of the land. But other than that, my parents had to rely on their own means. I was then a student at the French Lycée of Hanoi. When I obtained a scholarship to become a half-boarder there, my family was very pleased. I was very skinny and the scholarship gave me a free lunch six days a week, Saturday being also a school day in those days. Lunch at the Lycée provided more nourishing food than our ordinary fare. It was served *à la* French, with plenty of meat.

My grandfather shared his time between our ancestral home in Kim Bai and a small bungalow that he owned in Ha Dong. My grandmother and great-grandmother lived in Kim Bai. From Hanoi, we made the trip to Kim Bai quite regularly, about once every two months. Our visits usually coincided with seasonal festivals or commemorative services for ancestors. On each occasion, we stayed for a day or two, except for the New Year festival when the stay was longer. We were town dwellers and had the war not intervened, my experience of village life would have been limited to those short visits.

Our country was dragged into the Second World War following Japan's attack against Pearl Harbor. Trenches were dug, air raid drills were conducted, but for a long time hostilities did not affect us. Japanese forces were pushing forward farther and farther on land and in the Pacific Ocean. The only planes we saw in the sky were Japanese ones going to and from the nearby Gia Lam airfield on the other side of the Red River. Then, as the Allies struck back and the tide of the war turned, air alerts became more frequent. Japanese military bases were bombed. Sitting in the trenches, we could see American planes passing overhead on their way to attack the airfield, surrounded by the smoke blooms of antiaircraft fire. We still felt like we were observing a conflict involving other people, until Hanoi itself was bombed in the beginning of 1943. As a half-boarder, I went to school in the morning and stayed there until evening. After the afternoon classes, the half-boarders joined the full-boarders and did their homework under the eyes of supervisors, before they were allowed to go home. That day, having taken lunch in the school refectory, we were upstairs lying down during the regulatory half-hour siesta, when the alert sounded. We went downstairs, out of the building and over to the sports ground, now criss-crossed with open trenches. Soon, the planes came and the familiar noise of antiaircraft fire had just begun to be heard when loud explosions occurred all around us. From my trench, I could see columns of black smoke rising. The commotion lasted for quite a while. We emerged from our shelter after the all clear signal, safe but shaken. My family was living not far from the citadel. Our street ran between the town's power station and a Japanese army barrack. All these places were prime targets for American bombing. I was anxious to get home. There were rumors of many people killed. However, half-boarders were not allowed to leave until the evening; in spite of the special circumstances, the school stuck to its rigid rule. At last, I left the Lycée. The rickshaw sent by my parents was at the gate to pick me up. I was driven through streets without lights, past destroyed houses and fallen trees. War had truly come to our town. Thankfully, no one in our family was harmed. The next day, the authorities decided that all schools should close and children should be evacuated from the capital. We left for Kim Bai. Our ancestral home was full of close and distant relatives. Rather than a wartime evacuation, the atmosphere was like a school holiday combined with a family reunion.

The land where our ancestral home stood was believed to be part of an estate owned by the Nguyen since the sixteenth century. At that time, our ancestor Nguyen Tue was a minister of the court and held the title of count. As the family later on developed into several branches, the estate was parcelled out. We came from the youngest branch of the eighth generation. In the middle of the eighteenth century, the head of our branch settled in a corner of the original estate. His grandson, who made a fortune trading with Chinese merchants, purchased some land from neighbors to add to his block. My grandfather bought more land and extended the area to about two thousand square meters, quite a large size by Kim Bai's standard.

Transversal house (hidden under trees)

Altar house

Granary

Western house

New house

Gate house

towards the village

Si gate

N
E
W
S

An artist's impression of our ancestral home in Kim Bai (circa 1942).

Our compound occupied one of the best positions in the village, right in the middle of the Central Hamlet and close to the Communal Hall. On two sides of the compound, the land still belonged to other branches of the Nguyen family, except for only one or two small plots sold by impoverished descendants to outsiders. In the 1940s, the heir to our eldest branch decided to leave Kim Bai to make a living in town and he sold his land, which adjoined our compound, to my grandparents. He also sold his house—a cottage with a thatched roof and earthen walls—to be taken down and rebuilt elsewhere. His was the fourteenth generation after the count. It was sad to see him sell his piece of land and leave the place of his roots. As he belonged to the eldest branch, his land may have been the very place where our first ancestor had his home, four centuries ago.

Homes in the countryside were generally cottages with a small garden or orchard. Ours was built like a sprawling villa in the city. Nearly the whole compound was taken up by brick buildings and paved courtyards. Only here and there was some space left for flowers and trees. In fact, the compound contained not one house but several, built at different periods.

The oldest was the altar house and an adjoining building called the transversal house, because it stood at a right angle to the altar house. The latter was first built in the eighteenth century, probably with a thatched roof and earthen walls. After about five or six decades of tropical climate, houses made that way had to be rebuilt. Family elders recalled that each time when rebuilding took place, the altar house was given a new orientation. Succeeding generations in our branch had had only one son to continue the line and this was believed to be caused by the alter house facing in the wrong direction. Each time, a Chinese geomancer was called in to find a more auspicious orientation. The last time that this happened was in the 1920s, when the present house was built. As it was going to be a long-lasting construction in brick, my grandfather made a special effort to find a good geomancer, who again was Chinese. The geomancer shifted the house to another site and kept it facing southwest. South, by the way, was the orientation adopted by most houses in the Red River delta, as it exposed them to the cool southern breeze during summer. Whether the result of the geomancer's choice or not, the fact is that since then, there have been more male children in our family.

The altar house was a simple rectangular structure divided in two lengthwise by an internal wall. Its high roof covered with red tiles had no ceiling. From the inside, all the beams and tiles could be seen. On the ridges of the roof were sculptures, made in mortar, of dragons and clouds. The front part of the house was formed by a long open space running from one end to the other. Its size was as large as five rooms joined together and was therefore said to have "five rooms," although there were no partition walls. It served as lounge and dining room during the day, and became a sleeping area at nighttime. The back part also had "five rooms." The three rooms in the middle formed the altar area and were separated by partitions from the other two rooms, one at each end. The altar area was the sacred place where our ancestors' spirits were worshipped. It contained two altars. The main altar at the center was dedicated to the Nguyen ancestors. A smaller altar, on the right, was for our maternal ancestors. Normally, such an altar was not required because the ancestor cult was celebrated by male descendants. However, some of our forefathers married into families which had no sons, and the cult of their wife's ancestors fell to them. Many Buddhist families had in their altar room also a place to worship Lord Buddha, but our ancestral home had no such place.

The main altar was about five or six meters deep. It consisted of a low, large square platform and two high tables, placed end to end. Urns, incense burners, candle holders and other objects required by the cult were displayed there. During the ceremonies, the platform and tables also provided room for flowers and for the offerings of food and wine. At the far end of the altar stood the tabernacle, a miniature temple with intricate carvings and painted in red and gold, the traditional colors of our country. Set on a higher level than the tables, the tabernacle housed our ancestors' tablets. Normally, its sliding doors were shut. They were opened only on the anniversaries of the death of our ancestors and at traditional festivals, when the tablets were taken out for the ceremony of worship.

A drum and a gong were placed at the front of the altar. Their beat announced the start of ceremonies. Between them sat a pair of elephant tusks which was there, not for decorative purposes, but probably because it was presented to our family on the occasion of the bestowing of a title on an ancestor. Behind the tusks were two sword racks, each holding four long swords. Two rows of flags and parasols lined the sides of the altar. The swords, flags and parasols were symbols of authority and rank, bestowed posthumously on our ancestors by the court of Hue. In times of old, mandarins going out on official duties had soldiers marching in front carrying their flags and swords, and other soldiers marching behind, holding parasols to shelter them from sun or rain. Some flags were rectangular, others triangular and they were of different sizes and designs. The parasols were large or small, depending on the ranks. The swords were long and heavy, with delicate carvings of Chinese characters on both blade and handle. Sadly, these priceless treasures, as well as many other family heirlooms, were all lost during the war with the French and the communist revolution.

On the left of the altar house was the transversal house. The two houses, at a right angle to each other, formed two sides of a rectangle and followed a traditional pattern for village homes. In fact, until the end of the nineteenth century, all houses in the countryside had to be built in accordance with a rigid set of rules. The average house was just a rectangular cottage facing a courtyard. Wealthier people added to this a transversal house. They were allowed to extend each of these two houses but had to keep to the same floor plan. It was not permitted, for instance, to build another transversal house on the other side of the courtyard; such an arrangement was reserved for houses of high mandarins in the capital. Storeyed houses were also forbidden for the same reason. Our transversal house was a brick building with a tiled roof and walls only on three sides to provide shelter for paddy-grinding, rice-pounding, rice-sieving, preparing food for family festivals, etc. . . . . In other words, it was a working area. Next to this building was the kitchen and behind the kitchen, the granary. The fowl range and pigsty could be found farther back behind the granary.

My great-grandmother and grandparents generally started the day by having early morning tea in the altar house. They sat on two wooden settees set up in the middle of the house, the ladies on one side, grandfather on the other. Between them was a narrow table on which was put a tea set with a very small teapot in red earthenware, not much bigger than an egg, and even smaller teacups in porcelain. The set looked like miniature toys. Grandfather prepared the tea himself. He would drink one or two cups, then have a smoke on his water pipe, drawing deeply from it and making it sing like a boiling kettle. Sometimes, he would call me over to hand me a cup. The highly concentrated black tea was bitter and I never liked drinking it, especially in the morning before one had had anything to eat. After the midday nap, there was another tea session, this time with a bigger teapot and bigger cups, and a much more palatable tea because it was not as strong. As a matter of fact, the tea taken in the afternoon could be excellent when it was perfumed to the scent of the lotus flower, the jasmine flower or, most precious of all, the *ngau* flower of our own garden. Besides the tea sessions and the meals which were taken there during the cold season, the altar house was very much the domain of the women. Great-grandmother was then nearing ninety, her eyesight failing, but otherwise enjoying good health. She did not need any special help and could go about by herself within the compound. However, most of the time she remained seated on the settee. She and grandmother slept in the front room on two adjoining wooden beds, so that grandmother could look after her mother-in-law and help her if she got up during the night. There were no such things as individual bedrooms. Several wooden platforms were set up in the altar house. During the day, covered by rush mats, they served as a lounge for visitors to sit and have tea. At mealtimes, they became an eating area, with the family sitting around trays of food. In the evenings, cleaned, with the mats changed and mosquito nets installed, the platforms were transformed into beds.

The transversal house, too, was female territory. And so, of course, was the kitchen. How many times had I been expelled from there by my grandmother! She was very firm that only girls should be in there. "Heroes of the kitchen corner!" she would chastise us boys before telling us to go back to our study room. Still, I was drawn there by the smell of my favorite dishes being cooked, like bean curd casserole, caramel pork and a lot of others. Moreover, I was quite good at tasting the food to see whether it had been cooked to the right texture or whether it had got enough salt, sugar, or the right combination of spices. Often, I was called by the ladies to the kitchen to give my expert opinion on the dishes they were cooking.

In front of the altar house and parallel to it was a two-storey building called the new house. Built in the 1930s, it was the only storeyed house in the village and probably, in the whole canton. As mentioned earlier, its shape recalled the Mountain of the Twins in the geomancer's prophecy. The three rooms downstairs were used as lounge, guest room and my grandfather's study. The guest room became the boys' study or games room during the summer vacation. Grandfather worked and slept in his study. His platform of blackwood had a smooth and shiny surface which kept wonderfully cool in summer. I have fond memories of the new house, where we boys had our quarters, for we slept in the two rooms upstairs. It was also there that grandfather taught me the Chinese script, which we called *chu nho,* or scholarly script. A knowledge of that script is essential to a thorough understanding of the Vietnamese language, but schools had stopped teaching it. In the summer of 1943, my grandfather decided that it was time to fill that gap in our education. He started teaching us four boys. After a couple of weeks, however, the other three left for Hanoi to have private tutoring in preparation for the coming academic year. I was the only one who did not need tutoring and, therefore, stayed back in Kim Bai. At first I felt left out but soon became absorbed in my new studies. Each day after the morning meal, I went to grandfather's study and prepared the black ink by dipping an ink stick in water, then rubbing it hard against a stone slab until an ink of required thickness was obtained. I learned to use all the muscles of my right arm in this rubbing operation, so as to warm them up for the writing session. Then, I put out on the desk his writing panoply of brushes of different sizes, most of them having bamboo handles but some with handles in shining silver. When everything was ready, grandfather came to the study and the lesson started. A big rectangular panka fan was suspended from the ceiling. I listened to grandfather while pulling the fan.

Grandfather began his career as a teacher and stayed in that profession for ten years before he was appointed to head a prefecture. He was a good teacher who adapted his teaching to the needs of his pupil. Instead of making me learn by rote a number of Chinese characters in the traditional way, which was dry in the extreme, he taught me the characters in the context of Vietnamese and Chinese classical literature. Each day, he took a passage of the *Story of Kieu,* a 3254-verse poem acknowledged as the masterpiece of our literature. As I read the verses aloud, he wrote down all the words which came from Chinese script, at the same time explaining and commenting on each verse. Where other poetry may directly describe, Vietnamese poetry commonly alludes and suggests. Just as a few dots of ink in a painting can suggest so much, a few words of poetry can create a whole mood. Often the poet makes reference to some story taken from classical Chinese literature, and he gives to his poem, by that brief reference alone, a new dimension. For instance, in the early part of the *Story of Kieu,* the heroine said in response to the advances made by her lover:

> Even with deep red leaves and vermilion threads,
> We still must depend on our parents' consent.

"Deep red leaves" and "vermilion threads" both allude to ancient Chinese stories. To a knowledgeable reader, their inclusion gives to the above verse the poetic meaning and depth of feelings associated with those stories. This is the story of the vermilion threads. Vi Co was a young student, still very much after the pleasures of life. Returning home one evening after a merry session with friends, he saw an old man reading a book in the moonlight. The man had beside him a bag full of vermilion threads. Something out of the ordinary about the old man led Vi Co to approach and ask him what it was that he was reading. The old man said: "In this book are the names of men and women destined to be joined in matrimony and these threads are to tie them together." Vi Co was in high spirits so, repressing a chuckle, he said to the old man: "My name is Vi Co, can you tell me who it is who will be my wife?" The old man replied: "Indeed, I should not divulge Heaven's secret prematurely, but for you I am prepared to make an exception. Come and meet me tomorrow morning at the market place." Next day Vi Co went to the market and saw the old man already there. "So," asked Vi Co, "where is my future wife?" The old man said, "There she is!" and pointed to a half-naked three-year-old girl playing nearby. At once, Vi Co saw himself as the butt of a joke and was furious. Losing all control, he hit the small girl on the head with his stick and in the commotion that ensued, he slipped away. Years later, as a mandarin, he duly married the adopted daughter of his superior. They were in love with each other and lived happily ever after. One day his wife was washing her long black tresses when Vi Co happened to pass by her room. At that moment, he noticed a big scar on her head, and her story came out. Coming from a poor family, she had been orphaned and came to be adopted by a high mandarin. Vi Co realized that indeed it was she who had been the small girl in the marketplace so long ago. When Vietnamese texts mention "vermilion threads" or "the old man in the moonlight," they refer to a predestined union that transcends the love between a man and a woman.

The phrase "deep red leaves" alludes to another story of love promises exchanged.

I had known by heart many verses of the *Story of Kieu* and enjoyed their melodious rhymes and surface meaning, but grandfather's commentaries opened my mind to the real depth and richness of that work. I was thrilled. The solitary summer months without any companion of my age passed quickly. I also occupied myself with learning Chinese calligraphy. Grandmother looked upon it with much pride. As I was then very thin, she constantly urged me to have more to eat. "Only those who eat enough can learn," she said, quoting a well-known proverb. As a matter of fact, I found out myself that it was very difficult to use my brush well on an empty stomach. Good brushwork required total control of your right arm which was inclined to be shaky if you felt hungry or tired. We Vietnamese liked to eat what we called "the end parts" of fish or fowl; for instance, the head and tail of a fish are more appreciated than its body and chicken feet are much sought after. One popular belief, however, was that if a scholar were to eat chicken feet, his arm would shake and his calligraphy would suffer. It was a belief that I had never subscribed to, but whenever grandmother was present, chicken feet were something I was not allowed to touch.

The following summer, I was back in the village and grandfather resumed his teaching. I had by then made enough progress to learn the Confucian Four Books, not in their totality of course, but the first two—the *Great Learning* and the *Doctrine of the Mean*—and extracts from the *Analects* and from *Mencius*. At the same time, grandfather introduced me to Tang poetry. It was pure joy. He had a complete collection of Tang poems, printed with wooden plates in Vietnam or China, probably at the beginning of this century. The characters were bold and beautifully composed. How I wish now that that collection had been kept! In the manner of scholars of his days, he made a small circle in red ink next to the words he most enjoyed reading, so, when I opened a book, I would read first the poems that had the most red circles. Many Tang poems were so beautiful that some of the pages were almost covered in red circles. It was like discovering an endless treasure. In many poems, I could not read all the words nor could I completely comprehend the meaning, but even two or three verses would often suffice to reveal a magic beauty that led me passionately to search for new discoveries.

At about the same period, I began reading *The Story of the Three Kingdoms* in Chinese. Grandfather was away from the village for a few weeks. I took out the first volume of *The Three Kingdoms* from his bookcase more out of curiosity than anything else. I did not think I could read it, having studied Chinese for an aggregate of three or four months only. To my surprise, I went easily through the first pages and continued on. Lying on a hammock in the guest room and using my foot to swing it to find relief from the stuffy heat, I read avidly and with trepidation the stratagems of heroes and villains, the tales of loyalty and treachery, the fortunes of war and the fate of men in those stormy times. *The Three Kingdoms* along with other Chinese classics such as *The Warring States, The Water Margin* and *The Journey to the West* were parts of our own cultural legacy. Their heroes and heroines were familiar already from folk stories. Now I found them all over again and learnt more about them and their exploits from the richest literary veins themselves. When grandfather came back, the whole household was talking about my ability to read *The Three Kingdoms* in its original text. It was grandmother who broke the news to him. Grandfather was pleased indeed, but characteristically kept a sense of proportion. *"The Three Kingdoms,"* he said, "is the easiest of Chinese historical novels. All students started their reading with that novel."

Grandmother also kept all the sheets of paper that I used for practicing my calligraphy. It was a special, absorbent paper, as Chinese is written in vertical lines from top to bottom and from right to left. Our people considered Chinese characters as the "script of saints and sages" and extended their respect to the paper they were written on. It was not to be thrown away together with rubbish, or put to any lowly uses. Thus, grandmother took special care in collecting my papers and storing them away in a safe place. She showed them to her husband proudly. Grandfather, however, was content to respond with a smile. I knew that he considered my calligraphy still very immature.

The new house was parallel to the altar house, at a distance of about a dozen meters. Linking the two was a roofed hall, open to the garden and trees on both sides. The family took their meals during the summer in that well-ventilated area. In front of the new house lay a large courtyard, paved in square red bricks. The newly harvested paddy was dried there before being stored in our granary.

There was another building in the compound called the western house, but we seldom went there. It was built in 1929, in a style brought into the country by the French and therefore called western or modern. It had a ceiling, large windows, and was partitioned by internal walls into separate rooms. The name western also indicated its position, the western side of the compound. My grandfather gave the house to his younger brother, who had a business in Hanoi but owned no land in the village. My great-aunt died there in 1940 of tuberculosis. Since then, the house had been left vacant most of the time. Only at important ceremonies was it opened, to entertain village notables. When we children returned to Kim Bai for the summer holidays, we tended to keep away from it. Although my great-aunt had died several years earlier, we were still fearful of catching tuberculosis, an incurable disease in those days.

All the houses, except for the transversal house, were decorated with innumerable boards carrying Chinese inscriptions carved in the wood. There were vertical boards, hung in pairs on walls and pillars and called "parallel sentences." A sentence could be composed of up to seven or eight characters. There were horizontal boards, hung high on walls or across lintels. Some boards had only three or four very big characters. Others contained whole poems in smaller characters. The boards were painted and lacquered in various combinations of black, red, gold and silver; for instance, gold characters on a red background or silver characters on a black background. Some characters, made of mother-of-pearl inlaid in the wood, shimmered with all the colors of the rainbow. Apart from the boards, the houses had no other decorations, pictures or paintings. But the boards were everywhere. Their shining colors gave a rich and festive look to the rooms.

The boards were presented to our family on occasions such as the reception of some honor from the court, or when my grandfather was promoted to a higher rank, or again, when my great-grandmother reached the age of seventy. The inauguration of a new house was also such an occasion. Big celebrations were held and guests brought these boards as presents. Their value resided, of course, not only in the quality of the wood, carving, paint and lacquer, but even more in the thoughts they expressed and in the artistry of their calligraphy. Not every scholar could write the large characters to be carved on the boards. These were the work of master calligraphers. Calligraphy in our home region tended to favor an angular or "nervy" quality of stroke, designed to show "all the thews and sinews" in each character. Most boards in our ancestral home came from that school and gave an impression of strength, but also of formal rigidity. A few had characters with softer and rounder lines, which were more pleasing to the eye. They were written by scholars belonging to a different school of calligraphy. The characters on some boards were written in a clear and "regular style" and I could read them, or at least I could look them up in the dictionary. Many calligraphers, however, prided themselves with writing fast; they often used a "running style," or even a faster "grass style," which reduced the characters to a maze of indecipherable loops. "Like wriggling worms!" people would mock their style. But the highest compliment that one could pay a calligrapher was to say that "flying dragons and dancing phoenixes" came out from his brush. As a teenager, I was not able to read the grass style, but did sometimes see those mythological creatures appear. I used to take my midday nap lying in a hammock in the new house's guest room. In that room was a horizontal board with a long poem written in grass style. The characters of the poem were painted black over a background of golden clouds and the board itself was framed on all four sides with elaborate carvings of dragons painted in red. Dozing off in the oppressive heat of early afternoon, I would wake up suddenly and see the characters on the board springing up to life. For a brief moment, red and black dragons were dancing together before my eyes in a confused manner.

The words on the boards were mostly consecrated formulas expressing compliments and good wishes. A large horizontal board in the front room of our altar house had the four characters *Dai Gia Bi Phuc,* which expressed the noble reminder that "A great family is destined to be happy and fortunate." Most parallel sentences and poems were in the same vein. But some boards were particularly prized by my grandfather, either because they were written by renowned poets of his time—his friend Licentiate Duong, who wrote our family chronicle, was one such poet—or because they referred to salient events in our family's history. All the boards, however, were lost in the turmoil of the 1940s and the 1950s. Many of these works of art, I was told, were chopped up by the troops billeted in our compound to make firewood. Our family had kept a complete record of all presents received on the occasion of celebrations, including the texts of all decorative boards. Alas, that document too had been lost. Our ancestral home was occupied by French troops from 1950 until 1954. When the French left, the communists moved in. We were never allowed to go back there.

My grandfather built the altar house and its adjoining transversal house in the 1920s to provide better accommodation for his old mother, who stayed back in the village and did not follow him on his mandarinal postings. Besides a courtyard, the rest of the land was left to trees and gardens. In particular, our compound had a number of old and tall trees giving it coolness and shade and making it look like a secluded rural retreat. Grandfather was the son of a Taoist scholar. He would have liked the compound to stay that way, for the day when he would retire. But his career decided otherwise. He became a high official in his hometown Ha Dong. As Kim Bai was so near, he used to go back there to celebrate important family functions such as the anniversary of the death of his father. Friends, colleagues, surbordinates joined him on such occasions. As he rose high in rank the number of his guests increased. In the late 1920s, he built the western house to entertain them. Soon, this proved to be insufficient and the new house was built. Then, a larger courtyard was needed to park the guests' rickshaws and even cars which had made their appearance in the country. Our ancestral home became a group of brick buildings, very comfortable to live in, but a far cry from the traditional village cottage that I had learned to love in poems and folk songs. The arbor of *thien ly* was not there, and neither was the thatched roof on which dewdrops shone like gold in the morning sun.

Grandfather managed, however, to preserve a few old trees. In the front yard was a row of tall and thin areca nut trees, whose fruit was an essential ingredient to betel chewing. A *long nao* or camphor tree stood between the altar house and the new house. It was the tallest tree in the compound, taller even than the roof of the two-storeyed new house. The sap of the *long nao* had medicinal qualities and the whole tree produced a nice fragrance which kept away flies and mosquitoes. Its wood was good to make furniture. Three pomelo trees bore each year hundreds of fruits as big as a melon, full of juice and very sweet. The front yard had two tropical flower plants called *ngau* and *moc*. These were usually planted near places of worship and, therefore, treated with special care. Our *ngau* and *moc* were enclosed in raised brick planter boxes. The *moc* flower is a miniature jasmine, with white porcelain-like petals. The *ngau* must be quite old, as it was twice or three times the size of a normal *ngau* and its branches reached up to our first-floor windows. Its small and numerous yellow flowers bloomed in spring at about the same time as the *moc* and their fragrance filled the whole courtyard. Behind the altar house was a large tree called *sau* which bore small and acid fruits and when marinated in a mixture of fish sauce, vinegar, sugar and chili, produced a favorite tidbit. Ask any Vietnamese from the north about the marinated *sau* and his mouth will water at the mere mention of it.

The front yard was decorated with two three-legged concrete urns, as tall as a man. At the conclusion of anniversaries and festivals, the gold and silver votive papers were brought from the altars and burnt in the urns. In a corner of the yard and leaning against the wall was a raised goldfish pond built to the shape of a half-moon. In the middle of the pond rose a miniature rock-mountain, with its miniature bonsai trees. Most prominent among them was a *si* tree, of the same species as the one which gave to the village gate its name, with countless roots hanging down to the surface of the water. Even the snails living around its base were miniature in size. Here and there in the mountain were tiny earthen temples, bridges, cottages and figurines of wood gatherers carrying their packs home, old men fishing at a stream, chess players enjoying a game and a sage contemplating the beauty and mystery of nature. Such sceneries adorned many a garden, be they owned by scholars, businessmen, farmers or artisans. The Taoist dream of retiring to the mountains to live among the trees and the clouds and away from the cares of this world lay close to the Vietnamese heart. The rock-mountain, miniature trees and goldfish pond were more than a popular hobby; they were part of that dream.

The compound was surrounded on all sides by a high brick wall, which gave it a rather forbidding aspect. It had an imposing gate house with a green tiled roof showing the traditional curved lines, heavy iron gates and a guard room on top. What was special about the gate house was its position, tucked in one corner of the compound. From the village's entrance to our place, one had to follow the edge of the compound along its whole length before reaching the gate. Then, one had to make a sharp turn right, enter the gate, walk half the length of the front yard and make another right turn to face the new house. Next, one had to go through the new house and through the hall before coming to the inner center of the compound, which was the altar house. Many visitors intrigued by this roundabout route put the question to my grandfather. He replied that it was chosen on the advice of a Chinese geomancer, without giving any further explanation. Actually, the new house and the gate were built at the same time in the 1930s, some ten years after the altar house. The same Chinese geomancer was invited back and he made some radical recommendations. Firstly, he would place the new two-storeyed house right in front of the altar house, at a distance of only a dozen meters, thus blocking the latter's view completely. This went against a basic principle in geomancy, for to block a house's view would be to block the progress of its occupants. Secondly, the gate was to be built in a corner and oriented in such a way that part of it was hidden behind a hedge. Such a position did not bring out the imposing character of that construction. However, my grandfather accepted the recommendations. I was never given an explanation, but his reasons probably had to do with the prophecy of the Mountain of the Twins. Possibilities of high achievements existed in Kim Bai, but the way to the top was particularly difficult to find, according to the prophecy. The geomancer must have been inspired by it, for what he set out to do was to transfer the geomantic characteristics of the land of Kim Bai onto our compound. It was difficult to reach the peaks of the Mountain of the Twins. Accordingly, the geomancer made it difficult to get to the inner center of our compound. He hid the altar house behind the new house, devised a tortuous route to get there, placed obstacles on the way, put the gate house out of place. He counselled against some basic rules in geomancy to reach for a higher reward, that our family may benefit from the auspicious character of the Mountain of the Twins. Four centuries ago, the prophecy came true with the ancestors of our first generation. Now, the geomancer aimed to ensure that it would continue to hold true for their descendants.

4. School Holidays in Kim Bai

Summer vacation lasted three months, from mid–June to mid–September. After 1942, as the economic situation worsened and Allied air attacks became more frequent, there were no more holidays on the seaside for our family. Instead, our parents sent us to Kim Bai. At times, we were a group of up to ten boys and girls and it was great fun. But often, I found myself there with only my brother Dong as companion, who was then only seven and six years my junior. I felt lonely and missing out on all those exciting things happening in the capital. At the end of the academic year, when the subject of vacation in the village came up, all of us children asked to remain in Hanoi. Or if we had to go to Kim Bai, it should be only for a short time. We argued that a few weeks' change of air should do enough good for our health; more importantly, we needed tutoring so as to be ready for next year's studies. I was then a skinny child and often sick, but I did well at school, so these arguments were of no use to me. Every year, I stayed in Kim Bai for the whole duration of the school holidays.

It was not all holiday and play, but also work. My grandmother was nearing sixty, but remained very active and industrious. She abhorred idleness, which she said was not only a vice, but also a disease. The wife of a retired mandarin, she could have spent old age in leisure, yet chose to immerse herself in work. Like other women in Kim Bai, she made paddy into polished rice and went to the market to sell it. Soon, our group fell into the rhythm of village life. We got up early. Grandmother always was up at the crack of dawn. I learned how good it was to start a day in that way. It gave me a wonderful feeling of physical well-being and the reassuring thought that a whole new day lay ahead of me. To get up late in the country, when the sun was already high and the house empty because everybody had gone to their tasks, would really mar my day. Food was cooked and the family sat down for the first of the two main meals of the day. Then, the men went out to the fields and the women brought their wares to the market. In tropical countries, the best time of the day is early morning, after the rest given by a night's sleep and when the air is still cool and fresh. As the folk saying goes:

In a year, how many months of spring can there be,
In a day, how many hours of early morning can one have!

Such precious moments have to be put to good use; that is why the habit of rising early is so prized. Begun early, the day also ended early. Dinner was eaten in late afternoon and by dusk it was nearly bedtime. Between the two main meals, people usually had a snack of some sort. Around midday, children would be seen going out of the village carrying woven baskets containing food and drink for those working in the fields. Food generally meant sweet potatoes, manioc or corn, either boiled or grilled. Drink was either black tea, or, if in season, green tea made from freshly picked leaves. Out in the open under a burning sun, nothing could quench a thirst better than a bowl of steaming green tea. It looked greenish and was strong and bitter. Taken hot in hot weather, it made one perspire profusely. Many villagers were just as addicted to that green tea as to tobacco or liquor. After the snack, everyone had a siesta. Men and beasts repaired to some shaded places to rest. Trees were few and far between in the fields but, here and there, brick huts had been built for workers and travellers to shelter from the heat. In the village itself, all activities came to a stop. The red brick paths were deserted. Even dogs disappeared into the shade and stopped barking. Only the chirping of birds was to be heard, and from time to time rising above it, the strange crow of a rooster greeting the blinding light of the midday sun. Siesta-time did not last long. After half-an-hour or so, activities were resumed. The short nap acted like magic to clear one's head and refresh one's body for the afternoon's work.

Our group of teens and pre-teenagers included two of my grandfather's children, two or three of my great-uncle's children and five of us: my elder brother Hong, my younger sisters Trang and Giang, my younger brother Dong and myself. Following the morning meal, we all worked to make paddy into rice, all except for Dong who was still too young. Firstly, paddy had to be ground to break the husk and free the grain. Rotating the mill was a heavy task performed by the men in our household and we boys took turns to relieve them. Grains of rice came out of the mill mixed with their husks. Then came sieving, which was done by the women and girls. The sieve was a round and flat bamboo basket, loosely woven. On a sieve shaken in a circular motion, the heavier rice grains went to the bottom and were separated from the lighter husks which congregated on top. A girl who knew how to sieve well was a pleasant sight to watch. She would be seated on one of those low stools very much in use in the country, her body and legs at once in an elegant yet modest pose. Her long and graceful arms would move the sieve rhythmically. Rice grains and husks would roll faster and faster in the sieve until all the grain finally fell through, leaving only the husks. It was a charming picture, especially when the girl was attractive, as many in Kim Bai were. My sister Trang soon got the knack of doing this task and my grandmother watched her approvingly. "The family who will have that girl as a daughter-in-law," she said, "will be very lucky indeed."

Sieving had to be done two or three times before the bulk of the rice was clear of husks. Next came winnowing, to blow the last of the husks away. That was also a girl's task. Pounding followed, to take off the reddish-brown bran from the rice grain. The rice was poured into a cement mortar set into the ground. A long tree trunk served as a lever. At one end of the lever a pestle was attached, with its head covered in metal. Two or three people stood at the other end. They pushed their side of the lever down with their feet, the pestle came up and then, as the pressure on the other end of the lever was released, the pestle came down pounding on the rice. I enjoyed the slow and rhythmic pounding, in which both men and women participated. It was usually a time for singing to the tempo of pestle hitting mortar. Making paddy into rice being one of Kim Bai's main activities, the sound of rice pounding could be heard all day long. My memory associated it with summer afternoons, when the sun was at its fiercest and everything seemed to stop, except for that slow cadence which induced me to sleep. The final job was to separate the white rice from the bran. That meant sieving again, by the women.

> Five men,
> Holding two poles,
> Into a cave,
> They direct a flock of white ducks.
> What is that?

Villagers at work liked to sing, recite poems or pose short riddles like the one above. Males would be grouped on one side, females on the other. The men would start by challenging the women to find the answer to a riddle. The women would respond, then throw a riddle back to the men. Questions would go back and forth until one side either could not answer or ran out of riddles. The contest could go on for quite a while, as villagers not only had a good collection of riddles but also improvised new ones. The answer to the above riddle, by the way, is eating rice. The five men with their two poles are the fingers of a hand holding the two chopsticks, the cave is the mouth and the white ducks stand for white rice. In those working sessions, we sang and taught one another poems taken from the rich folklore of our region. More exactly, we recited them in a modulated voice to bring out the music in our tonal language. They were short poems of no more than two or four verses. Each of us had a repertoire of them. They mirrored the lives of our people and expressed the whole range of their feelings, but those I have come to love best were rather sad ones which spoke of love and duty, of the homesickness of the young bride for the village of her birth, of the pain of separation as the soldier prepared to leave for the border. Out in the fields, the white egret presented a lonely and sad sight, for it was most of the time wading by itself along some deserted ditch. Rarely would one

see a flock or even a pair of egrets. Thus, the white egret had come to represent in folklore the young wife whose husband was away and who toiled by
herself to bring up a family. This is the poem of the egret:

> Like the white egret wading along the river bank,
> She was carrying a provision of rice for her husband.
> Softly, the sound of her crying could be heard.
> "Please darling, go back to our village," he told her.
> "To look after our mother and our children.
> For to the border, in the mountains of Cao Bang,
> I have been called to go."

As the pounding developed into a cadence, a voice would rise. Firstly,
it would shyly recite a few verses. Then, as it grew bolder, the modulation
would appear and gain momentum. Eventually, everyone in our group
would chant their poems, instead of just reciting them.

My grandmother was busy moving from one group to another. She sat
down to teach the girls how to sieve. She held the basket of rice and poured
the grain down while behind her, someone agitated a big fan to blow the
husk away. She interrupted the pounding to see whether enough bran had
been taken off the rice. At midday, we all stopped for a snack of boiled
potatoes, or manioc, or corn on the cob. It was time for grandmother to
launch into one of her discourses. She liked to tell us ancient tales and
fables in verse, chanting them in traditional style. Her favorite fable was a
long one. She did not always remember all of it. Often, she improvised and
her verses did not rhyme well. But she was totally absorbed in it and we
were all listening attentively. I cannot remember all the verses, but the gist
of her story was clear. Once upon a time, the Lord in Heaven bestowed on
humanity peace and self-sufficiency. Everyone had enough to eat and enjoyed security. No thieves or robbers caused any need for a door to be
locked or bolted. They should have all been happy and contented, so the
Lord thought, but it was not to be. After a while, people started coming to
Him, asking for special grants and privileges. Day after day, their numbers
increased. Human greed really had no limits. The Lord in Heaven thus
became angry and decided to teach mankind a lesson. This he did by granting each and every request he received:

> My young man! whatever you want,
> I will gladly give to you.
> You want trouble and disorder?
> I will give trouble and disorder to you.

Hence the troubles of the world, grandmother concluded. Even after
this long time, mankind still did not seem to have learned the lesson.

My grandmother also reminded us repeatedly of a proverb, which
seemed to sum up her attitude to life:

It is not difficult,
To learn the ways of high living.
But how to live a poor and humble life,
That is indeed difficult to learn.

I have often wondered what made her have such a stoical and rather dour view of life. Her own family was rich and she had married into one that was poor. My grandfather had obtained his licentiate degree, but it was still many years before he entered the mandarinate, and even then it took him many more years to move out of the lower ranks. So, it had not been easy for my grandmother. However, the latter part of my grandfather's career was a remarkable success and he reached the top of his profession. Perhaps, my grandmother wanted to tell us that anyone could make the transition from difficult beginnings to wealth and honor. It was when confronted with adversity that coping and remaining true to oneself was difficult. Therefore, it was necessary for us children to be trained in manual work so that, when the need arose, we could adapt. I believe that, in those early years of the 1940s, my grandmother already had some premonition of the tremendous upheavals that would shortly affect our country, our society and our own family. She wanted us, the young generation, to be able eventually to face adversity and to see it as a challenge.

After the bran was removed from the rice, our day's work ended. Nothing from the paddy was thrown away. The bran, boiled and mixed with marsh lentil, served as pig's feed. The husk was used as fuel in the kitchen. The white rice of Kim Bai sold well at market because it was well clear of husks and had the right color and taste. Our people's main trade secret was the pounding. If not pounded enough, the rice would retain too much bran and would not be white enough; at the same time its taste would be too strong. If too much bran was removed, however, the rice would become rather insipid and tend to break.

In town, we used to have white rice. Most villagers, on the other hand, ate rice with plenty of bran left, which made it reddish when cooked. That "red" rice was more nutritious and a good prevention from beriberi, a disease common in the tropics and caused by a deficiency of Vitamin B. When in the village, we continued to have white rice, but every few days my grandmother, who had a quite modern and scientific outlook in spite of never having gone to school, would give us a meal of red rice. We children rather liked it, mainly because it was a change. A more special treat was broken rice, which came out in small pieces from the mortar after the pounding, and was not sold at market. Steam-cooked and mixed with fried onions and spices, broken rice is delicious. Many Vietnamese living abroad missed their broken rice. I did so in my student days in France, until the day I went into an Arab restaurant and discovered that its couscous was a good substitute to the broken rice at home.

Grandmother also wanted us boys to go out and work in the fields. As all our rice fields were let to tenants, she asked her cousin, whom I called Great-uncle Mayor, to take us to his fields. His response was not enthusiastic. "They have worked hard enough at school during the year," he told her, "let them enjoy their holidays." Still, one morning, the four of us found ourselves walking behind the mayor and his buffalo and heading for the open fields. Two of us were carrying the heavy plough. At the plot of land to be tilled, the mayor attached the plough to the buffalo and gave us a demonstration. Then, he let us take turns to handle the plough. The other three did not do too badly, but I found it very hard to press the ploughshare down so that the furrow would be deep enough. Also, to make the furrow run straight was a problem. Fortunately, the buffalo was quite used to working in the fields. It knew when to stop and to change direction, so my problem was only to deal with the plough. We managed to finish the plot as best we could. The mayor did not say whether or not he was satisfied with our work. "If they are bright enough to study at school, they should be able to work in the fields when they have to," was the rather oblique comment that he gave to my grandmother at the end of the day.

My grandmother often went to the market to sell rice and buy provisions for the family. She took the girls with her, to teach them how to buy and sell, and how to bargain with decorum. She did not approve of boys going there, saying that we should stay home and read books instead. But I can still see myself walking on the dike with her group of market goers, while the Lichee Field below was still wrapped in morning mist. Market days were the life of the countryside and thinking of them brings back fond memories of my youth. Grandmother was usually dressed in an old tunic of black gauze over black trousers. On her feet, she wore a pair of flat wooden clogs. Behind her came two or three members of our household carrying full baskets of rice. Although close to sixty, she walked at a fast pace and I had almost to run to keep up with her. Along the way, she kept up a steady flow of conversation with other market-going villagers, her ringing voice and laughter rising above the chatter of the group.

Market days were common to Kim Bai and a dozen or so neighboring villages. Five of them took turns to hold the market, according to a sequence which Kim Bai villagers had put in rhyme, so as to better memorize it. It ran as follows:

The first day, the market meets in our village,
The second day, it moves to Mai,
The third day, to Quan,
The fourth day is the turn of Chuong,
The fifth day, that of Dong.
The sixth day, the market returns to Kim Bai,
The seventh day is again Mai's turn,

The eighth day, Quan's,
The ninth day, the meeting is at Dong, not Chuong,
For Chuong is where the market goes on the tenth day.

On the eleventh day of the lunar month, the same ten-day cycle started again, and again on the twenty-first. As all lunar months have thirty days, there was no problem of dealing with the odd day out. Every day, it was market day at one of the five villages.

I know little of Quan, except that a foremother of ours, many generations ago, came from there. Dong, or Cat Dong by its full name, had a strong tradition of scholarship like Kim Bai, and could boast of several holders of the doctorate in the past. One doctor named Ha Ton Quyen was a poet of note, reached a high mandarinal rank, and, under the reign of Emperor Ming Mang (1820–1840), undertook an unusual diplomatic mission. He was given a ship and ordered to sail to Batavia, today's Indonesia. Outwardly, it was for trade, but his real task was to see whether the Dutch and other western powers had any design on our country. At that time, parts of south and east Asia had already fallen under European domination, although our country was still spared. The Vietnamese court could see the threat coming. Other ships were sent to Penang and Calcutta to keep an eye on the British and a diplomatic delegation went to France and England. However, no action was taken following those missions, and the country was hopelessly unprepared when French warships moved in to bombard our ports, some decades later.

Mai was a big village serving as the seat of a canton. Its people had a fierce temper and a tradition of opposition to authority which, at times, verged on lawlessness. Folklore had it that they could be found among rebels and bandits who appeared during periods of insecurity. Under the French regime, the villagers of Mai were known for their illicit activities in brewing rice brandy, then a government monopoly. Now and then they got into trouble, but for most of the time the police turned a blind eye and let them go about their business, provided it was conducted in an unobstrusive manner. Everyone in our region knew that when women from Mai, carrying baskets on their heads, went through one village after another shouting "Who wants to buy cakes?" they had in fact rice brandy undercover in the baskets. People bought their brandy, not only because it came from a neighboring village, but also because it was quite good and strong. Moreover, it was cheaper than the legal brandy, which was heavily taxed. Finally, Chuong was the colloquial name for Phuong Trung, the seat of our canton and a wealthy place, with many brick houses and wide brick lanes running deep into its hamlets. All the dozen or so villages in our group, whether large or small and having their own markets or not, were relatively well off. Their land was fertile. When the harvest was poor on account of the weather, our region suffered from scarcity, not from famine. Even in

1945, when over one million people died in north Vietnam, out of a population then of twelve million, it escaped the terrible calamity.

Once or twice a month, the market was held on a bigger scale and called "main market." It was there that my grandmother used to go, often to buy provisions in preparation for a family festival. She would bring home basketfuls of fruit, vegetable and other produce as well as chickens, ducks, even pigs if it was for an important occasion. A main market day brought a festive atmosphere to the village. People looked forward to it, the women in particular, for market crowds were predominantly female. It was women who did the selling, the buying and the bargaining. Men worked in the fields and would go only on special occasions such as required by the buying of seeds or farm implements. Country markets were also places where people met, exchanged chit-chats and gossips. Women made more use of such opportunities than did men, who had other venues for social contact. For women, the market provided the only regular setting for social life outside the family circle. Young men, too, looked forward to main market day, for girls from the village and neighboring places would be there. Even when work in the fields was demanding, they would take a few moments off, quickly go home to change into better clothes and drop in on the market. There, buying a cake and a cup of tea, or inquiring about various wares that the girls were offering for sale, they would try to strike up a conversation and make new acquaintances. Otherwise the segregation of the sexes gave young people scant opportunity to meet.

Markets in our region offered a variety of cakes, savories and other snacks. To me, a market trip would be incomplete without tasting some local delicacies. Crab noodle soup, rolled rice cakes to be eaten with a spicy fish sauce, deep fried balls of dough, all looked so inviting, but my grandmother would not always let me have them, as they were exposed to flies and other insects. I could buy cakes that were steamed and under wrap. There was a good choice of rice cakes stuffed with a filling of meat, vegetable or sweet bean paste. I often had *banh khuc,* a cake which had no meat, only flour, vegetable and some bits of fried spring onion. *Khuc* is the name of a spinach that grows wild in the fields. Boiled and mixed with flour, it made the cake green and gave it a delicate aroma. During the war, my mother used to make *banh khuc* for sale at the market. Every morning I woke up to the smell of steamed cakes wafting out of the kitchen. I do not know how much money she made. In any case, the cakes never went to waste; when not sold, they were a welcome addition to our evening meal.

In the winter, I liked to have a kind of sandwich made of two rice wafers with a filling of sweet millet paste. Described like that it may not sound very appetizing and in fact, it was quite cheap. But I was especially fond of it. The thin wafers were grilled over a bed of charcoal and became crackers the size of a dinner plate. The sweet millet paste was piping hot on a cold morning. Its color was a beautiful gold. The wafers crumbled in my mouth. Moreover, millet had always carried a special connotation for me. It evoked the fleetingness of time and the impermanence of wealth and fame. Whenever I had it, it brought back to mind one of the favorite stories of my childhood, "The Dream of the Golden Millet."

A scholar who had failed more than once at the examinations stopped one day at an inn. He met a Taoist priest and their conversation soon turned into a monologue by the scholar complaining about his adverse fate. The owners of the inn were cooking a pot of millet. The priest who had said little finally handed the scholar a headrest—of the hard kind made out of bamboo and used by country people—and told him to have a nap, he would feel better on waking up. As soon as the scholar lay down and let his head rest on the bamboo, he found himself being successful at the examinations and entering a mandarinal career. His whole life unfolded. He married, had several children, his career brought him great fame and honor. Then his own sons graduated and had brilliant careers themselves. Grandchildren came to his family in abundant numbers. Step by step, he reached the ripe old age of eighty and prepared himself for the final journey home, when he woke up suddenly. He realized that he was still in the same inn, with the priest seated next to him. The golden millet in the pot was still not cooked.

Of the five markets, the most picturesque was that of Chuong, the seat of our canton. Built on a piece of land between the dike and the Hat River, Chuong market had numerous shade trees. This together with its position on the river bank meant that it remained cool in summer. It started to fill up quite early in the morning. Sitting on a root of banyan tree, I watched line after line of villagers making their way on the dike towards the market. The bamboo poles on their shoulders bent into arcs by the weight of the baskets on both ends. In spite of their heavy loads, the villagers marched gingerly, while chatting all the way. Country girls liked to chant folk poems and I can still hear them telling about the hard work they had to do all year round, except for Tet, the New Year season:

> The first month, I stayed at home to celebrate the Tet.
> The second month, I raised silk-worms,
> To make cloth for selling at the market in the third month.
> The fourth and fifth months were taken up by the rice harvest.
> The sixth month, I sold the fruit of the longan and the lichee.
> The seventh and eighth months, I sold sweet corn and other produce of the fields.
> The ninth and tenth months were again harvest time, this time the main harvest.
> At the end of the year, I got married to a scholar,
> Who did nothing but eat and rest!

On the other side of the river, groups of people were waiting to be ferried across. They were also chatting noisily and calling for boats. The Hat River at that place was about twenty meters wide but the water was shallow and only waist-deep. When the market was not meeting, people simply pulled up their clothes and waded across. But that was not possible on market day, especially with heavy baskets to carry. So the small boats did a brisk trade. Very soon, all was people, produce, noise and activity. The countryside burst into life on main market day. To fully take part, one had to be there early, because the rush of activity did not last very long. After three hours or so, people started to leave. Villagers used to say, "Either you go early to market, or you do not go at all." A market emptying was a melancholic sight. It reminded me of the emptying school ground on the last day of the school year, when it was finally time for friends to say good-bye.

Every year on the tenth day of the first month, a big festival was held at the Chuong market. Nowadays, Vietnamese celebrate the Tet over three days, but traditionally it was longer and lasted seven days. In our region, the practice was to extend it even a little more, so that it ended with the Chuong Festival. This was the first public festival of the year and also the most important. People came from all villages in the region and even from places farther away. Everyone wore their best clothes. There was of course a lot of things to eat, as all the dishes each village was famous for were on sale. Competitions were organized, the two most popular being rice-cooking for teenage girls and for young men. The girls had to light a fire in the open and cook a pot of rice in the fastest time, while carrying a one-year-old baby who was not a member of their family and keeping him from crying. As an added difficulty, each girl was given a toad which should be kept inside a circle drawn in the ground. The baby was not accustomed to the girl and did not like the presence of the crowd, the toad also was frightened and wanted to jump back to its pond. It was, therefore, not easy to keep the two of them still while the rice was being cooked. The competition, so the elders said, was to test the mettle of the girls who would soon become housewives and should be able to deal with the multiple problems of running a household. The crowd enjoyed itself greatly, but the competitors had a hard time keeping the fire on while the baby cried and the toad jumped. Once, however, I saw a girl who remained in control throughout. Somehow, she managed to pacify the baby despite the noise, the crowd and the smoke. As for her toad, it was so sluggish that it refused to move even when prodded. Her rice was kept boiling, while she chatted merrily with her friends.

The men also had their rice-cooking competition. True, cooking the family meal was not their responsibility and the kitchen was female territory. But they had to know how to do it. What would happen if mother, wife and sister were away? Moreover, did not our Master Confucius say that "gentlemen must have all-round skills"? On a bank of the Hat River, a row of rice pots was arranged on their tripods with firewood at the ready. The young men started from the opposite bank in their small boats which were just big enough to hold them. They had to use their hands to paddle and reach the other bank. There, staying in their boats, they must with their wet hands strike matches, light a fire, and keep it going as their boat swayed and drifted away. It might take them up to one hour to cook the rice in those conditions. Few could avoid falling into the chilly waters. But they all had a good time and were given the rice they cooked to bring home. The winner, in addition, received a pair of live ducks. Other games were played, such as "human chess." The "chessmen" were teenagers, boys on one side and girls on the other, all smartly dressed, the boys in blue or green tunics and the girls, their young faces made so much more mature and attractive by make-up, in orange or pink dresses. Very much in demand too were the astrologers and fortune-tellers. New Year was the time when new resolutions were taken, new decisions made; many people needed to get from them assurance and encouragement. Last, but not least, a traditional Vietnamese opera was performed. Libretti were based on romances from Vietnamese and Chinese history. Actors and actresses wore splendid costumes and heavy makeup which indicated whether they were heroes or villains. Green-faced traitors met their death at the hands of loyal servants of the King whose faces were painted red. All sang, danced, and mimed to the accompaniment of drums, wind and string instruments. There was much to do and to enjoy. But the main reason for the Chuong Festival was social. It was for meeting and talking, most of all for seeing and being seen. A folk ballad ran:

> On the tenth day of the New Year,
> Let us go and enjoy the Chuong Festival.
> There in the crowd,
> Everyone will have eyes only for himself.

After the festival, the nice clothes were folded and put away in the trunks. People got ready to resume their normal lives. Tet was over.

We worked or studied only in the mornings. Afternoons were free for reading, playing games or going out as we pleased. Our village, and indeed the whole canton, was safe territory for us, as nearly everyone knew who we were. My grandmother never worried about where we went. Most afternoons, we boys roamed the countryside, each armed only with a stick to keep dogs away. Often we visited other villages for a game of soccer. We played on all sorts of grounds, from bare fields cracked by drought to grassy pastures full of water puddles after the rains. Twisted ankles because of potholes were frequent occurrences and it was quite usual for both teams to retire at the local herbal medicine man after a match, for injured players to be treated.

Birds and fish abounded in the country. Most families in our village had a pond, where fish were raised to provide a secondary income. Our own pond lay beside the main path leading from the village gate to the Communal Hall. From the edge of the pond, an old fig tree spread out in a most unusual fashion, for it projected itself horizontally towards the middle of the water, instead of upwards. Its trunk and branches were convenient places to sit and fish while keeping watch on village activities. I never had any success with fishing there. Not that I lacked patience; I could spend a long time sitting still. But somehow fish never took my bait; whereas my two younger sisters and even my brother Dong, who had just started school, caught them easily. We also took potshots at birds, using slingshots. Great care was taken in finding a forked stick of the right shape, made of guava-tree wood, a very tough wood with a beautiful shine similar to that of the crepe myrtle. I never brought down any bird that way. However, I was quite good at catching young birds in their nests before they could fly and raising them. I was especially keen to go after a small species of sparrow which had black feathers, a black beak and a lively chirp. Some became tame and could be let out among the trees of our compound. They would stay there and, at nightfall, would return to their cage.

Our region enjoyed security, but the memory of attacks by bandits was still alive and village defense was tight. Each village had a number of guards chosen by rotation among the young men. Armed with staves and using bullhorns to sound the alarm, they patrolled the hamlets at night, pounding their staves on the brick lanes to manifest their presence. In case of emergency, every villager—male or female, young or old—had to join in. Village rules set down in detail the rewards given to guards and other citizens for the capture of outlaws, as well as the compensations they received in the event of injury. If a person was killed while defending the village, he would be buried with all due rites and his family would receive a pension.

Our family owned two guns and employed a permanent guard. We knew that our village was safe, as otherwise my great-grandmother and grandmother would not have stayed there and we children would not have been sent there for the summer vacation. Still, people kept talking about robberies and bandit attacks which took place not so long ago. As soon as darkness fell, all gates were closed and the village became a fortress. At no time when I was there was Kim Bai attacked, but trouble did happen to neighboring villages separated from us by a few kilometers. It was frightening in the night to suddenly hear the grave and dramatic call of bullhorns being blown repeatedly. The whole village woke up and the menfolk went to defend the gates. On some occasions, rescue parties were sent to help our neighbors. If they were not, we made as much noise as possible with our drums, gongs and bells to frighten off the attackers. All of a sudden, the memory of insecurity in times past came back to us. We were grateful to be inside our impregnable wall of bamboo, but I often thought of the shopkeepers out in the market place. They were either Chinese migrants or Vietnamese coming from other places to open their business. Not being members of our community, they were not allowed to settle inside the village enclosure. Of course, being so near, they could expect to get help quickly. But how exposed they must have felt when evening fell and the village gates were shut. As for us boys, we were determined to defend our ancestral home. Contingency plans were drawn up in case our compound was surrounded by bandits. Perhaps we treated these preparations more like a game, but the underlying fear was real enough. We made bows and arrows of bamboo and spent a lot of time in practice shooting. The pomelos in the garden, which were as big as coconuts, were ideal targets. We succeeded in piercing and spoiling many of those delicious fruits. More difficult targets were the nuts of the areca palm, which village people chewed with betel leaves. The bunches of small nuts were perched on top of the tree, which had just a long slender trunk measuring up to seven or eight meters high. To drop a bunch was considered by our group the highest mark of bowmanship.

On days when the sky was clear and a light wind was blowing, the distant sound of flutes could be heard over the countryside. It came from kites flying so high that they could hardly be seen, yet their music was diffused everywhere. What was special about the kites, and I can remember nothing similar in other countries I have visited, was that they were enjoyable not only to watch, but also to listen to. Many people in our village prided themselves with the ability to make kites which flew well and produced a melodious sound. Some gained such a high reputation that villagers could recognize their kites, by the sound alone. Flying kites did not have to interfere with work. A group of farmers would go out to the fields in the morning, fly their kite, tie it to a stake and let it stay up in the sky while they worked. Its sound provided them with background music, which climbed to a high pitch when the wind blew strong and became low and grave as the wind subsided. Sometimes the music dropped quickly, like a siren running out of steam. This meant that the kite itself was coming down.

The monsoon arrived in the north in the later part of summer. Every year, villagers hoped for it to come early, so that the fields could be tilled and worked in time for the new crop. The last part of the dry season was very stuffy and hot. The hard soil cracked. Fields were deserted. The rains were always slow to come, and they always came with the same ritual. In the afternoon, black clouds would gather menacingly on the eastern horizon, bringing lightning and thunder. But after a while they would disappear. Several days—even weeks—followed in the same pattern and villagers became worried. They climbed the dike looking at the horizon for any harbinger of coming rain. Tension mounted and old people started reminiscing about droughts of years past. Then one afternoon, monsoon rain finally came, roaring in with unbelievable speed. We hardly had time to run home to bring in things which had been left outside. Water poured down from the sky and in no time our courtyard was flooded. We rushed out into the open to let the cool rain shower down on our bodies and to try to catch fish, which came in from ponds and drains. Next morning, the fields returned to life. Everywhere, people were busy working the soil and building up small ridges to keep water in the rice fields. It was a time as bustling as festival time. Only those who have lived in the country can know the excitement and sense of renewal that came with the rains. The torpid heat was over. A new and promising season had started.

A most enjoyable activity in summer was swimming in the river. Country people always took a bath late in the afternoon after the day's work was done and dinner was taken. "A filling meal, a cooling bath," that was how a proverb said a farmer's day should end. Most people in our village bathed in their own pond, the stagnant water of which was, however, not always clean. I preferred to go across the Lichee Field to the Hat River. The clear water running over white sand was a delight to jump in. On a hot day, many villagers of the riverside village of Sao would come to the beach for their bath. Men and boys went swimming in the middle of the river, while women and girls shyly stayed close to the bank. They were in the water up to their waists and wearing brassieres, so that only the soft lines of their white shoulders and arms could be seen. Since ancient times, river bathing was a pleasure of rural life enjoyed by all. The story was told of our Master, Confucius, as he went from one country to another offering himself for public service, but unable to find a ruler enlightened enough to use his talents. One day, relaxing in the company of some close disciples, he asked them what they would like to do most in life, if given the choice. One replied that he would like to administer a large country, surrounded by enemies and affected by war and scarcity; in three-years' time, he hoped to make that country strong and secure. Another said more modestly that he would like to administer a middle-sized country; within three years he expected to provide for its people a comfortable life. A third said that he would like to serve the king and be in charge of the Office of Rites. These disciples all took it upon themselves to realize their Master's unfulfilled aspirations for public service. Another disciple, Zeng Dian, was playing his lute and did not reply.

> "What about you, Dian?" the Master asked him. Stopping his music, Zeng Dian replied:
> "I dare not say, because mine is so different from the aspirations of the others."
> "Go ahead and say it!" the Master insisted. Zeng Dian then said:

"As spring nears its end, with a few friends, to go and bathe in the cool water of the Ni River."
On hearing this, Confucious sighed and murmured:
"I am like you, Dian."

The Hat River had a deep and wide bed as it came towards the Lichee Field. On meeting the Field, the river bent its course and made a big loop. Past the village of Sao on the other side, it started running over sand and became narrower and shallower until at one place it was reduced to a fordable stream. Then, past the sandbank, it grew larger again on its way south. That open sandy stretch was a most inviting place for bathing in summer. I would go there early in the morning, when everything around was quiet and still and the river itself seemed to stop its flow. As I plunged into the coolness and swam in the company of hundreds of small fish, everything else was forgotten. In the autumn, there were mornings when a dense layer of mist rose above the river surface into the cold air, and the warm water was like a balm to my body. Even princesses of legend, who rarely ventured out of their high-walled palaces, gave in to the simple pleasure of river bathing. I have recounted earlier the two legends of the Heavenly Prince of Phu Dong and the Spirits of the Mountain and the River. As a matter of fact, our history books carried not two, but three ancient legends originating from the first dynasty. The third legend was that of the Condemned Immortal.

Chu Dong Tu was an immortal who committed some mistake and was sentenced to be exiled to Earth. There he led the life of a poor fisherman having no home and staying among the reeds on a sandy bank of the Red River. King Hung Vuong's daughter, Princess Tien Dung, one day decided to go out of her palace for a boat trip. The season was summer, the weather was hot. As the princess' party passed by a sandbank, she found it inviting and decided to stop for a cool dip. Troops cordoned off the area and hung curtains all around so that the princess had the privacy to enjoy her bath. Chu Dong Tu, who was on the bank, found himself caught on all sides. Not knowing what else to do, he buried himself under the sand to hide. It happened that the princess chose to have her bath next to the spot where he hid and as she came up from the river and female attendants poured perfumed water over her virginal body, the sand was washed away and Chu Dong Tu's presence was revealed. Immediately, he was arrested and led away to be executed for he had committed the most serious crime of lèse-majesté. But the princess put a stop to it. She said that as her body must belong to only one man, and as Chu Dong Tu had seen her bathing, it was Heaven's will that she become his wife. The fact that he was a poor fisherman must not make any difference. Messengers were dispatched post-haste to the capital to report matters to King Hung Vuong who flew into a rage and sent the army to surround the area, with orders to arrest Chu Dong Tu and bring the princess home. But that night, a violent storm descended over the area and the troops could not move in. Next morning, they could not find the sandbank anywhere. In its place, there was a big depression which soon filled with water and became a lake. Chu Dong Tu, the immortal, had left the Earth to return to the realm of Bong Lai—the fairyland where immortals resided—and had taken with him his new royal bride. Whether they left in a rocket and the depression was caused by its blast-off, the story did not say. The setting for Chu Dong Tu's legend was the nearby province of Hung Yen, where the lake can still be seen. But I have always thought that the young princess, who loved river bathing, would also have liked the sandbank of our Hat River and stopped there, had her boat passed by it on a sunny summer day.

5. Our Family

Scholarship

Our family has been one of scholars since the end of the fifteenth century, probably even earlier. Few of our ancestors gained academic titles; in fact, only six over a period of four hundred years. The first three generations were highly successful at the examinations and in public service. Then followed eight generations during which we could claim just one diploma, until my grandfather obtained his. Yet, our family has kept to its scholarly pursuits. Only once was there a change. The head of our tenth generation became a trader. His son, however, returned immediately to the family tradition.

My grandfather was a man of few words, but there were times when sipping a cup of tea perfumed with the scent of the *ngau* flowers of his garden—his favorite drink—he was in a mood to talk about our ancestors. Those generations of unsuccessful scholars, he said, did not lose heart and remained committed to their vocation, although many experienced severe hardship. Referring to them, he quoted the proverb: "Pages are torn, but the spine of the book must be kept intact." This well-known proverb is often used to say that even when down and out, a family should endeavor to keep up appearances. Grandfather, however, did not use it in that sense. He wanted to show us the will of our ancestors to persist with studies in spite of failures at the examinations. His own father tried repeatedly for a diploma until an advanced age. It was not unusual in those times to see white-haired old men mixing with young hopefuls in a crowd of candidates, even father and son sitting at the same session. "When time finally caught up with a generation," grandfather said, "the hope was transferred to the next one. Whatever happened, the spine of the book must be preserved and studies pursued, so that one day the family could resume with academic success."

It is not difficult to understand why our people wanted to remain scholars. Vietnamese society was traditionally divided into the four classes of scholars, farmers, artisans and traders. A scholar who passed the civil service examinations and became a mandarin, joined the elite group which ran the country under the king's leadership. Scholarly families without academic titles tended to drop out of the top class after a few generations. Their descendants turned farmers, artisans or traders, while men from these three classes who could obtain a diploma moved into the upper group. Families moved up and down constantly and the scholarly class kept renewing itself. What was remarkable in our case was that our ancestors managed to stay on as scholars all through four centuries.

Untitled scholars did not have an easy life. Many of our ancestors were teachers and some of them earned a living not much better than that of poor farmers. But, successful or not at the examinations, all scholars were given respect and consideration by society. Author Duong Quang Ham, a student of my grandfather, explained it in his book on Vietnamese literature, which became a textbook for all secondary schools in Vietnam:

> Scholars were men of high character who shared the same goal in life, that of preserving the righteous ethics and strengthening public morality. Some may be engaged in a career to serve the king and country, others may teach and educate the younger generations, still others by their virtuous life may be models for others to follow. All scholars commanded the respect and obedience of the population, although many may not be given any honours or mandarinal positions.

In the popular concept, scholars were men who followed "the ways of saints and sages." High regard was accorded, in particular, to teachers who imparted their knowledge of "the ways" to the common people. A pupil was accepted by his teacher at a ritual ceremony after which a relationship akin to that between father and son was established. Indeed, in some parts of Vietnam, the same word *thay* was used to call both one's father and one's teacher. Pupils brought presents to their teacher at seasonal and family festivals. They came and lent a hand whenever their services were needed. In the 1940s, more than twenty years after he had stopped teaching, there were still former pupils of my grandfather coming from far away provinces to attend the anniversary of his father's death. Students usually formed an alumni association to provide material support to their teacher in his old age. Even when a student had gained high position and honors, he must maintain the same attitude of deference and respect towards his former teacher. "Now as then, one and the same" was the rule of conduct required.

A story in our family lore relates to an impoverished ancestor who had no diploma and therefore no high rank in the village. He could rarely afford to buy meat, yet there was nothing he loved more than a cup of rice brandy to be savored with tidbits of meat before a meal. At every village festival, he received a piece from the most coveted part of a pig, its head, because those who cut the meat at the Communal Hall to divide it among villagers respected him as a scholar and put him above protocol. Next to our ancestral compound lived a family of scholars who had known better times. When I was a little boy, Bachelor Bo was a retired teacher. An old gentleman with a pink complexion and a strikingly beautiful white beard coming down to his chest, he was very friendly and often played with us children. "In his time, he went to the imperial capital to sit for the doctorate!" villagers talked about him in a deferential voice. Normally, only those with a licentiate—or four-certificate degree—could aspire to become a doctor. Bachelor Bo, who only had a three-certificate degree, made the trip to the capital because he was among the brightest bachelors of his class and his father was the head educational officer of a region. He failed in his attempt and never became a mandarin. He had not made much money as a teacher and after retirement, had to sell parts of his family plot, some of which were bought by our own family. He no longer owned a pond, so made use of ours which was situated outside our compound. Other people used it too, but out of respect for him, everyone would keep out when he was there. Bachelor Bo had the habit of washing his feet every day and taking a very long time doing it. Others had to wait, and he would get into a temper if some youngsters, not aware of the etiquette, walked towards the water before he had finished.

Success came to but a few of the scholars. Candidates competed for a limited number of places in the state examinations, which took place once every three years. Bachelors and licentiates were selected at regional competitions conducted in a small number of centers, while doctors were chosen at a national competition in the capital. Those who failed at a session, or missed it for whatever reason, had to wait three years. The wait could be longer. At first, examinations were organized only if and when the king needed to recruit "good and wise men" to serve the country. Triennial sessions were introduced by King Le Thanh Ton in the fifteenth century and they became the rule, but wars and internal conflicts often resulted in them being abandoned. Under such a restrictive system, many were those who never made it through the examinations, despite their literary talents. My great-grandfather was one such scholar. He showed great promise as a student. People said that for him, success would only be a matter of time. Yet, he kept failing one session after another. He turned to teaching and many of his students graduated, but he himself remained without academic titles, all his life an impoverished scholar.

Our village Kim Bai belonged to a region which could pride itself for having produced a large number of graduates. Thanh Oai, our prefecture, figured prominently in The Register of High Graduates which listed all holders of the doctorate since early times. At nearly every session, there was one from our prefecture, sometimes there were even two; an impressive record considering that the number of new doctors at a session rarely exceeded fifty—most of the time it was well below that figure—and Thanh Oai was one of some 160 prefectures in Vietnam. Perhaps that had something to do with our region being close to the capital, because after the Nguyen dynasty moved the capital, and with it the doctorate examinations, further south to Hue in the nineteenth century, Thanh Oai's high rate of success dropped. In Kim Bai, intelligent boys who were keen on studies received help and encouragement. Literary competitions were organized periodically, in which a panel of scholars gave money prizes to the best essays. It was customary for teachers not to charge students from poor families. Old people recalled "the good old times" when conditions in the country were peaceful and prosperous, and scholarship highly considered; in those times, village guards kept watch on young students in the evenings. If, passing by the house of a student, the guards did not hear him reading books—to read aloud a text was the traditional Vietnamese way to memorize it—they would report to the village council and the student's parents would be fined! Bright students carried the hope of the whole community.

When my grandfather died, an old man told me: "It seems that I can still hear him reading classical texts and chanting poetry when he was a student. It was a resonant voice. Just by listening to him, I could tell that he would go far. Now that voice has fallen silent." When he sat for the licentiate examinations, there was great excitement. Our family, after so many generations without success, had high expectations of him. Village folks knew of his talents. They sensed that success was bound to come. A large group of people made the trip from Kim Bai to Hanoi, a day's march away. Led by a former village mayor, they were to attend the ceremony announcing the results.

The mayor was from the Chu, a prominent family in Kim Bai. He was my grandfather's maternal uncle and a figure well-remembered by later generations. He held his office when France had just imposed its protectorate. Government authority did not reach very far out into the countryside. Villages had to defend themselves against bandit attacks or encroachments by neighbors. A tough village leader, Mayor Chu had the reputation of being himself something of a ruffian and a bully during his youth. He built up his family's assets in a way which made some envious people gossip that the methods he used were not always aboveboard, but when he presented himself as a candidate for mayor, there was very little opposition. Those were turbulent times. The need was not for a scholar with a soft voice. Our villagers made a good choice because Mayor Chu served them well. His son, whom I called great-uncle, told me that he was a big man of great physical strength. Knowing the son, I could imagine what the father was like. Great-uncle still worked at sixty in the fields like a young man. He had a huge appetite. I had seen him eating a whole chicken, which in itself was nothing really extraordinary, but in this case, there were just one or two bones let when he had finished. The rest of the bones were all eaten, his strong teeth cracked them as if they were prawn crackers.

A serious incident occurred at the village one day when Mayor Chu was out. People from a neighboring place alleged that several of their water buffaloes had been stolen by our villagers. They accused the mayor himself of having, along with others, committed that offense. A large group of men, armed with sticks and knives and in a very angry mood, descended on Kim Bai. Our people withdrew behind the gate. Insults were thrown back and forth between the two sides and the assailants were on the point of storming the gate when the mayor returned. He rolled up his sleeves, seized a big knife and rushed to the gate, ordering that it be opened. Standing in the middle of the way, he invited the other people to come in, saying:

> You can go anywhere you want inside the village to look for your buffaloes. If you find them, they will be returned to you and we shall deal with the culprits fittingly. But if you cannot, then, before leaving this gate you will have to deal with this knife.

The risk was too great for anyone to take up the offer. At any rate, a violent clash was avoided.

The year when my grandfather sat for his examinations, Mayor Chu had already retired. In his fifties, he had settled down to a quieter life with his three or four wives. The day the results were announced, the Kim Bai group led by him joined the crowd assembling on the Examination Grounds. Everything was ready, the ceremonial platform erected for members of the panel, the elevated seats, the parasols, the multicolored flags and banners, the soldiers and attendants. The high mandarins of the panel arrived, dressed in ceremonial robes of blue, purple or green brocade. Preceding them was a board held high by soldiers for everyone to see, which bore four big characters *phung chi cau hien,* meaning: "On orders of the king, in search of good and wise men." The mandarins took up position in their seats high above the heads of the crowd. The names of successful candidates were called out. On hearing these words: "Province of Ha Dong, prefecture of Thanh Oai, canton of Phuong Trung, village of Kim Bai...," Mayor Chu knew that it was his nephew. Without waiting for his name, he jumped up high and clapped his hands with joy. Unfortunately, at that time our menfolk did not wear a belt with their trousers; these were only held in place by twisting the material around the waist, sarong-like, so that when the mayor jumped up, his trousers came down in full view of the thousands of people attending the ceremony. That episode of "the mayor's trousers coming down" was still told by villagers years later.

The Three Teachings

The Vietnamese people traditionally follow the teachings of Confucianism, Taoism and Buddhism. Their conception of life and the universe, their religious beliefs and code of conduct in society, all rest on the three teachings. These have been likened to the three feet of an urn, a representation showing that our system draws its stability from the support of all three of its components. If one is taken out, the system collapses. The three may compete with each other, but it is also by leaning on each other that they derive their strength. All three came to us from China, including Buddhism which originated in India. Although the earliest Buddhist priests in Vietnam were Indians who arrived by sea, our main Buddhist schools traced their sources to temples in China. After thousands of years in our country, the three teachings, which could also be called ways or paths, have acquired a Vietnamese character of their own and become a fundamental part of our culture.

In our family, the dominant influence has been Confucian teaching. Our ancestors were scholars brought up in the study of the Four Books and Five Canons of Confucianism. It has often been said by Western scholars that Confucianism is a way of life, not a religion. True, Confucianism is predominantly a set of rules of conduct in life and society. It does not worship any deity. But it places great importance on the cult of ancestors. Many Vietnamese, when asked about their religion, would reply that theirs is the cult of ancestors and in their minds, the cult is inseparable from Confucianism. At the center of our cult is the family, understood in the sense of an entity which encompasses all generations, those having existed in the past, the present ones as well as those yet to come. The concept of the family as an entity over time is commonly expressed in our behavior and language. Thus, the mention of a happy event or an achievement is usually preceded by this ritual formula: "Thanks to the merit inherited from our ancestors." The following sentence appears at the beginning of our family chronicle:

> He who inherits the merit acquired by his ancestors for many generations, has children and grandchildren in abundance.

We believe that whatever a person can achieve in his lifetime does not depend solely on his actions; it is also determined by the heritage of virtue and merit that he has received from his forebears. Under the ancient monarchy, this causal link between the generations was recognized by the court which awarded posthumous ranks and honors to ancestors of high mandarins. Just as we are dependent on past generations for good or bad fortune, so will the consequences of our own actions be transmitted to our descendants. To many Vietnamese parents, the material wealth such as house, land or jewelry that they may pass on to their children is considered secondary to the spiritual heritage which all parents, whether rich or poor, will leave behind.

Each generation is a stage in the life of a family. Stages come and go, but the family stays on with the transmission from one generation to the

next. One can see how important it is, in our system of belief, for the lineage
to be carried forward. Without a male heir, the name would be lost and the
family would disappear. Such was the prevailing conception in former
times. Nowadays, people may not attach the same importance to the principle of male heredity, but until recently, it was a real tragedy for a Vietnamese family not to have a son. Many generations of our own family had
gone through anxious periods just because a son was late in coming, so
pilgrimages were made to pray for an heir at temples and geomancers called
in to change the orientation of the family home. Family to us has a sacred
character and the ancestor's cult is, properly speaking, a religion. Ancestors
are spirits which our people invoke in prayers. With the Lord in Heaven and
Lord Buddha, they form our traditional trinity, as expressed in the following prayer commonly used by Vietnamese:

> I beg the Lord in Heaven, Lord Buddha and our Ancestors to witness my
> action, to protect our family and give it their blessings.

In every Vietnamese home there is an altar to the ancestors set up at
a place considered to be the most dignified in the house, usually close to
its center. Since 1975, Vietnamese refugees have kept up their cult, despite
their being away from the motherland. Ancestor worship is carried out
where the descendants happen to be living, according to the rule: "Wherever descendants are, so too are their ancestors." Since my parents went to
reside in France, they have continued to hold the ceremonies of worship,
just as they would have done if they had stayed in Vietnam. There, anniversaries were accompanied by copious meals bringing together family members and guests; in Paris, they are simple ceremonies with of offerings only
rice and a few dishes, sometimes just some flowers and fruit. But the spirit
in which they are celebrated remains the same. My mother often reminded
us that food offerings are not essential, they are more of a social requirement. With reverence and sincerity, she said, our prayers will reach the
spiritual world of our ancestors, no matter what we offer on the altar. Ancestors are remembered not only at anniversaries, but at all festivals of the
four seasons, such as the Mid-Autumn Festival in the eighth lunar month
to watch the bright full moon, the Double Five Festival in the fifth month
where children are given fermented glutinous rice and a great many kinds
of cakes to eat and, most important of all, the Tet festival. The special food
for each festival is presented as an offering to ancestors before the family
partakes of them. The new rice brought home after the harvest is cooked
and served on the altar. A beautiful flower from the garden, home-grown
fruits from the orchard, some choice food obtained at the market, they are
all placed first on the altar as a mark of remembrance towards our forebears,
whose spirits, we believe, would always stay near to protect the family and
support its endeavors.

The cult of ancestors existed well before Confucius. The Master upheld that ancient tradition. He extolled its virtues and built upon it the concept of *hieu*—filial piety—which together with that of *trung*—loyalty to the king—became the cornerstones of the Confucian code of moral conduct. His teachings on ancestor worship brought Confucianism into the realm of the mystic and supernatural, and made it a true system of religious beliefs. "Serve the dead as you would have served them had they been still alive, serve the departed as you would have served them had they been still present," he said. In the *Book of Rites*, he noted that a descendant worshipping his ancestors should endeavor to "hear what has no sound and see what has no form."

Confucianism being the official doctrine of government, scholars must be well-versed in it if they were to stand any chance at the civil service examinations. As he grew older, however, a scholar would find himself drawn more and more to the writings of Lao Tse and Chuang Tse. These provided him with a deeper insight into the meaning of existence than Confucian teachings. They helped him accept more readily the disappointments and vicissitudes of life.

Whereas Confucianism spoke constantly of duty and strivings regarding oneself, one's family and one's country, Taoism advocated a simple and peaceful life in harmony with nature. Man should avoid conventional social obligations and refrain from doing anything that would upset the natural order of things. Lao Tse's doctrine was one of detachment and of "no action." It had a particular appeal to those of our ancestors who met with failure at the examinations and saw their dream of serving king and country vanish, or those who could not even compete at the examinations because they were on the wrong side of the political fence. Among them, the one most attracted to Taoism was the head of our eleventh generation, my great-grandfather. He started with high hopes for a mandarinal career, but those hopes were not realized. Moreover, an adverse fate continually dogged him throughout his life. He never knew his father, who left home when he was a newly-born baby. As a young man, he set out for the Mekong delta to bring his father's remains home but had to turn back before reaching there. When he was nearing forty, first his wife, then his only son, died. For a pseudonym, he chose a name which broke with family tradition. Most of our ancestors had pseudonyms starting with the word *Phuc*, such as Phuc Ninh for our third ancestor and Phuc Thien for our fourth ancestor. *Phuc* is a basic term in our culture. It means happiness which derives from benevolent action. For a Confucian family, to have Phuc as a name component was very much in character. My great-grandfather, however, took the purely Taoist pseudonym of Song Son Dat Dan, or Hermit of the Mountain of the Twins, the mountain here being that of our village's prophecy. Old Taoist scholars retired among the clouds and pine trees to live, close to nature and away from society. In his old age, my great-grandfather also became a recluse, but the Hermit of the Mountain of the Twins never left his village. The Mountain was a creation of legend and it remained for him a dream.

Every scholar was an aspiring poet with at least a few poems or essays to his credit. The best loved poems in our language were Taoist or Zen in inspiration. They had that element of mystery and mystique which stood them apart from the down-to-earth poems of the Confucian school. When my grandfather retired from the mandarinate in 1940, his friends and colleagues organized a farewell function. Many were mandarins like him, others became teachers, writers or businessmen after they graduated. Together, they were the cream of scholars in the north of Vietnam. When the cups of wine had been filled up many times, a beautifully bound book, its—as yet blank—pages made of best quality rice paper, was brought out and placed on a low desk which was itself installed on top of a carved platform in blackwood. An attendant ground the black ink. A row of brushes were kept ready. As the music went on and songstresses entertained the party, the scholars took turns to sit on the platform in front of the low desk. Leaning forward, they dipped a brush in the black ink and, in a slow and purposeful motion, wrote in the book complimentary pieces addressed to grandfather on the occasion of his retirement. From time to time, grandfather was asked to respond, which he did by writing in the book poems of his own. In the life of a scholar-mandarin, Confucianism was the dominant "way" when he was shouldering social responsibilities and serving his fellow countrymen. After he retired, and in leisure pondered on the philosophical meaning of existence, Taoism took over. The day he "hung up the seals of office" marked the start of the change. As I can recall, many pieces in that book took up traditional Taoist themes. Written in the mode of ancient poems of the Tang period in China, they alluded to the peace and quiet that a man had earned after having fulfilled his duties in public service; now he could enjoy "his fields and gardens" with a heart "cold as ice," meaning completely detached from the pursuit of fame and wealth.

The strength of Buddhist faith in our family has fluctuated with the generations. Buddhism has been like a deeply embedded seed which remained dormant in some periods, but developed and blossomed in others. It is interesting to note that development, when it took place, was brought about by the maternal side. Thus, our foremother of the fourth generation was a devout Buddhist whose influence on the family's religious attitude extended to the next generations. The same could be said of our foremother of the ninth generation. In my grandparents' time, Buddhism was to us more of a tradition than a religion. That was during the first half of this century, when Buddhism registered a general decline in Vietnam. My grandmother came from a village with an ancient Buddhist tradition; however, she married into a strict Confucian family and came to live in Kim Bai where most people went to temples only at important festivals. My grandfather was not interested in the religion. I do not recall having seen him in a temple, or reading a Buddhist text. Kim Bai's pagoda was old and small, with a sole residing bonze and some young novices. They lived on some small plots of rice fields allocated to them by the village, and on financial offerings by the faithful. Our family made its contributions. I remember one important occasion when a large brocade hanger to decorate the main altar was presented to the pagoda. The hanger was still there when I last visited the pagoda before leaving Kim Bai. But an indication of the low priority accorded to the religion was that, while our village developed greatly in the 1930s — a new market and a new school were built, new roads were laid — renovation of the old pagoda was not contemplated.

At the age of three or four, I was "given" by my parents to a temple, in a religious ceremony. To give children away was a quite common custom, which had its origin in both Buddhism and popular superstition. As a Buddhist gesture, it was meant to show nonattachment to even the things dearest to one's heart. Popular superstition had it that demons and malevolent spirits would not look kindly on families with an abundant progeniture; they would come and take the children away. These had, therefore, to be made "children of a temple" in order to receive the protection of its spirit. Times have changed, but until a few decades ago, people in the country often told visitors that the children who could be seen in their house were not really theirs, but belonged to such or such temple and were only "adopted" by them. A devout Buddhist family would give their children to a Buddhist temple. My elder brother and I were given, not to our village's Buddhist pagoda, but to a temple situated next to Kim Bai where a Snake Spirit was worshipped. Of course, we were not physically given away, or separated from our family for any length of time. It was only a religious ceremony, after which we went home, as "children of the Snake Temple."

The legend of the Snake Spirit can be briefly retold as follows. Long ago, there lived a fisherman and his wife. They worked hard to scrape out a living, never complained about their poverty and were always trying to be of service to others. They were happy together with, however, one sad thought: they had no children. They gave alms, went to many temples to pray, but as time passed, their chance of having children grew more remote day by day. They entered into old age when the wife miraculously became pregnant. Their joy was without bounds. But as suddenly as joy came, tragedy struck. The woman gave birth, not to a human, but to a snake without a tail. She died. Her husband did not survive her for long. Villagers were shocked by what happened. They could not understand why a couple who had not harmed anyone and had done nothing but good met with such a tragedy at the end of their lives. "Mysterious are the ways of Heaven," they could only tell themselves. One day, the Snake without a tail appeared. Holding supernatural powers, it helped people in distress, cured those affected with grave illnesses. Soon, prayers from people far and wide were answered by that benevolent spirit. In particular, couples without children were blessed with a family. The grateful population of our canton built a temple which soon attracted the faithful from all over the province, especially during the holy season of Tet. The big crowd going to the Chuong Market Festival always stopped there to offer prayers. Once every year, my brother and I, along with our uncles, cousins and other relatives who were also "children of the Snake Temple," attended a service held by our family to give thanks to the Spirit. The service was celebrated in springtime when the Temple was at its best, for it had a magnificent camelia garden. Red, pink and white flowers were in bloom. Each of us was given a branch of camelia as a lucky charm to bring home. There is a tail end to the Snake story. It was quite frequent in the country to cut the tails of dogs, but such practice did not exist in our canton. No dog's tail was ever cut, in deference to the Snake Spirit. For our people believed that the sight of a tail-less dog might sadden the benevolent Spirit by reminding it of its infirmity.

I do not remember whether I was formally inducted to the Buddhist faith or not. As a child, I rarely went to the village pagoda. My grandmother would go there for prayers at the three main anniversaries of the Birth of Lord Buddha, his Enlightenment, his Death and at a few other festivals. Once or twice a year, a special altar was installed in our ancestral home and Buddhist bonzes were invited to come and celebrate ceremonies such as those for the Wandering Souls in the seventh month. Otherwise, our home did not have a permanent altar to worship Lord Buddha.

A change took place in my parents' generation. My mother belongs to a family with strong Buddhist roots, whose members have all been inducted into the religion and all carried a Buddhist religious name. A cousin of her great-grandparents became a nun in the Buddhist temple of Xom, the village with the molasses cakes between Ha Dong and Kim Bai. The story of that nun would touch many a Vietnamese heart because it resembled so much that of Thuy Kieu, the heroine of Vietnam's literary masterpiece. Thuy Kieu had to sell herself as a prostitute in order to save her father from financial ruin and imprisonment. Our nun's father, Hoang Nguyen Thu, was at the end of the eighteenth century the Military Governor of Lang Son, a mountainous province bordering China and throughout the centuries a frequent battlefield between Vietnamese and Chinese. At that time there was no war between the two countries, but a troublesome situation with large bands of Chinese bandits operating on both sides of the border.

In an engagement, the governor was captured by Chinese bandits and as a condition for his safe return, his daughter had to become the wife of the bandit chief. Later, she managed to leave China and return to Vietnam. Well versed in literature and poetry, she wrote a moving account of her life. After a few years back home, she announced that she would be leaving family and home again, this time to find refuge in the House of Our Lord Buddha. Then, she cut her hair and entered the nunnery at Xom.

Like grandmother before her, my mother adapted herself to the customs and habits of her husband's family. She attended temple service only at important festivals. We children were brought along and on these occasions, I must say that I was more interested in mingling with the crowd and in the midday meal, than in the religious proceedings. Most temples served excellent vegetarian food. When the dishes were brought out, an uninformed person might think that he was at the wrong place, for in front of him on the table were displayed several dishes of meat and seafood. What looked like meat or seafood was in fact just soya bean curd shaped into pork ribs, chicken wings or prawns in batter. In spite of being wholly vegetarian, the food served had a great variety of flavors and textures. A temple meal could be quite a feast, enough to please the finest gourmet. After our family returned to Hanoi in 1948, my mother started going to temples regularly; war and suffering had brought her back to her Buddhist roots. It was in that period when she set up an altar in our Hanoi home. The Buddha she worshipped was — and remains — Quan The Am or Buddha of Mercy, the literal meaning of Quan The Am being "the one who hears the sufferings of the world." Everyday she lit incense and prayed before the altar. It was through her that I developed an interest in the religion. Thanks to her example, Buddhism for me ceased to be just a tradition and became instead a personal involvement. Every Sunday, she went to the temple to attend commentary sessions on Buddhist Canons. She did not make any of us adolescents come with her, we were left free to choose whether or not to come. But she did need someone to accompany her to the temple and back, and between my elder brother and me, the task usually fell to me because he was always out with his friends and was never home at the right time.

A cycle rickshaw was called for her. I followed behind on my bicycle. We usually went to one of the large temples close to the center of the city. Before the war, the crowd at temples was generally middle-aged and female, but since then, the Buddhist church has enjoyed a revival. Wherever we went, there was a sizeable group of men, many of whom were middle-class intellectuals and civil servants. Also present were young students from both sexes. The boys were dressed in white "western" trousers and shirts, while the girls stayed traditional in their black silk trousers and white long dresses which fluttered as they walked; they looked demure with their shining dark hair neatly tied in a ponytail and coming down to their waistline. The majority of the faithful were still women; in the temple, our group of men kept to one corner of the hall. Everyone sat on the cool enameled brick floor. I knew many temples in Hanoi well. Then in my final years of secondary school, I often went after classes into a temple to sit in the quiet hall in front of the altars, not for any prayers or meditation, without even lighting a stick of incense; I just stayed there for a few moments before going home. My mother knew of my inclination. We sometimes discussed the meaning of Buddhist parables, but for reasons which I could not explain, I was reluctant to go in with her and attend the Sunday sessions. When I finally decided to do so, she was very happy. Alas! she was soon to be disappointed. After several sessions, I stopped going in and again stayed outside to wait for the end and accompany her home. I found myself completely out of tune with the priests' commentaries. I could not agree with the arguments used, the examples given, the lessons drawn. Somehow, they did not fit in with the way I felt and thought. I never had that problem with commentary sessions on Confucian and Taoist texts. Yet in my heart, I knew that in the teachings of Lord Buddha, there were answers to my problems, assurances to pacify my doubts and a goal to justify my instinctive faith. Lord Buddha said that there were many different paths that one could take, many different ways to follow his teaching. I realized that among those many paths, I would have to search for my own.

6. Family Gatherings

Members of our family lived in different places, my great-grandmother and grandmother in Kim Bai, my grandfather in Ha Dong, my parents, uncles and aunts in Hanoi and other provinces. They saw one another often, but the large gatherings when everyone was present took place only twice a year in our ancestral home, at the New Year and on the anniversary of the death of my great-grandfather.

The Anniversary

In our cult, the important dates are anniversaries of the death of ancestors. Not all ancestors' deaths are commemorated. Traditionally, anniversaries are observed only for the last four generations. In my grandparents' time, some twenty ceremonies were celebrated each year in our ancestral home in Kim Bai. For distant ancestors, a simple worshipping service was followed by a meal for family members. For ancestors of more recent generations, relatives from the village and elsewhere came, more offerings were displayed on the altar, and after the service, all visitors stayed for a meal. The most important anniversary, of course, was that of the nearest ancestor, who was then my great-grandfather. It fell on the nineteenth day of the sixth lunar month, which corresponded to a day either in July or in August, depending on the year. That was during the summer vacation, when I stayed in Kim Bai.

One month before the event, preparations were made to ensure a sufficient provision of rice. Pigs and fowl were bought, so that there was enough time to fatten them. The compound was cleaned up to receive the many family members and guests who came for the duration of the ceremonies, which lasted three days. Wooden platforms were set up in all houses, to serve as an eating area during the day and a sleeping area at night. We were in the midst of summer, before the monsoon season. The nights were warm and dry and all that people needed to sleep was a platform, a rush mat and a mosquito net. The last one was a requirement of city folks. Those living in the country would dispense with it. With a hard headrest made of wood, bamboo or stretched leather, they could lie down anywhere

73

and go to sleep, blissfully ignoring attacks by mosquitoes. The western house, normally closed, was made ready for the visitors, some of whom were students of my grandfather when he was a teacher back in the 1910s. With members of other branches of our extended family attending, the anniversary was the largest gathering of the year. Relatives who left Kim Bai to pursue a career in the civil service or in business came back for the occasion. Their country cousins welcomed them with pride, but also—as one could sense it—with a certain feeling of inferiority. For they were the ones who dared not get away from the village, to go and try their chance in the prosperous cities.

I stayed in Kim Bai only for the summer months, yet had begun to feel somewhat like a villager towards my peers who remained in Hanoi. I had the impression of being isolated. In particular, I missed the radio and newspapers. The war was raging in the Pacific. Steadily, it had been moving closer to us. Almost daily now, we could hear or see Allied planes flying in the direction of Japanese bases near Hanoi and in the western mountains. They had gained control of the airspace and were passing quite low over our region, occasionally shooting at a car passing on the highway. We knew that the fate of our country would depend on the outcome of the war. But Kim Bai had no electricity for listening to the radio and newspapers were circulated only in Hanoi and the big towns. I had news only once every few weeks, when my father visited Kim Bai. From the grounds of my great-grandfather's tomb where I went to wait for him, he could be seen five kilometers away as his bicycle came out of the Thanh Oai township. His bag was full of newspapers. I was so excited that I could not choose which of the several week-old papers to read first; I just jumped from one headline to another. But more interesting still was what my father discussed with my grandfather as they sat on the wooden settee in the altar house, grandfather preparing a fresh pot of tea for his son. My father gave the latest news from the capital on the war. I let my imagination wander on the vast spaces of the Pacific Ocean where mighty battles in the air and on the sea were joined by Japan and the Allies. However, my elders were more concerned with what would happen to our country. They believed it impossible that the situation, in which Vietnam was dominated by both France and Japan, could last. Sooner or later, one of these two powers would get rid of the other and that one would be Japan, which held the military upper hand. But the war in the Pacific had not been going well for Japan. What would happen if Japan were to lose?

A few days before the anniversary, my uncle, elder brother and cousin came back, each riding a bicycle and having plenty to say about what was going on in town, the movies they saw, the games they played. Their talk made Kim Bai appear even more of a backwater to me. But there was work for us to do. The altar and all cult instruments had to be cleaned. My grandfather directed us to do this task, instead of the servants. He himself supervised us. At times, while we were working he would take out from a bookcase near the altar an old handwritten book. Its pages were full of holes made by bookworms and termites. He sat down to read, and his thoughts seemed at once to move away from our group and from what we were doing. Was it a book of poems from his father, the Hermit of the Mountains of the Twins? I wondered but did not dare to interrupt him and ask. Parasols and flags were brought out in the courtyard to be dusted, and that was the only time of the year when we could see the rich colors of the flags, for the altar room where they were kept remained constantly in the dark. Then, all brass instruments were taken out and polished. The big chandelier hanging above the altar was lowered and disassembled. The incense burner, an urn with a round belly and three sturdy legs in which aloes wood was burnt during ceremonies, was too heavy for us to move; two robust men were needed to carry it outside. There were candle holders of different sizes, in particular a pair about three feet high in the shape of a crane standing on the back of a tortoise, both animals being symbols of longevity. The long samurai-type swords were drawn out of their scabbards. With a brush we spread a light coat of oil on the blades before putting them back in. Finally, the tabernacle with all its intricate carvings had to be wiped free of dust, a very time-consuming chore. We had to climb up the altar and clean every nook and cranny, brush all the mythical beasts and birds, flowers and clouds carved into the wood. Grandfather himself dusted his father's portrait and the tablet carrying his names and titles. It took us four boys nearly a day to do everything in the altar room.

We then moved to the new house where, in the lounge, stood an array of eight weapons, each made of a brass head set on top of a wooden shaft about two meters long. The heads were in the shape of a battle-axe, a cleaver, a mace, a coiled snake and other shapes which I cannot quite remember, but they all looked fearsome. We took the weapons out of their wooden stand, slowly, as they were quite heavy, and put a coat of polish on the brass heads. In ancient times, such arms were used by commanders engaged on horseback in single combat, as their troops looked on and stood ready to pounce on the enemy if their leader succeeded in bringing down his opponent. Warriors in those times handled a variety of weapons, designed both to inflict injury and to frighten their adversaries, and the eight weapons we had were among the most commonly used. Such weapons were no longer used for fighting, but as ornaments found mostly in temples. Called *bat bao,* or the eight precious weapons, they stood at the entrance of temple buildings to guard them against evil spirits. At festivals, they were carried at the head of processions. In our new house, the eight precious weapons retained their symbolic value. Planted on their wooden stand and arranged in the shape of a fan, they were placed next to the main door. Any person entering by that door was confronted by them. Even when we received our most distinguished guests, the weapons were kept in their place. The guests had to go around them to move into the lounge.

Several days prior to the anniversary, female members of the family returned to the ancestral home to help prepare the food, my mother ahead of everyone else due to her position as the wife of the eldest son. The transversal house and kitchen echoed the sound of knives chopping food, rice being ground to make cakes, meat being pounded to make *gio cha*, a pork sausage similar to mortadella of which Vietnamese were very fond. By the eighteenth, the day preceding the actual anniversary, the family was back in full strength. Ceremonies started in the afternoon of that day. In a simple service the doors of the tabernacle were opened. My great-grand-father's tablet and portrait were taken out and displayed in front. Rice and a small number of dishes were served on the altar. The purpose of the ser-vice was to invite the ancestor's spirit to sample some of the offerings to be made the next day, hence its name *Tien Thuong*, meaning "a taste of the offerings." The service was short. There was time on the eve of the anniver-sary to talk, exchange news and for travellers to tell about places which would forever remain mysterious to those who stayed back at home.

Since my childhood, I had dreamed of the western mountains which stood on the horizon and were believed to be the cradle of our race. They were not far away. I could see them from our village; yet I never went there. I only heard relatives describe how the green foothills rose gently up to the mountains and how, from up there, one could see the rich and fertile soil of the delta shine under the sun as if it was coated with oil. How inviting the plain must have been to the ancestors of our race, I thought, that they left their secluded highlands to venture down there and settle, millenniums ago. The mountainous region bordering China also held for me a special appeal. Under the Mac dynasty, my ancestor Nguyen Uyen served as a mandarin in Thai Nguyen and Cao Bang. For a long time, he was thought to be our first ancestor, and he was still the best known among ancestors of early generations. Those two provinces were infested with malaria, but visiting relatives also told us of their wealth and natural beauty. Thai Nguyen had a group of three lakes, hidden from all sides by high moun-tains. The lakes were so large that they were given the name of Ho Ba Be, or the Three Seas. A traveller weary after a long journey in the highlands, would suddenly discover behind the mountains the calm waters of an in-land sea dotted with small islands, and myriads of boats plying between prosperous settlements on the shore. Cao Bang, on the Chinese border, had long evoked images of war and suffering. Countless battles between the Vietnamese and their aggressors took place there. In the end of the six-teenth century, it became the scene of a long civil war. Defeated by the Trinh in the delta, the Mac retreated to Cao Bang and managed to stay there for sixty years. That meant sixty more years of fighting between them and the Trinh. The husband in the poem of the egret, which I learned to sing while pounding rice in Kim Bai, was drafted to go and fight the Mac in Cao Bang. Yet, those who went there spoke of a fertile valley nestled in the mountains, where it was good to live and where springtime brought out a profusion of peach and apricot blossoms. Cao Bang in the spring was so beautiful that it reminded people of the old legend of Luu Than and Nguyen Trieu. These two friends went up the mountains together one day and stumbled into *Dao Nguyen*, the Paradise of the Peach Blossoms inhabitated by fairies. They stayed on and married two beautiful maidens. After a few years, however, they became homesick and left *Dao Nguyen* to return to their village. But *Dao Nguyen* did not belong to the human world, and one year there lasted as long as one century. The two friends felt lost in the world they came back to; their parents, relatives and acquaintances all had died centuries ago. They went back to the mountains to try and find the Paradise again, but could not. "I wonder whether *Dao Nguyen* was any more beautiful than Cao Bang in the spring, when the blossoms came out," said a traveller. Seated under a pomelo tree laden with young fruit, I listened avidly. Our ancestor Nguyen Uyen must be no stranger to the wonder of the Three Seas or to the splendor of spring in Cao Bang. Did he write about his time in the mountains? As he was a scholar and a member of the Academy, I felt sure that he had.

The village's traditional band came to play religious music in the evening. Called *Bat Am*, or the Eight Sounds, its instruments derived from the eight natural elements that produced sound: calabash, earthenware, leather, wood, stone, metal, silk and bamboo. The band was composed of amateur musicians who performed at religious ceremonies in the Communal Hall and were also available to play at private functions. The musicians sat on decorated mats in front of the altar. They played traditional pieces devoted to the spirits of departed ancestors. Family and guests sat around to listen. Villagers crowded into the inner courtyard. The altar at night was an impressive sight. The brass, gold and lacquer all glowed in the light of dozens of candles and gave to the room a strange brightness. The sweet scent of aloes wood burning in the urns mingled with the fragrance of incense sticks. The sixth lunar month was the height of summer, on the eighteenth day the moon rose a bit late, but was still big and bright. I can recall with what enjoyment we listened to the rhythmic and melodious music, as incense floated in the air and moonlight shone over our altar house. It was a strange tradition that the only reward received by those musicians was a good meal. Their talents earned them no social consideration, only derisive comments from villagers, as shown in this proverb: "Puffing your cheeks and scratching your lips to get a mouthful of glutinous rice!"

The next morning, people were up early. There was great excitement among the children, for pigs were going to be killed. The animals made a deafening noise as young village guards carried them from the sty to the steps of the pond where their throats were cut and they bled to death. Steaming hot water in large cauldrons was poured on to shave off their outer skin and hair. A crowd of onlookers, mostly children, stood by and once we were given an on-the-spot anatomy lesson by my grandfather. He taught us the name and function of different organs inside the pig, recalling that in his time, that was the way students learned how organs in the human body looked. The guards did their job expertly and swiftly; in no time, the pigs had their dark skin removed and were turned into white carcasses. Then, they were opened up, cleaned and soon it was over. The carcasses, offal and blood were brought into the kitchen, the rubbish thrown into the pond for the fish and the steps swept clean.

Three services were held that day, corresponding to the three daily meals. The morning service consisted of cups of perfumed tea, which my grandfather prepared and presented to the altar on a carved tray inlaid with mother-of-pearl. The main ceremony took place at about ten o'clock in the morning. The altar full of food offerings looked like a banquet table. Indeed, the fare served was that of a traditional banquet. It started with cups of rice brandy and appetizers consisting of boiled pork tripes, chicken giblets and a specialty of northern Vietnamese cuisine, duck blood pudding. The brandy served on our altar differed from the usual colorless brandy. It was made from black rice which gave it a reddish color, and had been buried for many years to mature. Then came a variety of soups: swallow's nest soup, shark fin soup, and a soup made of a seafood called by the imaginative name of dragon's beard. Next came some special dishes: sautéed abalone, pork rind, to be savored with the brandy. Rice followed, served with meat pies, boiled pork, chicken and sautéed vegetables. Dessert included lotus seeds cooked in syrup, a custard-like sweet made of soya bean and sugar, and various fruits. When everything had been displayed on the altar, candles were lit, incense sticks and aloe wood were burned, and the service commenced. Witnessed by the rest of the family, my grandfather walked to the altar, sounded the drum and the gong, and knelt down. It took him a long time to say—in a low voice not audible to us—the prayers and consecrated formulas inviting our ancestor to accept the offerings. After a while, grandfather got up and poured rice brandy into the cups on the altar. By that gesture, he expressed his belief that the offerings had been accepted and the banquet in the realm of the spirits had started. Then, he bowed and knelt again several times. After he had finished, family members took turns to come before the altar. Being of the youngest generation, I was nearly last. Eagle-eyed, my grandmother watched all of us youngsters to see whether we knew how to kneel and bow in good style. She never liked my style. "Next time, watch your grandfather again and see how he does it,"

she told me. A few years earlier, the main ceremony was conducted according to a more formal ritual. The entire household performed the rites before
the altar at the same time. In the first rank was my great-grandmother,
behind her my grandparents, great-uncle and great-aunt, then down the
generations until us great-grand-nephews and nieces and lastly the other
members of the household. One rank followed another in a row extending
from inside the altar house to the verandah outside and down the hallway.
The scene was one of great solemnity. But grandfather had decided to
simplify the protocol.

After our immediate family had finished, the ceremony was opened to
other relatives and guests. The band returned. Meeting at the gate house,
the musicians formed into two lines. Playing music, they slowly marched
towards the new house, entered it by the two side doors, went through its
lounge and out into the hallway, then into the altar house. In front of the
altar, the lines joined together, band members bowed and played a few
pieces before separating again to settle on both sides of the altar. There,
they rested and only struck up a tune for important guests, such as the
prefect of Thanh Oai or village delegations.

Visitors brought offerings of incense sticks, votive papers, betel leaves,
areca nuts, flowers, fruit and various kinds of food. There was an abun-
dance of lichee and jack fruit, which grew well in our region. Flowers were
mostly white lilies and white or pink lotus, the lotus bunches usually coming with lotus pods full of green seeds, which were delicious to eat. There
were impressive-looking food offerings made by the association of grandfather's students, the village council, high officials and wealthy guests. For
instance, a suckling pig roasted to a beautiful dark red color and placed on
a yellow brass tray; a boiled head of a pig sitting on a bed of cream-colored
glutinous rice in a red-lacquered wooden tray; boiled capons richly
decorated with flowers; tray after tray of cooked glutinous rice, some with
white coconut meat, others with yellow beans, still others with monordica,
a fruit which gave to the rice an orange color. The colors of the offerings,
the shining brass instruments, the red and gold furniture, all combined to
give the altar room a festive look. In fact, the whole atmosphere at the anniversary was festive. The occasion was not a sad one. My great-grandfather died a long time ago, in 1909. Only my great-grandmother cried a
little.

After his offerings were brought in and incense sticks were lit, a guest
was invited to proceed to the altar. As he knelt and bowed to our ancestor,
a member of our family, standing next to the altar, knelt and bowed back
to him. That was the rite of *dap le*, or reciprocation. The guest not being
a member of our family, his paying respects to our ancestor was gratefully
acknowledged but must be returned. Therefore, my father or one of his
brothers had to stand ready near the altar. It was an established ritual

that the guest would protest and beg our family not to reciprocate, while my father would insist in doing so. Their exchange, done in good spirit and usually with a lot of banter, went on until the guest had to accept because other people had arrived and were waiting to perform the ceremony. But as my father had knelt and bowed to him, the guest must return the compliment; so after completing his rites to the altar, the guest turned to face my father, then knelt and bowed to him. Whereupon my father, this time the recipient of the guest's gesture, had to reciprocate once again. Once more, he knelt and bowed to the guest and there ended the rite of reciprocation.

A more delicate situation developed when a visitor of my grandfather's rank and age group presented himself. As the honored guest stepped out in front of the altar, the band started playing religious music. But, seeing that my grandfather had placed himself next to the altar to reciprocate, the guest objected, the band stopped and negotiations began. In this case, however, it behooved the guest to be adamant, not only out of consideration for my grandfather's position, but also because as an old man, it would be too much for him to kneel and bow repeatedly to guests. Finally, a compromise was reached, according to which my grandfather would stand on one side of the altar and limit himself to bowing, while on the other side his eldest son, my father, would perform the full rite by kneeling and bowing to the honored guest.

Following the ceremony, it was customary for all relatives and guests to stay for the midday meal. Food was served in round brass trays placed on wooden platforms, or at tables for guests of high status. Each tray provided for four or six persons; it should be an even number because odd ones were considered unlucky. Strict rules of precedence were observed and those sharing a tray must be of similar rank. To place someone at the wrong place would cause loss of face and resentment, which could last a long time. The number of dishes, the parts of pig or fowl served also depended on the guests' status. As the midday meal progressed and rice brandy was consumed, our ancestral home resounded with cheerful talk and laughter. The anniversary became an occasion to be enjoyed, by hosts and guests alike. As a family, we were gratified by the large attendance, for it was a measure of our standing within the community.

My grandmother went from one group to another to express thanks and to invite people to eat:

> "Your presence at the main anniversary of our family is much appreciated," she said. "I beg you to feel at home and share this ordinary meal with us."
> "We are privileged to be here," the oldest member of the group responded. "Please do not worry about us and consider us as members of the family."
> "But you are not eating anything! And we have been indeed failing in our hospitality," thus saying, grandmother would add another dish to the tray or

pour more rice brandy into the cups. There would be a chorus of protest: "We have had far too much to eat and drink!"

Then, grandmother moved to the next group. Vietnamese were by nature shy and guests needed to be constantly invited to eat by the hosts. Country people, in particular, would automatically refuse anything offered the first time and would only accept after having been pressed several times to do so. It was a kind of social game that people played. My grandmother pushed it to the limit. She was determined that guests at our house consumed plenty of food. She pressed on and on even when, I suspected, the guests already had had enough. But no one bore any grudge against her. On the contrary, she was widely praised for being warm-hearted and generous. It may happen that there were not enough guests for a tray; instead of making them wait, someone from our family had to sit in to make up the number. He would not eat, only be present there. That duty often fell to my father and his brothers. On the anniversary day, they may have taken part in several meals, without in fact having eaten. As the guests departed, each of them took home a gift pack comprising a plate of meat, a plate of glutinous rice and some fruits.

Among village officials, the lowest in rank was the crier, whose role was to make public announcements. He did so in the evening before people retired to sleep. Going from one hamlet to another and beating on a hollow block of wood to attract the villagers' attention, he shouted in a loud voice the announcements. There was only one crier in each village and he being of the lowest rank could not share a meal with anyone. So, at public festivals as well as private functions, he sat alone on a mat in front of a tray of food, a lonely figure amid the noise made by others and the fellowship enjoyed by them. King Le Thanh Ton, who ruled in the second half of the fifteenth century and was one of our greatest kings, was also a poet. He expressed his sympathy for the humble village crier in a poem:

> I, a village crier, endowed with a big voice and a long breath,
> When people heard me, they knew that it was not a matter to be trifled with.
> My woodblock resounded to the four corners,
> Issuing orders to young and old.
> Making announcements for all to hear...
> At festivals, I sat at my leisure, a whole mat for myself.

Everyone could see that the poem was not simply about a crier, it also applied to a king. For there was something in common between the highest and lowest official in our land. Neither could share, in public, a meal with anyone else.

Then, there were the beggars who, after the meal was finished and the guests had gone, were admitted into our compound and given some decent food.

Elders recalled that, when my grandfather was a mandarin, the anniversary was celebrated on a much grander scale. Colleagues of his, civil servants working under him and a lot of other guests attended. In addition to pigs, an ox was killed. A detachment of rifle soldiers was posted to guard the village. My grandfather took the precaution of sending the soldiers to Kim Bai for the anniversary following an incident in 1934, which my mother recalled vividly. An award had been given by the court to my great-grandparents, posthumously to my great-grandfather, in person to my great-grandmother who was then eighty-one. Crowds came from all over the canton and places further away to watch the arrival of the court representatives. On that occasion, Kim Bai's gates were opened to all comers. Mandarins in ceremonial robes conducted the ceremony of bestowing the awards. Their wives, my mother noticed, wore a profusion of gold jewelry. The official guests stayed in our ancestral home. A banquet was held in the evening, amid great rejoicing. In the middle of the night however, my mother woke up to the cries of "Emergency! Emergency!" Quickly, she picked me up—I was then a boy of four and still sleeping with her—and went out into the inner courtyard. There was great commotion. Menfolk were running to the walls of the compound, their swords drawn. Flames shot up in the sky, quite close, although they did not seem to come from within our compound. From outside came the clamor of a crowd. Voices were shouting: "The mandarin's house is on fire. Everyone must go in and help fight it!" Those voices did not belong to people in our village, my mother noticed, and she realized that bandits had set fire to a nearby cottage and raised the alarm that our home was burning. They hoped to move in along with other villagers, under the pretext of fighting the fire. Once in, they could lay hands on our valuables. But what they were after in the first place, my mother believed, was the gold and jewelry belonging to our guests. The bandits pushed and smashed against the iron doors of the gate house which, fortunately, held firm. "Bring the ladder here!" a voice was heard. They were trying to scale the walls.

From inside the compound, our people shouted: "There is no fire here! Those climbing in would be cut down! Villagers of Kim Bai, don't fall in with the bandits' ploy!" The women and children gathered in the altar house. Trembling with fear, they all prayed to Lord Buddha and to our ancestors for protection. Men in our household had put tables against the walls and jumped on top of them. Holding big torches to light the area and brandishing their swords and knives, they kept warning the crowd outside: "Don't climb in or you will be cut down! There is no fire here!" For a while there was a stalemate; then a bullhorn was heard sounding the alarm, followed by other bullhorns. Village guards were coming! People would wake up in fear of impending dangers at the staccato calls of bullhorns in the night, my mother said, but these were now music to her ears.

They announced that, at last, rescue was on the way. In no time, the bandits vanished, the villagers dispersed and calm was restored. But the ladies could not go back to sleep. Spending the rest of the night drinking tea and chewing betel, they told each other horror stories of bandits.

After that incident, my grandfather also bought some guns and hired an ex-soldier to guard our ancestral home. But, as Vietnam was a French protectorate, no Vietnamese was allowed to own rifles which could be turned against colonial troops. Our family could only get shotguns. As it turned out, the guns were never used against bandits, only to shoot doves, wild ducks and geese.

The third service of the anniversary day was held before the evening meal. The next day, the last ceremony took place, after which the votive papers were taken from the altar to the big urns in the front yard and burned. The papers came in two colors, gold and silver. Once burned, so our people believed, they would become gold and silver in the realm of the spirits, ready for our ancestor to spend. A quick meal was served, then the visitors left. As my peers said good-bye and merrily jumped on their bicycles to return to the city, I felt miserably left out. Once again, I was seized with the depressing thought of being stuck in the country while exciting events passed me by. School would not resume for another two months. Until then, I would have to stay in the village. The compound looked deserted.

But I was called by my grandfather into his study. He greeted me with a smile and a twinkle in his eyes. "Now we can get back to Chinese script and Tang poetry," he said.

The Tet

Tet is the first festival of the year and the most important of all festivals. All Vietnamese like to return to their village for Tet. As the year draws to an end, they could feel in their bones the appeal of the ancestral land. The tinkle of New Year poles, the ancestral home with smoke rising from its chimney, a soft drizzle falling over tall areca nut trees, all must be there to give to the Tet festival its full flavor. Since 1947, war, then partition, then war again and exile have prevented me from going back to Kim Bai. Thus, an essential ingredient of Tet has been missing for me.

Women and children were usually the first to return. The men, kept in town by their work, followed later. My mother, being the eldest daughter-in-law with special responsibilities in the family, usually left Hanoi with us children three or four days before the year ended. Two rickshaws were needed for her and my younger siblings. My elder brother and I on our bicycles formed the escort. The winter landscape was bleak.

Lifeless fields lay bare under grey skies. From time to time, we only saw
a white egret take off on its solitary flight. My fingers on the handlebars
were numb from the cold wind. But travellers on the highway were all in
good spirits. They were returning home, like us, to "send off the Old and
welcome the New," or going to the market to buy provisions to celebrate
Tet. When an air alert was on and everyone had to clear the highway and
take shelter under a large tree—so as not to be seen by Allied planes—there
was conversation and laughter as if between old acquaintances. At the
village of Xom, our caravan stopped for the family's favorite cake. I held
the steaming hot cake in my hands for a long time before opening its wrapping of leaves and savoring the delicate taste of flour and molasses blended
together. Going out of Xom, my brother and I raced ahead on our bicycles.
There was no more need to escort the rickshaws. We were already in home
territory. On entering Kim Bai, we could hear around us the welcoming
tinkle of New Year poles. These were long trunks of bamboo with earthenware representations of animals suspended on top; swayed by the wind,
these banged against one another to produce light ringing sounds, like
those of small bells in a temple. The poles were planted in every garden to
frighten off evil spirits. According to popular superstition, Lord Buddha
had warned the spirits that all places with those poles were put under his
protection and that they must keep away from them.

It was said that Tet was the time for people to rest and enjoy themselves, but for the eldest daughter-in-law, it was certainly not a restful time.
My mother had to look after everything, from the preparation of offerings
to the provision of food for a household of thirty people. Although the servants and other women in the family lent a hand, the main burden fell on
her shoulders. With grandmother, she had to get up before everyone else,
at five o'clock when it was still dark and bitterly cold. The two went to bed
after everyone else, having seen to it that everything had been tidied up. I
remember one Tet when my mother dropped on her foot a heavy brass tray
used for serving food that she was carrying. The foot became so swollen
that I suspected a bone may have been cracked. Despite great pain, she continued to be up and about, fulfilling her duties without uttering a single
complaint.

For Tet, the Vietnamese traditionally had two kinds of cakes, one
round, the other square. In the olden times, the round cake was thought
to take the shape of the sky and the square one that of the earth. Both were
made of glutinous rice. In the round cake, the rice was just plain boiled,
then pounded into a smooth pastry. In the square cake, it had a filling of
beans and meat. By far, the most popular of the two was the square one,
called *chung*. Our family cooked both types of cake, but to me, the high
point in the preparations leading to Tet was the wrapping of the *chung* cake.
By then, most of the family had come back. Only two more days separated

us from the New Year. Women and girls sat on wooden platforms in the transversal house, forming a circle. Between them were baskets of rice and beans, plates of pork meat and heaps of rush leaves to wrap the cakes. My mother, my aunts, my teenaged sisters, all were there working. The men and children gathered around them. Tet was a time of family reunion, not the extended family as on my great-grandfather's anniversary, but just our immediate family. Even my great-uncle and his children were not present. There were no guests, no friends, only ourselves. Everyone participated in the conversation, laughter rang out like firecrackers. At times, grandmother came and sat on the edge of the platforms to listen to our jokes or to tell us one of her philosophical tales.

A family like ours needed several dozens of *chung* cake. The wrapping session could take the best part of an afternoon. Two kinds of *chung* cake were prepared, with salt or with sugar. Our family had a special liking for the sweet ones. I have never tasted any better sweet *chung* cakes than those made by my mother. She had a way of combining the beans, meat, fat and sugar into a delicious filling. When the cake was cooked, the filling became dark red, while the glutinous rice on the outside took on the green of the rush leaves. The result was as good to the eyes as it was to the palate. Since leaving Vietnam, my mother has continued to make sweet *chung* cakes at the New Year to remind us of past festivals spent in our homeland. The only thing missing is the green, as fresh rush leaves cannot be obtained in Paris. For children, the wrapping session grew in interest towards the end, when miniature cakes were made with the leftovers of rice and filling. A common sight during Tet was children playing with those minuscule *chung* cakes, often suspended by a red thread from their wrists. The cakes wrapped in rush leaves were boiled in big cauldrons. The cooking took many hours, ending late at night. We sat in front of a row of cooking fires, enjoying their warm glow, talking and eating sweet potatoes roasted in the embers. To the happiness of reunion was added the excitement and promise of an imminent festival, for the year was fast drawing to a close.

The *chung* cake could be eaten cold or steamed hot. Another way, which I particularly liked, was for it to be fried crisply and served at breakfast. Tet was the time for all kinds of good food. In fact, food was an important part of all festivals in a country where, all year round, the people worked hard and lived frugally. At festival time, they rested and had something better to eat than the usual diet of vegetables and rice. Everyone, whether rich or poor, looked forward to some special fare at Tet, the premier festival of the year. "Even though not well-off, one should live well during the three days of Tet," was the counsel given in a proverb. Each region, each family had its own traditional dishes. The ones served in our family were chosen because they were good to eat, of course, but also for the special meaning that Tet gave to them. For dinner on the last day of the year, we had only one dish, a river fish called *am* cooked in rice gruel. In Vietnamese, the word *am* also means dark. Our tradition required this fish to be eaten, so that all things dark would go with the old year and the new one would start in brightness. The thick, long-bodied fish was boiled in rice gruel with onions, ginger and a lot of pepper. The family assembled for dinner in the altar house. The men sat on chairs at tables, the women and children on wooden platforms. From the kitchen, steaming pots were brought up. We dipped spring onions, Chinese cabbage, celery and various fragrant herbs in the hot gruel. The fish, simply boiled, retained all its flavor. With the rice and vegetables, it made a complete meal, very good to have in the cold weather.

At midnight on New Year's Eve, religious services were celebrated at several places to mark the transition from the old year to the new. It was traditional in our family to observe also, at that time, the custom of "the first caller." That most important event usually took place, for other people, in the morning of the new year. In our case, however, it was just after midnight that the first caller came.

According to popular belief, the fortune of a household in any one year would depend on the first person to call on it at the New Year. But how to choose the right person, one who could bring good luck to your family? One could pick someone rich, or in high office, or with a distinguished background, or just a good friend, but how could one be sure whether he had good luck or not? Furthermore, a person might have it one year, but another year, because the stars which governed his life were positioned differently, his luck might change completely. For the same reason, to be invited to be a first caller could be embarrassing. One was touched by the honor, yet the responsibility was overwhelming. What would that family think, if some misfortune befell them? Our own family, fortunately, had no need to ask anyone to "first call" at our ancestral home, for as a rule my grandmother herself was our first caller, and it had been like that every year for as long as I could remember. Our good or bad fortune thus depended only on ourselves. We did not owe thanks to anyone, nor could we blame anyone. How and when did that tradition of ours start? And why was it that the first caller was my grandmother and not my grandfather, the head of the family? I do not know the answers but wonder whether that was not a piece of advice given by an astrologer or a Chinese geomancer.

As midnight approached, we celebrated a service at our ancestors' altar, then grandmother led a family delegation to the village's Buddhist temple. The night was as black as ink. We followed one another, guiding ourselves by the flickering light of a kerosene lamp and taking care not to step outside the brick lane. The small temple was an island of light, overflowing with people. Grandmother made offerings to the altars and spent a long time praying. When she finished, it was midnight and the first day of the year had begun. Firstly, from somewhere in the village, a string of firecrackers exploded. Another explosion was heard, then another. The noise came from all the hamlets. Village guards at the gates beat their drums. After presenting our good wishes to the bonze, we returned home, bearing gifts of food and flower. The iron gates were closed and grandmother called out for someone to open them. My father, her eldest son, was waiting. He greeted her and invited her to be the first caller to tread on the soil of our ancestral compound. She obligingly accepted. The same ritual was followed each year. After her return, a service was held at a specially erected altar in our compound, in honor of the celestial envoys who were looking after the affairs of the earth. The envoys were believed to be replaced every year at Tet. The service was to farewell those who departed and to welcome their successors. After that service, everyone went immediately to bed, so as to be up early the next morning.

The first day of the year was one day when no one could linger in bed. A lazy start would augur badly for the whole year. Even as children, we would not wait to be woken up by our parents. After breakfast, we changed into new clothes. My great-grandmother and grandparents wore red brocade dresses. Other men and boys had blue ones. Women and girls came out of their room in beautiful long dresses of red or pink velvet. During the year, I usually wore western style clothes. Tet was the only time when I dressed in the national costume. I felt a bit strange and clumsy in white trousers and a blue brocade dress, with a black turban around my head, but soon got into the special mood of Tet. The ceremony in front of our ancestors' altar began. My grandfather knelt down to invoke the spirits of our ancestors. He called upon them to protect the family and help its members in their endeavors during the new year. Four times he knelt down, touching the ground with his forehead. Then he bowed three times. Following him, my great-grandmother, then grandmother and the rest of the family performed the same rite. We did so at two places, the central altar for the Nguyen ancestors and the smaller altar for our maternal ancestors. Last to go in were the children and I well remember that it was an occasion for uncontrollable mirth. Our obeisance to our ancestors was interrupted by giggles, and we would be rolling on the mat instead of kneeling down. Such a thing never happened at services commemorating the death of an ancestor. No doubt the fun and excitement of Tet had something to do with it. Family elders looked on and laughed too. Normally, an irreverent attitude before the altar would be severely reprimanded, but this was the first day of the year. Parents abstained from scolding because to do so would bring bad luck both to them and the children. Any manifestation of temper had to be avoided on that auspicious day. After the religious ceremony, my great-grandmother and grandparents went to sit on the two carved wood settees in the middle of the altar house. There, they formally received the good wishes of family members and gave to each of them money wrapped in red paper.

This was called the ceremony of "welcoming another year of age." The first to present them with good wishes was my father, the heir and head of the next generation. Then came the heir and head of the generation which followed his, my elder brother. Other members followed according to rank, my uncles, aunts, then us and younger cousins. We all had to say something, so each had prepared a little speech. According to an ancient tradition, we would have to kneel down twice before the oldest surviving member of the family, who was my great-grandmother, then nearing ninety. But she would not allow it and only accepted that we bowed to her. As a member of the fourth generation, I presented my good wishes to her, to my grandparents, to my parents, to my uncles and aunts. Each time I received some money wrapped in red paper. At the end of the round, my pockets were weighed down by coins, all brand new and shining. Drinks were served. We had champagne — imported French wines were much in fashion — in which we dipped finger biscuits. Even the ladies, who normally would not touch alcoholic beverages, would take a sip of champagne after much prompting. Red lacquered boxes were opened to show their attractive display of crystallized pineapple, cumquat, lotus seed, tomato, also sweet potato and marrow, all very sweet and in their bright colors of red, orange, cream and green. We ate the preserve to make the year itself bright and sweet. Also during Tet, Vietnamese very much liked to munch on watermelon seeds, grilled and dyed red, which we cracked open with our teeth. Following drinks, the family went out to the front yard to watch the display of firecrackers. Suspended high in long strings from the roof of the gate and the first floor of the new house, they made a deafening noise and filled the air with smoke and the smell of gunpowder. Soon, the yard was covered with shreds of red paper, omens of good luck and prosperity.

The firecracker display brought to an end the morning's ceremonies and we settled down to playing cards, an activity inseparable from Tet. Young and old became absorbed in it. Gambling was normally forbidden in my family. My mother had always been very firm about this. Her own family had suffered from gambling addictions and we children were taught to eschew it. But Tet was an exception. We were free to play whatever card game we wanted. Mother herself, however, never touched a card. As a matter of fact, the only three people who did not sit down to play cards during Tet were my great-grandmother, grandmother and mother, the three eldest daughters-in-law of three generations in our family. Everyone else played. Our elders played a game called *to tom*, a precursor of today's mahjong and more of an intellectual exercise than a mere game of chance. The rules were rigid and numerous, requiring complex calculations. Although quite young then, I already knew how to play it and was always happy to be asked to take the place of an elder who had to be absent for a while. Sometimes I "sat in" and played a few games, with grandfather among the other players. That was a thrill. Men prized themselves for being skilled at the game. To be referred to by other scholars as a high calibre *to tom* player was a mark of distinction, even a recognition of intellectual prowess. A group of *to tom* players—five people sitting in a circle on a wooden platform—usually produced a great deal of talk and laughter. Conversation among them often bubbled with wit.

Women and children played simpler games. My grandfather was a man of stern character and rather distant, but during Tet he shared a lot of fun with the family. At times, he even left his game of *to tom* to come and play cards with us. On one such occasion, we were playing the game of *bat,* which was based on the number ten. You won it if your cards added up to ten or were nearer to it than those of your competitors. If your total exceeded ten, you were out of the game. On the cards were pictures of people, animals or flowers. We used to get a laugh out of giving the cards not their accepted names, but nicknames. One card in particular represented a woman with a plain and sad-looking face. We called it "Aunt of Don Thu." That "aunt" was grandfather's concubine and Don Thu the name of her village. Grandfather took her as his concubine with the full consent of his wife. "Aunt of Don Thu" lived in our Kim Bai home, but for one reason or another, the arrangement did not work. After a number of years, she left to return to her village. That happened not so long ago. We kept talking about her but of course not in my grandparents' presence. That Tet, I was about twelve. We were playing a game of *bat* when grandfather joined our party. With him there, our card table became a center of attention and other people gathered around, giving advice to players, making jokes and chatting merrily. The card we called "Aunt of Don Thu" was the seven which, if you got it first round, was not a good sign because seven was probably not high enough to win you the game and yet, with a second card you were likely to exceed ten. I drew the seven and let escape from my mouth: "Tough luck, Aunt of Don Thu again!", forgetting that grandfather was present. Fortunately, everyone burst out laughing and grandfather, in a generous mood, also laughed heartily.

We were all keen to play cards but could not play for long. Relatives and other villagers kept coming with their season's greetings and we always had to break up to greet and entertain them. A colorful event was the visit by the canton chief, who arrived on horseback at the head of a delegation of officials. Wearing a black satin dress with a wide belt in red silk wrapped around his waist, his head under a shiny black turban, he cut a stately figure. Officials followed him on foot. Behind them came porters carrying offerings. My father came out to meet them at the gate; a welcoming string of firecrackers was lit, which made the horse jump wildly. The delegation paid their respects to our ancestors' altar, wine and crystallized fruit were served, and then came the exchange of greetings. The canton chief had a powerful baritone voice. With the help of wine, his greetings were delivered loudly and in flowery language. Other delegates followed suit. As the meeting progressed and more wine was consumed, the greetings became louder and more elaborate. On our family's side, my grandmother had a vibrant voice and a spontaneous laugh that had won her much affection. Whereas her husband expressed himself briefly, she always responded with a verve equal to that of the visitors. The sound of voices and laughter echoed up the gate house. As our guests left, they were bidden farewell by another explosion of firecrackers.

After lunch, we still were not left alone because now, on top of receiving guests, members of the family had to call on those who had visited us to return the courtesy. It was a busy day for everyone. Not until the evening, after dinner had been taken, could we finally concentrate on playing cards. Some of us continued to play until the early hours of the morning.

On the altar were offerings of traditional round and square cakes and special dishes prepared for Tet, most of which were based on chicken. Chicken in the Vietnamese scholarly language is *ke* which, in our colloquial language, means money. Thus, people believed that by eating chicken at Tet, they would have plenty of money during the year. On the first day of Tet, two big capons were boiled in two very large pots—the pots must be large enough so that the birds were intact from crest to feet—after which they were placed on two brass trays and decorated with flowers. One capon was sent to the Communal Hall as an offering to the village deities, the other went to an altar especially set up in honor of the deities who presided over our ancestral home. Several dishes for the feast of Tet had a base of chicken broth, such as swallow's nest soup and dragon's beard soup. We had bamboo shoot soup too, which normally was not a prized dish for banquets, but the shoots here were taken from a species of small bamboo special to our region called *truc sang*. These shoots had a delicate flavor and were the only ones tender enough for my old great-grandmother to eat. The next day, it was customary for our family to have a dish called *kim tien ke*. There can be no better name for a Tet dish, for these three words all mean money. My mother was especially good at preparing that dish, which was a great favorite of mine. It was she who introduced it to the Nguyen family after her marriage and such was its success that since then, every year it was on our menu for the second day. Its three layers of chicken, fat and ham were marinated in sweet brandy, then grilled over charcoal and served on a bed of lettuce. On the third day, we usually had a noodle soup prepared with chicken, prawns, pork sausage and flavored with a special condiment taken from a species of beetle called *ca cuong*. That condiment is one of the most ancient and expensive in our food. History books recorded that, as far back as the year 181 B.C., a basket of such beetles was among the tributes sent to the Han Court in China. These beetles have at the base of their neck a single drop of an oily substance. Just a tiny portion of that drop would suffice to give a delicious aroma to a whole bowl of soup.

The second day of Tet was marked by visits. The first to arrive was my great-uncle. As head of a junior branch, he stayed in Hanoi to welcome the New Year with his own family. Early on the second day, he returned to the ancestral home, riding a rickshaw and accompanied by one or two of his children. Grandfather waited for him before celebrating the day's service at the ancestors' altar. Great-uncle knelt and bowed. He presented to his mother, his elder brother and sister-in-law his New Year's greetings. His nephews, nieces, grand-nephews and grand-nieces took turns to wish him a happy New Year and to receive from him the traditional money gift. These formalities over, great-uncle immediately joined a game of *to tom,* for he was a very keen player. Aunts of mine who were married visited with their husbands and that meant to us children more greetings and more coins. Other relatives and friends would also make the trip to Kim Bai on that day. Some came in their motor cars and created quite a stir in the village, as cars were still a rarity in those days.

Among the visitors on the second day, two people stood out in my mind. The first one was a former student of grandfather who, eventually, married his niece and became head of a prefecture. Uncle Prefect Tam, as I called him, belonged to the old school of learning based on the scholarly script. A favorite pastime among scholars was for a person to write a poem and for others to respond by producing other poems on the same theme and using the same rhymes. It was akin to "variations on a theme" in Western classical music. Tet and the coming of spring have inspired many a poet and every year, Prefect Tam had a poem to show to his former teacher. But he was quite reluctant to produce it and only did so after much prompting. Finally, he recited the poem in modulated tones. Grandfather and other elders, who had all stopped their games of *to tom* to listen, congratulated him warmly, expressing appreciation of the subtleties of wording and in-spiration. Then, grandfather said that such good poetry deserved a response and he immediately improvised a four-verse poem with the same rhymes, also to celebrate the festival of renewal. Uncle Prefect Tam got up and made a deep bow to his teacher. He praised the response with much eloquence, saying that grandfather's poem had expressed the feelings that he himself had wanted to express in his own poem but had been unable to do.

The second personage was a widow and businesswoman who owned a large shop in downtown Hanoi called Hoa Tuong. As was the custom in Vietnam, she was herself called Mrs. Hoa Tuong, after the name of her shop. Rumored to be among the wealthiest business people in Hanoi, she personified the independent and resourceful woman often found in our society, who did not fit into the traditional mold of Confucian teaching, according to which a woman "when unmarried should obey her father, when married should obey her husband and, on her husband's death, should follow her son." She had three boys and a girl and was distantly related to my grandmother. The boys were my grandparents' adopted sons. Wealthy people in business often asked high officials to "adopt" their sons. This was not an adoption in legal terms, simply a practice to obtain more social standing. My grandfather had other "adopted" sons and daughters, not all of them from rich families. Some were village people who belonged to his household and had followed him to various provinces in the course of his career.

As part of our family, Mrs. Hoa Tuong and her children participated in all our celebrations and anniversaries. They always joined us for the New Year on the second day. They came in a big car, bringing expensive presents such as imported French wines and biscuits, rare fruit such as the renowned oranges of Bo Ha in the Northern Highlands and the imperial bananas, so called because they were sent each year as tribute to the emperor in Hue. Tet was also the season in the north for a special type of mandarin which went by the name of *cam duong*, or sugar orange. True to its name, it was perfectly sweet with absolutely no trace of sourness. Bigger than the usual mandarin it had a very thick skin and big segments full of juice. In the cold northern winter, the juice was chilled. I have never eaten more delicious mandarins, not in the south where our family moved in 1954, not in all the foreign countries where I have stayed. Once, on a visit to Taiwan, I was told that sugar oranges like those in north Vietnam were available. I immediately bought some. Unfortunately, although they looked the same they did not have the same flavor and sweetness.

Peach branches covered with pink blossoms and bowls of flowering narcissus were traditional New Year decorations. Narcissus, in particular, was *the* flower of Tet. Nowadays when spring comes to our Melbourne garden, narcissi grow profusely—some white, some yellow. In Vietnam, narcissus is a rock plant difficult to grow and, therefore, very precious. Bulbs had to be nicked for buds to come out, according to an ancient art taught by older ladies to the younger ones. Narcissus bulbs came from the mountains in the north or were imported from China. They were bought as Tet approached and nicked in such a way that flowers would bloom right on the first day of the New Year. If these seemed likely to be late, the bulbs were put in lukewarm water to speed up the process. In the opposite eventuality, they were left outside in the cold night air to retard flowering. When ready, the bulbs were displayed in porcelain bowls, with water and pebbles, in an arrangement similar to the Japanese *Ikebana*. The delicate beauty of the flowers, the bulbs' white roots hanging out under water and the pebble arrangement combined with the classical lines of the blue porcelain bowls to make an exquisite tableau. But more than shape and color even, it was the fragrance of the narcissus which became associated in my mind with the New Year and its message of renewal. In Australia, as the flowers first come out in the middle of the year, their sweet smell brings back to life the Tets of my youth. Suddenly, the refugee away from his homeland feels hope being reborn within him, and he gears himself for a new beginning.

The ceremony of "sweeping the tomb" took place on the fourth day. By tradition, it started at dawn. Late starters were viewed with disapproval, for one must not make the ancestors wait on that day of all days in the year. I can not recall my grandfather participating in the ceremony—perhaps this was on acccount of his age—but all male members of our family were there. From an early age, I had been allowed to join the party. Going out in the open fields, when everything was quiet and still and the promise of a new day lay ahead, always gave me a special feeling of elation. Winter in the north meant a persistent drizzle and a penetrating cold. Our party of twenty people or so was led by a cousin of my father, who belonged to a senior branch of the extended family and had held the position of Deputy Mayor of Kim Bai. I called him Uncle Deputy. My great-uncle the mayor, although a Chu and not a Nguyen, was also in the party, because over several generations the two families had intermarried and some ancestors were common to both. The misty rain was all around us. Flat and empty fields stretched far into the still dark horizon. We walked in single file on the narrow paths that served as boundaries to the rice fields. It was slippery, our feet were wet and our clothes spattered with mud. But in the gentle light of dawn, the countryside assumed a poetical beauty. Like an ink painting, shapes and lines were indistinct and the colors but different shades of grey. Villages appeared vaguely in the distance. The fields were silent, no sound of bird or animal could be heard. Here and there, silhouettes of men in single file were seen, carrying on their shoulders shovel and hoe. They were fellow villagers on the way to perform the same ceremony as we. Only short greetings were exchanged with them; it was as if everyone's mind was turning inwards and towards the past.

We visited all ancestral graves, starting with that of my great-grandfather. The graves were mounds of earth, some still as large as newly-built tumuli, but others and more ancient ones had been reduced to the size of a tea chest standing solitarily in the middle of a field. At each grave, we used hoe and shovel to clear the grass and weeds. Then, we built the earth up and made the mound square and upright again, before lighting incense and offering prayers. Lastly, votive papers were burned. Elders recalled the time and life of the ancestor buried there to the young people, for whom each year's ceremony was an occasion to learn something more of the family history. Some graves lay within our village's boundaries, others lay farther away in the neighboring villages of Kim Lam, Cat Dong and Van Quan. Although the graves covered a period of three centuries, their actual number was not high because many generations of ours consisted of only a single branch. By the time we had finished, it was only mid-morning. On our way home, we passed by graves which had been weeded and hoed. Red incense sticks were planted on them, some still burning. Ashes of votive papers floated around. While earlier in the day they had looked forlorn in the fields, the graves seemed to have acquired a life and warmth of their own. A few, however, had been left unvisited and the mayor would tell us their sorrowful stories: the family line had ended or the descendants had all left the village. Often, he stopped our procession, went over an untended tomb, cleared it and lit some sticks of incense over it. The *Story of Kieu* contains a famous passage about the young Kieu who, on the day of sweeping the tombs, saw an abandoned grave and took pity on it. She enquired and was told that it was the grave of a songstress, long renowned for her beauty and talent. But the songstress died alone and destitute. Only a kind-hearted admirer came to give her a simple burial and since then, no one had ever visited her grave. "How fragile was the fate of those blessed with beauty!" lamented Kieu. Little did she know that her own fate would not be so different from that of the songstress. That passage was one of the first that I learned from the *Story of Kieu*. During our own "sweeping the tomb" ceremony, I saw that my great-uncle was also moved by the same feelings as the heroine of our best loved literary work.

The ceremony over, we left Kim Bai. It was customary for my mother to return to her own family on the fourth day of Tet. My parents took us back to Hanoi and from there, they went to her village, which was only a few kilometers away. Not all the children accompanied them, only one or two each time. They stayed there only for the evening meal. In the countryside, the Tet festival would continue until the seventh day of the New Year, when the poles were taken down. But schools in Hanoi resumed one or two days earlier, and to us, going back to school marked the end of Tet.

7. The Village Community

"A village is a small state," said a proverb. "The laws of the king have to give way to village customs," proclaimed another. Since olden times, villages in Vietnam had enjoyed extensive autonomy. The king's government, although it appointed village chiefs, concerned itself only with the collection of taxes, the conscription of men and the maintenance of public order. Each village organized its life according to its own customs and regulations. In the beginning of the eighteenth century, village autonomy was further strengthened when communal authorities became elected by the people. Our old political system was a peculiar combination of absolute monarchy at the national level and democracy at the village level. All citizens had their say in the conduct of communal affairs. They participated in deliberations at the Communal Hall and elected the village council. Positions in the council were open to all. Traditionally, each village had a written document setting out the rules and regulations governing communal life. The name of that document underlined the democratic character of the system. It was called *Huong Uoc,* or the Village Contract and was signed by all citizens.

Fellow villagers shared strong bonds of solidarity and loyalty. In the old days, solidarity extended to the point of collective responsibility. Should an offence be committed by a member, the whole village was reprimanded by government officials. If taxes collected from its citizens failed to reach their target, the village had to make up the difference. The good reputation of the community must be upheld by all. One village's bylaw stipulated that "disputes should be settled by the people involved in them. If the parties came to fighting and shouting abuses at each other, thereby making the community a laughing stock for outsiders, then both parties would be fined." To have a native son graduate and become a high mandarin meant that the village itself would benefit, for the mandarin would see it as his duty to further the interests of his community. In the 1930s, my grandfather did much for Kim Bai. Four centuries ago, under the Mac dynasty (1527–1592), our village had the good fortune of producing as many as four doctors who all became high officials. Consequently, the Mac period was one of great development and prosperity for Kim Bai; in fact, its golden age. The village where a dynasty originated became something of a second

95

capital. Whenever the king returned there, the court followed him. Palaces and offices were built to accommodate the monarch and his entourage. Even when the king was not in residence there, all mandarins who happened to travel near the village in the course of their duties would stop to pay their respects to his birthplace. Outside Co Trai for instance, the village of the Mac kings in the eastern part of the Red River delta, a ceremonial platform was erected for the mandarins to perform their act of worship, facing in the direction of the village. They would not go in there; being the king's own, the village had become a forbidden place, like the forbidden city in the royal capital. Important positions in the army and civil service were given to natives of the king's village. Often, these were appointed as close attendants to the monarch and would control the access to his chambers.

Village solidarity remained strong during periods of violent change, such as the aftermath of a civil war. Vietnam has had a long history of internal conflicts. From the sixteenth to the nineteenth centuries, the Vietnamese were fighting against one another, more or less continuously. Rival dynasties partitioned the country. New forces emerging from the south challenged traditional rulers from the north. When a dynasty fell, its followers and their families were persecuted. Villages which were too closely allied with the defeated regime would suffer too. Certainly, the fate of the king's village would be sealed. Time and again, our history had shown a victorious side razing to the ground the village of its enemy, destroying all its ancestral tombs and leaving no trace for the population to remember the former rulers. But thanks to their traditional autonomy, most villages would survive a change of dynasty. Life behind the bamboo enclosure would continue very much as before, under a new ruling house. Rarely a village would betray its citizens and hand them over to the new authorities. On the contrary, those on the losing side could always expect to get help and temporary shelter from their fellow villagers. They knew that if they survived the critical period of persecution, they could always come back and re-integrate into the community. Ancestors from two branches of our family occupied high positions under the Mac dynasty. When that dynasty fell under the attacks of the Trinh, both branches had to flee the capital, of course not to go back to Kim Bai, for the village would be the first place where the victors would look for them. Where they went for refuge and for how long they stayed away, we do not know. But one branch has since disappeared. The other branch, our own, met with untold tribulations. Our third ancestor died in tragic circumstances. The rest of the family, however, succeeded in returning to Kim Bai. After an absence lasting as many as ten or a dozen years, they were accepted back within the community. Furthermore, they were able to regain possession of most of their land.

In times of war, when having to flee from the scene of hostilities, a Vietnamese would instinctively seek the protection of his village. I remember that, as the conflict with France threatened to break out in 1946, Hanoi was evacuated. My family knew where it would go and so too did most of my friends. We were not too worried about having to leave Hanoi and exchanged addresses, as if we were saying good-bye at the start of the summer vacation. "If you pass by my village, look me up," we said to one another. One friend, however, had no forwarding address to give. "I do not know where we will go," he said. "But where is your village?" we all asked, convinced in our minds that at such a time, one could only think of going to one's village. He explained that his people had been living in Hanoi and had lost contact with the place of their origin. "We have spent all the Tet festivals in town," he added, and his voice suddenly carried a note of sadness.

Ceremonies and festivals played an important part in village life. They contributed much to bind people together. Kim Bai had no festivals known all over the country like that of the Heavenly Prince in my grandmother's village, or a market day celebrated by the whole region like the New Year Festival in Chuong. Kim Bai's festivals were only held for the benefit of the village community. There were many in a year, with the two main events taking place in spring and autumn. I knew little of them since they coincided with the school terms, when I was away. The first festival was for the village what Tet was for each family. At Tet, family members gathered to worship their ancestors' spirits and celebrate the arrival of a new year. A month later, the villagers got together to worship Kim Bai's deities and usher in a new cycle of seasons. The sacred tablets kept on the altars in the Communal Hall were taken out and carried in a solemn procession through all hamlets. After they were returned to the Hall and the religious ceremony had ended, a communal meal for the men followed. In the evening, music and dance were performed in the Hall's courtyard for the enjoyment of the population. The second festival was held in the autumn to pray to the village's deities for a bountiful crop. Between these two events, there were smaller festivals. Every month or so, villagers had an occasion to stop their work routine and participate in a day of celebration and entertainment.

All citizens were entitled to contribute to the village feast and take part in it. From the age of twelve or thirteen, a boy could have his name registered in the village roll and, following an admission ceremony in the Hall where money and food offerings were made, was allowed to partake of the communal food. To begin with, he was only given his portion of meat and boiled glutinous rice. Then, having reached the age of eighteen, he would qualify to go and eat in the Communal Hall with the other citizens. In prosperous times, our village sacrificed an ox and several pigs at the principal festivals. As the economic situation worsened in the 1940s, the ox was spared and the number of pigs dwindled. Still, the excitement and sense of occasion remained undiminished and few people would ever want to miss a communal feast. Among those who left Kim Bai to work in town, many made the trip back to attend the main festivals. More specifically, they wanted to be present at the feast in the Communal Hall. "A morsel at the Hall is worth a platter of meat in one's own kitchen," people used to say. The criteria for determining village precedence were based on age and merit. The place of honor, in front of the altars, was reserved for holders of high diplomas and mandarinal ranks. In my grandfather's time, he was the only person qualified to sit there, but abstained from attending, perhaps because he did not want to have to eat by himself. Two rows of wooden platforms covered with rush mats were arranged on the two sides of the altars. Heading the rows on the right side were the four oldest men in the village, all past the age of seventy and known as "the four pillars." Current and former members of the village council headed the rows on the left. Behind them and the old men came the rest of the citizens.

I was too young to take part in a meal at the Communal Hall, but had the opportunity to go to a formal meal at the place of my great-uncle the mayor. The Chu was one of Kim Bai's prominent families. Their private function was attended by a large number of guests and village protocol was observed. My mother was quite excited. She treated the occasion almost like my first communal meal and carefully explained to me the rules of behavior, what to eat and when, although, being a woman, she had never attended a village meal.

On the strength of my school diploma, I was allowed to attend the meal while still underaged; moreover, the mayor made me jump ranks and sit with adult graduates. Three elders shared a food tray with me. They were kind enough to make me feel at ease. The tray contained soup and a number of meat and vegetable dishes. The meat was neatly cut and arranged to show four clear portions. Any risk of confusion must be avoided, for to eat into someone else's portion would be the worst of manners. Protocol set down precisely which part of the pig was served to whom. To the table of honor—or tray of honor, for everyone was sitting cross-legged around the trays of food—went the best parts of a pig, taken from its head and collar. For a citizen to be served the wrong piece of meat was a slight which could lead to bitter acrimony. Cutting and distributing meat at village functions was not a task for every butcher. Such task required a thorough knowledge of protocol and local customs. I read in history books that a king in ancient China chose a man to be his prime minister solely on his talent for cutting meat at public ceremonies. That man never made a mistake which caused recriminations. "He must have an inner sense of justice and of the rites," the king said, and indeed the butcher proved himself to be a very good prime minister. Now I began to understand something of the king's wisdom. We started the meal by drinking rice brandy while sampling appetizers. I accepted the first cup offered by my elders.

The strong brandy took away my inhibitions and shyness. I remember that we had pork blood pudding, which was not as refined as duck blood pudding, but on that day it seemed to me particularly tasty. The thin slices of belly of pork, simply boiled and eaten with fish sauce and pickled cabbage, were also delicious. As the meal progressed, I joined in the spirit of togetherness. Wine and food made everyone merry and the mayor's house resounded with talk and laughter. I found myself talking and laughing too, among those people who were all my elders but now had accepted me as one of theirs. I understood why the first communal meal was so important. To the young, it was something like their graduation to adulthood and to full citizenship in the community.

When I think of my country, my mind often turns to the village of my youth. Walking through rice fields at harvesttime among the golden paddy; swimming in the cool waters of the Hat as autumn mist covered the Lichee Field; greeting the new year behind the bamboo enclosure in the warmth and trust of the village community; it was there, in Kim Bai, that I began to feel the thousand ties which bind a person to his homeland. Since then, in every place where I have lived, the countryside has held for me a special appeal. Abroad during my career as a diplomat, I became attached to a country only after going out of the cities and spending time in a village, among open fields where I could sense the presence of the land all around me.

The village to us Vietnamese is home. We never say that we are "going" to our village. Always, we are "returning" there, to the place of our roots. Generations of our family had lived in Kim Bai in an unbroken chain since at least the fifteenth century. Our ancestral home was built on a plot of land owned by our family from times immemorial. Our forefathers lived and worked there; when they died, they were laid to rest in rice fields which, since their times, had been the property of our family. The links with the past could be seen everywhere. They were never more apparent to me than when we went from one rice field to another to sweep the tombs in the yearly ceremony. In doing so, we crisscrossed the generations. From an ancient forebear who died three hundred years ago, we would come to a much more recent grave, then in another field, it would be back in time to an earlier ancestor. Sometimes, my uncle, the deputy mayor, could not tell to which generation belonged the grave that we were sweeping, although he was sure that it was one of our ancestral graves. Or he would suddenly recall that a tomb was missed, and we had to retrace our steps. In this haphazard manner, we journeyed back and forth into family history, at each year's ceremony.

In Kim Bai, a large village with a population of about one thousand, the community was closely-knit, almost like a large family. Many villagers were in fact related, either by blood or by marriage. Even in my early teens and not living permanently there, I knew practically every villager. At any rate, I could say for certain who belonged to Kim Bai and who did not. Paths and lanes going into every corner of the village's hamlets were familiar to me. The bamboo enclosure gave me an almost physical sense of belonging and security.

All families in Kim Bai owned some land. The very poor ones would have about one-third or half an acre. An average farmer would have one or two acres. Landless people did not stay; instead they left to find work in town or venture farther away to the new lands of the south where they became plantation workers. Our village had no big landowners, over whose fields "the white egret could fully spread its wings," to use a popular way of describing large properties. Land repartition in the Red River delta was completely different from that of the Mekong delta in the south, where big landowners may hold thousands, even tens of thousands of hectares, and a man could see his fields stretch out of sight in the horizon. In our region, the land was parcelled everywhere in small plots, most of which were not larger than half of an acre. A family owning six or seven acres was already considered as fairly well-off.

Poor farmers supplemented their incomes by working as tenants. Landlords in our village did not necessarily own a lot of land. Many people let out their rice fields because they pursued occupations other than farming, such as teaching, trade, medicine, the civil service. Throughout the generations, our own ancestors were scholars and never worked in the fields. There were times when they became impoverished and led a life of privation like poor farmers, but the few pieces of land that they owned continued to be let out. Between landlords and tenants, rich and poor people, the difference in lifestyle was not great. For all, it was a life of work and frugality. Our family was the wealthiest in Kim Bai, yet my grandmother drove herself as hard as any sixty-year-old villager I knew. She did not eat meat everyday. Her diet consisted mostly of rice, fish and vegetable dipped in her thick bean sauce. Special fare was prepared for us town dwellers when we returned to Kim Bai. Grandmother made us work during our holidays—albeit not too hard—for there was no question of her letting us idle the time away. Life in Kim Bai was characterized neither by "exploitation" of poor peasants by rich landlords nor by "class struggle," as latter-day Marxists would claim in their ideological model. Injustice and exploitation could occur where a few landlords owned most of the land and enriched themselves from the toil of their tenants; such a situation would be made worse if those owners were absentee landlords, with no other relationship with their tenants than the economic one. In the densely populated Red River delta, where land was scarce, there could not have been many such rich absentee landlords. Certainly, there were none in Kim Bai and neighboring villages. Very large landholdings could be found only north of the delta, in the highlands. There, during the French conquest at the end of last century, many battles took place and villagers fled from their villages. The French seized the abandoned land and granted it to their settlers and to French companies. When the situation had settled and the villagers came back, they could not claim their land and had to work as tenant farmers for the new owners.

Rich and poor villagers of Kim Bai were part of the same community. The ties between them had been forged through generations of living together and sharing common responsibilities. There was much more to their relationship than just economic power and greed. In any case, village hierarchy rested on age and scholarship, not wealth. At public ceremonies, a rich landlord would be placed at a lower rank than a civil servant or a scholar. Should a conflict erupt between villagers, village elders would intervene to bring about a solution. Like a family, a village would seek to settle its own affairs as far as possible without recourse to an outside authority. Our traditional culture, based on the search for the Middle Way and for harmony, had always shunned extreme positions and conflicts. Emphasis had been on restraint and compromise. Moreover, many tenants were related to their own landlords, and family spirit would come into play to temper any excessive imbalance that may exist in their economic relationship.

This is not to say that the traditional land system should have been kept unchanged. In a country of farmers, justice must ultimately mean that tenants become owners of the land they work on. Such was the objective of the land reform undertaken by the nationalist government of South Vietnam in the 1960s, which granted ownership of the land to tenants. At the same time, landlords were indemnified for their loss. That successful reform was carried out peacefully, unlike what happened in North Vietnam. After the communists extended their control in 1954, villagers were divided into "poor peasants" and "rich landlords." Each village was fixed a quota of "rich landlords," whether in fact they existed or not. A campaign of hate was launched against them. Then, they were brought before "people's tribunals" to be tried for "crimes" that they had committed in the past. Villagers were forced to find or invent crimes with which to denounce their fellow villagers, their relatives, and, the cruelest of cruelties, their own parents. The 1956 campaign of so-called agrarian reform in North Vietnam accounted for the death of tens of thousands of innocent people, whose landholdings were confiscated by the state. Then, instead of giving land to the poor, communist policy forced them to give up what little land they had. Eventually, all peasants were dispossessed by the regime. All became proletarian workers in collective farms.

1945 was the last year our family celebrated a traditional Tet. A few months after Tet, a chain of events was started which changed the course of our history. In March 1945, as defeat in the war was imminent, the Japanese finally decided to get rid of the French. On the evening of the eighth—I was then going to school in Ha Dong and staying with my grandparents—we had just finished dinner when a heavy rumble was heard over the small town. There was no air raid alert, so it could not have been American planes. We went to the verandah, which looked on to the road linking Ha Dong to Hanoi, and saw Japanese army lorries rushing past. There were hundreds of them, all packed with troops in full battle gear, some trailing artillery pieces. That day, I had homework to do for a coming test at school, but I knew that something far more important than a school test was going to happen. Leaving my books aside, I went up to the first floor balcony to watch the lorries passing by in the evening darkness with hardly any lights on. A few hours later, cannon fire rolled in the direction of the capital, signalling the end of the colonial regime. It took only one night of fighting to make Vietnam "independent." A new government was installed by the Japanese, but it had not time to consolidate. Japan soon lost the war and, taking advantage of the power vacuum which ensued, the communists launched their revolution. Events happened in quick succession. French troops were sent to reoccupy Vietnam. The communists agreed to let them come into the country. A period of uneasy coexistence ensued. Then, war broke out in December 1946.

My father, who at the time owned a small bakery in Hanoi, stayed there as long as possible to keep the business going. My elder brother and I kept him company while the rest of the family went back to the haven of Kim Bai. French troops were stationed in many sectors of the city and exchanges of gunfire between them and Vietnamese guerrillas occurred nearly every night. One morning, after having finished the night's work of looking after the baking and delivery of bread, we were told to leave Hanoi immediately. Hostilities would start that very evening. Without any sleep, we packed our things on top of the rear wheel of our bicycles and set out in streets which were almost empty, most people in our area having fled already. We dared not go past the old citadel, now occupied by trigger-happy French troops and avoided the main streets where one could run into French soldiers patrolling in their jeeps, their submachine guns at the ready. By a roundabout route, we got out of the city. The town of Ha Dong had also been evacuated, although there was no French presence there. My grandparents' bungalow was deserted but for a servant who had remained behind to guard the property. In our ancestral home in Kim Bai, the whole family had congregated. All houses in the compound were occupied. Even the transversal house, which was opened on one side and was normally used as a working area, had been equipped with platforms for people to sleep. That night, we had just gone to bed when a muffled sound like that of distant thunder was heard. The thunder did not stop. It went on and on. War had begun.

The haven of Kim Bai could not shelter us for long. Early in 1947, it became exposed to enemy attacks. On their first foray into our village, the French captured my father and elder brother and took them away as prisoners. The rest of the family fled to a small village in the Lichee Field. We stayed with acquaintances in that village, but many people from Kim Bai had to camp in the lichee groves. Each lichee tree served as a prop to a small tent and each grove became a little hamlet. During the day, people crowded there. At night, when French troops had returned to their camps in Ha Dong, everyone slipped back into Kim Bai, to leave again early the next morning. However, the Lichee Field was uncomfortably close to the dike, which was only a few hundred meters away. We could hear the noise of tanks and trucks passing on the dike, sometimes even the voices of French soldiers. The latter did not venture into the Field, but after a few weeks, our family thought it safer to have the Hat River between them and us. We crossed the river and sought refuge in the village of Sao, on the other bank. Many people from Sao had previously served in our household. My own wet nurse came from there. My family stayed with the Phat's, whose head was a former corporal in my grandfather's personal staff and whom I called Mr. Corporal. His wife was nurse to both my younger sister Giang and my younger brother Dong. Our group was composed of my great-grandmother, my mother with six of her children, and my youngest brother's nurse. My grandfather stayed with the former mayor of Sao. My uncles and aunts moved to other places in Sao with their families. But my grandmother chose to remain in Kim Bai to look after our ancestral home. She fled to the Lichee Field whenever the French came, and returned home after they left. As she could not take care of great-grandmother, that responsibility fell to my mother, her eldest daughter-in-law, and therefore great-grandmother was staying with us.

We lived in the Phat's house for nearly a year. Our situation was difficult. Separated from her husband and her eldest son, my mother could only rely on the help of myself and my two teenaged sisters. Our savings in gold, silver and jewelry were taken by French soldiers when they entered Kim Bai. Our financial plight was at times desperate. We had enough rice but could hardly buy any meat and, some days, we even went without that essential ingredient in Vietnamese food, fish sauce. Our meals usually consisted of rice and boiled water spinach, the staple diet of the poor, with from time to time an additional dish of small fish cooked à la casserole and made very salty, so that less of it was consumed. "We are fortunate to have enough rice to eat," my mother would say to comfort us. "Many refugees have to mix potato or manioc with their rice." Returning from the market, she would sometimes take the three of us grown-ups aside and tell us that she could only get a little meat, therefore we should leave it to great-grandmother and the younger children. On rare occasions when there was meat for everyone, what a change a morsel of boiled pork dipped in fish sauce made to a meal! An ancestor of mine was so poor that only at a special festival like Tet could the family afford a dish of meat. While other members happily enjoyed the meat at the beginning of the meal, he kept his portion until the end. "Let me give you this advice," he told them. "By having meat with your last bowl of rice, you would get the impression of eating the whole meal with meat." I did not follow my ancestor's advice, but certainly wartime scarcity helped me understand his message a little better. The Phat's thatched house had only two rooms. We had use of the larger one. Our hosts moved into a smaller room on the side. We were nine and our stay was long, but their welcome remained the same as on the day of our arrival. They helped us as much as they could. Faithfulness and constancy were virtues most valued in our culture. Although circumstances had changed—they were members of our household before, now we were refugees relying on their hospitality—their attitude towards us remained true to the precept "One and the same, now as before." In Sao and in neighboring villages, people opened their arms to refugees like us. Very quickly we were made to feel safe and at home.

From Sao, I often had to cross the Hat to go back to Kim Bai. That year in the rainy season, the Hat turned into a huge and threatening river. Because of the hostilities, the dam upstream was not properly manned. Boats were not quite safe during the day as they could be spotted and machine-gunned by French planes. People had to wait until evening to cross, except for the villagers of Sao, who just swam over, using their special style of swimming known as "standing up." Taking off their clothes on the river bank, they folded them neatly in a pile and put them on their heads. They went into the water with one hand on the pile keeping it steady and swam with the other arm, kicking with both legs, body being kept vertical and head above water. On reaching the other side, they put their dry clothes back on and went about their business. It was a fast and most convenient way of crossing the river. I tried to learn it but could never quite keep my body vertical. So I had to use other less specialized style of swimming. The problem, however, was the clothes. It meant that I could cross the river only with someone from the village who could hold mine as well as his. Besides, the river was wide and the current strong. It was safer to have company. My own forte was the backstroke and I could swim for hours on my back. But in a flood-swollen river, that was by no means the best way to swim. For one thing, I could not see what was coming towards me. The river was full of logs, branches and debris of every kind. I had to rely entirely on the directions of my companions who, with their heads above water could see what was coming towards us. Once, however, we got caught in a big clump of marsh weed and were in serious trouble as the weed slowed down our movement and the clump carried us farther and farther along downstream.

We finally managed to reach the other bank, exhausted and miles away from our intended crossing spot.

During the time in Sao, my family was engaged in various enterprises to provide us with some income. My mother made cakes for our hostess, Mrs. Phat, to sell at market. We raised silkworms to produce cloth for the family. It was an absorbing occupation; we could really see the worms growing before our eyes and in no time they became cocoons of silken threads. We put the cocoons in boiling water to unwind the threads, which took on a golden color. The whole courtyard was filled with their pungent smell. After the silk had been removed, the chrysalis was not thrown away; when grilled, it became a tasty and nutritious tidbit. Food was scarce during the war and I well remember the thrill of having grilled silkworm chrysalises in my pocket, still warm from the fire. But silkworms were extremely delicate creatures and so many things could go wrong with them. The weather might be too hot or too cold; they might be exposed to rain or draughts. Accidents were all too easy and one's hard work might be destroyed in an instant. Of all the problems, the most pressing was to provide enough mulberry leaves for the worms when they reached the final stage of growth before spinning their silk. It was then that they ate noisily and gluttonously and even a room with only a few baskets of worms would sound like a roof under heavy rain. I was responsible for the supply of leaves, but despite planning, something unexpected always happened. If they did not get enough food, the worms would die or at best be unable to produce much silk. The pressure and urgency were great. I had to rush from village to village and, at times, even venture fairly near the front line to buy the leaves.

Our main—and most successful—enterprise was making conical hats. My sisters Trang, Giang and I went to the canton Chuong to learn how to make the hats with Teacher Hien's wife. Teacher Hien was for several years our house tutor in Hanoi, hence his title of teacher. At the time he was studying for his baccalaureate or final secondary school examination. After many sessions without success, he married and returned to his village, Chuong. Coming from a well-off family, he led a comfortable life even during the war. Chuong was, at that time, still some distance from the front line. Teacher Hien always offered us good hospitality and good meals, which meant a lot in wartime. He was also glad to have someone whom he could trust, to talk to about the war and the way things were going in the country. People like him were considered as intellectuals by the communists and had to be careful of what they said and to whom they said it. I was, however, his former pupil and as close as a family member. He and I used to stay up talking late into the night. Soon, my sisters and I became quite proficient at making conical hats. I made the bamboo frame on which my sisters then sewed the latania leaves. We manufactured hats of a nicely balanced shape and with a smooth and shiny surface, for my sisters only used good latania leaves and were careful not to break them when they sewed. We produced between ten and twenty hats each day. They sold quite well. The money earned helped to buy meat and other luxuries such as sugar, soap and medicine. My grandfather had not shown much interest in our hat-making activity. But one day, he came to visit with great-grand-mother and sat down for a while to watch us work. He did not leave until he had seen some latania leaves and a few sticks of bamboo transformed into a pretty hat, ready to be worn. Not a man prolific with compliments, he had high praise for our workmanship and described our products as "art-istic."

Often, I travelled to remote areas to buy latania leaves and to sell hats. Hostilities had pushed the markets deeper into the hinterland of the west and some were meeting, under tree cover, at the very foot of the hills. I had always wanted to go to those hills. Standing on the dike of Kim Bai and watching the western mountains turn purple against the glow of the setting sun, I had dreamed that someday I would find myself in the highlands retracing the steps that, millenniums ago, our Viet ancestors had taken to go down and settle in the delta. But I never was able to go that far, only to the foothills of the mountains. The region I went to was some distance away from the front line and ground action by the French was not a threat. However, bombings and strafings were daily occurrences. Anything that sounded like a plane would send people running for cover. What was feared most were sudden attacks by paratroopers dropping down from the sky and giving one no time to flee. Yet, in such a tense situation, villages we went through offered friendliness, reassurance and trust. As soon as they knew that our small group came from Kim Bai and Sao, a neighboring region, villagers were all willing to offer hospitality and lend a helping hand. My grandfather was, of course, a well-known public figure, but I found that many people also knew of my father, who had worked in the central ad-ministration in Hanoi and not in the provinces.

We were caught by the monsoon one day as I went on one of my mar-ket trips. Our hats and cloaks made of latania leaves were dripping wet be-fore we found shelter at a tea stall. Some people from a nearby village were sheltering there too. On learning that I came from the Nguyen family of Kim Bai, they invited us to stay the night at their place, as rain continued to pour down and soon it would be dark. There was no way we could have gone on to our destination, so we did not wait too long before accepting their kind offer. Their thatched cottage was small with little furniture ex-cept for the ancestors' altar and a wooden platform. We had just settled down when other villagers appeared. Word had gotten around that we were in the village. A well-dressed man of about forty, said that he had met with my father and asked us to be his guests. Not being able to say yes or no, we let the villagers decide for us on what to do. Eventually everyone, including our first hosts, left for the man's house. By then it was dark. Rain kept falling. We came to a nice and well-lit place, a cottage with a thatched roof over wooden walls and a brick floor. Several wooden platforms could be seen in the room. In front of the ancestors' altar stood a long narrow table flanked by two wooden sofas, where we sat. The corporal, who led our party, and I were treated as honored guests. It appeared that our host had some matter which came up before the Hanoi City Council many years ago and my father, a public servant at the Council, had dealt with it fairly. Even after such a long time, our host was glad that I happened to be in his village, and he could, in some measure, repay the kindness. As we talked, the sound of chopping knives came from the kitchen and the sweet smell of cooking rice floated towards us. Soon, food was served. On the tray were dishes of boiled chicken meat and giblets, sautéed vegetables, clear chicken soup, pickled cabbage, simple country fare quickly prepared for unheralded guests. In the warm atmosphere of fellowship, we ate heartily, without waiting to be pressed by our hosts as we would normally do. I had hardly had any chicken since our evacuation to Sao. The fish sauce, too, was deliciously tasty compared to the rather cheap sauce that my mother bought for our daily meals. That night, I slept on a platform next to the altar, feeling happy and at ease, just like at home after a good meal. Rain had driven the mosquitoes away and sleep came quickly. Next morning, we got up early, but our hosts had been up earlier and we were treated to another meal before resuming our trip. Those years of war spent in the countryside have left deep marks in my memory: the constant danger, the terrorized shouts of villagers calling on family and neighbors to flee, the humiliation of being defenseless. But I also recall the intense solidarity of people in the country, and the many acts of kindness which filled my heart with gratitude.

However, my market trips became suspect to the communist authorities. Friendly villagers told us that our group was being followed by the secret police. My mother wanted me to stop, but I managed to continue for a few more times, arguing that if the communists wanted to arrest me, they could always do so, whether I went or stayed at home. Corporal Phat took the precaution of never leaving me alone, for people had disappeared that way, after they were arrested by the police in the absence of witnesses. For more than twenty years, the corporal was in my grandfather's service. He only returned to live in Sao when grandfather retired. He was not a soldier—the title of corporal was an honorary rank he received—but worked as a civilian in grandfather's personal staff. He had known me since I was born and liked to tell of the days when he looked after my meals and took me to school. "In spite of the fact that you had an egg every morning, you were so thin," he reminisced, adding "but you were a very bright boy, I could see that!" He himself was thin and very tall, one of the tallest Vietnamese I had known. I never felt safer crossing the swelling Hat River than in his comapny, as he was expert in swimming "standing up" style, and was so relaxed and tall that one had the impression he was not actually swimming, but walking on the river bed. Corporal Phat knew well the region leading to the western highlands. He had acquaintances in many villages and we were never short of places to stay. I very much enjoyed the trips made in his company. They gave me opportunities to meet with people and discover more of our countryside, but more and more we could feel the unwelcome presence of the secret police on our tail. Then, one day one of my uncles disappeared. All of us ran frantically from one village to another to find out his whereabouts, but no one could tell us what had happened. After a few weeks, he walked home. The reason given for his kidnap and arbitrary detention was that the police had just wanted to talk to him. After that incident, there was no question of another market trip for me.

The village life which I knew no longer exists today. Our traditional system had been called a "village democracy." Under communist rule, the autonomy that villages enjoyed vis-à-vis the central government and their democratic setup have been abolished. The traditional ceremonies and festivals have been abandoned. The communists sought to break up village solidarity by sowing division and hatred among villagers. They were against the ancient ties and traditions which had given each village its distinctive character. Their aim was to destroy village spirit. The village community and the family had been the two pillars of our society. Throughout the history of our nation, these two institutions had cushioned the effects of frequent political upheavals and protected the common rights of our people against excessive encroachments by the government. Now, the communists were out to destroy family and village spirits, so that nothing would stand between the individual citizen and the absolute power of the party apparatus. Children are taught to spy on their parents. Villagers are made to hate one another. But how can a political regime, no matter how dictatorial and ruthless it is, prevail over the Vietnamese family spirit? As for the Vietnamese village, it had existed as a community since the earliest times. Through the centuries, it had developed in response to the needs and aspirations of our people. The communists wanted to impose on it a model of class struggle taken from a foreign ideology. In the long run, they cannot succeed, and I feel sure that the age-old village spirit will one day rise again.

II / The Source in the Mountains

8. The Family Chronicle

The origins of our family went back to the fifteenth century. Our earliest known ancestor lived in Kim Bai, five hundred years ago. From him down to the present time, we have been able to establish a continuous line of sixteen generations.

The family chronicle kept in our Melbourne home came from my grandfather. It was written in the scholarly, or Chinese script. Up to the beginning of this century, the Vietnamese language had two components: the colloquial, used in everyday life and the scholarly, used in government business and as a vehicle for learning. The colloquial language was written with characters adapted from the Chinese. After the scholarly language was abolished in the 1910s, the colloquial one—which, in the meantime, had been romanized—became the "national language." My grandfather graduated and started his career under the old system. Like other scholars of his generation, he continued to use Chinese script in his writings, in preference to the newer script. Grandfather did not specify when the chronicle was written. I believe it was in the early 1910s, after he had succeeded in tracing an earlier ancestor of the Nguyen, thereby extending the knowledge of our lineage up to the fifteenth century. The text mentioned my father's birth in 1907, but gave no indication about his next brother, who was born in 1913. Thus, it should have been written between those two dates or, at any rate, not very long after 1913. Two texts of the chronicle existed, a draft in grandfather's own calligraphy and the official chronicle of our family in the calligraphy of his friend Duong Ba Trac.

In the old tradition, a descendant should not write the chronicle of his own family, but should ask a close friend to do it. The original idea could have been to gain more objectivity, although what a friend may feel freer to do is to praise the family's merits and achievements; it is hard to see that he would criticize or write bad things about it. In any case, what often happened was that a descendant actually wrote the chronicle and the friend only copied it. To me, this tradition underlined the value of friendship in our culture. Close friends were like brothers; indeed, the culmination of friendship was, as in the case of the three warrior-heroes in the *Story of the Three Kingdoms*, to take the oath of brotherhood. What better way to link your best friend to your family than by asking him to write its chronicle?

阮
族
譜
記

金方青河
牌中威東
社總府省

The cover of the chronicle. The four large characters stand for "Chronicle of the Nguyen family." The smaller characters stand for "Province of Ha Dong, Prefecture of Thanh Oai, Canton of Phuong Trung, Village of Kim Bai."

It was also a nice way to keep a friend's calligraphy, for scholars considered calligraphy not only as an expression of a man's personality but also, when it was well executed, a work of art. Moreover, I believe that the tradition may help save some family histories from being lost. Insecurity has often marked our people's lives. In troubled times, a family may lose all its documents and find itself cut off from its roots; that had happened several times in the history of our own family. It could, therefore, be a useful insurance to have someone else with the knowledge of one's family lineage. Regrettably, this endearing tradition of ours has vanished. With the onset of the communist revolution in 1945 and several decades of war which followed, how many Vietnamese have had the opportunity to sit down and write their family history, let alone ask a friend to write it?

Duong Ba Trac, the close friend whom my grandfather asked to write our chronicle, was a leading nationalist figure. A graduate of the Licence Examination, he was known to us as Licentiate Duong, Duong being his family name. Vietnamese are normally called by their personal name but, as a mark of respect, grandfather's friends were referred to in our family by their surname. Licentiate Duong and grandfather attended the same school and graduated in the same year. He engaged in political activities against the French regime and was imprisoned in 1907. After his release, he declined to enter the mandarinate and adopted an attitude of noncooperation with the protectorate. Grandfather, for his part, became a mandarin. In spite of their divergent political attitudes, they remained close, as did their families.

Several younger brothers of Licentiate Duong studied under grandfather. One of them was our prefect-poet of Tet, who married grandfather's niece. Licentiate Duong was a well-known writer, many of whose poems became so popular that they were mistaken as folk poems. Children learned them at school. His calligraphy was quite different from grandfather's. Its round and feminine-looking characters showed the sentimental disposition of a poet, whereas grandfather's were quite lean and angular. I was too young to remember Licentiate Duong. During the Second World War, he and some nationalist leaders fled the country for Singapore, then under Japanese occupation. There, they organized opposition against the French domination and were groomed by the Japanese to take over the leadership of the country when the time would come for them to bring down the French regime. But Licentiate Duong contracted a malady and died in exile.

After retiring in 1940, my grandfather translated the scholarly text of our family chronicle into the popular language, using the romanized script. In the translation, he added a great deal of information concerning his father's generation. However, he did not bother to bring the scholarly text up to date for by that time, that script had become a relic which only a few of the young generation could read. Also, by then, the friend who "wrote" the original text had left the country and was destined not to return.

Both scholarly texts were kept in our ancestral home. When French troops began making incursions into our region early in 1947, grandfather gave me the responsibility of keeping them. Kim Bai had become unsafe and our family was preparing to move to a village in the Lichee Field. The last months had been traumatic for him. First, news came that his house in Ha Dong was burned to the ground as the communists implemented their scorched earth policy and set fire to the town. Then, his only surviving brother died. Soon after, my father and brother were captured and taken away by French troops. Kim Bai was attacked by the French who pillaged our ancestral home. Grandfather's own health deteriorated and now, he was going to have to leave his village.

I was called to his study and found him sitting at the same place where he used to teach me the Chinese script, with the two copies of the chronicle on the desk in front of him. He looked tired and worried.

"I want you to take these books and keep them safe," he said.

Instead of giving me the books, he opened a copy and started reading. I stood next to him and waited. After a while, he asked me: "Have you read the family chronicle?"

I was rather surprised by the question and replied quickly: "Yes, I have."

"No, I mean this text," he said, pointing at the copy he was reading which was written in the old scholarly language. "Can you read it?"

"Yes, I can," I answered, "although there are a few words that I do not understand."

He went back to reading, then told me: "We are lucky that we still have

GIA PHẢ HỌ NGUYỄN 阮

Cây có nghìn cành muôn lá, bởi có rễ sâu; nước có nghìn dòng muôn phái, bởi có nguồn dài; người có nghìn con muôn cháu, bởi có đức của Tổ-Tiên để lại. Vậy sinh ở nghìn năm về sau mà muốn biết được tự nghìn năm về trước, tất phải xét lại dòng rồi, thế hệ, thì mới biết được đực của tổ tôn để lại đã lâu đời mà con cháu ngày một thêm đông vậy.

x

Họ NGUYỄN ta cụ Tổ đời thứ nhất đỗ tiến sĩ năm Hồng-Thuận thứ ba đời nhà Lê (1512) làm quan đến chức thượng Thư, phong tước Ba, tên huý là NGUYỄN TUỆ 阮鐩 (Tổ tỉ không còn biết).

Cụ Tổ đời thứ hai đỗ Tiến-Sĩ năm Đại-Chính thứ sáu đời nhà Mạc (1536) làm quan đến chức Thanh Hình Hiến Sát-Sứ ở xứ Thái-Nguyên, tên huý là BÁ UYÊN, tên thụy là Ôn Tĩnh Tiên sinh (溫靜先生). Tổ tỉ thứ người họ Phùng tên hiệu là TỪ ƯỚC (慈約).

Từ đường và phả ký họ ta vào khoảng hai trăm năm nay, bị cướp đốt phá mất cả. Về sau chỉ nghe mà ghi chép lại, không thể biết rõ được.

Bản phả ký cũ chỉ thấy biên Cụ Tiến-sĩ Thanh-hình-Hiến Sát Sứ, huý BÁ UYÊN (伯淵) là cụ Tổ thứ Nhất, nhưng xét trong đăng khoa lục (sách ghi tên các cụ đỗ

The chronicle in the new "national script" using the romanized script. This was typed circa 1942. My grandfather added the scholarly characters to the names. The photo shows the first page of the chronicle, starting with these lines: "A tree has countless branches and a dense canopy of leaves, because its roots grow deep into the soil. . . ."

these books. All the documents in Ha Dong have been destroyed. You should take them with you whenever we have to flee. Do not leave them behind. We must not lose them."

He appeared now in a more expansive mood and went on: "Several times in the history of our family, chronicles have been destroyed and our ancestors have had to reconstruct them. Your great-grandfather's generation and mine spent a great deal of effort searching for our roots. When I was young, our first ancestor, the Count, was unknown to us. We could only trace our lineage back to Ancestor Nguyen Uyen who...."

I cannot remember another occasion when grandfather had talked to me about the chronicle, but he had just started when some guests came to see him. He stopped talking, gave me the books and did not return to that subject.

At that time everyone of us had, within easy reach, a bag containing valuables and other belongings, ready to be grabbed when the alert was given and we had to flee. The books were constantly kept in my bag. They went with me to our refuge in the Lichee Field, then farther away to the village of Sao. After my grandfather died, the front line moved closer to Kim Bai. My family decided to leave the communist zone and join my father in Hanoi. I took grandfather's copy with me while the official chronicle was left in the safekeeping of grandfather's youngest son.

My uncle and I were of the same age and as close as two brothers. He was, in fact, a few months younger than me. Physically, we could not have been more different. He was tall and strong; when fourteen he already measured five foot nine. As a child, I was very thin and often sick. He left me way behind in martial arts and sporting activities. At school, however, I did quite well, while he often had difficulties passing from one grade to the next. After a few years, we were separated and went to different grades. In spite of all that, we got on very well together. Family members usually call one another by their rank, but being playmates, we could not call each other "uncle" and "nephew" all the time; that sounded so distant and formal. So we borrowed a more informal mode of address from the French: *toi* and *moi*. My grandparents and parents all implicitly accepted it, but my great-uncle did not. He often chided us with his acid tongue. "What has the *toi* and *moi* got to do with the Vietnamese language?" he asked. "That combination is fit for a pig's language."

We spent together the last day of my stay in Kim Bai. As we went through grandfather's bookcases, my heart suddenly swelled with ominous forebodings. All those books that I may never see again! Like someone trying to save a few possessions from a house on fire, I feverishly took out all those which I could not bear to lose: some books in grandfather's handwriting; the collection of Tang poems with which he had introduced me to the magic of Chinese poetry; *The Three Kingdoms*, my very first Chinese novel; the Confucian Four Books which grandfather taught me in those hot summer mornings while I slowly pulled the panka fan to and fro. Alas! we were going on a hazardous trip and I had other things to carry than books. My grandmother and mother refused to let me take the additional load. They told me that in wartime, the most precious thing was life: "Even if you can save those books now, one day they will disappear, like all material possessions we have. But under the protection of the Lord in Heaven, Lord Buddha and our own ancestors, our family will continue. It is our first duty to see that it will do so and develop. As long as life remains, everything else will." Thus, the books were left behind. Afterwards, I sometimes told my mother that I still regretted not having taken those books, at least two of them. One was produced on the occasion of grandfather's retirement. In it, he wrote poems in scholarly language and friends and colleagues wrote their poems addressed to him. My grandfather was not really a poet. However, in the manner of all scholars in those days, he did have a number of poems and I would have loved to be able to keep some. The other was the record of all texts on the decorative boards received by our family. These could have given us some insights into grandfather's career and our family's history. My mother's reaction was serene. "As Buddhists, we should eliminate the term 'regret' from our vocabulary," she said. "What happened has happened. Let us not dwell in the past."

My family left Kim Bai at the end of a winter night. Great-uncle Mayor came to take us to the place where we were to meet with the guide. We took leave of our great-grandmother who was lying in bed in great pain, having broken her leg a few days before. My mother opened the mosquito net and knelt down to talk to her. "Grandmother," she said softly, "we beg your permission to leave."

No reply came. She repeated her words and this time, great-grandmother uttered a groan. Was she acknowledging our farewell or only groaning because of the pain? I could not say. "Please, rest yourself until you are well again," my mother continued. "We will send medicine home as soon as we can." We took leave of grandmother, who remained very calm. As my mother cried and could not decide to go, she led us out of the altar house, saying: "Don't be late and make the guide wait!"

She patted us on our backs. To me, she said: "You will be able to go to school in Hanoi. Try to do well."

She saw us off at the gate of our ancestral home and quickly closed the heavy iron gate wings back, so as not to draw anyone's attention in the still sleeping village. We made our way in the dark, trying to make as little noise as possible. Fortunately, all dogs in the village had been killed, on order of the authorities, as their barking would reveal the presence of guerrillas to the enemy, and the silence of the night was not disturbed. The Si Gate was closed but our party slipped out, one by one, through a hole made in the bamboo enclosure. We crossed the deserted highway and reached the open fields. All had gone well so far. Then, there came a hitch. The guide was not at the rendezvous. The place was a small brick hut serving as shelter to farmers working out in the open. Instead of the whole group waiting for him, which would make us look too conspicuous, Great-uncle Mayor decided to go ahead with the rest of the family while I stayed back. "He will be here," he said confidently. "I know him well, he is only late."

It was still dark, although dawn was soon going to break. Squatting low on the floor of the empty hut, I saw in the distance a communist patrol heading towards me, their silhouettes clearly visible against the sky. My first reaction was to hide, but the fields around the hut were entirely bare, with not a single tree. I thought that my best bet was to stay just where I was and act normal. The patrol was composed of five or six men, well-armed. I was relieved that they belonged to the regular army, not to the local militia, and no one had recognized me. They were, however, very suspicious of why I happened to be there, so early and so near the front line. I told them that I was going to my maternal village with my father. I had started ahead and was waiting for him. They deliberated and decided that I would have to come along with them. I tried to gain time until I saw our guide approaching. In a loud voice, I called out to him: "What took you so long, father? The maternal village is far away. We are late!" He was an eastern medicine man, fortyish, wearing a black tunic and carrying only an umbrella. He took the cue immediately and shouted back: "A neighbour was ill. I had to stay and give him some medicine." Thus, posing as father and son, we succeeded in talking our way out. Hurrying our steps, we soon joined the family group. Our guide was in high spirits, having succeeded in "rescuing" me from the communist soldiers. Great-uncle Mayor left us in the care of the guide and returned to Kim Bai. A few months later, we learned that while working in the fields, he was caught up in a crossfire and killed by a French bullet.

Now reunited, our group made way towards Ha Dong. My youngest brother Dao, who was three, sat in a basket suspended at the end of a pole carried by his nurse over her shoulder. Except for my sister Trinh who was only seven and the guide who had just an umbrella, we were all carrying our belongings in large bags. My eleven-year-old brother Dong had charge of all our wooden clogs which were strung together and quite bulky. For the trip, an uncle gave me a dark flannel "western" suit bought before the communist revolution and still almost brand new. With that suit, which was a bit too long and large for me, I went barefoot, but I had on my head a felt hat made in Paris, also dating from pre-independence days. I was lucky that the communists did not notice my western suit—it was still quite dark when they apprehended me—for they could have wondered how the son of an eastern medicine man in the country could own such a suit. As we approached the front line, gunfire opened up. The French were launching an attack! People were fleeing in our direction, but our guide decided to press on. He said that we should try to reach the Catholic village—the one with the statue of Saint George and the dragon. Once there, we would be safe, for the French would not attack it. Following their usual tactics, communists troops withdrew before the French and luckily for us, the attack actually followed another direction. So the way was clear towards Ha Dong, which we reached late in the afternoon. The next day, we were in Hanoi. The chronicle was handed over to my father. Meanwhile, one of my uncles had also returned to Hanoi and he had with him the version in Roman script. Thus both versions were now safely in my father's keeping.

I went to France for my university studies and was there in 1954 when Vietnam was divided. I did not return to Hanoi. My father moved our family to Saigon. Six years earlier, we had left our village each with a bag. Now the family had to be on the move again, leaving the north for the south of the country, each person carrying a suitcase. All other things gathered by us during those six years were left behind, including the photographs to help us keep the memories of that period of our lives. Once again, we had to start anew. The chronicle, of course, went with the family to Saigon.

In 1963, on being transferred from London to our diplomatic mission in New Delhi, I spent some time in Saigon. War had flared up again, as communist North Vietnam launched its aggression against South Vietnam. My father gave me the original draft to keep, as it would be safer with me abroad. Also, I was the only member of the family able to read the old script. With it, I took a copy of the modern version which my father had brought up to date with information relating to my grandfather's generation. Since then, these documents have been with me through my postings in India, France, Japan and following the great calamity of 1975, to our haven in Australia. As I write this story of the Nguyen of Kim Bai, they are the only written documents handed down from earlier generations.

I do not know what happened to the text kept by my uncle. He went into the communist army in 1949. Did he succeed in preserving the chronicle during all those war years lasting until 1954? Since 1948, he and I have not communicated. We had been so close until then. Events beyond our control caused our lives to diverge. He stayed in the communist army, while my life and work were tied to the free regime of South Vietnam.

In a passage of the chronicle, my grandfather wrote: "We could find in the old chronicle mention only of our second ancestor...." Thus, an older chronicle existed, which he had consulted. I had heard family elders mention that chronicle, but never saw it. It probably dated from the time of our eleventh ancestor, my great-grandfather. In 1862, members of our extended family met to discuss the resumption of our ancestral cult and to reconstruct the chronicles of different branches. These measures were taken following grave events which I shall describe later. The old chronicle would have been the product of that collective effort. I believe that most probably it was kept in our Ancestral Shrine.

9. The Ancestral Shrine

Each extended family in Vietnam traditionally had a place to worship its common ancestors called the Ancestral Shrine. The Nguyen Ancestral Shrine in Kim Bai was built on a block close to our ancestral home. All known ancestors of our family were worshipped there, but on the altar was placed a single tablet bearing this inscription in scholarly script: "Our Original Nguyen Ancestor." This ancestor, whose time lay beyond the reaches of our memory, stood at the center of our cult. At ceremonies, it was his spirit whom we invoked in the first place, spirits of known ancestors were invited to join in and to receive the offerings as secondary participants.

A keeper was in charge of the Shrine. He organized worshipping services at seasonal festivals. "Once a year," to quote our chronicle, "in the beginning of the second lunar month, all family members assembled at the Shrine to worship our common ancestors and to express attachment to our roots." Proceedings on that occasion were rather similar to those at anniversaries celebrated within our home. Early in the morning, a pig was sacrificed. Food offerings were prepared as members from different branches started arriving, bringing with them incense, voting papers and flowers. The worshipping ceremony started with the keeper, who was the head of our eldest branch, first invoking in prayer the spirit of our original ancestor, then calling out the names and titles of all departed ancestors since the earliest generations. It was a long and arduous exercise because the old man was reading from a text written in scholarly script and many of our ancestors' names, taken from ancient Confucian books, were extremely difficult to read. Moreover, their titles were long and many. I remember standing among family members, waiting for him to finish so that we could go in and perform the rite of kneeling and bowing in front of the altar. We did so by group of two or three people of the same rank. I came from the youngest generation of our branch, which was itself the youngest branch in the extended family, so my turn was very low down the line. Naturally, a meal followed the religious ceremony, and the atmosphere turned into one of fellowship and enjoyment. That annual function of the Nguyen of Kim Bai came after the Tet, which was celebrated within each family unit, and preceded the village Spring Festival. Only after these festivities over would our people finally set their minds back to work and another laborious year would begin.

The Shrine was built in 1936, but the sacred tablet on the altar dated from almost two hundred years ago. It was made to specific requirements laid down by an age-old tradition for all ancestral shrine tablets. A flat and rectangular piece of wood, it was of a larger size than the tablets on the altar in our home. On each of these smaller tablets was written the name of an ancestor but, as has been noted, the large tablet in the Shrine had no individual name, only the family name. The small tablets were meant to last for four generations as within each branch, our ancestors' cult was celebrated only up to the great-great-grandfather. When a man died and his son took over the cult from him, the tablets of ancestors of five generations before were taken off the altar and buried. From then on, these forebears would only be worshipped at the Ancestral Shrine, alongside those of other branches of the extended family. The sacred tablet in the Shrine, however, was meant to stay there forever. It was not to be replaced, or buried, at any time. It should for always stand there as the symbol of the permanence of the family. According to a popular belief, its wood was indestructible and "would not rot for one hundred generations," because it was taken from a tree called *tao* which could live for one thousand years. Was that popular belief correct? No one could say, for the solidity of the *tao* wood had never been fully tested in our country. No sacred tablet had lasted for very long, not because rot had set in it, but because no ancestral shrine had been able to survive for very long. As a result of natural calamities, insecurity, war, political upheavals or the decline of families, most ancestral shrines disappeared after no longer than a century or two and when they did, the tablets they housed disappeared too.

In the five hundred years of our family's history, there had been three ancestral shrines. The first one probably dated from the early sixteenth century. At that time, our branch of the family had two brothers, both men of wealth and power. These two forefathers would, understandably, have wanted a fitting place for the cult of the Original Nguyen Ancestor and it was believed that the old Shrine was built by them. It was a spacious building, looking like a temple—as our family tradition recalled—and well-furnished with tables and platforms in precious wood, ornate commemorative boards and cult objects in brass. The heir to our eldest branch usually was named Keeper of the Shrine. Expenses related to the Shrine were met by donations and bequests from family members. Records showed that until the eighteenth century, our Shrine received from the various branches a great deal of land, called cult land, which was cultivated by its keeper. The Shrine also served as a repository for our family's history. The Nguyen Register—our equivalent of the western family tree—was kept there, as were the chronicles of succeeding generations. The register was updated at regular intervals, while it was the duty of each generation to write a new chapter to the chronicles, not about itself, but about the generation that preceded it.

At the end of the sixteenth century, our third ancestor found himself on the wrong side of a dynastic war. When the Mac were defeated by the Le, he and his family had to flee to escape persecution, leaving behind all properties in Kim Bai. What happened to the Ancestral Shrine during their absence, which lasted for over a decade, was not clear. It may have been looked after by other branches of the Nguyen, whose members were not high mandarins under the Mac and therefore did not have to flee their village. At any rate, the Shrine was neither destroyed by the new authorities, nor seized by other people, as would often happen to properties belonging to losers in a war. It survived. When our branch returned to Kim Bai, the Shrine again was the recipient of donations of land. The chronicle mentioned that successive generations continued to give land all through the seventeenth century.

In the following century, all branches in our family suffered a decline in their fortunes and the Shrine became less well-endowed. However, it was still an imposing place, which explained why it was among the first places that bandits, who overran Kim Bai in the middle of the eighteenth century, directed their attention to. The Shrine was sacked. Cult objects, ceremonial swords and flags, gongs and drums, heavy platforms, tables and commemorative boards, all were taken away. Then, the bandits set fire to the building, which burned down completely. The family's archives, kept in the Shrine, were destroyed.

Security only returned to our region several decades later. Our extended family, by then impoverished, managed to build a second Ancestral Shrine on a very modest scale. It was just a small cottage with bamboo walls and a thatched roof. Most of the cult land had disappeared. The keeper continued to celebrate the cult at the Shrine, but with dwindling donations, ceremonies became fewer and fewer. Sometime after the turn of the nineteenth century, the annual function attended by all family members ceased to be held. A low point had been reached in the history of the Nguyen family, whose branches seemed to have lost touch with one another.

Then, the pendulum swung again. The tenth ancestor of our branch, who lived in the first half of the nineteenth century, was a successful businessman. He took great interest in the family's history. The Shrine which, after a few decades, was already in need of repair, was a matter of concern for him. He never saw the first Shrine, but had heard it described by his grandmother, "looking like a temple" and rich in furniture and cult objects. "I want to build a fitting shrine," he often said, "to those forefathers who had built such a grand memorial to our ancestry as the old Shrine." His intention was to pull down the existing Shrine, build another place of worship and equip it with new furniture and decorations. Proceeding by stages—like the good businessman he was—he started by having commemorative boards made, which would decorate the future Shrine. These included a large horizontal board to be suspended above the Shrine entrance, bearing in Chinese characters the words "Ancestral Shrine of the Nguyen Family," two other horizontal boards each bearing a poem and a pair of vertical boards bearing parallel sentences, to be hung inside the Shrine. Our ancestor was a scholar turned businessman. He himself wrote the poems and parallel sentences to honor the memory of his forebears. Well-known calligraphers were invited in to write the large characters on the boards; then, wood-carvers were hired to work on them and painters came to put on the gold leaves and red lacquer. The boards were installed in the existing Shrine, while waiting for the new place to be built. A few years later, our ancestor bought expensive timber from the northern highlands and had it sent down the Hat River to Kim Bai. He planned to start work on a new shrine in 1836, after having completed a business trip to the south of the country. He died on that trip. With his death, our family found itself in difficult times again and there was no more question of building a shrine.

The problem of the Shrine did not come up again until 1862, when a special meeting of the extended family took place there. The meeting was convened following the recovery of the Cu Hau's papers, an event of special importance in our family's history. Family members decided to restore the annual ceremony of worship, which had been abandoned for over fifty years. They discussed the Shrine and agreed on the need to have a new and larger place of worship. However, financial resources were not available and the assembly could only conclude that: "As for following on our forefather's footsteps and extending the Ancestral Shrine, that will have to be left to the coming generations."

By the twentieth century, the Shrine had fallen into dilapidation. In 1936, my grandfather came into possession of a piece of land in the Middle Hamlet, just behind the Communal Hall. This well-situated rectangular plot measured 372 square meters. After consulting the heads of all branches, he built a third Shrine, then donated both land and building to the extended family. In the village's Land Register, these were recorded as "the common property of the Nguyen family."

The new Shrine was a brick construction, the size of an average cottage. It had three "rooms" without any partition walls. The altar to our Original Ancestor stood in the middle. On both sides were wooden platforms, tables and chairs for use of family members during ceremonies, and cabinets to hold the family's records. Around the block ran a perforated brick wall with decorations in plaster of flowers and of the Chinese character *tho,* meaning longevity. The building opened into an attractive garden planted with small trees and shrubs of the kinds usually seen near temples and pagodas. The shrubs were chosen for their big and variegated leaves of red, blue, green and yellow hues. The trees of different sizes from the taller orange trees to the shorter mandarin and cumquat trees exhibited their round and golden fruits. The jasmine and *ngau* blossomed in spring and their flowers added perfume to the tea served as an offering on the altar. There were dahlias and camelias. A narrow pebble path wound its way from the gate to the Shrine, bordered by a dark green grass with very fine and long leaves called *toc tien,* or fairy's hair. On the front verandah, blue porcelain pots were lined, holding trees such as pine reduced in size— although not as small as the Japanese bonsai—and bent into shapes of dragon and phoenix. Right next to the gate stood a miniature bamboo grove no more than two meters tall. The black-stemmed bamboo with yellow stripes belonged to a rare species highly prized by our people. My grandfather especially wanted it to adorn the Shrine of his ancestors, for in our culture, bamboo was a symbol of the gentleman-scholar, whose "character was as straight as a bamboo stem" and for whom wealth and power meant little, for his heart, "hollow like the bamboo trunk," was devoid of wordly ambitions. The garden retained a rich and dense vegetation all year round. The trees, shrubs and flowers of different shapes, sizes and colors made it look much larger than it was. During the summer holidays, I often went to the Shrine to enjoy its garden, for our ancestral home was all courtyard and apart from some big trees, had no garden. More particularly, I was looking for bird nests. Small black sparrows with a lively chirp liked to build their nests in orange trees and always a few nests could be found there, quite low and within easy reach.

The seat of our cult was transferred to the new site. My grandfather bought new cult objects, but the altar came from the old Shrine and naturally, the sacred tablet installed in the latter part of the eighteenth century was preserved. Having pride of place in the new Shrine were the commemorative boards presented by our tenth ancestor in the 1830s. A century later, his wish of having a more fitting place of worship was finally fulfilled by his grandson. The boards were the oldest heirlooms kept by our family. They dated long before those which decorated our ancestral home. At the end of the 1940s when I last saw them, they were over a hundred years old, yet still retained their original colors and shining lacquer. Unfortunately, I do not remember the poems and parallel sentences that they carried. When war submerged our village, all furniture and decorations in the Shrine were lost. What use could these boards, sacred and treasured relics of ours, be to other people besides their weight in firewood, one must wonder. Thus, only a decade after it was built, our new Ancestral Shrine had ceased to exist. The shell of the building still stood, but the Shrine had gone. With our country subjected, since then, to more wars and to a communist regime whose aim has been to undermine family ties, who could say when the Nguyen of Kim Bai would be able to get together again and have another Ancestral Shrine.

Of the documents kept at the Shrine, the oldest and most precious to our family were papers belonging to an ancestor known as Cu Hau. These were the only written evidence of our lineage to have escaped the destruction wrought by the bandits in the eighteenth century. For a very long time, they went missing. Our family regained possession of them in 1861.

10. The Cu Hau's Papers

Searching for ancient documents to establish a family's ancestry is an extremely difficult task in Vietnam, often an impossible one. Change has been the rule, stability an exception. Vietnamese families have moved up and down the social ladder in rapid succession. Wealth has never lasted for very long. It has always been dispersed. In all extended families, rich and poor branches could be found; within each branch, there have been rich and poor family units. A deeply-held belief of our people was expressed in this proverb:

> Who can be wealthy,
> In all three of his families?
> Who has to endure
> Poverty for three generations!

The three families of a man are his own, his mother's and his wife's. Our traditional society had no rigid classes and nothing like the entrenched nobility in feudal Europe, India or Japan. Its distinctive character was a constant movement form one class to another. Everyone could aim for the top, through studies and by presenting himself to the civil service examinations. Change could occur after a span of no more than a few generations, as indicated in the above proverb, because things usually moved in a certain way in our society. Unsuccessful scholars or people belonging to lower social categories were strongly motivated to move up. They sent their children to school and made them spend much of their time with "their lamps and books." Maybe success would not come in the first generation, or the next, but with perseverence, it would finally be attained. At the other end of the social scale, a mandarin brought wealth to his family, but his descendants may soon become spendthrift and lazy. They would neglect their studies and fail at the examinations. As a result, the family would go into decline. In prosperous times, a family would build an ancestral shrine in memory of its forebears, put land aside to provide for the cult, keep records for future generations. During periods of decline, however, cult land may have to be sold, the shrine may fall into disrepair, family members themselves may have to leave their village in search of a living; in such circumstances, chronicles would not be written and documents handed down by earlier generations might even be lost.

Apart from these changes in family fortunes, there were also other factors. Many dynasties had followed one another on the throne of Vietnam.
Each time a new ruling house came to power, it tried to eradicate all
vestiges of its predecessor. Palaces were razed, records of the fallen regime
destroyed. Not only the former dynasty, but also its mandarins would go
down in defeat and have their possessions taken. Many family archives
were lost in that way. War and insecurity also took their toll. Ever since the
sixteenth century, our country has hardly known a prolonged period of
peace. If it was not war against foreigners, it was war amongst contending
Vietnamese dynasties. Insecurity often plagued the countryside, caused by
rebel movements or simply bands of brigands. One of the worst periods in
our history, in terms of loss of ancient documents, was the Chinese domination in the fifteenth century (1414–1427). The Ming aimed to stamp out
our literary heritage and make Vietnam a mere cultural appendage of
China. All books they could lay their hands on, whether prose, poetry, history or law, were either burned or taken away to China. Of the many
authors under the Ly (1010–1225) and the Tran (1225–1400) dynasties—
that golden period of Vietnamese classical literature—we know only the
titles of books they wrote and some extracts which have survived in anthologies. The bulk of their works was lost. From the forest of our ancient
literature, only a few trees remained. Last but not least, another great
destroyer of our historical records has been the tropical climate. Books and
other paper documents are quickly damaged by dampness or eaten away
by white ants. Inscriptions on wooden material cannot last longer than two
centuries or so. Our people have never been good at the art of preserving
ancient relics. For all the above reasons, there are not many Vietnamese
families who can trace their roots back to more than ten generations.

Our family has, since the sixteenth century, undergone several critical
periods in which it was almost cut off from its roots. The first period came
with the fall of the Mac dynasty, at the end of the sixteenth century. Our
ancestors had to flee, abandoning home and village. Chronicles and
records may have been lost in the upheaval. Families caught in such a situation, if they escaped with their lives, still faced a real danger of being
dispersed. Hiding their real identity under assumed names, always apprehensive of being discovered by the new authorities, their members may
soon lose touch with one another. After a number of years, links between
branches may be severed. Thus, two branches of our family were believed
to have fled Kim Bai to escape persecution. Our branch was able, eventually,
to return to the village; but of the other branch, nothing more was known.
Although our people were back in their haven of Kim Bai, the trauma they
suffered was such that, of the three generations of ancestors who were
mandarins under the Mac, two would soon disappear from our collective
memory. Clearly, a persisting fear had inhibited the family from recalling

the times and lives of those ancestors; consequently, younger generations quickly forgot about them. Only in this century could we find out again who they were. None of their graves had been preserved. Our first two ancestors died while the Mac were in power; being high mandarins, their burial places would have to be built into large tombs. Sitting amidst open and flat rice fields, such tombs used to be considered as landmarks by travellers and it would have been difficult to lose trace of them. That ours were lost suggested that they had been destroyed, either by the advancing Le army as it passed through our region on its way to the Mac capital, or by some zealous officials in the violent period immediately following the change over. Certainly the people of Kim Bai were not involved, for our Ancestral Shrine, located within the village bamboo enclosure, had been left untouched.

In the eighteenth century, rebels and bandits roamed our region. Kim Bai fell prey to them time and again. Our extended family suffered to such an extent that it took the efforts of three generations to retrace our ancestry. We shall describe that crisis in detail in the next pages.

Until the beginning of this century, all our family's documents were written in the scholarly language, using the Chinese script. Then, the colloquial language using a new Romanized script became the national language. My grandfather belonged to a generation which knew both Chinese script and the national language. His children however, were only taught the new script. My father's generation could not read old documents. When I started learning the Chinese script in 1943, I was the first one in two generations to do so. Papers belonging to my great-grandfather, who died in 1909, were still kept in our ancestral home, many of them already damaged by weather and insects, but my scholarly language was not good enough to read them. The change of script created a rupture in the generational chain of knowledge. Given time this problem, which was national and not particular to our family, could have been remedied by having old documents translated into the national language, as grandfather did with our family chronicle, and by training more people to read the old script. But the communist revolution in 1945 and the 1946–1954 war intervened before anything could be done to save our family's documents.

In that period, all books and written materials left by my great-grandfather and grandfather were destroyed, except for the chronicle. When the war ended, there was nothing left to be saved. Our loss was as total as the one suffered two centuries ago at the hands of the bandits. Today, I cannot quote a single poem or literary piece written by my ancestors, although we have been for five hundred years a family of scholars and my great-grandfather, in particular, was known to have kept himself busy with essay and poetry writing.

In the eighteenth century, Vietnam was nominally under the Le dynasty but real power belonged to the Trinh overlord. The ruler Trinh Giang was a cruel and tyrannical man. In 1732, he killed a Le king to put another one on the throne. His spendthrift policies caused heavy taxes to be imposed on the population. Resentment was widespread in the country. Several rebellions broke out to challenge the Trinh's rule. Bandits operated in the open in many parts of the Red River delta. It took the central government thirty years to pacify the country. During that period, recalled by later generations as "the great calamity," our village was pillaged many times and had to abandoned for long periods. Many families lost their fortunes and were scattered away. Our Ancestral Shrine was burned down. The family register and chronicles deposited in the Shrine were destroyed. After the turmoil, some elders got together to put down on paper what they could remember. The new chronicle, my grandfather noted, "was based purely on recollection, without any written evidence." The earliest ancestor that our elders could remember was Nguyen Uyen, who lived in the sixteenth century and is now known as our second ancestor. Only two centuries after his death, Nguyen Uyen's father, the Count of Hung Giao, had been completely forgotten. Of our third ancestor, himself a deputy minister at the Mac Court, only a name remained, not his real name but a pseudonym used by the family to invoke his spirit during ceremonies commemorating his death. From the fourth generation down, precious little was recorded about the lives and careers of our forefathers. Even information of a sacred character such as the location of their graves and the anniversaries of their death was in some instances missing. As a result of the great calamity, our family even lost its links with a recent past.

Fortunately, a person who lived before those troubled times had in his papers information relating to our family's ancestry. It was known that those papers had escaped destruction at the hands of bandits. He was Cu Hau. Hau was not his name but an honorific title, and Cu a term of address which Vietnamese use for old people. Like other villages with a tradition of scholarship, Kim Bai had an Association of Literati to promote culture and learning. People who donated land to the Association received the honorific title of Hau and the Association would celebrate the anniversaries of their death after they had passed away. Cu Hau lived in the early part of the eighteenth century. Our seventh generation had two branches; he was probably the second son of the eldest branch. A scholar without academic diploma, he served as keeper of the Nguyen Ancestral Shrine. Normally, that responsibility rested with the heir to the extended family, in other words, the eldest son of the senior branch, but often it was delegated to another family member. In this case, Cu Hau's elder brother, Nguyen Du, was a mandarin who pursued a career away from the village. Cu Hau replaced him and assumed the duties of administering the cult land, maintaining the Shrine and celebrating the ceremonies of worship.

It was possible that Cu Hau either died during the period of bandit attacks, or soon after, because his papers were already missing when a new chronicle was compiled following the return to normal conditions. The Nguyen family knew that the papers existed but, in the decades that followed, all its branches fell into hard times and no search could be made. As time passed, the papers were not forgotten but, like the old Shrine, they grew in importance in our people's minds. The old told the young about a hidden treasure which held the keys to our past. "We have been a family of scholars for many generations," they said. "Many of our ancestors won high diplomas and had rewarding careers in the service of the state. We do not remember who they were and in what period they lived, but they must be mentioned in the Cu Hau papers. At the time when all our ancient chronicles were burned by the bandits, those papers were saved." No one knew where the papers were, but hope continued to be entertained by the elders: "The papers were only misplaced. When found, they will reveal a golden period in our family history." Meanwhile, the family was in serious decline. Success at the examinations had not come for several generations. Poverty had become our lot. The need was to encouarge the young to persevere with their studies. "Our family was once rich and powerful," the young were constantly reminded. "The cycle will soon turn. Success and prosperity will be with us again."

Indeed, at the start of the nineteenth century, a revival occurred. The tenth ancestor of our branch quickly made a fortune in trade. Nguyen Quang So was a man intensely proud of his lineage. "His aim was to uphold the merits of our forebears and lead the way for future generations to follow," wrote my grandfather. He was convinced that Nguyen Uyen, then the only ancestor known to have obtained the doctorate and reached the high ranks of the mandarinate, was not an isolated case. "One mandarin cannot assemble such wealth as to built the old Ancestral Shrine," he said. "There must have been others." With material means at his disposal, he set out to search for the papers in earnest. But a century had passed since Cu Hau's lifetime. Already it was the generation of Cu Hau's great-grandchildren and his branch had dispersed. As related in the chronicle, our ancestor discovered that "Cu Hau's eldest grandson had left Kim Bai and, subsequently, his whereabouts were unknown. Before leaving, he handed the papers to a younger brother, who took over from him the responsibility for the worship of our common ancestors. Then, those documents were mislaid." Apparently, the younger brother had died and some of his children had left the village—in those times of economic difficulties, many people went to look for work in towns. It was not possible to know who had the papers for safekeeping. The search ended there, for the time being. When our ancestor died, his only son was three years old. It looked as if, as a treasure, the Cu Hau papers would be forever hidden from us.

Nothing was done in the next two decades until, as a young man, Nguyen Dinh Dat took up from where his father had left. The papers could not be found in Kim Bai. Hope rested with them being kept by a relative who had left the village. Although our family, after having enjoyed a brief period of affluence, was again in difficult circumstances, Nguyen Dinh Dat managed to reestablish contact with relatives at many places. He travelled widely in the Red River delta, went up the highlands and mountains of the north at the risk of catching malaria. He journed to Lang Son on the Chinese border, where some of our people were established as traders. He visited other relatives living in Thai Nguyen and Cao Bang, where centuries ago our ancestor Nguyen Uyen resided as a mandarin. In his trips he restored links with family members who had gone away a long time ago. The papers were found on one of those trips, in 1861; precisely where and in what circumstances the chronicle did not say. But it made clear that the merit belonged to Nguyen Dinh Dat, who was my great-grandfather. The following passage showed him playing the central role:

> The papers left by Cu Hau were only recovered in the fourteenth year of Emperor Tu Duc (1861). In the first lunar month of the following year, Nguyen Dinh Dat called a meeting of all members of our extended family at the Ancestral Shrine in order to lay down the rules for our cult and to put again on record the chronicles of different branches.

Thus, some one-and-a-quarter centuries after they were missing, the papers were safely back in our hands, a result which said much of my great-grandfather's perseverence and conviction. He must have felt elated, yet it was said that on reading those papers which for so long had captivated the family's imagination, his reaction was one of disappointment and shock. Our people had thought that the papers would carry a register of ancestors worshipped at the old Shrine; in other words the ancient genealogy of the Nguyen, as well as information on the lives and careers of these ancestors. Had that been the case, Cu Hau would have been the savior of our family's history. But the data my great-grandfather found only went back to the sixteenth century. There was no mention of any ancestors whom he did not know, no reference to that golden period which generations of ours had talked about. Clearly, the papers were intended to help Cu Hau celebrate the cult and administer the cult land. They were not used to record family history.

Of these papers, my grandfather wrote:

> Thanks to (them), we now know that the cult land bequeathed by our ancestors dated well back in time. The first six generations of ours all had left land, including ricefields, gardens and ponds, to provide for the cult. They all had deposited records and chronicles in our Shrine. By misfortune, the Ancestral Shrine was pillaged and burned down by bandits with all its contents.

The shock to Nguyen Dinh Dat came from the cult land. A large part of Cu Hau's documents was concerned with descriptions of land donated by family members to the Ancestral Shrine. In our tradition, before dividing their estates among their children, parents usually set aside some land for the eldest son, who had charge of the ancestors' cult. Well-off people would also leave some land to the family's ancestral shrine. In both cases, the land was called cult land, or to use a more literal translation of the Vietnamese term *huong hoa,* "land to provide for the flame and incense on the ancestors' altar." A cult land differed from ordinary land by its almost sacred character. It was not considered as the property of the person receiving it, but as land entrusted to him for purposes of the cult. He could not dispose of it as he pleased. If a family were to suffer hardship, its cult land would be the last to go, and a decision of the family council was required before it could be sold. It was known that our family owned large landholdings under the Mac dynasty in the sixteenth century and that we remained wealthy following the change of dynasty at the end of that century. But Dinh Dat never knew that our Ancestral Shrine owned so much cult land. The many acres of rice fields, ponds and gardens mentioned in the Cu Hau papers would form quite a large estate by Kim Bai's standard. However, he was shocked to find that they were all presently in other hands. How did it happen that they were lost? Other branches were alerted and my great-grandfather called an urgent meeting of the extended family in the beginning of 1862. That it fell to him to take such an initiative was interesting to note. Our branch was the most junior of the family. It would have been more proper for the senior branches, on whom rested the primary responsibility for our cult, to act. However, while our branch had known a degree of revival, others continued to stay down and some even had dropped out of the scholars' class. Although from the youngest branch and only a young man of twenty-six, Nguyen Dinh Dat was taking over the leadership of the extended family.

The plenary meeting of 1862 was the first to be held in that century and the only one recorded in detail in the chronicle. The most important problem was, of course, ownership of the cult land. The assembly found that the land had been taken over by other people; not recently, but fifty or sixty years ago. Whatever right our family may have had before, prescription had applied in favor of those in possession. To quote the chronicle:

> ... [because] the papers were misplaced for fifty or sixty years, the land bequeathed by our forebears had been cultivated by others. As a consequence, anniversaries and festivals in memory of our ancestors could not be properly celebrated.... [When the papers were recovered, the land had been usurped] for a long time and it was not possible any more to claim it back.

There is a certain mystery about what actually happened to the cult land. The belief in our family was that all the land was usurped after the papers were "misplaced" by Cu Hau's descendants at the beginning of the nineteenth century. I do not think that misplacement of the papers by itself could have led to usurpation of the land. More likely, the loss was caused by breakdown of family ties and the fact that those in charge of the land—the shrine keeper and his descendants—had left. Cu Hau's grandson must have gone away from Kim Bai at the end of the eighteenth century and later on some of his great-grandchildren also left. Other people must have seized upon that opportunity to take our land. Moreover, I cannot help wondering why Cu Hau's descendants had to leave their village, if our cult land was so extensive. To go away from one's birthplace was not a decision taken lightly. Especially in the case of Cu Hau's eldest grandson, heir to his branch, who had to relinquish his responsibility for the cult and hand it over to a younger sibling. Why could the descendants not stay on and cultivate the cult land for a living? Very likely, the land described in Cu Hau's papers was that which existed in his time or the beginning of the eighteenth century. But by the next century, much of it had probably been disposed of. Indeed, the Nguyen prospered until the end of the seventeenth century, then a downward trend started. Some land may have been sold to help family members in need, or for the upkeep of the old shrine and for the building of a new shrine following the destruction wrought by bandits. Thus, the amount of land illegally appropriated by others may not have been as large as suggested in the chronicle.

Why was it that "for fifty or sixty years," our family did not react to the loss of its cult land and anniversaries and festivals in memory of ancestors were "not properly celebrated?" Obviously, our extended family had broken apart. Branches had lost touch with one another. Before Cu Hau's descendants left the village, no one raised with them the question of who was going to look after the Shrine and administer the cult land. Three decades later, in the 1830s, the problem of cult land never crossed the mind of our tenth ancestor as he planned on establishing a new shrine. Fortunately, the papers were recovered and, because of them, our people were jolted into action. It was then too late to get the land back, but steps were immediately taken to restore family cohesion. The plenary meeting decided to reestablish the yearly ceremony of worship in which all branches participated. There had been a gap of over half-a-century since the last ceremony.

Cu Hau's paper did contain a wealth of information on more recent generations, including the membership of all branches, the location of ancestors' graves and anniversaries of their death. Apparently, Cu Hau did not only look after the Shrine, he also helped other family members celebrate the cult within their own branches, which explained why he needed to have all the above information at hand. His papers covered only the four generations which preceded his, because within each branch, the cult did not extend further than four generations. If Cu Hau had copied all the records kept in his time at the old Shrine, how much more of our ancestry would we know? He noted in his papers that in the six generations preceding his, "all generations had deposited records and chronicles in the Shrine." When we know that in the Vietnamese tradition, people wrote chronicles to relate the time and life, not of their own generation, but of their parents, grandparents and more distant ancestors, it is safe to assume that in Cu Hau's time, our lineage was established at least back to the Tran dynasty in the fourteenth century. As it happened, that early part of our history was wiped out at the hands of bandits in that disastrous period of the eighteenth century.

From the written evidence provided by the papers, my great-grandfather and family elders compiled a new chronicle to replace the previous one which was quite sketchy as it was based mainly on recollection. They were also able to draw up a register of members of all known generations. In those two documents, which were from time to time complemented and brought up to date, was contained the history of our extended family, while the chronicle in my possession dealt mainly with that of our branch. Until 1948, the documents were kept in our Ancestral Shrine. During the hostilities, all furniture and decorations of the Shrine were lost, but it is not entirely impossible that the documents may have been saved by someone and are waiting to be recovered someday, like the Cu Hau's papers of two centuries ago.

11. The Nguyen Brothers

Two names belong to our village's legend. An old saying about them runs like this:

Nguyen Huyen, Nguyen Tue,
The two brothers.
At the same session,
They won the golden board.

In the high examinations of old, the names of successful candidates were written on a board painted gold which was displayed in front of the Palace of High Learning in the capital. To win the golden board became a more refined way of saying that someone had passed an examination. From a village of scholars which had produced a large number of graduates, what did the Nguyen brothers do to be remembered in such a way? When did they live? The saying had been transmitted by generations of villagers; every child knew it, yet until the 1910s, no one could say who the brothers were. Being Nguyen did not mean that they must necessarily be our direct ancestors. Nguyen is a surname quite common in Vietnam. In Kim Bai itself, there were several Nguyen families which I believe may have started as branches of the same extended family, but had become separate.

When my grandfather grew up—he was born in 1879—our lineage was known only as far as Ancestor Nguyen Uyen, who lived in the sixteenth century. The brothers were figures of legend, but he could not help associating them with a belief in our family that we descended from a long line of scholars and several ancestors of ours had obtained high diplomas and mandarinal positions. That strongly held belief did not quite fit in with the family's history as we knew it then. From Nguyen Uyen, who was made a doctor in 1535, until this century, a span of nearly four hundred years, we could count only one more graduate, a licentiate at the beginning of the eighteenth century. Such a record was hardly impressive. Many scholarly families had done much better than us. To take just one instance, my mother's family, the Hoang of the village Dong Ngac, can boast of five doctors under the Restored Le dynasty alone (1592–1788). So, how could our family belief be explained? Moreover, why did the people of Kim Bai also share that belief and consider us as being the leading scholarly family in the village? There were obviously some missing links. Our tradition of scholarship had probably been built up since early times, but the men responsible for it had gone out of our collective memory. Could Nguyen Huyen and Nguyen Tue have been amongst them?

Cu Hau's papers were found to contain less than what our people expected. They were a disappointment. Yet, like seeds planted in the soil which took time to germinate, half a century after they were found the papers would trigger another search for that "source in the mountains," where lay the origins of our family. A careful study of the papers revealed to my grandfather that the generations immediately preceding that of Ancestor Nguyen Uyen left a large amount of land to the Ancestral Shrine and appeared to enjoy great wealth. The Shrine itself was probably built by them. No names of earlier ancestors were given, but the way these were referred to in the papers suggested that they had had careers even more distinguished than Nguyen Uyen's. More and more, my grandfather came to believe that the golden period remembered by our people was that of Nguyen Huyen and Nguyen Tue. I believe that he spent time searching for the brothers' identities after his father died in 1909. In accordance with Confucian tradition, he took a year's leave of absence to mourn his father's death. In that time of mourning and contemplation, his mind naturally turned to the past and to family history. From indications given in the Cu Hau's papers, he set out to find whether there was any relationship between the brothers and our family. He talked to family and village elders but found on their part a strange reluctance. They all tried to discourage him. Some said that the brothers were ancient figures of legend, about whom information had since long been lost; it would be futile to go after such information. Others were against the very idea of trying to know who Nguyen Huyen and Nguyen Tue were. "Let a legend stay as a legend," they said. My grandfather was taken aback by their reaction. It was only later, when he succeeded in his quest, that he understood the reason.

Reasoning that the two brothers must have been successful at the highest civil service examination, that is, the doctorate, my grandfather started his search at the Temple of Literature in Hanoi. There, the names of those who graduated as doctors since ancient times were kept. Dedicated to the cult of Confucius, the Temple was the sanctum of our traditional culture. The *History of Dai Viet*, written in the second half of the fifteenth century and the earliest one preserved in Vietnam, recorded that King Ly Thanh Ton "had the Temple built in 1070. Statues of Confucious and of his closest disciples were installed there. Ceremonies of worship were held in all four seasons. The Crown Prince went there for his studies." The first civil service examination in the history of the country took place five years later, in 1075. King Le Thanh Ton, the great king of the Le dynasty, ordered in 1484 that all graduates of the doctorate—the elite of the nation—

have their names carved in stone to be preserved for posterity. The stelae bearing their names were erected in the grounds of the Temple and can still be seen today.

I have never been to the Temple of Literature. It was located just outside the city of Hanoi, to the south of the ancient citadel. On the way to Ha Dong and our village, I always passed by it. From the road, it appeared distant, almost untouchable to the common man. Tall trees with wide branches, which had been there for centuries, hid most of the Temple from sight. The place looked like a dark and deep wood. Nowadays, countries open their temples to the public and even use them to attract tourists. In my youth, our Temple of Literature stood in isolation, an object for reverence from afar. The thought never occurred to me to enter its grounds and look at the stelae, although I knew that my ancestors' names were on them.

My grandfather found on the stelae that the two brothers became doctors at the 1511 session, twenty-four years before Nguyen Uyen graduated. The gap was that of a generation. Several pieces of the puzzle had now fallen into place. The brothers were from our village, they bore the same surname as us, they belonged to the generation of Nguyen Uyen's parents. There remained, however, the need to establish the links of ancestry. The search for historical documents was long and difficult. Grandfather did not have access to government archives or to public libraries. He had to rely on books kept by other scholars in their private collections. Old editions published in a limited number of copies were rarely reprinted and scholars used to copy by hand the books they wanted to keep. It was several years before he could lay his hands on the right document, which was a register compiled by Nguyen Hoan and other authors, and published at the end of the eighteenth century. Entitled *Register of High Graduates in the Dynasties of Dai Viet*—Dai Viet or The Great Viet was then our country's name—it listed the names of all people who passed the doctorate examinations from the beginning until the last session under the Le which was held in 1787. Each name was accompanied by a few biographical notes and these provided grandfather with the information he was looking for. He noted in the chronicle:

> The Register set down that in 1511, Nguyen Huyen and Nguyen Tue were both successful at the doctoral examinations. It added that Nguyen Tue was Nguyen Huyen's elder brother and that his son Nguyen Uyen was made a doctor at the 1535 session.

The relationship was thus established. An earlier ancestor had been found. That result vindicated grandfather's belief and was a source of great pride to him. Triumphantly, he wrote: "This matter has been proved right! No further doubt can be entertained! I now put on record that Nguyen Tue was the ancestor of our first generation."

The Temple of Literature in Hanoi built in 1070. Stelae bearing the names of those who graduated as doctors are erected on the grounds.

The two brothers became mandarins under the Le dynasty. They stayed on to serve the Mac who overthrew the Le in 1527. The *Register* mentioned that Nguyen Tue was a minister of the Mac Court and received the title of count. Nguyen Huyen rose to the position of governor of a region. After sixty-five years of Mac rule, the Le were restored to the throne. High mandarins who worked for the Mac and their families were persecuted. Their villages also suffered. The victorious Le never forgave the Mac for having taken the throne from them and considered them not as defeated enemies but as traitors. Historians of the Restored Le, whenever they used the word Mac, always preceded it with the word *nguy*, which means usurper. That label stuck to the Mac.

The reason for the negative attitude adopted by elders, on hearing that he sought to establish a link between the brothers and our family, was now clear to grandfather. Our family and village went through a traumatic period after the collapse of the Mac regime. Those who tried to dissuade him from launching into his search did not themselves remember who the two Nguyen of Kim Bai were. But they still had in memory the warning of danger, even after so many generations had passed.

Nguyen Tue's son, Nguyen Uyen, was himself a high mandarin of the Mac; yet, later generations felt no apprehension in recalling him. The links with him were always maintained. Many aspects of his remarkable career

Doctors' stelae sit on tortoise backs and are supposed to last for a thousand years or more—the life of a tortoise.

were lost for a time, then rediscovered, but his name did not suffer from the same official ostracism as those of his father and uncle. I believe that was because Nguyen Uyen graduated, started his career, retired and died, all under the Mac. For him, there was no switch of allegiance. Nguyen Tue and Nguyen Huyen however, were mandarins of the Le who opted for the Mac at the change of dynasty. This counted against them, although they had died half a century before the Le came back. In those times, death did not put matters to rest. Their descendants and the villagers of Kim Bai sought to avoid the wrath of the Restored Le by hiding their ties with the two brothers. Soon, they themselves forgot and were it not for the popular saying, the identities of Nguyen Huyen and Nguyen Tue would have stayed forever in oblivion.

Grandfather never seemed to be bothered by the fact that our ancestors made their names under a dynasty much stigmatized by later historians. He did not talk much about them, but whenever he did, it was with admiration and pride. "To shoulder the burden of office in that tumultuous period," he said, "was a real test for a scholar-mandarin. Our ancestors did achieve much, for the first part of the Mac reign had been marked by unprecedented order and prosperity." After a pause, he added: "It is not easy to do right for your country, your family and yourself, all at the same time." In saying this, perhaps grandfather was also thinking of his own time and the difficult choices that he himself had had to make.

12. Family Traits

The chronicle left by my grandfather is a short document of ten pages or so. Written in the concise and condensed manner of a Confucian classical text, in which each Chinese character is carefully chosen and everything unnecessary has been cut out, it provides just the basic information on our family's history. Each generation was outlined in a few sentences, most of which were taken up by the names of ancestors, anniversaries of their death and places where they were buried. Our second ancestor, who lived to be over seventy and whose career was particularly long and varied, was given less than ten lines. Fortunately, many stories about past generations have been transmitted orally down to our times. Some of them I have learned from my grandmother and other family elders. Most were told to me by my parents, who also gave me eyewitness accounts of more recent events. My mother, in particular, is a treasure trove of family stories. Thanks to her excellent memory she is able to remember exact quotations of what was said some sixty years ago, from the time when she came into the Nguyen family as a young bride. "Being the wife of an eldest son, I expected plenty of responsibilities and a difficult period of adaptation," she told us, "but it turned out differently." Her in-laws let her have all the time she needed to settle in. Then, just a year after her marriage, she gave birth to a healthy boy. "My position in the family was firmly established," she said with a smile. "My mother-in-law did not let me do anything else but take care of the baby." She spent much time in the company of my father's grandmother, who told her about family customs and traditions. Mostly, the old lady liked to tell stories of olden times and in that way, my mother said, she learned more about the family history than by reading the chronicle or other documents on our ancestry.

Our chronicle shows a rigid adherence to the patriarchal system and to Confucian ethics. There is nothing about the maternal side of all our generations, besides the names of our foremothers. Essential information such as their social and family backgrounds, the villages where they came from, are absent. It is as if, once married into the Nguyen family, they were absorbed by it and their origins and distinctive characters ceased to matter. In the Vietnamese language, the word for maternal side is *ngoai*, meaning outside, while paternal side is *noi*, or inside. Our chronicle deals only with the latter, the side which is "in." As mentioned earlier, two generations of our family were responsible for the cult of maternal ancestors, but even in such instances, the only indications given by the chronicle are the names of those ancestors and the anniversaries of their death.

Daughters of our family also received scant attention. They only appeared in the chronicle from the eighth generation, in the eighteenth century. Of earlier generations, only sons were mentioned. "A daughter is born to you," so goes a popular saying, "to another family, she will belong." In our traditional society, marriage meant a radical break, almost a severance of ties between the bride and her family. She would only return to her parents' home on rare occasions, once or twice a year perhaps. That explained why our old custom was for the bride to cry at her wedding and refuse to leave home. Relatives had to convince her to obey the wishes of her parents and it would be some moments before she would finally agree to go, still crying profusely. In many instances, this was not just an attitude dictated by social custom. The bride must have felt a genuine sadness and apprehension at parting with her own family and heading for a new life in an unknown family environment. While a son's wedding meant an addition to the family, a daughter's was a loss. In my grandparents' time, the marriage of a daughter was an event both joyous and melancholic. I remember well my aunts' weddings. The bridgegroom and his party came to ask for the bride; both families happily enjoyed the occasion until the moment the bride came out of her room crying. The assembly fell silent and I could see that my grandmother was crying too. Everyone left for the main ceremony at the bridegroom's place, everyone except my grandparents. By tradition, they stayed back because their daughter now belonged to another family and they must not appear to be interfering. Some of us children, being too young, were also left behind. The house suddenly looked empty and sadness showed on my grandparents' faces. Grandfather, normally so composed, now walked aimlessly in the courtyard, in and out of the altar house. The daughter he had raised and who had been at his side all those years was now gone. He would see her only from time to time, on brief visits. She had become a member of another family and had acquired a new loyalty. Times, of course, have changed. When the turn of my own generation came, marriage no longer meant such a radical separation. The bride was not required to cry and her parents were welcome to join in the celebrations at the bridegroom's.

Confucian ethics placed a woman, at all stages of her life, in a position of dependence. She must "defer to" her father when still unmarried, her husband after marraige and her son when in widowhood. This was reflected in the chronicle, which recognized to our foremothers a role secondary to that of their husbands and sons. Vietnamese women, however, have never quite fit the Confucian mold. As a matter of fact, relationship between the sexes in the early period of our history was on a remarkably equal footing. Men and women freely chose their partners in marriage. Warriors who fought under the Trung Sisters against the Chinese occupants in the beginning of the first century came from both sexes. After that period, Confucian influence spread from China and social norms became more and more male-dominated, although until the fifteenth century, our laws still recognized to women equal rights in such matters as inheritance and marriage. To some degree, the ancient tradition of equality has continued to survive and reality has never totally reflected Confucian teachings. Vietnamese women have, hidden under their gentle demeanor, a strong personality. Their role as wife and mother and their contribution to the family have been far more important than envisaged in the Confucian model. While deferring to their husband's position as family head, they have remained in charge of most of the day-to-day running of the family, administering its budget, looking after the children's education, and so on. It is not for nothing that they have been called "generals of the interior."

Several women played vital roles at critical junctures of our family's history. They were mentioned, albeit briefly, in the chronicle but remembered more fully through oral tradition. Our family survived the upheaval caused by the defeat of the Mac dynasty in the sixteenth century, thanks to Trinh Khiet, the wife of our third ancestor. The respect and gratitude that she commanded were only second to those that later generations showed towards Nguyen Uyen, long thought to be our first ancestor. As recently as the second half of last century, our family was still trying to find Trinh Khiet's tomb, the location of which had been forgotten. Nearer to us, my great-great-grandmother was credited with saving the family from dropping out of the scholars' class. She took over the helm after her husband died on a business expedition. All his money was lost, but she managed to raise three young children and, in particular, give to her son a proper scholar's education.

As we know so little about their background, it is difficult to assess the contribution made by our foremothers in terms of attitude, outlook, religious belief, or even money and property. It is believed that their influence had tended, over the generations, to temper our rather rigid adherence to Confucian norms. In some periods, it had helped bring out a development of the Buddhist faith. Wealthy families often gave their daughters to poor but promising scholars and in such marriages, the wife would bring to her husband a dowry to help meet the family's expenses. That may have happened in some generations of our family. The chronicle mentioned that our ninth ancestor inherited all the land and property left by his in-laws. Part of the capital with which our tenth ancestor started his business was believed to have come from his wife. During the impoverished generations, women worked to provide a living so that the men could devote themselves to their studies. Their supportive role was acknowledged in the chronicle. They raised silkworms, wove cloth, made paddy into rice, sold textiles, rice and other products at markets. Like other women in Kim Bai, they worked hard and did well in their market activities. Often, they provided the main source of family income. Scholar-husbands, while they may enjoy a high status in the village, usually earned very little money. The women, true to the Vietnamese tradition, made sacrifices and endured hardship to give the men the opportunity to study and gain honors. As in the words of the young wife, in this popular ballad:

Please, dear husband,
Stay with your books and your studies,
Let me do the tilling of the fields,
And the transplanting of the rice seedlings.
Let me work on the weaving loom. . . .

The main keepers of customs, traditions and oral history have been women. Most of the old stories I know have been told by my mother and my grandmother. As they were housewives, they had more time to spend with the children than the men who went out to work. My mother knows the members of the extended Nguyen family, their ranks, the branches to which they belong, better than does my father. Often she told stories about our ancestors to my wife instead of me; just as it was she, and not my father, who learned of them from my grandmother. The line of transmission has been mainly from mother-in-law to daughter-in-law. Often, if not always, our foremothers survived their husbands, some by a very long stretch. In my great-grandmother's case, it was forty years; in my grandmother's, eighteen years. They were the living bridges between the generations.

From the first ancestor to my grandfather, in a space of some four hundred years, there had been eleven generations of our family, a rather small number compared to other families which may have counted up to fifteen or sixteen generations in the same period. In our case, a generation took up, on average, as many as thirty-six years. Sons generally came late to our ancestors. Several of them were over forty before they had a male descendant. Moreover, sons were very few. All through the first five generations, our lineage was maintained by a single male branch. The situation improved afterwards and several branches appeared, but while the others developed, the one son pattern frequently came back to our branch. Only in my grandparents' time, did ours finally reach the traditional goal of familial happiness which was "an abundant flock of children and grandchildren." But for a long period, the survival of our line had remained uncertain as it depended on an only son. This sole thread was a source of great anxiety and many generations were obsessed by the fear that the lineage might be lost. Down to my grandparents' time, the fear had persisted. Grandmother kept reminding us that what our family needed and valued most was "children, more children." She herself gave birth to twelve children, eight of whom survived. "From such insecure periods," she told us, "we must feel particularly grateful that our family has finally been able to grow and prosper."

In the society of old, scarcity of male children was looked upon with great apprehension. People saw in it a warning by Fate that the worst possible eventuality—the end of the lineage—might befall the family. In the hopes of having more sons, our ancestors did what customs and superstition in those times prescribed them to do. They gave alms, offered prayers at temples, called in geomancers to modify the orientation of our altar house. Other people in their situation would also move family graves, but this our ancestors never did.

The custom of moving graves was quite common in our region. A grave could be moved after three years had passed since the burial. The ceremony usually took place at night as the realm of the dead was associated with darkness; if it had to be done during the day, great care was taken to shield the grave from the source of life, the sun. Its rays should not be allowed to reach the remains. The procedure consisted of digging up the grave and taking the bones out of the coffin, cleaning them with scented water and transferring them to a smaller coffin, then reinterring the remains at another location. Some families followed that custom as a matter of course. But in most cases, graves were moved only in the event of unfortunate occurences, such as a serious illness or disability in the family, the lack of an heir or persistent business losses. People believed that such bad fortune could be remedied by having ancestors' graves relocated in a more auspicious geomantic position. It was recalled that at a difficult juncture of our family's history, consideration was given to moving some of our ancestors' graves. That happened in one of our first six generations, for the story indicates that our family was still wealthy enough to afford the services of a master geomancer. The man had arrived recently from China with a high repute. He was invited to our ancestral home and treated like an honored guest. While waiting for "the right time" to go and find auspicious geomantic locations, the guest toured the countryside, consulted our family chronicle and studied his books. Ten days soon went by. Our people asked no questions and continued to provide the geomancer with whatever he needed. Another ten days passed and our ancestor tactfully enquired whether the geomancer would want to see the family graves. "You may then tell me which ones need to be moved," he added. "I am afraid the right time to act has not come yet, please bear with me a little bit longer," the geomancer replied.

He did not speak Vietnamese. Our ancestor communicated with him by writing, using classical Chinese. Early one morning, he awoke our ancestor to let him know that "the right time" had come. The two set out for the fields around our village. The geomancer visited all our family graves and spent a great deal of time examining their positions. When he had finished, our ancestor thought that he would next choose the new locations, but the geomancer headed straight back to our house. There, he sat down to engage in a long communication, by writing, with our ancestor. According to him, those geomancers who had placed our graves where they were had done a very good job. The location of each grave was well-chosen; moreover, all graves were linked together in an auspicious pattern. "If you move one grave away, the whole pattern will suffer irreparable damage. Your family would gain if, for now and for the future, all graves were left in their places," he wrote, adding "Only in unavoidable circumstances, such as when ordered to do so by the authorities or when a road is built running over them, must you move the graves."

At the end of the exchange, the geomancer offered this reflection: "Families who are given talent and a capacity to reach the heights have to contend with difficult problems. That is the way of Fate. The way to the top of the mountains is never easy."

The next morning he left, refusing to take any fees. He said that he did not have to choose any new locations and, in any case, had taken advantage of our hospitality far too long. Since then, it had become a tradition in our family not to move any graves. In our region, original graves were usually built in rectangular tumuli. When newly established, they were about two meters long and one meter wide. Over the years they would get smaller and smaller but would keep their rectangular shape. The smaller graves of a round shape which looked like small drums in the fields were those that had been moved. On the day of sweeping the tombs, our party would sometimes find three or four graves close to one another in a plot of rice field, and it was by their shape that we could recognize which ones were ours.

Our ancestors were scholars of the conservative school who kept rigidly to the path of examinations and public service, or failing that, teaching. They would not try other fields of activity, except for one brief interval in the tenth generation. They even shunned occupations such as medicine, astrology or geomancy, which were often taken up by untitled scholars, but regarded by the traditional school as less orthodox. In addition to the conservative streak, several of our ancestors seemed to share the trait of being late bloomers. Success did not come to us either early or easily. Our second ancestor reached the high mark of his career—a diplomatic mission to China—at the age of seventy. My great-grandfather gained the reputation of being a fine scholar, but he never won "the golden board." He turned to teaching his sons and the success which eluded him only came to the next generation. His eldest son, my grandfather, started slowly by first obtaining the bachelor degree, then at the next session, which was three years later, the licentiate degree. Bright students—and he was one—could have jumped the grades and become licentiates at their first try. Once in the mandarinate, he was bogged down and stayed in the same starting position for years before receiving any promotion. His career ultimately brought him to the top of the mandarinate, but not without other stagnant periods and with him having to go through each and every rung of the administrative ladder. Results achieved by our family had been through persistent efforts and step by step progress. As with climbing to the peaks of the Mountains of the Twins, we learned that in life there were no easy shortcuts, but one had to patiently follow a winding path.

"Who has to endure poverty for three generations?" asked the proverb. Our family had, and it had also enjoyed wealth for more than three generations. Perhaps as a consequence of our character, the cycle of rise and decline in our case had stretched over a much longer period than that indicated in the proverb. We managed to remain wealthy in the first six generations. In the next two centuries, except for a brief interval, poverty became our lot. More seriously for a family of scholars, eight generations of ours could claim just one academic diploma. By failing to make it through the competitive civil service examinations, our people were kept in the lower social class of "untitled scholars."

The recovery had started in my grandparents' time. When I grew up, we enjoyed a comfortable life, but many of the stories told by elders were still about hardships suffered by ancestors of not so long ago. When we sat down to a good meal, one with a dish of meat or two, my grandfather often reminded us that our ancestors were poor and would seldom have had such a meal. The nadir, he told us, was reached in the eighteenth century with our eighth and ninth generations. The family could afford to buy meat only on special occasions such as Tet. For the rest of the year, meat was served only when our ancestor received his portion at village festivals. That portion would be shared among the whole family. Grandfather told us how our ancestor would save his small share until the end of the meal so that he would get the impression that the whole meal had been eaten with meat. There were also times when our family did not have enough rice and had to cook it mixed with sweet potato and manioc. Care was taken not to let other people know of our plight, for as teachers, our ancestors held a high position in the village community. The rice pot would be quickly hidden away if a visitor should appear at mealtime. Here, my grandfather would pause to smile before adding: "But all the neighbours knew because they could smell potato and manioc being cooked." Grandfather himself, as a student, often had just boiled vegetable to eat with rice, and salt to dip the vegetable in, instead of the more expensive fish sauce.

When spending our school holidays in Kim Bai, we often had boiled sweet potato or manioc as a midday snack and were quite fond of it. We could not understand the stories of poor people having to mix it with their rice. Why! Potato and manioc would make the rice taste better, we thought. We talked about it so much that grandmother agreed to cook for us the rough red rice that country people used to have, mixed with slices of potato and manioc. "You will have it for a week," she told us. "Let us see how long you will like it. Do not forget that poor people have to have it the whole year." The first meal went wonderfully well. The sweet potato and manioc gave sweetness and flavor to the rice. It was like some kind of cake. I found it so good that I ate it just by itself and hardly touched any vegetable or meat. At the next meal, it became less appetizing and, after a few days, that very sweetness and flavor put off my appetite. I missed rice, the unmixed rice thought to be tasteless but which, I now realized, had a taste so delicate that one never grew tired of it. In a popular saying, rice was likened to "gold" and the water which helped it grow, to "silver." The meaning of that saying was brought home to me, as well as that of grandmother's oft repeated admonition: "To waste a single grain of rice is to commit a sin."

In North Vietnam, winter temperature could drop to ten degrees Celsius but the cold was made worse by humidity and a biting wind coming from the landmass of China. However, "impoverished scholars," in our language *han nho,* a term which can be translated literally as "scholars suffering from the cold," continued to wear clothes made of thin material more appropriate to the heat of summer. As teachers, our ancestors earned little. In the old Confucian tradition, teaching was a vocation and a duty more than a career. An unwritten rule laid down that students from poor families should receive their tuition free. Teachers were presented with gifts in kind such as fruit, chicken or a plate of glutinous rice on occasion of season festivals; rarely were they paid their fees in money. To make ends meet, they might have offered their services as calligraphers, while their wives engaged in petty trade. I remember the spectacle of impoverished scholars who had set up calligraphers' stalls at the local market as the year drew to a close. Using big fat brushes, they wrote large Chinese characters on red paper for people to stick on the doors and walls of their homes; the characters were expressions of good luck and good wishes to greet the coming of Tet. Most were old men, their grey hair hidden under black turbans, some with long beards of silvery whiteness. Dressed in a double tunic of white cloth on the inside and thin black gauze on the outside, they all looked thin and frail. "My ancestors must have been like them," I told myself. The wrists and hands which came out of the black sleeves of their tunics were all skin, bone and sinew. A group of deferential customers and onlookers formed around them; we were all shivering in the cold and I imagined that I could never write good calligraphy in such conditions, for my hands would shake terribly. Yet, when those old and wrinkled hands held a brush and dipped it in the black ink in preparation for writing, they gave out a surprising impression of strength and suppleness. I can still see them moving the brush in firm and purposeful strokes and making elegant characters appear on the red paper, shining in their wet black ink.

At the best of times, village teachers did not have a prosperous life. Our impoverished ancestors in the eighteenth century were much worse off. At that time, the country was racked by civil wars. Our own region suffered from wave after wave of rebellion and banditry. Villages were pillaged, people ruined. Few families were left which could afford to send their children to school. Scholarship itself became devalued. Our ancestors, however, continued with their teaching. True to the Confucian tradition, they "accepted their poverty and sought to find joy by following the ways of Saints and Sages," said my grandfather quoting an ancient precept. At that point of the story, my grandmother usually intervened to tell us another of her favorite tales, this time about the king of Ngo, a country in ancient China. The king owned fabulous treasures, never in history had there been a man as rich as he. Whenever he came out of his palace, thirty-six parasols made of gold shaded him. Following his death, he found himself walking alone on his last journey. No mandarins or servants waited upon him and he was not able to take any of his treasures with him. He met another man.

> "Who are you?" the king asked.
> "I was a fisherman in the kingdom of Ngo," the man replied.
> "Do you know who I am?" said the king.
> "No, who are you?"
> "I am the king of Ngo," said the king who was rather annoyed by the question. "He should have recognized me by the robe I wear," he thought.

But then, he looked at himself and did not see his golden brocade robe. He was dressed in simple cloth like the fisherman.

The two got on talking. The king was mostly interested in whether the man was rich or poor in his life and what he left to his children on his death. The man replied that he was poor; the only material thing he could give his children was a small boat. He said:

> "With a boat, they can fish and spread their nets in rivers and out in the sea, they will not have to depend on anyone else for a living." After a pause he continued: "With a boat, they can go anywhere they want, from the River Ngo to the Sea of So, any port can be their haven. With a boat, they are free men."

The king listened to the man, but still found it hard to understand that a man could be happy to leave his children just a small boat.

> "You left only a boat!" he commented.
> "By doing good things and avoiding harming others," said the fisherman in a whispering voice, as if to himself, "I strove to earn some virtue and merit.

I do not know how well I have succeeded, but that was the real heritage I wanted to leave to my children."

Thus on his final journey, the king of Ngo learned that he was no more than any other man in his kingdom. "My companion the fisherman," the king mused, "may be even richer than me, in the virtue and merit that he had acquired for the benefit of his descendants."

My grandmother ended her tale by repeating, in a singing voice, some of her favorite verses:

> The king of Ngo,
> Shaded by thirty-six gold parasols....
> On his last journey,
> He was on a par
> With the poorest fisherman in his kingdom.

Family records show that the Nguyen have been blessed with longevity. An ancient proveb says that "from antiquity to our time, few people have reached seventy." In our part of the world as in the West, three score and ten have been taken as a crowning landmark in a person's life. Many of our ancestors lived to be over it. The head of our second generation was still actively involved in public service, even in his seventies. His son, who died a violent death away from his ancestral village, came close to seventy. The same trend had continued through the ages. In particular, our foremothers usually survived their husbands to live well past that proverbial age. Of the generations closer to us, my great-great-grandmother reached the age of seventy-eight. My great-grandfather died at seventy-four, his wife several decades later at ninety-six. My grandfather lived until sixty-eight, my grandmother until eighty.

More than a sign of good heredity, longevity was in our beliefs a favor bestowed by Heaven. To generations of ours anxious for the arrival of a son, that belief had brought comfort and hope. A family deserving of such favor, they thought, must surely be able to overcome its problems and survive.

I remember, since a child, having heard about another trait in our family. Elders never sat down to tell the children about it the way they did with other stories of the past. They only touched upon it in their conversations, with an air of mystery in which one could detect apprehension, but also pride. In almost every generation, it was said, "We have had people going to far away lands, wherefrom many failed to return." The "going away" could be traced, like many of our family's traits and traditions, back to the sixteenth century and to Ancestor Nguyen Uyen. A mandarin, Nguyen Uyen was sent to Thai Nguyen and Cao Bang in the mountainous region of the north. That remote region was looked upon with fear by Delta people, for few who went up there could escape from either the attentions of rebels and bandits or the effects of an unhealthy climate. However, Nguyen Uyen survived his stay in the mountains. Later in his life, our people recalled that he was called upon to undertake "a hazardous journey to a place far away," but no details about the place or the journey were remembered. I found in ancient history books that Nguyen Uyen went in a tribute mission to China in 1580, when he must have been close to seventy. Not only was this an arduous journey for a man of his age, but also in the diplomatic circumstances of the time, our envoys did not know when, or even whether, the Chinese Court would let them go home. Nguyen Uyen came back. Calamity fell on the next two generations. With the change of dynasty, our family had to flee and stay away from Kim Bai. Of the head of the third generation, very little was known except that he had, at one point, been forced to live the life of a fugitive, "moving from place to place." Even his name was forgotten. And yet, as I was to discover, he was a titled mandarin holding a high position at the Mac court. But, like his grandfather, he became the victim of political changes and such was the traumatic effect on our family that later generations forgot completely about him. His son also appeared to have been kept away for a very long time from his native place. However, he came back and died there. In the eighteenth and nineteenth centuries, adverse economic conditions forced many of our kinsmen to leave their village and find means of subsistence elsewhere. The chronicle simply noted that "they went away and their trace was lost."

The tradition of "going away" has continued with the present generations. In the late 1920s, my father went to France to further his studies. On the same trip was a student friend, the son of a colleague of grandfather, from our own province of Ha Dong. After two years, the friend contracted tuberculosis and died in Paris. This unfortunate accident should have had nothing to do with my father's stay abroad. But the news came as a profound shock to our family. It revived the centuries-old apprehension about people going away and failing to return, especially with my father being the eldest son. Grandfather, who had visited France, tried to make the family take an objective view of the matter, but great-grandmother would not listen. She refused to take any food until orders were given for my father to immediately stop his studies and take the next ship home. Those of our people who went away did so for a variety of reasons. But whatever the apparent reasons, I believe there must have been a strong desire to venture beyond the familiar setting of their lives. The call of distant lands seemed to have cast its spell on them. I myself came under it. Although attached to my ancestral land, I felt the intense need to move out of it and widen my horizons. After finishing high school in 1950, I asked my parents to send me to Paris for university studies. They wanted me to go, but finance was a problem. They had lost nearly everything in the war and were trying to rebuild the family's assets. Already with seven children to provide for, it would not be easy for them to carry the additional expenses of supporting my stay abroad. Furthermore, as my father was the head of his branch, his duty was to help other family members. Just at that moment, my grand-mother escaped from the communist zone and joined us in Hanoi. Without any hesitation, she said firmly that I should go. "Every generation of ours had people going afar," she invoked family tradition. "Since he shows good promise of succeeding in his studies, it is right that we should send him to France." As for the financial commitment, she expressed her confidence that everything would turn out right, but quoting this commonly used proverb:

The Lord in Heaven created elephants,
He also created enough grass to feed them.

The tradition of going afar revealed an adventurous and daring side of our character, which was perhaps the counterpart to our cautiousness and conservatism. Time and again in recent generations, our family has shown a willingness to pioneer new ways and take up formidable chal-lenges. Early in the nineteenth century, my great-great-grandfather Nguyen Quang So was the first Nguyen of Kim Bai to engage in wholesale trade and he chose to break new grounds by cooperating with Chinese mer-chants and by pursuing his activities abroad as well as in the south of the country. Vietnamese had traded with Chinese for a long time, although rarely as partners. Our ancestor joined hands with them in what would now be called joint ventures. The south was a comparatively new field for trade, but he saw the vast opportunities it offered. On both grounds, he achieved considerable succes. As we know, he lost his life in the south. In 1904, my great-uncle Nguyen Tam Tiep left home and country as a young man of sixteen to fight against French domination. France was then a great world power. He certainly knew that the fight against colonial rule was an uphill battle and that what lay ahead for him were long years of hardship in exile. He left, not to return. Thirty-one years ago in 1960, my eldest brother Nguyen Trieu Hong led a military coup against the Ngo Dinh Diem re-gime. South Vietnam was fighting against communist aggression from the north, the threat to its survival was becoming more and more acute; yet the regime could not command popular support. My brother, a colonel in the army, tried to bring about a change. But Fate took a hand. He was killed in the first hour of the uprising while inspecting his troops on the battle-field.

"Men scheme their endeavours, Heaven decides of their success," says a traditional precept. These elders of ours did what they thought they must, however difficult the challenge and even at the risk of their lives.

13. The Continuing Search

To praise the efforts made by his father and grandfather to delve further into our ancestry, my grandfather used the term *quang tien,* which means throwing light on the past. According to Confucian ethics, a pious son should uphold the virtues and merits of his ancestors; to do so he must strive to learn about them. The philosopher Tsang, an eminent disciple of Confucius, called that duty *truy vien,* a term which can be translated as both to remember one's distant ancestry and also to search into it. My grandfather had left us the chronicle. My father, after he returned to Hanoi in 1947 during the war, searched patiently through the largely destroyed government archives to piece together his father's career. Their examples were before my eyes; yet, it would be a long time before the "source in the far mountains" which my grandfather alluded to in the chronicle, would beckon to me.

At first, the chronicle was a precious book given me for safekeeping. After my grandfather died, it became a treasured relic. Each time I looked at it, the image of him sitting in his study in the ancestral home teaching me how to write Chinese characters came back to mind. I knew the content of the chronicle; more correctly, I had read it a few times. Then, I went abroad for my studies and stayed there to pursue my career, coming back to the country only for short stays. For years, I did not see the chronicle. When once again it was given to me for safekeeping, this time by my father, I was already in my late thirties. I took it with me abroad. Reading it again after a gap of some twenty years, I was surprised to find it so concise and brief. I told myself that I should put down in writing all that I knew about our history. I should get in touch with elders to learn more from them and to transmit their knowledge to younger generations. The presence of the chronicle seemed to urge me on. Our family had lost its ancient documents, but I could search in history books for information about those of our forefathers who had achieved high positions and honors. Grandfather's chronicle started with two particularly successful generations. In the old days, a graduate of the doctorate brought fame to his family and to his entire village. Two brothers graduating at the same time was the material of which legends were made. But that was not all. In the next generation, another doctor followed in the footsteps of Nguyen Huyen and Nguyen

Tue. Could such results have come to our family, all of a sudden? Just as a tree needed time to take roots and come to fruition, I believed that our tradition of scholarship must have been cultivated long before. Earlier ancestors of ours, now forgotten, must have been scholars with academic titles.

If the cycle of rise and decline held true, our family should have known an earlier period of prosperity, some two or three centuries before the brothers. I would place that period either under the Ly (1010–1225) or the Tran (1225–1400), two of Vietnam's most powerful and glorious dynasties. The Ly were strong enough to even attack China, their troops going into Guangdong and Guangxi provinces in 1075. Under the Tran, our people became the only ones in mainland Asia to defeat the Mongol invaders. In a space of four years (1284–1288), Kublai Khan's army was decisively beaten by the Vietnamese, not once but twice. During the Ly and Tran dynasties, our national territory extended to the south at the expense of the Kingdom of Champa. Several military expeditions were sent there and against Laos in the west. That period was also one of the most creative in the arts. Classical prose and poetry blossomed in what could be considered a Vietnamese equivalent of the great Tang era in China. Learning and scholarship prospered. The first literary works written in the everyday language of the people appeared. Those were times of great opportunity for men of talent and ambition. Perhaps my own forefathers were among the many who had distinguished themselves and gained a mention in the nation's history books. Perhaps, their names were there, in those books, waiting for a descendant to discover them.

The first documents I directed my attention to were the registers of high graduates. Historical records are sadly lacking in our country, but fortunately those on the holders of the doctorate are not. All the names of doctors since the first examination in 1075 have been preserved. I knew of at least two complete registers, both published in the latter part of the eighteenth century, one by Nguyen Hoan called the *Dai Viet Register of High Graduates*—in which my grandfather found the link with our first ancestor Nguyen Tue—and the other by Phan Huy On entitled the *Southern Sky Register of High Graduates*. Besides the names, the registers contain short biographies of the graduates and therein lies their interest because Vietnamese names, by themselves, do not give any precise indication on family relationship. All the Nguyen, or the Tran, or the Le are not related. The village where a graduate came from and some details about his career are needed to ascertain his origin. However, the problem with both registers was that they were not readily accessible, as only a small number of copies existed in the country. Also, they were written in the old scholarly language, which I could only read with great difficulty. We were then in the 1960s.

In that decade, ancient books started to be translated into the modern language. I learned that a translation of Nguyen Hoan's compilation was available in Saigon. But then, the war intensified in Vietnam while prolonged peace talks, in which I was involved, took place in Paris. I had no time to devote to family genealogies. I only returned to my quest more than ten years after the war had ended and my family had taken refuge in Australia. On a visit to Paris and following a laborious search in libraries there, I finally had the two translated volumes of the *Dai Viet Register* in my hands, one morning in 1986. With some trepidation, I looked for the doctorate session of 1511, the year of the two brothers' success. As their names appeared in front of me, I could imagine how my grandfather felt three quarters of a century ago. The information he was looking for was there before him, and it could not have been clearer or more precise. "Nguyen Tue," it was written, "was Nguyen Uyen's father and Nguyen Huyen's elder brother. Father and son, elder and younger brothers, all graduated." It was as if the author had written it specifically for the benefit of our family, knowing that one day, we would search for it in his book. "No further doubt can be entertained!" exclaimed my grandfather. People were skeptical, some even critical, of his endeavor to establish the identity of the brothers. But he was proved right and, of course, by his time the old antagonism toward the Mac dynasty belonged to history. I could feel his excitement and joy. Now, I was following in his footsteps and trying to find in the same book some clues to our earlier ancestry. Starting from the 1511 examination, I went further back in time and carefully read through lists of doctors. Names from the prefecture of Thanh Oai appeared frequently, underlining the prominent position held by our region in the field of letters. I recognized villages close to ours and which I knew well. Where were the descendants of doctors who became high mandarins, I wondered, for in several of those villages, there were no large ancestral homes, no imposing gates, no vestiges which recalled the prosperous times of old. Slowly, I came to the first doctorate session ever to be held in Vietnam, in 1075 under the Ly dynasty. Disappointedly, I found that there were no Nguyen of Kim Bai among the lists of doctors.

Going back to 1511, I then moved down to more recent years and was not looking for any particular information, when came an unexpected windfall. Nguyen Tue, his brother Nguyen Huyen and his son Nguyen Uyen were thought to be our only high graduates. To my surprise, another Nguyen of Kim Bai appeared in the register, whom I think must be Nguyen Uyen's son and the forgotten head of our third generation. "Nguyen Hoang," as the register made clear "hailed from the village of Kim Bai in the prefecture of Thanh Oai. He graduated (in 1571) at the age of thirty-eight."

The following year—1987—on another visit to Paris, I obtained a microfilm of the *Southern Sky Register* in the old scholarly language. I found in it valuable information which helped me reconstruct the careers of our first three ancestors, but this book confirmed what I had learned from the other register, that there were no Nguyen of Kim Bai on the golden board of the doctorate before 1511. The brothers were, indeed, the first doctors ever to come from our family, or our village. Could our earlier people be holders of the lower diplomas of baccalaureate or licentiate? I have no way to know, having not come across any register for such diplomas.

Next, I turned to history books. After the Ly and Tran dynastic periods, however, very few records were left. The Tran dynasty was followed by years of instability which led to Vietnam falling under Chinese domination in 1414. That domination lasted only thirteen years, but proved disastrous for our historical records and literary treasures, nearly all of which were either destroyed or taken to China by the occupants. All the history books that we have today were written after that fateful period. Of the two major works on Vietnam's history, *History of Dai Viet* was written in 1479 and *Mirror of Vietnam's History* much later, in 1884. Both works are, as far as those early dynasties are concerned, fairly general and basic. I was not able to find anything about earlier generations of our family in the first work. As for the second, I have only succeeded in consulting a few chapters. So far, my quest has proved fruitless. But it will continue. There are still many documents which I know exist, but have not been able to lay my hands on. Others I do not know about must be held in archives and libraries. It is said that of the lost records of the Ly and Tran dynasties, some are still kept in China, while others have found their way to Japan. I am confident that, in the coming years, we would stand a better chance of retracing an earlier phase of our family history.

Three legends held the keys of our village's past: the Two Nguyen Brothers, the Mountain of the Twins and the name Kim Bai. The first legend helped my grandfather trace the roots of our family back to the fifteenth century. The Twins in the second legend predicted the brothers' concurrent success at the examinations and following grandfather's discovery, the Mountain of the Twins also became associated with our family. Our own history seemed to merge into our village's. The third legend remains unexplained. When and how was the name Kim Bai taken? Would the same link be found there with our family?

We know that the name Kim Bai existed before the eleventh century as well as the Ly dynasty. It was believed to date from a golden period in the village's history, when its citizens held high mandarinal positions. Could these citizens be our own ancestors?

Nguyen, our family name, is the most common name in Vietnam. Millions of people are Nguyen, who may not be at all related. Among them, a distinction can be made between those families which have always had that name and others which had changed theirs to Nguyen. After taking power from the Ly in 1225, the Tran killed all members of the royal family; moreover, in order to eradicate from the people's minds the name of a dynasty which had stayed on the throne for over two hundred years, the new rulers ordered all the Ly in the country who were not related to the fallen dynasty to drop their name and become Nguyen. A sizeable part of the population thus joined the mass of Nguyen, making it by far the largest group of Vietnamese sharing the same family name.

We are not original Nguyen. I had always thought that our ancestors were Ly who changed into Nguyen in the thirteenth century, until my father told me, one day as we discussed about the family's origins: "I heard that our original name was not Ly, but Le." I was taken aback. I could understand that having been Ly, we were forced to become Nguyen by edict of the Tran dynasty. But if we were Le, why did we have to change? What made us do so, and when? My father offered no explanation. "It must have happened very long ago," he said. "The reasons for the change have been forgotten, inevitably so."

Indeed, the earliest ancestor whom we know was already a Nguyen. He was Nguyen Tue, born in the latter part of the fifteenth century. The change of name had occurred before him and, probably, in times very far away for I can find no tradition or belief handed down within our family which gave an explanation for it. But it puzzled me that our forefathers had taken such a step. Vietnamese do not change their surname, unless for very compelling reasons. The family, in the sense of an entity over the generations, has a sacred character in our system of ancestor worship. Each generation has the duty to uphold the family name and pass it on to the next.

There may be strong private reasons to change one's name, such as in the old days when a guardian considered a ward as his own son and gave him his name, and the ward accepted it as a sign of gratitude. The same thing may happen between an aged master and the favorite disciple who was going to succeed him. Rich and powerful men with no male heir may leave their name and their properties to a son-in-law. I do not believe that any such private reasons could have motivated our ancestors, for we have always been a proud, independent and rather conservative Confucian family. In the annals of all dynasties can be found instances of high mandarins who were "allowed" by the king to take the royal family name as a reward for their particularly meritorious services. However, no Nguyen dynasty existed before the fifteenth century and therefore, such a signal honor was not the cause for us being Nguyen. On the other hand, an ignominious punishment could be meted out to members of the royal family who had committed serious offenses; they were stripped of their royal name and forced to take a "common people's name." Fortunately, this also did not seem to have been the case for our family. Our first ancestor Nguyen Tue graduated and became a mandarin under the Le in 1511, less than a century after that dynasty came to power. In those times, strict checks were made on the candidates' antecedents and Nguyen Tue would not have been allowed to sit for the public service examinations if his close forebears had done something very wrong and been obliged to change their name from Le to Nguyen.

I believe that we have been Nguyen since long before Nguyen Tue's time and that only very compelling political reasons would have made us change our family name. Vietnam's history has been marked by periods of violent turmoil, especially at the change of dynasties. Those in the service of the fallen dynasty had to flee with their families to escape persecution and death. Our family had known one such period at the end of the sixteenth century, following the collapse of the Mac dynasty. Then, our name was preserved, but it was concealed. Eventually, even his own descendants could not remember what the personal name of the head of our third generation was. It was quite possible that, in an earlier crisis, our family was faced with an even greater danger and the name had had to be changed as a means to ensure the family's survival.

In the tenth century, the Vietnamese wrested their independence from the Chinese. The first dynasty was that of the Ngo, whose founder Ngo Quyen annihilated the Chinese in the battle of the Bach Dang River (938). Upon learning of this defeat, the King of the Southern Han was said to have burst out crying and decided to withdraw all his forces from Vietnam. Ngo Quyen ascended the throne in 939. At the time, the country's borders did not extend very far to the south and the king's rule was confined to the Red River delta and parts of the highlands to the north and the west. Thanh Oai, our region, was then one of the centers of power with its populous villages and fertile land spreading out from the banks of the Hat River. The hills and mountains in the west and a large marshy area in the south provided good cover for defense as well as places to retreat to in case of an emergency. The Ngo did not stay in power for long. Ngo Quyen died in 944. Soon after, numerous warlords set themselves up in different parts of the country. One of the best-known generals of the Ngo dynasty, Do Canh Thac, seized our region and built his capital at a place about five kilometers from our village. The ruins of his citadel can still be seen today. In 965, the country was divided into twelve principalities and the warlords were fighting against one another for the throne of the Ngo. The two main contenders amongst them were Do Canh Thac and a young warlord named Dinh Bo Linh. In 967, Dinh Bo Linh vanquished his rival, rallied to him the rest of the warlords and became the first king of the Dinh dynasty. He ruled until 979 when he was assassinated. The son who succeeded him was only six. On hearing this, the Sung dynasty in China sought to take advantage of the situation and sent an army to reconquer Vietnam. Before they set out to meet the foreign threat, the Vietnamese troops elevated their commander-in-chief to the throne, replacing the child-king. The general from the Le family, by the name of Le Hoan, defeated the Sung invasion and established the Le dynasty in 980. History books referred to his dynasty as the Earlier Le, to distinguish it from the Later Le who came to power in the fifteenth century.

Mindful of the risk of warlords challenging his rule, the Le king sent his twelve sons to take up residence in key areas of the country. In 993, his eighth son Tuong was given the title of prince and sent to our region. For sixteen years, until the end of the Le dynasty, he was our local ruler. Did our ancestors then have the family name of Le? Could they be related to Tuong or be part of that prince's entourage? Did our village receive the name Kim Bai during that period? Tuong proved himself to be no military leader; history books recorded that in 997, bandits plagued his fief and his father, the king, had to personally lead his troops in to restore peace and order. When the king died in 1005, six of his sons fought for the throne and three of them were killed. Tuong kept out of the struggle. It is not known what happened to him at the end of the Le dynasty in 1009. But if the answers to the above questions were affirmative and our ancestors were associated in some ways with Tuong, they would certainly have to flee to escape retribution from the new ruler. The lives of many people were affected by the upheaval and that was shown in an edict proclaimed by the new Ly king in 1010, ordering "all those who went into hiding to return to their villages." Probably, our ancestors were among those who stayed in their place of refuge for a long time. In the sixteenth century, our family's tribulations continued over more than a decade. Five centuries earlier, either they might have lasted longer or the danger must have been more pressing, for our ancestors to be driven to take the radical step of changing the family name.

As with the preceding generations, mine and those which follow will seek to throw more light on the past, to use the term that my grandfather wrote in the chronicle. The source in the mountains will be there to beckon them. The search, the conjectures, and the dreams will continue. But for the moment, let us put on record what we know about our family history. Here is the chronicle of the Nguyen of Kim Bai.

III / The Nguyen
of Kim Bai

14. First Generation—
The Count of Hung Giao

The following was written in the chronicle:

> The ancestor of our first generation was named Nguyen Tue. He obtained the doctorate third class in the year of the Goat, which was the third year of the Hong Thuan era under the Le dynasty. He served in the mandarinate, reached the office of minister under the Mac dynasty and on him was conferred the title of count. Of his wife, nothing is known.

The term "first generation" used here does not mean that Nguyen Tue was considered as the founder of our family. He was only the earliest ancestor known to us. Eighty years ago, before my grandfather established the relationship with him, our knowledge did not reach up to Nguyen Tue and our "first ancestor" was his son Nguyen Uyen.

The third year of the Hong Thuan era, when our ancestor graduated, was 1511 in the western calendar. On ascending the throne, a Vietnamese king chose for his reign a title, primarily so that the country could use it to count the years of his rule but, naturally, the name chosen also expressed the king's aspiration as to what his reign would be. King Le Tuong Duc took the dynastic title of Hong Thuan, which means Great Harmony. However, there was in his case a wide gap between aspiration and reality, for he started by killing his first cousin to appropriate the throne and would end up by being assassinated by one of his generals. By the beginning of the Hong Thuan era, the Le dynasty had been in decline for some time. It would not be long before it was displaced by the Mac family and Nguyen Tue himself was involved in one of the most controversial periods of Vietnamese history. Although we do not know when Nguyen Tue was born, the fact that he became a doctor in 1511 gave us an indication about his age. A petition submitted by a mandarin to the king in 1509 addressed the problem of "students under thirty with less than fifteen years of study . . . who have only passed a number of subjects in the doctorate examination" (and therefore have not obtained the degree). It went on: "If by luck they were made mandarins, a regrettable confusion would be created." From this opposition to people under thirty and not full doctors joining the mandarinate, we can deduce that most graduates at that time were thirty or over. Let us, therefore, say that our ancestor obtained the degree when in his thirties; in other words, he was born around 1475.

The doctorate was the highest degree in the examination system. It was not just an examination but a nationwide competition, held once every three years in the capital to recruit a limited number of mandarins. Candidates were required to have successfully gone through a regional competition. Historical records did not specify how many people sat for the 1511 examination, but they gave for previous sessions a number of candidates averaging five thousand. As forty-seven graduated in 1511, the success rate was in the order of one per cent. The examination comprised two stages, of which the first one called *Hoi* was eliminatory. By tradition, the *Hoi* took place in spring and its association with the season of hope and promise was not lost on the candidates. They knew that this was their chance to become part of the elite and play an active role in public affairs. They may even, one day, be in a position to realize a dream close to the heart of every Vietnamese, which was to render prominent services to the country, take a hand in its destiny, and in the words of the poet, "make their names known to the rivers and mountains." Such a chance came but rarely; at the earliest once every three years, but if conflict or troubles affected the country, the wait could be longer. Few of the thousands of candidates would be among the chosen. Doctors formed a very small and privileged group.

Of the duties of a king, Confucian ethics laid great stress on the choice of good and wise men to help him govern the country. A doctorate session was, therefore, an event of national importance recorded in detail by historians. The examination grounds were located in the southern quarter of the capital, now Hanoi. In my childhood, the grounds had been transformed into a residential quarter full of elegant bungalows for French colons and professional Vietnamese. But in former times, it was just a flat open camp in the shape of a huge rectangle, surrounded on all sides by three rows of hedge and a ditch planted with bamboo stakes. Security was very tight to prevent any contact between candidates and the outside world, and the grounds were protected like a military camp. There were no permanent buildings; at the approach of the examination, bamboo cottages were erected to serve as administrative offices. Most of the spacious grounds remained bare; on examination day, each candidate was assigned a place to set up a small canvas tent where he stayed to write his essays.

Candidates sat for a total of four subjects. In the first, called commentaries on Confucian classics, they had to write no less than eight essays on topics taken from the Four Books and the Five Canons, each essay to be of three hundred Chinese characters or more. In the second, they were required to draft a series of administrative documents, including three royal proclamations in the style of the Chinese Han dynasty, three royal decrees and three submissions to the king in the style of the Tang period in China. The third subject was composition of poems in the Tang style and literary essays in classical Chinese style. The last and most important subject was a dissertation on a theme chosen from ancient books or from history. This had to be of one thousand characters or more and was designed to test the candidates' general knowledge and judgment.

The scholars' training was based on Confucian texts and on commentaries made by ancient Chinese masters. At the examination, they must keep closely to those texts and commentaries. Any personal idea or interpretation could destroy their chances, for examiners would not countenance it. Even the style that a candidate used to write his papers must not be his own, but that of a given Chinese classical period. With such a training and examination system, it was not surprising that the country had an essentially conservative mandarinal corps, which modelled its art of government and behavior in public life on ancient Chinese precedents. These precedents were constantly referred to in submissions, statements and edicts. For instance, here is an extract from an order to the troops, exhorting them to the greatest sacrifice and issued by Marshal Tran Quoc Tuan at the time of the Mongol invasion in the thirteenth century. The order is considered as one of the most eloquent expressions of the Vietnamese spirit of independence; yet it began by a string of allusions to the deeds of heroes, not our own but those in ancient China:

> I have heard: Ji Xin risked his life to save that of the Han Emperor, Shen Yu exposed his back to spears to shelter the Prince of Zhao, Yu Rang swallowed live coal to avenge his master, Shen Kuai cut off his arm and died for his country. Jing De was a petty officer, yet he braved death to save Emperor Tang Tai Zong from enemy encirclement. Kieu Qing was a mandarin in a place far away from the capital, yet he publicly branded Lu Shan as a rebel. From antiquity to our times, which period did not have righteous men and loyal subjects willing to give their lives to the nation? If those people had clung to common attitudes and petty calculations, they would have died of old age in a corner of their homes, their names would not have been written in history books and remained there, for thousands of generations to see.

Nguyen Tue sat for the same doctorate examination as his younger brother Nguyen Huyen. Both went throught the *Hoi* stage, which means that they not only passed all four subjects but were also among the forty-seven with the highest marks. They were now assured of being made doctors, for the second stage was not eliminatory but served only to rank successful candidates. This stage was called the *Dinh* or Royal Courtyard, as it was held in the courtyard in front of the Hall of the Throne. There the candiates sat and wrote their papers. A stele erected in the Temple of Literature gave this account of the Royal Courtyard examination of the year of the Goat. It was the fourth lunar month, on the fifteenth, the auspicious day of the full moon:

His Majesty set as subject for the examination the principles of government from antiquity to our times. He appointed the Duke of Thieu, Great Teacher, as governor of the session, the Minister of Works as director, the Deputy Ministers of Finance and Public Service as inspectors and hundreds of mandarins to other tasks. The next morning, the candidates' papers were read aloud to His Majesty by the Minister for the Rites and the Head of the Censorate.... After having listened to the reading, His Majesty read the papers a second time before deciding on their ranks.

I have abstained from quoting in full the names and titles of the officials, which were quite long. The title of the Duke of Thieu, Great Teacher, ran over no less than forty words. As we can see, the examination was an event of special importance. The role of the king was stressed at the outset; he chose the examination topic and marked the papers after having twice acquainted himself with their contents. The panel was headed by the Great Teacher, a title held by the premier mandarin of the kingdom. More than half of the ministries, which numbered six, were represented on the panel with two ministers and two deputy ministers. Rites and protocol underlined the solemnity of the occasion. For candidates to write their papers in the Royal Courtyard was a special honor, even a kind of initiation as only high mandarins of the Son of Heaven were admitted there. In colloquial Vietnamese, doctors were called *nghe, nghe* being an office in the Royal Palace and a symbol of their position in the power structure. They formed a prestigious elite, all the more so because entry to their group was extremely difficult and restricted. In Nguyen Tue's time, less than fifty scholars in the whole country were made doctors, every three years. Talent alone would not suffice. Luck naturally played its role, but popular beliefs attributed a doctor's success to something special in his destiny, which made him the chosen one to receive a favor from Heaven.

Mandarins on the panel bore a heavy responsibility. The role of the monarch was formal and symbolic. Among the Le kings, only Le Thanh Ton, who ruled for thirty-seven years from 1460 to 1497 and was himself a renowned scholar and poet, took an effective part in the conduction of doctorate examinations. In 1511, King Le Tuong Duc was a young man of nineteen, in his third year on the throne. The real decision rested with the mandarins whose names and titles were recorded for posterity in full and who, therefore, were expected to exercise the greatest vigilance and care. In a way, the future of the country depended on them selecting the "right" people, who in our culture were men not so much of talent and knowledge as endowed with virtue and the intangible quality of wisdom. Candidates were thoroughly checked on their antecedents, moral character and any other aspects of their personality which could make them unfit for public office. Maturity of judgment was a main consideration and it could easily happen that a person was failed just because he was considered still too young. Recommendations made by panels may run something like this: A bright talent but too young, it would be better for him to wait and graduate at the next session.

The account on the stele continued:

> On the fourth day of the fifth month, His Majesty went to the Palace of Kinh Thien. Officials using trumpet loudspeakers announced the names of the new doctors. The assembly of mandarins in full Court apparel attended the graduation ceremony. On His Majesty's orders, officials of the Ministry of Public Service gave to the doctors their diplomas. Officials of the Ministry for the Rites brought out the golden board and hung it in front of the Palace of High Learning. The king also gave ceremonial dresses, hats, belts and a banquet to the doctors. The function to honour these good and wise subjects was very solemn indeed.

The forty-seven successful candidates were grouped in three classes. The doctorate first class was awarded to the top three graduates, each of whom received a prestigious title inherited from ancient times in China, *Trang Nguyen* or First Laureate, *Bang Nhan* or The Eye of the Honor List for the second and *Tham Hoa,* a delightfully poetical title meaning Searching Among the Blossoms for the third man. In the banquet given by the Tang Emperor to the graduates, the custom was for the two youngest doctors to be sent to the apricot garden to pick the most beautiful blossoms. The third man's title derived from that custom. Our ancestors Nguyen Tue and Nguyen Huyen did not obtain those coveted titles. As a matter of fact, none in our family ever did and even our village could not boast of ever having a doctor first class, in spite of its long tradition of scholarship. Nine graduates of that session were given the doctorate second class and thirty-five the doctorate third class. The two Nguyen brothers belonged to the last group.

On the golden board mentioned above, the new graduates' names were written in black ink over a background painted the color of gold. Before being treated to a banquet, the new doctors were given the honor of visiting the royal gardens. Like the other guests at the banquet, the Nguyen brothers only ate just enough of the food offered to them that good manners required. They kept the rest aside to bring home for parents and relatives. They would do the same during their mandarinal career, each time they had the honor to be called to a royal banquet. For the food given by a king was something special which a person must not eat all by himself. It must be saved to be shared, firstly with one's parents, then with other members of the family.

All those ceremonies recorded by the official historian took place in the capital. Now came a celebration deeply imprinted in the popular mind and so often sung by folklore, the Triumphal Return of the new doctor to his home village. Following the examination results, official messengers were despatched to bring the news to the places where graduates hailed from. Welcoming ceremonies were prepared. The Nguyen brothers already had been given a taste of triumphal return after they won the regional competition, on their way to the doctorate. As licentiates holding a higher degree, they were welcomed home by more notables and more people, those from all villages forming our canton of Phuong Trung. Now that they were doctors effecting their Triumphal Return, they were greeted not only by their village and canton, but also by the entire prefecture of Thanh Oai. On the appointed day, the prefect of Thanh Oai and his officials, notables from villages in the prefecture and, of course, the local population of several thousand people turned out to meet the brothers on their return from the capital. A new doctor going home was already an extraordinary event; the spectacle of two doctors in the same procession would be seen only once in a lifetime, in fact it would remain unique in the history of our region. As a mark of respect, the welcoming party did not wait at our village's gate but went to the boundary of the prefecture, some miles away from Kim Bai. Upon the new graduates' arrival, a cortege was formed and the triumphal march home began. Nguyen Tue and Nguyen Huyen, riding on horseback and preceded by flags and banners announcing their ranks, were each shaded by two parasols painted gold. Their parents, teachers and wives followed, each sitting in an open palanquin shaded by a parasol.

The cortege went to the Nguyen's Ancestral Shrine for the doctors to report their achievements to our Original Ancestor, then to our ancestral home for them to kneel and pray before our ancestors' altar. Oxen and pigs were killed to make offerings to the village's deities. A feast was prepared for officials and village folks. Festivities lasted several days. Although expenses were heavy on our family, they were a must, for village rules were quite explicit: the recipient of a new honor or diploma must declare it to the village community by means of a religious service at the Communal Hall followed by a feast, otherwise the village would not recognize it, even though it may have been the highest diploma of the kingdom or a very high honor bestowed by the king. Such was the autonomy traditionally enjoyed by Vietnamese villages. A poor graduate might have to postpone the celebrations until he had the means; in the meantime, he continued to be treated by village folks as if he held no diploma.

The honor conferred on a doctor extended to his village. From then on, he would not be called by his name, but by his title followed by the village's name. Both Nguyen Huyen and Nguyen Tue would be known as The Doctor of Kim Bai. Our village in that year of the Goat must have believed itself blessed by Heaven. It had not just a holder of the doctorate, but two. And what about the family having them as sons? The brothers became legendary figures. A saying to praise their academic prowess has been handed down among villagers until today:

Nguyen Huyen, Nguyen Tue,
The two brothers.
At the same session,
They won the golden board.

The Triumphal Return did not mark the end of ceremonies. The year of the Goat session was the first doctorate examination in King Le Tuong Duc's reign. "His Majesty believes," it was recorded on the stele, "that talent and wisdom are the lifeblood of the nation and should be constantly nurtured." Following the session, therefore, he appointed the second highest mandarin in the country, the Duke of Nghia, Great Guardian, to oversee the renovation of the Palace of High Learning, which was another name for the Temple of Literature, and the construction there of two new wings to house the doctors' stelae. Two years later, the king ordered that the new doctors be given the ultimate honor of having their names carved in stone and preserved for posterity in the seat of our nation's culture. The order was recorded in detail by the historian:

> His Majesty gave to the Duke of Uy, Minister of Works, the task of supervising the carving and erection of the slabs, the Minister for the Rites that of writing an introductory text, and high mandarins in the Central Secretariate that of being calligraphers.

The wings built in that time have since long gone. But under the shade of century-old trees, the stele bearing our ancestors' names can still be seen on the Temple grounds today. Preceding the honors list was an introductory text composed by the Minister for the Rites, exalting the merits of the Le kings and their enlightened way of encouraging scholarship. Addressing the new doctors, it gave them praise as well as a warning:

> Those scholars who have their names carved on this stone slab, how lucky they are! If they know how to prove themselves as loyal, honest and industrious subjects, then students of the future would point to their names in praise and seek to emulate them. But if they let their talents go to waste and behave like cowards who tie their own hands and know only to flatter, they would be the mockery of later generations.

Our family chronicle only briefly recorded that Nguyen Tue was a minister under the Mac dynasty and on him was conferred the *ba*, a title of nobility corresponding to that of count. I searched for more information about him in the history books written in this century, but they were only school textbooks containing few details. Nothing could be found there. I knew that I would have to consult earlier writings and, in particular, the two basic works on Vietnamese history, the *History of Dai Viet* and the *Mirror of Vietnam's History*. However, these were written in the old scholarly script and it was not before the early 1970s that I obtained a translation of the complete set of the *History of Dai Viet*. Having obtained it, I then put it away without looking at it. A full-scale war was taking place in South Vietnam, which was fighting for its survival against the communist North. The Paris Peace Talks had just ended, but instead of finding a peaceful solution to the Vietnamese conflict, they were followed by an all-out communist invasion. Left to itself, South Vietnam collapsed under the weight of the North Vietnamese army, armed and supplied by the communist bloc. Hundreds of thousands of Vietnamese had to flee their country to save their right to live as free men. Our family asked for asylum in Australia. Our first years here were extremely difficult. Only ten years after our arrival in Melbourne, did I find the time to read the *History of Dai Viet*, for the first time.

The *History* was compiled in the fifteenth century by Ngo Si Lien and added to in the seventeenth century by later historians. The part I was interested in was the Mac period and I found that the Mac did not have a history of their own. What we know about them was written by their enemy, the Le. Like all other Vietnamese dynasties, the Mac attached great importance to establishing their historical records, but when they lost the throne, all their records were destroyed. Those who wrote the Mac annals in the *History of Dai Viet* were mandarins of the Le and they wrote it in the seventeenth century, after the Le had been restored. They branded the Mac rule as illegitimate. Their work was biased and sketchy.

What happened was that by the start of the sixteenth century, a process of disintegration had started for the Le dynasty. Successive kings came to the throne at a young age and did not stay long. They could not come to grips with ruling the country. Power passed more and more into the hands of a military commander named Mac Dang Dung. In the sixth month of the year of the Pig (1527), the latter compelled King Le Cung Hoang to abdicate. I was reading the account in the *History of Dai Viet* of the seizure of power by Mac Dang Dung, the dramatic scene at the court where the Le mandarins deliberated whether or not to accept a new ruler, then the abdication and the pitiable death of the young Le king. After a few pages, I came to a passage starting with: "In the second month (of the year of the Rat [1528]), Dang Dung . . . promoted and conferred titles of nobility on fifty-six persons," and there followed a long list of names and titles. Among them, I read "Hung An ba Nguyen Tue" (Nguyen Tue, Count of Hung An) and was going on to the next name when suddenly, these words seemed to spring out at me and pull me back. I read once again. Then, I realized it. That was my ancestor. I felt as if, from a distant past, he had reached down to me. My heart beat faster with the joy of reunion.

The name attached to his title, Hung An, was not mentioned in any of our family documents. I later found out that it was not the correct one. As recorded by historian Le Quy Don, in a book published in the eighteenth century, the exact name was Hung Giao, a village close to ours and belonging to the same prefecture of Thanh Oai. The Mac dynasty observed the same rules of court protocol as those laid down by the former Le dynasty. Court precedence started with members of the royal family, then came the mandarins holding the following titles of nobility: *vuong, cong, hau, ba, tu, nam,* which could be translated as prince, duke, marquess, count, viscount and knight. The first title *vuong,* or prince, was normally conferred on princes of royal blood. Only in exceptional circumstances was it given to commoners, as its meaning was nearer to king than prince. It had happened that officials who performed outstanding services and received the title of *vuong* often began to think of themselves as royals and ended up by coveting the throne. Mac Dang Dung himself was made a *vuong* before he dethroned the Le king. Count was therefore the third highest title that a commoner could aspire to.

Protocol rules stated that those given a title of nobility would take a name to go with the title: "Dukes will take the prefecture's name, . . . marquesses and counts will take the village's name." Prefecture and village here did not mean their native place, for in that case our ancestor would have been called Count of Kim Bai, but the place where they were granted land. Under the Mac, ministers at the court like Nguyen Tue generally received the title of count. The higher titles of marquess or duke were mostly conferred on military commanders and on mandarins related to the royal family. Vietnamese titles of nobility were not hereditary. Sons of ennobled mandarins enjoyed certain privileges, such as being taught at special schools reserved for them and being admitted to the lower echelons of the civil service without holding a diploma, but they had to earn for themselves titles and honors. Throughout our history, there had never developed a stable and strong noble class which could act as a counter-weight to the absolute power of the king.

Nguyen Tue's career probably began before he obtained the doctorate. Winners of the regional competitions who became bachelors or licentiates, usually went into lower echelons of the mandarinate, then tried their luck with the higher diploma while pursuing their career. Some eventually graduated at a mature age, when already in the middle ranks of the administration. I believe that our ancestor came under that category, because when the Le fell from power sixteen years after his graduation, he was already among the top officials at the court. The mandarinate had nine grades, each divided into an upper and a lower echelon, or a total of eighteen rungs that a person had to climb to get to the top. Doctors, depending on the class they obtained at the examination, were appointed to functions ranking from the eighth grade to the sixth. Top graduates served in the capital, many of them going into the prestigious Academy. Those of the third class like Nguyen Tue and his brother would be made mandarins of the upper eighth class and sent to the prefectures. Following the customary career path of mandarins, they would work their way up from the prefectures to the regions, before being called to the center.

It is not known in what prefectures and regions Nguyen Tue served. His whole career was spent in troubled and unstable times. The Le dynasty, after an unprecedented period of stability and prosperity under the great king Le Thanh Ton, had entered a decline. Le Uy Muc ascended the throne in 1504 at the age of seventeen and turned out to be so cruel and bloodthirsty that he earned the nickname of Devil King. He killed his own grandmother for having opposed him being chosen to succeed his father. In 1509, he was killed by his cousin who became king at sixteen years of age. This king was a spendthrift who led a dissolute life devoted to wine and women. Rebellion and banditry broke out in many places. Support was needed from military commanders to keep the country under control and soon, it was they who controlled the country and the king. In 1516, the king was killed by a military commander. His successor, a fourteen-year-old boy, stayed on the throne for six years before being desposed by another commander. Those were difficult times for scholar-mandarins like Nguyen Tue, who were taught and trained in the Confucian classics. Their model was a stable, orderly society in which each and everyone knew where they stood and what was expected of them. When asked how the ship of state should be run, Confucius gave this simple answer: "A king should act like a king, a subject like a subject, a father like a father, a son like a son." By subject, he meant a mandarin in the service of the king. Now scholar-mandarins were faced with a confused and moving situation where the king did not behave as a king should, royal authority was not respected and those commanders who took power unto themselves certainly did not act like subjects of the king. They had to adapt and devise their own line of conduct instead of being able to rely on the teachings of saints and sages from ancient China.

Mac Dang Dung, the founder of the Mac dynasty, was a seventh-generation descendant of Mac Dinh Chi, a famous scholar and statesman living in the fourteenth century. A First Laureate at the doctorate examination, Mac Dinh Chi went in 1308 to China on a diplomatic mission and dazzled the Mongol court with his erudition and poetical talent. In the following generations however, as was the rule in our society where rise and decline often followed each other in quick succession, the Mac family became impoverished. Dang Dung earned his living as a fisherman before making his career in the army. When our ancestor obtained his doctorate, Dang Dung was an officer of high rank and a count. Ten years later, he was a duke and the commander-in-chief of all land and naval bases outside the capital. "His authority increased everyday, everyone looked up to him," noted the official historian. Mac Dang Dung began displaying the trappings of royalty. "Whenever he went out, he was shaded by goldplated parasols bearing representations of the phoenix; on the river, his boat pulled by footmen was built in the shape of a dragon. He went in and out of His Majesty's private chambers without any apprehension." King Le Chieu Ton saw the writing on the wall and plotted to get rid of Mac Dang Dung. Instead, he had to flee and his brother, a boy of sixteen, was put on the throne. The stage was set for the overthrow of the Le.

In 1527, when Mac Dang Dung made his move, our ancestor was serving at the court, in what capacity we do not know exactly, but considering the circumstances in which the new ruler made him a count, he must have been a viscount holding a deputy ministership or some equivalent post. He would be then in his early fifties. I found nothing in history books indicating that he belonged to the circle of Mac Dang Dung's followers, or that he was involved in any way in the many episodes which were to bring the Mac to power. It was clear that he was one of the mandarins who kept to their task of administering the country. But events would place him and his fellow mandarins before a choice, perhaps the most momentous that they would ever be called to make. They must decide whether to remain faithful to the Le king, or to transfer their allegiance to a new monarch. In the sixth lunar month of that year of the Pig, Mac Dang Dung left his seaside village of Co Trai, which he used as his headquarters, to return to the capital. He forced the young Le king, whom he himself had put on the throne five years before, to abdicate. Public opinion was favorable to him, as recorded in the *History of Dai Viet*: "At that time, mandarins and common people in the country all sided with Mac Dang Dung and welcomed him into the capital." When the mandarins assembled for the regular royal audience of the fifteenth day, the Le king had lost his throne but had not formally abdicated. The atmosphere of the audience, where the king was conspicuously absent, was dramatic. Mac Dang Dung was present, still bearing his title of Prince of An Hung, but power had already been gathered into his hands and the mandarins knew what he wanted. Some manifested their opposition in a violent manner; they shouted insults, even spat and threw ink slabs at him. Others refused to draft the proclamation of abdication when asked to do so. The majority of mandarins however, with our ancestor Nguyen Tue among them, acquiesced to the change of dynasty. Finally, a proclamation was drafted in the name of the Le king. "I am devoid of virtue and unable to carry the burden of state," said the proclamation. "Recognizing that the mandate of Heaven and the wishes of the population ... are in favour of Mac Dang Dung, Prince of An Hung, ... I bow to reason and cede him the throne." A few months later, the deposed king and his mother were forced to commit suicide.

Some comments need to be made on the attitude of the mandarins, a great many of whom went along with Mac Dang Dung's action. It would be easy to think that they had bowed to pressure in order to save their lives and positions. No doubt some had. But the true scholars among them were guided by other considerations. Central to Confucian teachings was the relationship between a subject—or mandarin—and his king, a relationship governed by two cardinal rules of conduct as far as the subject was concerned. The first rule expressed the duty of loyalty; it commanded that a loyal subject must not serve two kings. The second rule was a counterpart to the first and took into account the need for change. Taken from the teachings of Mencius, it stipulated that the king must come after the people and that the people's wishes were one with the mandate of Heaven. The duty of loyalty, therefore, could cease if the king had lost the support of his people.

It took great personal courage to oppose Mac Dang Dung and publicly taunt him; those mandarins who did so knew that they would pay with exile, or their own lives. Their conduct would be duly praised in history books. It required a different kind of courage to assess what the people's wishes were. Loyalty to the king was a paramount part of the "virtue" for which scholars were selected for public service. Individualistic appraisal was not an intellectual process encouraged by the highly formalistic education system. For those trained in the Western process of intellectual enquiry, it would be difficult to imagine the agony that a true scholar must have gone through before arriving at the decision that the mandate of the Le had ended and that the people needed a new ruler. Old mandarins like Nguyen Tue—who had passed fifty—would have found it easier to stay with the old dynasty than to opt for change, to retire than to cooperate with the new regime. But the country had suffered too long from instability and unrest. The people clearly saw in Mac Dang Dung a strong man capable of restoring peace and stability. I believe those reasons were instrumental in making our ancestor overcome the prohibitions against "serving two kings." Perhaps in Nguyen Tue, we can also recognize the daring and adventurous side of our family character, which had manifested itself forcefully in recent generations. By coming out in support of Mac Dang Dung against the estab-lished monarchy, he showed himself to be a revolutionary unafraid of change.

After elevating himself to the throne, Mac Dang Dung conferred titles and high positions upon his relatives and close followers, an action which went down badly with the public. He was expected to bring in a new and untainted regime, yet had shown favoritism and nepotism. As noted by the historian, "Everyone was disappointed, confusion developed in the country." Mac Dang Dung saw his mistake. He sent officials out to seek the support of the great mandarinal families and invite their descendants to cooperate with the new regime. He went as far as honoring some of the mandarins who had publicly opposed him. At the same time and in order to create a climate of continuity and normalcy, he decided to retain all the government structure, rules and regulations of the former dynasty. Several months later, a list of fifty-six people, who could be described as the new ruling group assembled by Mac Dang Dung, were given titles and promotions. As we have seen, Nguyen Tue was in that group. Twenty-two high mandarins in that group had their names recorded in history books and among them, only nine were known as longtime supporters of Mac Dang Dung. The majority, our ancestor included, were simply mandarins who opted to serve the new dynasty. Having been accused of favoritism, Mac Dang Dung took care this time to promote the mandarins only to the next higher grade and rank. Nguyen Tue became a count and therefore at the end of the Le, he must have already been a viscount, a title usually given to those holding the position of deputy minister.

Mac Dang Dung would be castigated by later historians as a rebel and usurper who killed the Le king to appropriate the throne. The *History of Dai Viet* called the Mac rule illegitimate and not worthy to be put on a par with rightful dynasties. As a consequence, the annals of the Mac were written in smaller characters and presented as an appendix to those of the Le, whom the Mac had overthrown. Historian Le Quy Don, writing in the eighteenth century, entitled his account of the Mac period: "The story of rebellious subjects." However, neither he nor those who wrote in the *History of Dai Viet* could lay claim to objectivity. They were all mandarins of the Restored Le. The *Mirror of Vietnam's History*, written in the nineteenth century under the Nguyen dynasty, continued to chastise the Mac for "having treacherously usurped power." But the Nguyen emperors also held a grudge; in the sixteenth century, their ancestor Nguyen Kim fought against the Mac and died from poisoning, allegedly at their hands. In the first half of this century, new history books appeared in the modern language with their authors following the line set by ancient texts. Tran Trong Kim, whose *Vietnamese History* became a standard school textbook, even called Mac Dang Dung a traitor to his country for having "capitulated" to China in an incident we shall discuss later. It was not before the 1950s that efforts were made to more objectively examine Mac Dang Dung's role and reappraise his place in history. After centuries of being vilified by partisan historians, the Mac dynasty has now been rehabilitated in authoritative works such as *A New Vietnamese History* by Pham Van Son and *A History of Vietnamese Literature* by Pham The Ngu.

The Le dynasty started its downward slide before Mac Dang Dung came to the scene. The rot set in with the Devil King, who came to the throne in 1504. The *History of Dai Viet* had the following commentary about him: "The population became resentful, the roots of turmoil were to be found there." Only a century before, the Le had come to power as the nation's saviors. Their founder, Le Loi, brought the Ming domination to an end after an armed struggle lasting ten years. His grandson, Le Thanh Ton, ruled for thirty-seven enlightened years (1460–1497), in what was remembered as a golden age in our history. Our ancestor Nguyen Tue spent his young and formative years during the reign of that great king. Le Thanh Ton came close to the model kings of ancient China whom Confucian scholars learned about in books; he was intelligent and wise, showed great filial piety towards his mother, chose good men to help him run the country and treated them with regard. Under him, scholarship flourished, the king himself being a prominent scholar and poet. He reorganized the public service, set up a new governmental and administrative structure which was to remain in place for the next several centuries. In 1483, all laws and regulations were assembled and codified in a single text called the Hong Duc code, the first legal code in Vietnam; among its many features was the recognition of women's rights, probably unequalled anywhere in the world at that time, such as the equal claim of daughters and sons to their parents' inheritance and the right of women to choose and divorce their husband. Agriculture developed; specialist mandarins were appointed to look after the country's dike system. Le Thanh Ton strengthened the army and sent it south to conquer the Kingdom of Champa and west to attack Laos, while keeping the borders with our giant neighbor to the north safe. In short, advances were made in every field of national endeavor under this enlightened scholar-king.

But Nguyen Tue's mandarinal career took place in a quite different climate. Le Thanh Ton's son was a good king but then a succession of bad kings brought the dynasty into disrepute. For over two decades, the country was in turmoil. The traditional scholar that Nguyen Tue was must have, at first, hoped that the Le would recover and a good and wise king would appear. Instead, conditions kept getting worse. The last two kings were kings only in name. Power rested with military commanders who were fighting among themselves. The people longed for peace, security and the rule of law, something which the Le family looked increasingly incapable of providing. Mac Dang Dung made his reputation as a pacifier and a champion of law and order. He suppressed, in the name of the Le king, several rebellions led by insurgents and insubordinate commanders. He built up a strong following, not only among warriors but also among scholars, who increasingly saw in him a strong leader able to pull the country out of its predicament. More and more, the population looked up to him. When he finally decided to take over the mantle from the Le, in 1527, it was a simple formality. As has already been quoted, from the *History of Dai Viet*, "mandarins and common people in the country all sided with Mac Dang Dung and welcomed him into the capital." The historian who wrote this was a mandarin of the Restored Le. Thus, for Nguyen Tue and many of his fellow scholars, the signs were clear: the people had suffered long enough, the time had come for a change.

Later historians who condemned the Mac rule as illegitimate also chose to ignore the fact that, with the end of the Le, our country had entered upon a confused period of division and conflict. From the sixteenth to the nineteenth century, Vietnamese fought among themselves for political power, more or less continually. No dynasty could rule the country long enough to lay an undisputed claim to legitimacy. A decade after the Mac took power in 1527, a movement to restore the Le took hold in the south and civil war started. In 1592, the Mac were defeated. The Le dynasty was restored, but while the Le king represented legitimacy, all power belonged to the Trinh overlord. This state of affairs led to a revolt by the Nguyen under a banner proclaiming "to destroy the Trinh and support the Le." For nearly two centuries, the country was divided again. War was fought between the Trinh in the north and the Nguyen in the south, both sides claiming to uphold the legitimacy of the Le. In the second half of the eighteenth century, from the Tay Son mountains in the center of the country rose a "hero in rough cloth"—a man of the people—who defeated both Nguyen and Trinh and became emperor under the name of Quang Trung. At the battle of Dong Da in 1789, Quang Trung annihilated a Chinese expeditionary force tens of thousands strong and put his name on one of the most glorious pages of our military history. But he died soon afterwards and, after only two generations in power, the Tay Son dynasty crumbled. In 1802, Emperor Gia Long, a descendant of the Nguyen overlord in the south, succeeded in unifying Vietnam under his rule. Division seemed to have come to an end. But it was not long before our country succumbed to pressure from European powers. France invaded and by 1884 had imposed its domination. With such a prolonged period of upheaval, the notion of legitimacy had lost its clarity. Everyone claimed it. Might decided it. Truly, it was a situation summed up by this proverb: "He who wins becomes the king, he who loses is branded as a bandit."

Our ancestor may have become a minister right from the beginning of the Mac dynasty, at the same time as he was made a count, for office and title usually went together. I believe that he served under two Mac kings, Dang Dung (1527–1530) and his son Dang Doanh (1530–1540). It was unlikely that he would have stayed in office after 1540, having reached by then the retirement age of sixty-five.

In the hierarchy of mandarinal titles, ministers ranked below the *Tam Thai* or Three Great Dignitaries—Great Teacher, Great Guardian, Great Protector—and the *Tam Thieu* or Three Great Dignitaries of second rank. These were exalted titles taken from ancient times in China which the king gave to a few elder statesmen. Great dignitaries, however, were only honorary titles without any specific function. A minister headed one of the six ministries which formed the executive arm of government. He held the lower second mandarinal grade and ranked above the heads of other institutions such as the Censorate, the Eastern Cabinet or the Academy.

Nguyen Tue, as I discovered in one of the registers of high graduates, "rose to the position of minister for the Rites." In the hierarchy of ministries, the Rites stood third, below Public Service and Finance, but above the Army, Justice and Public Works.

The ministry dealt with all matters relating to rituals, ceremonies, protocol, religion, education and examinations. In a society where each man must know his place and codes of behavior were to be strictly followed, rites played an essential role. Everyone knows the Confucian maxim: "Learn the rites first, the letters second." In addition, the ministry fixed the calendar and chose auspicious dates for the holding of sacrifices and royal audiences. It interpreted the meaning of unusual phenomena such as comets, shooting stars, solar eclipses, even hailstorms, all of which were dutifully recorded in history books. Other information found its way in there too, such as: "Snakes appeared for twenty days in the Co Xa River," or "On the seventeenth day, a red and yellow mass of air appeared in the east, and yellow air dispersed all over the sky." Today, such information would be considered as of no relevance to the life of the country. In the old times, they were harbingers of grave events to come, and the role of the Rites was to explain them and propose preventive measures. If the country was affected by persistent troubles, or if bad harvests occurred in successive years, the king would expect his minister for the Rites to advise him on what ceremonies to perform in order to the placate the anger of Heaven. The Rites, thus, had a quasi-religious function. Vietnamese monarchies were not theocracies; still, a minister for the Rites enjoyed high moral prestige. Usually, he was an elderly scholar, belonging to the mainstream of his class, and well respected by his peers. That Nguyen Tue held such a position convinced me that our family's tradition of scholarship must have gone back long before his time.

Our ancestor may have headed other ministries, but only the Rites was mentioned in his biography because it was the highest position he rose to. He might also have been appointed to other bodies at the court such as the Eastern Cabinet or the Academy. The practice then was not to keep anyone in the same office for longer than two years or so. Mandarins were frequently transferred in application of a Confucian principle which stated that "a gentleman should not be a specialist" and therefore should be called upon to accomplish all kinds of tasks. This was also a good way for the king to prevent his officials from becoming too entrenched in their positions and gaining too much power.

A minister at the court may be called upon to perform a wide range of activities. At the king's audience, all matters of state were discussed in the presence of the assembly of high mandarins, civil and military. The king could ask anyone for advice and assign any task to him. For their part, all mandarins may submit their opinions, even if the matter under discussion lay outside the scope of their own administration. Such was the rule, although the mandarins would often play it safe and stay silent. The great king Le Thanh Ton tried hard to change that attitude, without much success. He used to make bitter remarks about mandarins who "stood like wooden statues or as if they were made of clay. . ., did not discuss the way to rule the country, had neither commended a good man to their sovereign nor sent away a bad one." In 1487, he issued an order making it compulsory for all in the audience to participate in policy deliberations. The mandarins were divided into three groups. Censors and inspectors were in one group, ministers and those responsible for implementing policy decisions in another. The last group was composed of dukes, marquesses, counts and military commanders. The order specified that whenever a matter was raised by the king, each group "should give a clear opinion, should not shirk its responsibility by remaining silent, or staying vague and just trying to echo the others." Officials were appointed to report on those mandarins who did not obey the order. However the atmosphere at the new Mac court would have been different. The Mac had just seized power, amidst popular expectation that the country would see the end of its troubles. The mandarins wanted the situation to change; that was the reason why they had made the difficult decision to break with the Le and rally to the new dynasty. Their part in the conduct of national affairs was an important one, the more so as the new king was prepared to seek out and take their advice in an effort to win over the ruling classes to his cause.

The Mac king achieved a remarkably smooth transition. Law and order quickly returned to the country. The main concerns of the new monarchy were defense and China. It was recorded in the *History of Dai Viet* that soon after he took power and even while peaceful conditions were prevailing, Mac Dang Dung gave instructions to reorganize and strengthen the army. No doubt he feared that the Chinese would take advantage of the change of dynasty to put pressure on Vietnam. Also, many mandarins of the former Le remained opposed to his regime and he was well aware of that particular trait of Vietnamese psychology whereby a population disaffected with a dynasty would often reverse its attitude once that dynasty had been overthrown. Failures were passed over, only achievements were recalled. In the case of the Le, the military feats accomplished by Le Loi to liberate the country from Chinese domination and the golden age under the enlightened Le Thanh Ton were still in everyone's mind. Although he had the situation well in hand, Mac Dang Dung knew that supporters of the Le could easily become an active opposition if there were government shortcomings or a bad harvest.

All Vietnamese dynasties recognized Chinese suzerainty, usually in a nominal way symbolized by the periodical sending of tributes. A new king had to be invested by the Chinese emperor before relations between the two countries were normalized. That was always a difficult problem for the Vietnamese, for the Chinese would profess indignation—how could anyone dare to overthrow a vassal of the emperor, ask questions, pose conditions, or interfere in Vietnam's internal affairs? Mac Dang Dung used a ploy already tried by other rulers before him. He sent an envoy to inform the Ming emperor that "the Mac family had to temporarily take charge of the country's administration because the Le dynasty had left no descendant." Unconvinced, the Chinese sent emissaries to Vietnam on a fact-finding mission. There, a special type of Vietnamese diplomacy came into play, "using flowery language and bribing the emissaries with vast amounts of gold and silver," as noted by the historian. The Chinese envoys returned to report that no descendant of the Le could be found and that the population accepted the Mac rule; consequently, they recommended that the Ming emperor formally recognize Mac Dang Dung's authority. This was rejected by the emperor who, however, consented to receive a tributary mission sent by the Mac. Although the investiture question was left pending, diplomatic missions were exchanged between the two countries. After three years on the throne and following a precedent set by the former Tran kings, Mac Dang Dung abdicated in favor of his eldest son. He said that he wanted to go back to fishing and enjoy it in old age. In fact, he continued to be very much involved in the nation's affairs.

His son Dang Doanh's reign lasted over ten years, from 1530 to 1540. It started inauspiciously, with elements loyal to the Le rising up in the southern province of Thanh Hoa, the fief of the former dynasty. It took the Mac two years to quell the revolt. Then word came that a marquess of the Le, who had taken refuge in Laos, had started a restoration movement with the help of the Laotian king. He was Nguyen Kim, whose descendants would establish the Nguyen dynasty in the nineteenth century. Nguyen Kim found a nephew of the last Le king and proclaimed him king at his place of exile in Laos in 1533. The movement could now appeal to the strong nostalgic attachment of the population towards the Le. As written in the *History of Dai Viet*, "From that moment, many warriors and men of talent in the western region bordering Laos rallied to the restoration." Nguyen Kim sent envoys to China to denounce the Mac usurpation. Seizing on the opportunity, the Ming court mobilized an army to go to Vietnam and punish Mac Dang Dung for having taken the throne of a Chinese vassal. The Mac were faced with a twin threat of civil war and external aggression. But for the moment, the threat was contained. Nguyen Kim's forces stayed back in Laos; they were not yet in a position to confront the Mac army. As for the Ming Court, it could not make up its mind to attack Vietnam. The mandarins in faraway Peking were full of fight, but those appointed to lead the expeditionary army were much more cautious. The Mac negotiated with the Chinese at the border; as a result, hostilities were prevented.

Meanwhile, the country enjoyed order and prosperity. Even historians of the Le had to recognize the almost idyllic conditions obtained under the reign of Mac Dang Doanh. This excerpt is taken from the *History of Dai Viet*:

> People going out on their business and other travellers did not have to carry arms or weapons to protect themselves. There was no thievery or banditry at night, cattle were left to pasture outside without the need of being brought home each day, only a monthly check was necessary and often it was not known to whom newly-born calves belonged.... Valuables dropped in the street were not picked up, gates needed not be closed, crops were plentiful and security prevailed within the country.

Other historians, also mandarins of the Le, wrote about honest public servants and a strict and fair application of the law. They noted that the tax burden was lightened and the price of rice and paddy kept falling following good harvests. Dang Doanh was a wise king who also did much to encourage scholarship and learning. He ordered that the national university be renovated and personally made an inspection there. Doctorate examinations were held every three years without interruption, in spite of the change of dynasty. In short, Dang Doanh's years were the great period of the Mac, their golden age. Mandarins who held positions of responsibility during that period could, justifiably, claim a share of the credit for the regime's accomplishments. For Nguyen Tue, these accomplishments would have amply vindicated his decision to rally to the new dynasty and he may have retired a contented man, towards the end of Dang Doanh's reign.

Dang Doanh died in 1540. His son Phuc Hai was an ordinary man, quite unlike his father. He liked song and dance, wine and women and would not listen to the entreaties of his mandarins. Furthermore, he suffered from epileptic fits. His grandfather Mac Dang Dung, then in his seventies, was left to carry the burden of state. At that juncture, military pressure intensified against the Mac from two sides. In the south, Nguyen Kim's troops came out of Laos to attack the provinces of Nghe An and Thanh Hoa. In the north, Chinese forces prepared to invade. What followed was one of the most bizarre incidents in the Mac history. This is how it was related in the *History of Dai Viet*:

> Mac Dang Dung and his suite went to the Nam Quan frontier gate with China. Bare-footed and with ropes tied around their neck, they crawled to the Ming command post and asked to capitulate. Presenting the register of lands and inhabitants of the country as a mark of submission, Mac Dang Dung ceded six mountain districts to China.

That disgraceful episode has damned Mac Dang Dung in Vietnamese eyes more than the "crime" of usurpation for which he was condemned by the Le. It made author Tran Trong Kim brand the Mac king as a traitor to his

country. Although the history of the Mac was written by their sworn enemies, it was accepted without question until recent times. No one doubted
the veracity of what the Le historians wrote. Only in the 1950s did some
authors begin reassessing the place of the Mac in our national history.
About that frontier incident, so damning to Mac Dang Dung, serious
doubts have been raised. It was pointed out, in the first place, that the Le
historians relied on Chinese sources, which were themselves based on
reports made to the Ming court by their commanders on the Vietnamese
border. It is a known fact that the Chinese generals did not want to get involved in a war with the Mac. Their problem was to make the bellicose
officials in Peking accept a peaceful solution. That could be the reason for
their portraying the Vietnamese in an abject posture of surrender and presenting the solution they proposed as a glorious victory for China. Secondly,
it is difficult to believe that Mac Dang Dung, an old king and experienced
warrior who was, moreover, the mainstay of the dynasty after his son Dang
Doanh's death, would be foolish enough to deliver himself to an invading
Chinese army. The Chinese had only to kill him or to take him prisoner,
and the Mac regime would have been decapitated. No Vietnamese leader
would trust the Chinese to the extent of risking falling into their hands.
Many times in our history, the Chinese had asked that the Vietnamese king
make the trip to Peking to pay tribute; each time, excuses were given by the
Vietnamese for not going. In 1596, after the Mac were defeated and the Le
restored to the throne, again a Chinese army was poised on our border
threatening to intervene and the Le king had to come to a meeting with the
Chinese at the border. He brought with him more than ten thousands
troops, just in case the Chinese might have some other ideas. Likewise,
Mac Dang Dung would not have gone to his meeting without a military
escort, let alone binding himself up as a prisoner.

An agreement was struck at that meeting between Mac Dang Dung
and the Chinese, by which China would call off the invasion and withdraw
her troops from the border in return for our country becoming a dependency, instead of a vassal state, of China. Six small mountain districts
would be ceded—the Chinese said that they would be "returned"—to
China and the Vietnamese would resume their tribute missions to Peking.
The Ming court approved the agreement and conferred on Mac Dang Dung
the military title of Supreme Commander of An Nam, An Nam being the
name that China gave to our country to show her dominance (it means
"The Pacified South"). Dependency, however, was only a fiction as China
was not allowed to interfere in Vietnam during the Mac dynasty. With the
acceptance of that fiction, the military threat in the north had disappeared
and relations with China were normalized. Mac Dang Dung could now
concentrate his attention to dealing with the forces of restoration in the
south.

But he died soon after in 1541. The Le camp went from strength to strength and set themselves up in the southern provinces. The country became divided. The war between the Mac, or Northern court, and the Le, or Southern court, would not end before the sixteenth century was nearly over. Good men and bad men were found on both sides of that war; there were shining examples of loyalty and dark deeds of treachery on both. Even the Le mandarins who wrote the *History of Dai Viet* did not systematically praise or criticize the main players of that period by the side to which they belonged. They expressed their admiration for Mac Kinh Dien, a son of the second king and the best of the Mac generals: "A kind, generous and brave man who was intelligent and good in strategy . . .; in spite of going through many dangers, he remained loyal and hard-working." The folklore of that period, which reflected the views and feelings of the common people, did not side with either the Northern or the Southern court. Unlike history books, no folk songs or poems ever condemned the Mac for usurpation. Their complaints were against the war and the sufferings caused to the population.

In those troubled and confusing times lived a famous Vietnamese prophet who must be mentioned here, for there were several indications linking him with our family, as will be seen in the next chapter. Nguyen Binh Khiem graduated at the 1535 doctorate examination, at the same session as our second ancestor Nguyen Uyen. A contemporary of Nostradamus, he left a treasure of prophetic sayings which Vietnamese believe still hold true nowadays. He was also a celebrated poet and the first scholar of his generation, having won the title of First Laureate. Considering his ability to discern future events, it is interesting to note that the First Laureate served the Mac who would later be condemned by historians as an illegitimate dynasty. A recipient of the Mac's highest honors—he was a minister and a duke—the prophet was also held in high regard by those at the Southern court. And while his advice was often sought by the Mac king, he also had opportunities to influence the turn of events in the south. In 1556, King Le Trang Ton died there without leaving a descendant. He was only a nominal king. Power was in the hands of Trinh Kiem, the army commander, who toyed with the idea of taking upon himself the royal mantle. Trinh Kiem sent a secret envoy across the lines to the north to solicit the First Laureate's advice. The story was told that the latter declined to give the envoy a direct reply. Instead, he took him to a nearby Buddhist temple. There, he told an apprentice monk: "Guard the temple, worship Lord Buddha, and the food offerings of the faithfuls will be yours to take!" The envoy reported the incident to Trinh Kiem who understood the allusion. His role should remain that of the monk. He sent officials out to look for other surviving members of the Le and never again would he, or his descendants, think of doing away with the Le. They became hereditary overlords and ruled under the nominal authority of the Le kings, a system similar to that between the shogun and the emperor in Japan. In that way, the Trinh enjoyed "the food offerings" mentioned by the prophet and they stayed in power for over two hundred years.

When he started his mandarinal career, at the bottom grade which was the lower ninth, Nguyen Tue's annual salary was fourteen *quan,* our ancient monetary unit. To give an idea of its value, one *quan* bought about one hundred kilograms of rice. Salaries in those times were low. A top mandarin belonging to the upper first grade was paid only eighty *quan* a year. But as they advanced in grade, the mandarins received other emoluments. On reaching the lower seventh grade, our ancestor would be given his first executive position as the head of a small prefecture. Tradition prescribed that all villages in the prefecture make welcoming gifts of money and rice to the new prefect. As he could have a few dozen villages under his authority, the gifts amounted to a substantial payment. From the fourth grade upwards, he was granted land, the amount of which increased with each grade. A minister belonged to the lower second grade, but Nguyen Tue received the salary and land which went with his title of count and which were in a bracket above that of the highest mandarinal grade. Historical records showed that, at the end of the fifteenth century, a count was given an annual salary of one hundred and six *quan* and the following grants of land: two hundred *mau* of rice fields as a hereditary grant (or about seventy-two hectares, a *mau* being about 3,600 square meters); two hundred and thirty *mau* of rice fields as a life grant (eighty-three hectares); seventy *mau* of mulberry fields (twenty-five hectares); one hundred and forty *mau* of rice fields (fifty hectares) as a hereditary grant to provide for the expenses of the ancestors' cult and the upkeep of tombs.

In addition, a count received about three-quarters of a hectare of land and a half-hectare of pond in the capital to build his residence. He was entitled to a suite of aides and servants. The above grants applied during the reign of Le Thanh Ton, when the country enjoyed great prosperity and stability. Under the Mac, following several decades of unrest, the actual land that our ancestor received might very well have been less. But it must still have been very extensive, by the country's standards. In the Red River delta, where for centuries the population had been heavily concentrated, five hectares of rice fields already made a man a wealthy farmer.

The rice fields and mulberry fields granted to our ancestor were taken from the public estates of a number of villages in our prefecture of Thanh Oai. Hung Giao, the name he took with his title, was one of these villages. A titled mandarin usually received land from his own region, which then became something like his fief. However, Nguyen Tue's position was not that of a feudal lord. On the one hand, his titles and privileges were tied to his mandarinal career and they could all be affected if his career went wrong. Under the ancient monarchy, a mandarin could easily lose title and function or be dropped to a lower grade; it was not exceptional to see a high official at the court being demoted to a junior post in a faraway province. In addition, the land given in life grants reverted to the state after the recipient's death and hereditary grants lasted for only thirty years, or the space of a generation. In his lifetime, Nguyen Tue must have also built up important private assets, for the Cu Hau papers mentioned that a vast amount of cult land was donated to the Nguyen Ancestral Shrine in his generation, which meant he and his brother. The Shrine itself was probably built, or rebuilt, during their time.

Nothing is remembered about his wife. The couple had only one son, who became our second ancestor. Old mandarins liked to retire to their native village, as the popular saying went, "to enjoy their fields and gardens." Nguyen Tue probably spent the last years of his life back in Kim Bai and was buried out in the fields beyond its bamboo enclosure. Mandarins' tombs were built according to well-established rules. As our ancestor held the second grade, his tomb was a square of eighty meters, whose inside was a square platform of raised earth of forty meters. The grave lay in the middle. A low brick wall surrounded the tomb. In the open countryside, no one could have missed such a large tomb. But the Mac rule came to an end half a century after Nguyen Tue died, and his tomb did not survive the monarchy he served.

Not only was his tomb lost. The memory of Nguyen Tue also became lost to his descendants. Fortunately, village folklore continued to remember the Nguyen Brothers' academic prowess and provided a clue which helped my grandfather retrace our lineage back to our first ancestor.

Nguyen Tue's younger brother Nguyen Huyen graduated with him at the same 1511 session. I had wondered whether the two were twins, as the prophecy referred to the Mountain of the Twins, but Huyen was in fact much younger. The *Southern Sky Register of High Graduates* noted that he "won the golden board on his first try," an indication that he was then a young man, probably in his twenties, or some ten years younger than his brother. Huyen obtained a higher rank, coming fifteenth out of the thirty five doctors who made up the third class, while his elder brother Tue only managed the twenty-seventh place. His career brought Huyen to the positions of administrator-delegate of a region, and first deputy minister of Justice. In his time, the national territory extended to the south only as far as Quang Nam province and the country was divided into thirteen administrative regions. At the head of each region stood a troika of delegates of the king, one in command of the army, the other of the administration and the third in charge of inspection. As administrator-delegate, Nguyen Huyen was the highest civilian authority in his region.

Like his brother, Huyen started as a mandarin of the Le dynasty. Did he stay on to serve the Mac? The question arises because both registers of high graduates made no mention of him being a Mac mandarin, while they made clear that his brother Tue reached this position under the new dynasty. Does that mean that Huyen had remained faithful to the Le and had left at the change of dynasty? I do not believe so. As a young doctor in 1511, Huyen was probably only in his late thirties when the Mac took power. He could not have achieved his high offices at that age. More likely, he was then only a middle-rank mandarin, whose transfer of loyalty was not deemed a matter worthy of interest by the authors of the registers. We have no indication as to the region where Huyen was appointed as an administrator-delegate. The thirteen regions differed in importance. Some like Thanh Hoa in the south and Hai Duong in the east of the capital Thang Long were strategic places where only trusted servants of the king were sent. Thanh Hoa was second in importance only to the capital itself; under the previous dynasty it was called the Western capital. As for Hai Duong, it was the home town of the Mac kings. With an elder brother in an influential position at the court, Huyen would be well-placed to obtain a good appointment, perhaps not Thanh Hoa or Hai Duong, but quite possibly one of the fertile and populated regions of the Red River delta. The positions of administrator-delegate and deputy minister both corresponded to the lower third mandarinal grade. Huyen's rank was, therefore, slightly below that of his brother, who as minister belonged to the lower second grade.

Of the two branches of our first generation, the younger one had disappeared. My grandfather wrote in the chronicle:

> No descendants of Ancestor Nguyen Huyen are known to have survived. His branch could have ended due to the absence of a male heir or because its descendants had gone away during times of trouble and contact with them was lost. We do not really know what happened.

Did the lack of a male descendant, that scourge which had plagued our family for so many generations, cause the disappearance of the second branch? I rather think that it was the "going away." The times of trouble referred to in the chronicle came with the collapse of the Mac. Our own branch fled from Kim Bai. It managed to survive and return many years later. The second branch might not have been so lucky. Whatever the cause, it is sad to think that a branch which began so auspiciously with a young and bright doctor—who subsequently had a very successful mandarinal career—was to vanish without trace, for the Cu Hau papers written in the eighteenth century contained no mention of it.

15. The Academician-Envoy

The passage regarding our second ancestor in the family chronicle reads:

> He was named Nguyen Ba Uyen and given the posthumous name of On Tinh Tien Sinh. He passed the doctorate third class in the year of the Goat which was the sixth year of the Dai Chinh era under the Mac. He held the position of inspector-delegate of the administrative region of Thai Nguyen. The *Register of High Graduates* recorded that he was a member of the Academy. His second wife came from the Phung family. Her pseudonym was Tu Uoc.

The name given in the chronicle was Nguyen Ba Uyen, but in the *Register of High Graduates* it was only Nguyen Uyen, without the middle name Ba. According to my father, the *ba* here was not a middle name, but a title. After family documents were destroyed in the eighteenth century, our people could only write down what they remembered, and the *ba* was mistaken for a name. That was quite understandable, my father said, because *ba*—meaning elder—was a middle name commonly given to the first son and when the chronicle was rewritten, more than two centuries had passed since Nguyen Uyen's time. Besides, up to the seventh generation, our ancestors' names used to have only two words, not three. It appeared, therefore, that Nguyen Uyen also received the title of *ba*—count—like his father. But I still have to find confirmation for this in history books or registers of graduates, to be sure. Indications about Nguyen Uyen in these documents, however, are extremely sketchy and consist in just a few pointers to a very long career. The posthumous name was conferred on him by the Mac court after his death. *On Tinh* means Moderation and Calm, *Tien Sinh* is an appellation addressed to elders, which can be translated as Honorable Sir.

Unlike his father, Nguyen Uyen has always been remembered by his descendants. The *Thanh Hinh Hien Sat Su*—as they usually referred to him, by his full title of Royal Delegate for Inspection and the Fair Application of Justice—was long thought to be their earliest ancestor. Family tradition recalled that he was a brilliant scholar, a mandarin who remained in active service until an advanced age and also, that he undertook a hazardous journey to a faraway place. My grandfather discovered that he graduated in the year of the Goat and became a member of the Academy. I was able to find additional information and draw a broad picture of his life and career.

Nguyen Uyen became a doctor in 1535, the sixth year of the Dai Chinh era, or era of Great Righteousness, a dynastic title taken by the second Mac king. He must have been born sometime between 1510 and 1515 because, as will be seen later, history books recorded that he went to China in 1580, a trip he could not have made later than in his late sixties or early seventies. He would have been, then, a doctor in his early twenties, or a full ten years younger than most other graduates. Although the registers of graduates do not mention it, he may well have been successful at his first try, like his uncle before him. When the Le lost the throne to the Mac, he was still a young student and would not have known the stress of a transfer of loyalty, especially since his father took the side of the Mac from the very beginning. He probably started schooling in his village at one of the many private schools run by scholars who had failed to gain a diploma. At about the age of twelve, he would have left for the capital, or the town where his father worked, to study under more qualified teachers. A few years later, he was ready to join a special college for mandarins' sons. There were three in the capital, admission to which was based not only on the father's mandarinal rank, but also on the son's rank in the family. As his father was a count and a mandarin of the second grade, and he an eldest son, Nguyen Uyen could go either to the Sung Van Quan or the Chieu Van Quan. The first one, whose name means College for the Exaltation of Literature, was reserved to eldest sons of mandarins of the first three grades and to cadets of those of the first two grades. The second, or College for the Advancement of Literature, admitted sons and eldest grandsons of dukes, marquesses and counts as well as eldest sons of mandarins of the second to eighth grades. I believe that Nguyen Uyen went to the first college, which was more exclusive and had a higher academic reputation, for he proved to be a very bright student who obtained his diplomas at a young age. In 1534, he went to the regional examinations, passed all four subjects and became a licentiate. He was now entitled to sit for a doctorate in the following year. To prepare for it, he joined the Quoc Tu Giam, or National University, an institution founded in the eleventh century under the Ly kings. There, he attended lectures given by learned academicians on Confucian texts and other subjects required for the doctorate. Exercises and essays were given to students every day. His workload was heavy, for there was only one year between the two examinations; if he failed, it would mean a wait of three more years. The university was built next to the Temple of Literature, where doctors' stelae were housed. The names of Nguyen Uyen's father and uncle were on one of the recent stelae. The young scholar must have dreamed to have, one day, his own name in the Temple. Unfortunately, although he did become a doctor, no stele was erected to commemorate his session. In the beginning of Mac Dang Dung's reign, the Mac managed to erect one stele for those who made doctors in 1529, but for some reasons never came round to have the names of doctors admitted at later sessions carved on stone for posterity.

With Nguyen Uyen's success, two generations of ours had won the golden board, a rare achievement in a society where families moved up and down quickly. The registers of high graduates acknowledged this, for in their short biographies, they highlighted the fact that he was Nguyen Tue's son and Nguyen Huyen's nephew and that "father and son, elder and younger brothers all graduated." The scholarly reputation of our family was made. It would remain long after our family had dropped out of the mandarinal class. "The Nguyen of Kim Bai" continued to be known throughout the region. Later ancestors who made their living as village teachers used to have students travelling from far-off places to study under them.

A total of thirty-two scholars were awarded the doctorate degree in 1535. Three obtained the first class, seven the second class and twenty-two the third class. Nguyen Uyen was among the latter. At that session, the prophet Nguyen Binh Khiem earned the title of First Laureate. Khiem's fame as a teacher and prophet was established long before he won a doctorate. He could have sat for it under the last kings of the Le dynasty, but abstained from doing so because, so it was said, he considered it unwise to come out and serve in those troubled times. He kept staying away in the first seven years of the Mac, until 1534, when he finally decided to enter the regional competition, the same year that Nguyen Uyen did. The next year, he was First Laureate at the nationwide competition. His coming out to serve the dynasty was an important success for the Mac. The prophet had found a king worthy of his allegiance! Those were halcyon years under Mac Dang Doanh's reign and the Mac looked set to rule for a long time to come. Strong ties of solidarity existed between fellow graduates. Nguyen Binh Khiem was then forty-five. Twenty years separated Nguyen Uyen from him. More than a fellow graduate, our ancestor must have looked up to Khiem as a respected elder and teacher. He may have stayed close to the prophet and I believe that the latter may even have been the go-between in Uyen's second marriage.

The prophet did not have to climb one by one the rungs of the mandarinal ladder like the other doctors. At once, he was appointed to a high position by the enlightened king Mac Dang Doanh. Within a few years, he became a deputy minister of Public Service, a very influential post dealing with nominations and promotions of officials. But the good Mac king died in 1540 and Nguyen Binh Khiem soon was disenchanted with the way things were going at the court. Using old age as an excuse—he was then fifty-one—he asked to be allowed to retire. King Mac Phuc Hai continued to treat him with great consideration in his retirement, asking him for advice and conferring on him honors and titles. By that time, the forces of restoration had established themselves in the south and their leaders also solicited, in secret, the prophet's advice. We saw in the last chapter how he counselled Trinh Kiem against the temptation of making himself king. He was also credited with helping Nguyen Kim's descendants find a place of refuge and a base for their future conquest of power. Nguyen Kim was the leader who started the campaign to restore the Le. After he died, allegedly poisoned by the Mac, power in the Southern court fell into the hands of his son-in-law Trinh Kiem. Nguyen Kim had two sons, both military commanders. One was killed by Trinh Kiem. The other son Nguyen Hoang, Duke of Quan, knew that he would be the next target. He sent a secret emissary north to see the First Laureate and beg him for guidance on how to escape the danger. This time, the prophet gave a direct advice. "Beyond the Hoanh Son range," he said, "you will find shelter for countless generations." Beyond the Hoanh Son mountains, in the southern portion of the country, lay a few poor and sparsely populated provinces conquered not long ago from the Champa. Situated far away from the traditional seats of power, which were the capital Thang Long held by the Mac and Thanh Hoa—also called Tay Kinh or Western Capital—held by the Trinh, exposed to attacks from the neighboring kingdoms of Laos and Champa, these provinces were certainly no place for a leader with political ambitions to go. Nguyen Hoang asked his brother-in-law to send him to guard the southern border and Trinh Kiem readily obliged. It was from there that, in 1628, Nguyen Hoang's son set himself up against Trinh Kiem's grandson and war between the Trinh and the Nguyen overlords began. It would be fought over almost two centuries. Not only did the prophet help Nguyen Hoang find a place of refuge, he also placed his descendants in a position to lead the Vietnamese people in their final and greatest surge towards the south. By the end of the seventeenth century Vietnamese colonizers, setting out from the provinces held by the Nguyen overlord, had settled on the Dong Nai River in a place now called Saigon. After a few more decades, the Mekong delta was theirs and they had reached the shore of the Gulf of Thailand. The historic *Nam Tien,* the March South started by our people millenniums ago from the Red River delta, had ended. With the conquest of the south, the balance of power shifted and it would be from there that a descendant of Nguyen Hoang reunified the country under the Nguyen dynasty in 1802. The prophet, who lived in a period of violent conflicts and rapid changes, was not bothered by considerations of legitimacy or loyalty to a king. He served the Mac but did not refuse to help also the Trinh and the Nguyen, the other contenders to the throne. Unlike the historians, he—a prophet—did not claim to say which side was right and which side was wrong in the national drama which was unfolding. His conception appeared to be very close to democracy, in that he saw the country as belonging to all and everyone was entitled to claim a share in it. As he exclaimed in a poem: "But the country is not anyone's patrimony!"

Nguyen Uyen's career could not be compared to that of his famous fellow graduate. But it was also a special one for the few indications that we have show it spanning over half a century and extending to a wide variety of fields. Of his mandarinal appointments, the family only remembered one, that of inspector-delegate to the region of Thai Nguyen. We do not know when he was appointed, but assuming that his career was one of smooth progression, he would have reached that position ten to fifteen years after graduation. A new doctor of the third class started at the upper eighth mandarinal grade. He would have to move up four rungs to reach the upper sixth, the grade of an inspector-delegate. As three years were normally needed to climb each rung, Nguyen Uyen, who graduated in 1535, would have been in Thai Nguyen circa 1550. One of three mandarins in charge of a region, an inspector-delegate's role was to administer justice and to exercise control over the work of all mandarins in his region, both civilian and military. He should find out, investigate and report to the king all instances of maladministration and corruption. He received complaints from the public; an order made by King Le Thanh Ton in 1471 stressed that he should be able to "express the secret sufferings of the people." In addition, he was consulted by the administrator-delegate on such important matters as nomination of mandarins and assessment of their performance. Of the three royal delegates, an inspector was the lowest in rank. The gap between him and the other two was large; he had only the upper sixth grade, while the military-delegate had the upper third grade and the administrator-delegate the lower third grade. Yet, he was held in high regard, even feared by the other two, for he functioned as "the eye and ear" of the king and had the right to look into their behavior and actions. The system rested on checks and balances. The two senior delegates were high mandarins, generally in their fifties, with a long experience of public service behind them. The inspector-delegate was a younger mandarin of middle rank only, who therefore posed no threat to his elders' positions, but exercised an effective control because he usually enjoyed strong political backing at the court.

A royal decree issued by King Le Thanh Ton in 1496 dealt with the choice of inspectors. It said: "Inspectors have the responsibility of censoring, therefore those chosen should prove to be strict upholders of the law, of upright character, fearless of the noble and mighty and must not have committed any wrong-doing themselves." It laid down strict selection criteria, not for inspector-delegates, who were appointed by the king, but for their deputies. These should be chosen among holders of a doctorate diploma, among civil and military officials who had passed a number of subjects at the doctorate examination but did not obtain the diploma. Probably, Nguyen Uyen had served as deputy inspector in one or two regions before becoming a royal delegate. When appointed to Thai Nguyen, he would have been in his late thirties, quite a young age for a delegate of the king. He gained a reputation of uprightness and that perhaps explained why, down the generations, the family continued to remember him as a judge and inspector, while his higher appointments at the Academy and as an envoy to China came to be forgotten. The *Thanh Hinh Hien Sat Su* has always inspired in me a certain feeling of awe. The word *Sat* in the title means to investigate, but it had another meaning, to kill. As a child, I took it in its second meaning and thought that our ancestor had had the power to kill. It was known that many inspectors struck fear among mandarins of their region. Maybe our ancestor did bring some corrupt officials to justice and to their death.

The administrative region of Thai Nguyen was situated in the mountainous areas bordering on China. Large and sparsely populated, it was — like the rest of the northern mountains — infected with malaria. Delta people dreaded going there, for few could escape the debilitating attacks of that illness. Those were places where "noxious gases emanated from the poisonous mountains," they said in fear. It said something of our ancestor's constitution, that, having been posted there, he then went on to lead an active life until a ripe old age. Thai Nguyen was also a haven for bandits, rebels and other fugitives of the law. Its military-delegate was traditionally an officer of high rank. The mandarins shunned the place. They preferred to stay in the Red River delta where land was rich, climate good and life more enjoyable. In normal times, delegates sent to Thai Nguyen were mandarins receiving their first royal assignment or those who did not pull much weight among the mighty and powerful at the Court. Nguyen Uyen may have been a young inspector-delegate placed for the first time at the head of a region, but when he went to Thai Nguyen, the place was one of great strategic importance for the Mac regime.

West of Thai Nguyen was the border region of Tuyen Quang. In 1527, when the Mac overthrew the Le, Vu Van Uyen was military-delegate in Tuyen Quang. He refused to serve the new dynasty and set himself up as an independent authority. His troops numbered several tens of thousands. After a Le king in exile was proclaimed in Laos, Vu Van Uyen rallied to him. In 1540, China made preparations to invade our country and Vu Van Uyen's forces were slated to act as vanguards for the Chinese. But, as we saw earlier, Mac Dang Dung succeeded in defusing the invasion threat and in normalizing relations with China. Having done that, the Mac turned against Vu Van Uyen. Twice in the following years, they launched big offensives to seize Tuyen Quang and get rid of that thorn in their side, but failed. For his part, Vu Van Uyen also made sorties out of his region, but was beaten back. On his death, his brother Vu Van Mat took over. In 1551, his forces made a foray into the delta and came close to the capital, forcing the Mac king to flee. Not only was Tuyen Quang a military problem for the Mac; under the Vu brothers, it prospered and attracted people from the delta who moved there to settle. Many traders also went there to engage in the commerce of forestry products.

Meanwhile in the south, the forces of restoration pushed out from Laos and occupied the Western Capital in 1543. By the mid–1540s, the country had been partitioned. The Mac authority extended over the Red River delta and all other areas to the west and the north, with the exception of Tuyen Quang. From the region of Thanh Hoa, where the Western Capital was located, to the southern border was Le territory. During the next two decades, a seesaw war took place, pitting against one another two outstanding generals, Mac Kinh Dien on the northern side and Trinh Kiem, the founder of the dynasty of Trinh overlords, on the southern side. Ten times, Mac Kinh Dien attacked the south. Six times, Trinh Kiem sent his troops north. Neither side could gain a decisive edge. In 1559, Trinh Kiem nearly obtained victory. Bypassing the delta to the west, he moved a sixty thousand strong army through the hilly areas next to the Laotian border, then swerved east. Joining forces with Vu Van Mat in Tuyen Quang, he quickly seized Thai Nguyen and all the northern provinces up to the Chinese border. He now had the Mac caught in a pincer movement as his forces attacked the delta from both the north and the south. The Mac fought on until 1561 when, in a masterly counterstroke, Mac Kinh Dien reversed the situation. Abandoning a defensive posture, he launched his forces against the Le capital in Thanh Hoa, while Trinh Kiem was away in the north. Faced with the danger of losing his own home base, the latter hurriedly called off his campaign. The stalemate was restored and the country settled in for a prolonged partition.

Nguyen Uyen probably stayed in Thai Nguyen for two years, the normal mandarinal tour of duty. At that time, Thai Nguyen's territory was quite large as it extended up to the Chinese border and included the province of Cao Bang. The region's wealth lay in its gold, silver and iron mines. Fertile valleys yielded a plentiful crop and forests were a ready source of timber. Cao Bang had a thriving trade with China. Before Trinh Kiem launched his 1559 offensive, in which his troops were to move far away from their bases in the south and reach up to the Chinese border, his generals cautioned him about overextending his lines of supply. He told them:

> Tuyen Quang, Thai Nguyen and Lang Son in the northern mountains are places where people are rich and money and paddy are in surplus. We will obtain the food from where we happen to be, so there is no reason to worry about supplies.

There was also an interesting story about the wealth of Cao Bang, which had become a separate province under the Trinh overlordship. In 1715, the Chief Censor—one of the most important mandarins at the court—was told to go as governor to Cao Bang. He protested against what he considered as a demotion, but it was explained that the overlord had wanted to reward him for his services by giving him a "fat" appointment. Mandarins posted there were the recipients of many extra emoluments and could quickly make a fortune. The Chief Censor understood the overlord's intention and gratefully accepted his commission.

An inspector-delegate was required by law to make frequent inspection tours and Nguyen Uyen must have known the area of Thai Nguyen and Cao Bang well. He may have even spent a good part of his time travelling. Either by land on winding mountain paths or on rivers through rapids and waterfalls, it took days to go from one district to another. Delta people who had been to the northern mountains usually came under their spell. Traders, mine workers, civil servants, many ended up staying there, or if they had gone back to the plains, often tried to return. In this century, several of our kinsmen went to settle in the mountains. They came home on the occasion of family festivals to tell us about peaks wrapped in autumn mist, strange birds and flowers and the sculptural beauty of tribeswomen. We listened to stories of cruel bandits, man-eating tigers, mountain genii who would become very angry if a traveller did not make proper offerings to their temples. Some of them suffered from malaria and had grown very thin and yellow-complexioned. Then, the festival over, they left again. Four centuries ago, our ancestor too must have been captivated by that region, and not only by its scenic beauty, flora and fauna, or such a wonder of nature as the lake of The Three Seas. Scholars dreamed of the calm of the mountains, of temples nestled in the heights looking out to the vast empty space, of recluses wandering among the clouds and under the pine trees. The mountains where a man like Nguyen Uyen could set aside his mandarinal responsibilities and let himself be part of the peaks above and the valleys below. "The wise may like the sea, but in the mountains the virtuous would find joy," said Confucius. I have never seen the lake of The Three Seas or the paradise of Cao Bang in springtime—having grown up in a country at war, I never had much opportunity to travel—but it seems to me that I have always known them. Perhaps they had settled, since Nguyen Uyen's time, in a corner of our familial memory so that I feel I can almost conjure them in my mind.

Our ancestor was appointed to Thai Nguyen at a time when neighboring Tuyen Quang was in enemy hands and acting as a pole of attraction to delta people. Vu Van Mat's forces, as we saw earlier, were strong enough to push into the delta. Thai Nguyen itself was threatened. The king would only send there delegates who enjoyed his full confidence, especially the inspector-delegate, his "eye and ear" whose responsibility was to ensure the loyalty and good conduct of government officials.

Nguyen Uyen obviously had a high standing at the court where his father, who might have retired by then, should still have had plenty of connections. It looked as if he was destined for the top offices in the ministries, or that he would join the Censorate, a logical place for an inspector to go. But I could find no information in historical documents to support this line of thought.

Instead, the evidence pointed to the calmer waters of the Academy. Both registers of high graduates indicated that the highest point of Nguyen Uyen's career was reached there. "He rose to be an academician," one of the registers stated. But there were eight different grades and functions in the Academy, which one was his? The other register was more precise: "He rose to be a reviser in the Academy." But manifestly this was wrong. A reviser read and checked government documents before they were published. He only held the lower seventh mandarinal grade. That could not have been our ancestor's highest appointment, for we knew that he had reached higher as an inspector-delegate. However, we can take it that Nguyen Uyen was a reviser at the Academy at some point in his career. He could have gained that junior position about three years after his graduation.

The Academy was not open to every mandarin, not even to every doctor. Only the most brilliant and learned doctors were appointed there and the king often chose his envoys to China among them. The Academy had a right to remonstrate against governmental wrongdoings, but mainly its work was in the fields of education and research, away from the pressure of day to day government. Some academicians had the tasks of reading books to the king and commenting on them for him. From their close contacts with the monarch they often became very influential. Others drafted the text of royal edicts, orders and proclamations or explained them in case of difficulty of interpretation. Academicians were also educators, the equivalent of today's university professors, and they ran the state examinations. The Academy was a prestigious institution, but in the mandarinal hierarchy, it came after such bodies as the ministries or the Censorate. Promotions were slower for academicians. Their Chancellor was only a mandarin of the upper fourth grade, whereas the Chief Censor had the upper third grade and a minister the lower second grade. In those times, grade was the common yardstick to measure all positions and a mandarin knew where he stood in relation to all others.

Nguyen Uyen would probably have worked at the Academy before he became an inspector-delegate. Then, there followed a gap of some thirty years before the next thing that we know about his career, a diplomatic mission to China in 1580. What did he do during all that time? We can only make an informed guess. By 1580, Nguyen Uyen very likely had passed the retirement age of sixty-five. It was rare to see mandarins stay on after that age; history books did contain cases of men over seventy, some over eighty, still in active service, but they were elder statesmen holding the highest grades and titles of nobility. We have no indication that our ancestor had such grades or titles, except for the *ba* which was attached to his name. He must have been engaged in some work requiring great continuity to be asked to stay on. I am inclined to believe that he was a historian. This belief is strengthened by the fact that he became an envoy to Peking, for being an academician and a historian were two attributes which would make him a highly qualified candidate for that assignment.

All dynasties took great care to write their historical records, a task entrusted to official historians. These worked under a tradition which required that the annals should never be seen by the monarch of the time. Thus, although mandarins and "servants" of the king, their independence of judgment was respected. Under an absolute monarchy, the profession of historian was not an easy one. The line between independence and deference to the king's wishes was very fine indeed. The "grand" historian of China, Si Ma Quan, courted the displeasure of emperor Wu and was metted out the most humiliating punishment that a man could suffer, castration. Our own history recorded this revealing incident under the Le dynasty. The great king Le Thanh Ton (1460–1497) wanted to read the annals of his reign. He ordered his chamberlain to go the Academy and see historian Le Nghia in secret. The chamberlain started by not asking a direct question; in the usual manner of scholars he raised a historical precedent in order to maneuver the historian into a position where the latter would not be able to reject his request. Naturally, his precedent was taken from ancient Chinese history. He said: "In former times in China, Fang Xuan Ling worked as a historian when emperor Tang Tai Zong wanted to see the annals. Ling refused to accede to the request. How would you say you compare to Ling?"

The question was double-edged as it referred to an incident in which Tang Tai Zong killed two of his brothers. Fearful of writing the truth, Ling only made a vague mention in the diary about "that incident in the fourth day of the sixth month." Having seen that omission, the emperor ordered Ling to record clearly what happened. By recalling that event, the chamberlain hoped to draw the historian into saying that Tang Tai Zong did the right thing by seeing the diary. However, Le Nghia was on his guard. He answered: "The Chinese historian did not faithfully record what happened, but only did so at the command of the emperor. I am afraid that he was not a good man."

Seeing that his maneuver had failed, the chamberlain went straight to the question: "His Majesty wants to read the annals of the first eight years of his reign." The historian replied: "It is not a good thing for a king to read the annals. The way Tang Tai Zong and Fang Xuan Ling behaved was criticized by later generations."

Brave words by the historian for these could easily be taken as a criticism against his king. The chamberlain pressed on: "His Majesty said that reading the annals would help him see past mistakes and change for the better." The historian remained firm: "His Majesty needs only to strive and do good deeds. There is really no need for him to see the annals." But the chamberlain repeated the request several more times and the historian finally bowed to the pressure. He produced the documents. King Le Thanh Ton read them and had them returned to the Academy. There was no mention that he asked for any change to be made to the entries.

Nguyen Uyen had impeccable credentials to be a historian. A doctor-scholar, he came from a family whose commitment and loyalty to the Mac dynasty were unquestionable. The qualities which made him a good inspector, integrity and impartiality, an ability to operate without fear or favor, were eminently required in a historian, who otherwise would be a mere scribe writing down what his master wanted him to. If our guess was correct, Nguyen Uyen would have been an academician assigned, probably along with others, the long and exacting task of writing the official history of the Mac. That would have explained why he had continued to stay in active service until such an advanced age.

The *History of Dai Viet* recorded that on the third day of the twelfth month in the year of the Dragon (1580), the Mac king "ordered Luong Phung Than, Nguyen Nhan An, Nguyen Uyen, Nguyen Khac Tuy, [eight more names followed] to go to the Ming country [China] for the yearly tribute."

I noted the name of the third member of the mission but had, at first, doubts that he was our ancestor. A mission to Peking was the most prestigious task that a mandarin could be given and an envoy to China usually held a very high rank, either that of minister or deputy minister. Nguyen Uyen was not known to have reached such high positions. Moreover, being born sometime between 1510 and 1515, he would be in his late sixties or early seventies at the time of the mission. Would a man of his age be chosen to undertake the long journey to Peking? On the other hand the trip to China would fit in particularly well with our family recollection of Nguyen Uyen having been in the king's service until a ripe old age and having "gone afar, with a risk of no return." We shall see why there was such a risk in his diplomatic mission. The word *uyen* in Vietnamese has several meanings; it was written in different ways in the old scholarly script, depending on the meaning. *Uyen* in our ancestor's name means profound, deep. I found that the envoy's name was written in the same way. But could there be another person with exactly the same name Nguyen Uyen? I checked carefully with the *History of Dai Viet*, and found none. As time went on, the conviction grew in my mind that the envoy may indeed be our ancestor.

Then, I went to Paris and got a translation of Nguyen Hoan's *Register of High Graduates*. It gave me a shock. By the strangest of coincidences, there did exist at the time of our ancestor another Nguyen Uyen, who was also a doctor and mandarin. Moreover, the *Register* stated that he "had gone in a diplomatic mission." So the envoy was him! I was taken aback, but wanted to get confirmation in the other register, that compiled by Phan Huy On, before accepting this new piece of evidence. Fortunately, I soon obtained a microfilm of the second register, written in the scholarly script. Phan Huy On's work is credited by scholars with more thorough research and accurate information than that of Nguyen Hoan. It has the added advantage of listing the graduates by prefecture, thus greatly simplifying the task of a researcher. Quickly, I found our prefecture of Thanh Oai and came to the short biography of Nguyen Uyen. There, on the screen, appeared the information that I was looking for:

> Nguyen Uyen was a man from the village of Kim Bai ... On the year of the Dragon under [King Mac] Hau Hop, four diplomatic delegations were sent out the capital of the Ming, to make up for the missing tributes. He went as deputy-ambassador...

As for the other Nguyen Uyen, who graduated in 1556, the register noted the following: "Nguyen Uyen was a man from the village of Nham Lang.... In the winter of the year of the Dragon under (King Mac) Hau Hop, was ordered to go in the annual tribute to the Ming...." It appears that both Nguyen Uyens went to China on the same diplomatic mission. It is not known what position the other Nguyen Uyen had, but our ancestor was deputy ambassador of the mission. In all probability, he was the envoy mentioned in the *History of Dai Viet*. Diplomacy was my profession and a cherished part of my life. Now I have discovered that its roots went deep in my family and could be traced back to the second ancestor.

The 1580 mission had more important objectives than just to bring tribute. As a matter of fact, no tribute was sent "yearly" to China. The timing of tribute missions was flexible and depended on the current state of relations between the two countries. Let us go back to 1540 and the agreement between Mac Dang Dung and the Chinese. In 1542, the Ming envoy came to the border to deliver the papers appointing Mac Dang Dung as Supreme Commander of Annam and a silver seal of office. By then, however, Mac Dang Dung had died and it was his grandson, King Mac Phuc Hai, who received the papers and seal. Following that event, envoys of the Mac were sent to China to "show gratitude" and pay tribute. The

Chinese sent new documents of appointment to Mac Phuc Hai and, in 1543, another tribute mission went. Then there was a gap of five years. In 1548, envoy Le Quang Bi was sent to Peking. It was an inopportune time. According to the *History of Dai Viet*, a marquess of the Mac named Pham Tu Nghi had rebelled against the king with the aim of putting the second son of Mac Dang Dung on the throne. Defeated by loyal forces, he retreated to the northern mountains with his troops, then crossed the Chinese border and wrought havoc in the two provinces of Guangdong and Giangxi. The Chinese were furious for not being able to contain him. They blamed the Mac regime for being behind that incursion and showing "insolence" towards China. They threatened to mount an attack against Vietnam. It was at that juncture that envoy Le Quang Bi arrived at the border on the way to Peking to bring tribute. He was detained by the Chinese provincial authorities who claimed that he was a false envoy. They did not allow him to proceed to Peking until fifteen years later! In the meantime, the Mac captured Pham Tu Nghi, beheaded him and sent the head to China as a proof that they did not approve of his activities. But the Chinese were still so angry that they returned the head. Such was the historian's version. Popular folklore, however, treated Tu Nghi as a hero. A man endowed with exceptional strength, he was said to have been sent north by the Mac to look after the security of the mountainous region next to China. Tu Nghi performed with great zeal and success, pursuing Chinese aggressors and bandits to their lairs in China, where he was killed. The Chinese cut off his head and sent it down the river back to Vietnam where it was picked up and reverentially buried by the border population. Many villages close to the border worshipped him as a guardian spirit.

Tu Nghi's death did not put an end to the envoy's woes. For years, he was kept in southern China. In 1563, when he finally reached Peking, he was compelled to stay there for three more years. He came back to Vietnam in 1566, eighteen years after he left. His hair was black and shiny when he set out on his mission; it was white as snow when he returned. He was not the only Mac envoy retained by the Chinese. Ten years before Le Quang Bi's mission, another envoy had gone and was refused leave by the Ming court. He was Nguyen Van Thai, a colleague of our first ancestor Nguyen Tue who, like him, was made a count by Mac Dang Dung after he seized the throne. Nguyen Van Thai took a Chinsese wife and spent the rest of his life in China. Le Quang Bi, for his part, continued to consider himself an envoy of his country during all the years he was kept in China against his will. When he came home, the Mac king sent the highest mandarins of the court to go and greet him at the border. Le Quang Bi was made a marquess and became a popular hero.

Over a decade followed without a diplomatic mission to China. Meanwhile, war continued between the Mac and the Le, or more exactly the

Trinh. After the 1559–1561 campaign in which they were pressed in their last defenses by Trinh Kiem, the Mac recovered. But in the next ten years, the initiative rested with the forces of restoration. The land in the south was poor and every year after the harvest, Trinh Kiem led his troops into the fertile delta to seize rice and other provisions. His objective achieved, he withdrew to start again in the following year. All that time, the Mac were kept on the defensive, except in 1565 when Mac Kinh Dien could mount a counterattack on Thanh Hoa. Trinh Kiem died in 1570 and a new situation developed. Two of his sons, Trinh Coi and Trinh Tung fought for his succession. Mac Kinh Dien in the north saw his opportunity. He led his army south and defeated Trinh Coi, who rallied to the Mac. Trinh Tung's troops fell back. The initiative now belonged to the Mac, while the Southern court was weakened by more internal conflicts. In 1572 the Le king, whose power was nominal, plotted to kill Trinh Tung, but was himself deposed and killed. Trinh Tung put on the throne a six-year-old son of the deposed king. All through the 1570s, Mac Kinh Dien launched yearly offensives against the Trinh. He was unable to gain any decisive breakthrough, but Trinh Tung was hard put to defend his territory. Such was the military situation in 1580, when our ancestor joined a diplomatic mission to China. It was a good time for the Mac to try and consolidate their external position. They were holding the upper hand in the war. Fourteen years had passed since the previous Vietnamese envoy was "freed" by the Ming court. The bad feelings on both sides had subsided.

The 1580 mission was special, being three or four times larger than a normal tribute mission sent either by the Mac or by the Le before them. In earlier instances, three or four names of envoys were recorded by the historian. This time there were twelve. With the administrative and support staff which included interpreters, secretaries, physicians and servants, no less than a hundred people must have set out for the trip to Peking. Probably, the delegation was the largest ever in the history of our relations with China. According to the eighteenth century historian Le Quy Don, the 1580 mission was not one but "four missions grouped together to bring to the Ming Court the tribute which had not been presented for many years." Thus, the large size of the mission was to make up for those missing in the past fourteen years, since Le Quang Bi came home. Being the third-ranked member of such a mission, Nguyen Uyen must have held a high mandarinal rank, certainly higher than a seventh grade reviser at the Academy, or a sixth grade inspector-delegate. He must have been high enough to attend royal audiences and been known personally to the king to be appointed an envoy to China.

To the Chinese, a tribute was an expression of submission and dependence towards China. To the Vietnamese, it was a means to keep relations with our large neighbor smooth and peaceful. At the start of every

Vietnamese dynasty, moves were made to gain peaceful coexistence with China through a recognition by the Chinese emperor, which took the form of the conferring of a title. In most cases, the title was *An Nam Quoc Vuong* or King of Annam, a king being a vassal of the emperor. The Mac, as we saw, only got the inferior title of *An Nam Do Thong Su,* or Supreme Commander of Annam. Tribute missions were sent, in order to periodically reaffirm the relationship. But whether considered by China as a vassal or otherwise, Vietnam's dependence was only nominal. The Vietnamese remained masters in their own country. Besides, Chinese suzerainty did not provide the Vietnamese kings with protection, either against external or internal threat. Vietnamese dynasties were changed when the people willed them to be so, and those dynasties which in desperation turned to China for help as a rule could not save themselves. In the nineteenth century, the French launched their conquest and for the first time in their history, the Vietnamese called for Chinese help against an external enemy. But China proved to be powerless and that put an end to the fiction of suzerainty.

Since antiquity, the Chinese had been prone to treat any non–Chinese coming to them with presents as subjects bearing tribute. As early as in 1109 B.C., envoys of the Viet people arrived in China bringing a present of white pheasants. Chinese history books recorded it as a tribute but, interestingly, they also recorded what the regent had to say on that occasion. He said that "since imperial authority did not extend over there, it would not be gentlemanly to consider those people as subjects." He ordered that the envoys be escorted home on "carriages pointing to the south," which showed that the Chinese knew then how to use the compass. The first real tribute sent by our country was to the Han emperor in 179 B.C. It was handed over to the Chinese envoy who came to Vietnam and consisted of "two tablets of white jade, one thousand sets of kingfisher feathers, ten horns of rhinoceros, five hundred shells with red stripes, one basket of *ca cuong* [a beetle used as a food condiment], forty pairs of live kingfishers, two pairs of peacocks." For his part, the Chinese envoy brought, from the Han emperor to King Trieu Da, "fifty quilted robes of high quality, thirty quilted robes of medium quality and twenty quilted robes of low quality [sic]." Through the centuries, the content of tributes changed. In the sixteenth century, tributes sent by the Le and the Mac dynasties were quite costly, including an important amount of gold and silver. I can find no records of what the 1580 mission brought to Peking, but we can get an idea from the following list of presents taken to China by a previous Mac mission in 1542. The list was given in historian Le Quy Don's book. It included four incense holders and flower vases in gold, two incense holders and flower vases in silver, one gold tortoise and one silver crane (probably serving as candle holders), twelve large silver trays. These were all cult objects made by Vietnamese goldsmiths and silversmiths whose artistry was highly appreciated by the

Chinese. Incense also was much sought after and over a hundred kilograms of different kinds of incense made out of sandal and other precious wood were sent. So fond was the Chinese of our incense that once, the Ming Empress had the luggage of the Viet envoys taken to her chambers and searched, for she suspected that the Vietnamese had rare incense which was not in the tribute but which their envoys brought for their personal use. Various silk materials were also sent, in particular the thin black silk used to make turbans and, of course, such favorite items as elephant tusks (thirty pairs) and rhinoceros horns (twenty). The horns were believed to have aphrodisiac qualities as well as being an antidote to poison. Moreover, it was said that one never gets drunk by drinking from a horn! Two items, however, were missing from the above list. They were two human statues of about five hundred centimeters in size and weighing some six kilograms each, one in gold and the other in silver. After the Chinese occupants were defeated and Vietnam recovered its independence in 1427, the Ming court accepted its loss but demanded the statues as a "compensation" for the death of two generals in the battle of Chi Lang, the last battle of the war. It was a demand to save face and the Vietnamese accepted it as a price for normalizing relations. The costly statues were part of every tribute sent by the Le dynasty to China. They were not mentioned in the Mac tribute recorded by Le Quy Don, but other authors stressed that the Mac king had to provide even bigger statues than those of the Le because the Chinese claimed that he was not a vassal but a dependent and therefore had to make a larger tribute. In any case, the 1580 mission must have brought with it a very rich tribute for it was four missions grouped into one and it would be quite in character for the Chinese to insist on receiving four times the value of a single tribute.

The sending of the 1580 mission was a diplomatic victory for the Mac. For a long time, they were without direct contact with Peking and had to deal with the provincial authorities in Guangdong and Guangxi. Now, agreement had been obtained for a large delegation to go to the Ming court. Was it just to pay tribute? Of course, a tribute mission never just paid tribute; it had a host of matters to negotiate with the Chinese government. Our envoys' first task was to establish contact with Chinese officials, those who decided on policy in Peking as well as those in the two Guang provinces who were in charge of the day-to-day relations with our country. Valuable presents were needed to gain audience with them, although the envoys must be careful not to appear as bribing their hosts. *Thuyet khach*, literally "a guest who talks and convinces," was our traditional image of a diplomat. It was a role much celebrated in ancient Chinese history. During troubled periods, when that country was divided into small states, a great number of talented men could be found travelling around, expounding their ideas on how to solve the problems confronting China and looking for good rulers to offer their services. Confucius himself was once a *thuyet khach,* much respected and listened to wherever he went, but able to find only one state where he could exercise his statesmanship, and just for a short period. Many of our envoys gained fame in China. They were trained in the same school of thought as Chinese scholars; like them, they were imbued with the teachings of Confucianism, Taoism and Buddhism. They would speak Chinese too, for our scholarly script already used Chinese characters and it was a rather simple matter for them to learn the spoken language. The Chinese, who thought of their country as the center of the world, were surprised to find people from a faraway place in the south who could discuss philosophy, literature and poetry on even terms with them. Such was the impression created by our envoys that a title was conferred on some of them by the Chinese court: "First laureate of both countries," meaning that they deserved to come first at the doctorate examinations in both China and Vietnam. It was an implied recognition by the Chinese that our culture and civilization were equal to their own. To cite an instance, Phung Khac Khoan, whom I believe was related to Nguyen Uyen's wife, was an envoy to Peking in 1597. He arrived at the Ming court when festivities were being held to celebrate the Lunar New Year. Chinese mandarins and foreign envoys all presented poems of praise and good wishes to the emperor. While the others wrote one, or perhaps two poems, Phung Khac Khoan wrote thirty. The emperor read them and wrote this commentary: "Which land does not produce men of talent!" There and then, he pronounced him: "First Laureate of both countries."

Having won the respect of his hosts with his culture and erudition, half of the envoy's work was done. He now could raise matters of state with them and be certain to get a sympathetic hearing. A few well-chosen words by the Chinese mandarins in their submission to the Son of Heaven would contribute more to the success of his mission than the rarest and most expensive tribute. In 1580, when our ancestor went to China, Vietnam was a divided country. The Mac had been waging a war with the Le for almost fifty years. They were always apprehensive to be caught between the Le forces in the south and the Chinese army in the north, a situation they had found themselves in prior to 1540. Following the agreement concluded in that year with Mac Dang Dung, China cut off her ties with the Le and maintained relations only with the Mac. Since then, she had stayed out of the Vietnamese conflict. The northern border had remained quiet. The Mac's foreign policy had one overriding objective: to keep China on their side and prevent any rapprochement between Peking and the Le. 1580 was an opportune time to resume contact with Peking. The Le camp was weakened by internal dissensions. Initiative in the fighting rested with the Mac. Our envoys were in a good position to impress on the Chinese that the Mac were winning the war and, therefore, that China was backing the

right side in the Vietnamese conflict. No doubt, the rich tribute and imposing size of the mission were intended to show the increasing strength of the
Mac regime.

Our scholars and poets used a metaphor for the trip from the capital
Thang Long (now Hanoi) to Peking. They called it "the three thousand *li*
journey." The actual journey was much longer, as a *li* was only about half
a kilometer. Furthermore, for reasons of national prestige, the Chinese
authorities wanted as many people as possible to see foreigners bringing
tribute to Peking. Tribute missions were made to wind their way through
the country, from one populated center to another. A mission from Vietnam usually travelled by land and river across the south of China, then
north through the deltas of the Yangtse and Hwang Ho to Peking. Depending on the itinerary established by the Chinese, it may take five months — as
in the case of our ancestor's mission — or up to twelve months. Our envoys
visited important cities, places of great historical significance or scenic
beauty, but they also had to climb high mountain passes and float down
dangerous rapids. It was a hard and exhausting journey. "As exhausting as
going in a diplomatic mission," a proverb said. For a seventy-year-old man
like Nguyen Uyen, and even for younger colleagues in their fifties or sixties,
the prospect must have been daunting indeed. Some envoys took their pre-
cautions before leaving. "If I die in China," I can imagine our ancestor telling his family, "and the date is not known to you, the anniversary of the
day I leave the country should be taken as that of my death, for the holding
of worshipping services." Besides the dangers of travel, no one knew how
long the Chinese would offer their "hospitality" to the mission. If the
drama of the previous mission was to be staged again, how many years, or
even months, could a seventy-year-old envoy wait to go home? Our family
tradition of "people going to faraway places, where from they may not
return" may very well have started with Nguyen Uyen's trip to China.

Being an envoy to the court of the Son of Heaven carried a prestige
perhaps unequalled by any other mandarinal assignment for China, the
Empire of the Middle, was the paramount power in our world. To represent the country there was to uphold national honor and prestige. China
was also a fountain of culture of which our people had been, since the
earliest times, the recipients. We could never forget the thousand years of
Chinese domination and could not, for a moment, ignore that massive and
threatening presence on our borders. But there was no denying our attachment to the cultural heritage we received from China. Over the centuries,
that heritage had been assimilated and had become part of our own culture.
The mission "to the north" was a source of inspiration for much poetry,
written by those fortunate enough to be in the journey, as well as by friends
and colleagues seeing them off. Many poems from the Tran dynasty, the
classical period of Vietnamese poetry, have been preserved. The following

is a much liked one by Le Quat, a statesman and poet living in the fourteenth century. Then a young man and an untitled scholar, Le Quat lived
in the poor and mountainous region of Thanh Hoa in the south of the
country. Hearing that a friend was chosen to join a delegation to China, he
took a boat up the coastline, passing through all the twelve seaports of the
delta, to say farewell to him at the border. His short and melodious poem
in the scholarly script was in the pure classical tradition. In just a few words,
it evoked in the mind of a Vietnamese reader the long journey of the envoy,
his successful career and, by contrast, the life of a recluse in the mountains
who chose leisure and peace of mind; the two diverging dreams of any
scholar! The poem was one of the very few not written by kings or addressed
to them, which found their way into the *History of Dai Viet*. The historian
quoted it in full. Entitled "Sending off Pham Su Manh on his journey
north," it ran:

> On horseback, may you safely go on the three thousand *li* journey,
> While passing through the twelve seaports, I return to my mountains.
> An envoy to the Empire of the Middle!
> A wanderer in a far corner of the country.
> You have won achievements and fame,
> While what I have is but leisure and peace.

Those who stayed behind could only imagine what the envoys were going to see: the Wu Ling or Five Mountains Range, north of Guangxi province and long believed to be our ancient borders with China; the Wu Hu
or Five Lakes where, in the words of a poem, "the visitor set out on a boat
trip, in the clear weather following a snowfall." So many places and historical events in China had become part of our own literary tradition: the
River Wu where Lord Hsiang Wu lost his last battle against the founder of
the Han dynasty and saw his dream to rule over China turn into smoke;
the imperial city of Loyang whose splendor was immortalized in many
Tang poems and the beautiful women of Soochow, sung by generation
after generation of Vietnamese poets who had never set foot on China.

A few days before their departure, the envoys were received in audience by King Mac Hau Hop, the fifth of the dynasty, who gave them his
last instructions and wished them well for their trip. Following the royal audience, the "hundred mandarins" of the court gave a banquet to farewell
the mission. There was a certain urgency about it because our envoys left
in the last month of the year, a rather unusual time. All Vietnamese wished
to celebrate Tet, the most important festival of the year, at home. Moreover, popular belief considered it not auspicious to start great and important endeavors at year's end. Let us wait, people would say as they quoted
the proverb: "Come the new year, days will extend and months will be
longer." No doubt, our envoys would have liked to commence their mission once Tet was over. But the Mac rulers were keen to resume relations

with China, broken thirty-eight years ago since the ill-fated Le Quang Bi's mission. Perhaps also, negotiations over the terms of the mission had been difficult, with the Chinese demanding the payment of tributes missing over the past period and the Vietnamese claiming for guarantees that delegation members would not be retained in China against their will. Chinese agreement to receive the mission was welcome news to the Mac king who implemented it without delay. Our envoys were not given the luxury of greeting the new year and setting off for their diplomatic journey when the days and months were "longer."

On the auspicious third day of the twelfth month, at an auspicious hour chosen by the Ministry for the Rites, they departed from the capital Thang Long. Ten days' travel and they arrived at the town of Lang Son, still a day's march from the official crossing place to China which was the Nam Quan pass. The name Nam Quan was imprinted in our national history. All the wars between our country and China had started at that pass, which commanded the easiest route from the north to the Red River delta. While in the south and the west, the Vietnamese fought to subjugate their neighbors and extend their territory, in the north they had to defend their own country against China. Nam Quan evoked memories of invasion, of battles fought against great odds and of the heroism of soldiers sent there to be the first to fight and to die. In peacetime, Nam Quan was on a main route taken by traders and immigrants. All our diplomatic missions started their journey north from Nam Quan and it was also from there that Chinese missions entered our country. Before reaching Nam Quan, the mission came to a pass believed to be guarded by a powerful spirit. Back in the third century when the Chinese ruled over the Viet country, they called it Demon's Gate, for it was said that nine out of ten of their people passing through it would never come back to China. They would be killed either by the deadly climate or in fighting against the Vietnamese. Our people worshipped that guardian spirit. Traders, officials, soldiers, all stopped there to make offerings. On the passage of the envoys, a large ceremony was held for them to make sacrifices to the spirit and pray for a safe and successful journey. A day before the agreed date to cross over to China the mission arrived at Nam Quan. The time had come for the envoys to take leave of friends and colleagues who had come all the way from the capital to see them off. That evening, they dined together, drank farewell cups and exchanged poems. Older envoys made last recommendations to their children. Ahead of them was a journey across mountains and rivers over tens of thousands *li*, one from which they may not return.

The next day at an auspicious hour, the gates of Nam Quan were thrown wide open and the Chinese welcomed the Vietnamese onto their soil. The tribute mission was on its way. "This journey lives up to the dream of a lifetime," wrote an envoy. As a scholar trained in the Chinese classics and well-versed in the culture and history of China, our ancestor was going back to the very sources of his learning; how thrilling it must have been for him! From poems written by envoys and some accounts of later delegations, we can get a good idea of what his trip was like. Members of the mission travelled in convoys of comfortable boats or carriages escorted by Chinese officials. They stayed in government guest houses and were entertained at every stop. The Chinese were sometimes guilty of not letting foreign envoys return home, but they always looked after them well. They did so with Le Quang Bi during the whole eighteen years they kept him as a virtual prisoner. Even unofficial representatives of the Le who were in China in 1540 when the Chinese switched their support over to the Mac, and who could not return to the south, were given house and land to live on.

From the border going north to Peking, travellers could go either by way of the province of Guangdong or that of Guangxi. In the sixteenth century, our tribute missions usually took the Guangxi route. Diplomacy played an important part in the first stage of their journey for, as we have seen, China's day-to-day relations with Vietnam were handled by provincial authorities of the two Guang provinces and not by the Ming court in faraway Peking. Our envoys met with those authorities in Kuei-lin, the capital of Guangxi. Much of the mission's success depended on the kind of impression they made on their hosts and how well they could convince them that the war was going the Mac's way. The Chinese report would reach Peking before their arrival and determine what welcome they would receive. Mandarins of the two Guang could make or break a mission. It was they who sabotaged the mission of envoy Le Quang Bi in 1548.

Once the diplomatic business was over, our representatives settled down to enjoy their journey across China. If the Chinese authorities wanted the envoys bearing tribute to be seen by the people, they also wanted foreigners to see—and be impressed by—the wealth and beauty of their country. From the rich valleys of the south to the fertile plains of the Yangtse and the Hwang Ho, their itinerary led them through large and prosperous cities: Nan-ning not far from the border and known to many Vietnamese, Chang-sha and Wu-chang farther north in Hunan and Hupeh provinces, Hankow on the Yangtse, which was the most important commercial center in central China at the time, and the southern capital of Nanking, former seat of the Ming dynasty. In the mountainous areas of Guangxi, they saw majestic landscapes of deep gorges and high peaks. As described by one mission:

> The Que River wound its way across an infinite succession of mountain peaks. Sometimes, wild animals of the forest came to the bank to drink, on seeing our convoy of boats, they roared and made fearful sounds.

And again:

On the Tuong River, our boats had to move very slowly. A little mistake could produce a disaster. The deep river made its way through the whole Hunan province before pouring its waters in the Tungting lake. For nearly a month, our boats negotiated the Tuong. It was a very difficult part of the journey, but one in which we could see the strangest and most magnificent landscapes.

Several of the places visited held a special significance for the Vietnamese. Changsha, the capital of Hunan, was the scene of a battle won by the Viet over the Han in 185 B.C. Then, Trieu Da ruled over a country called Nam Viet, or Viet of the South, whose territory extended over what are now the two Guang provinces and the north of Vietnam. He refused to submit himself as a vassal to the Han court, which reacted by forbidding the sale of all products in gold and metal, in particular agricultural implements, to Nam Viet. Trieu Da in anger led his troops north and attacked Changsha. He was, as a matter of fact, a Chinese commander who conquered our country from a Vietnamese dynasty, the Thuc, in 207 B.C. But ancient history books, including the *History of Dai Viet*, appropriated him and treated his as a Vietnamese dynasty. They anchored the belief that our northern border was originally the Wu Ling mountains north of Guangdong and Guangxi. As a result, scholars often wrote of the Wu Ling with nostalgia as our natural boundaries and our envoys to imperial China stopped at the old battle place in Changsha to recall the glory of time past, when the Vietnamese advanced close to the Yangtse River. Under the Ming in China as well as under the Mac in Vietnam, Confucianism was elevated to the rank of a state doctrine, well above Buddhism and Taoism. Temples of Literature dedicated to the cult of Confucius were found in large cities and provincial capitals. Our envoys never failed to visit those temples which happened to be on their way. Close to the end of their journey, they made a pilgrimage to the prefecture of Khuc Phu in Shantung province, to worship in his native place the one whom the Vietnamese, like the Chinese, honored as "Teacher of ten thousand generations." It was customary for tribute missions also to honor the memory of Si Nhiep, a governor when our country was under China's rule, by paying a visit to his home district in Guangxi province. Chinese governors were best forgotten—some became notorious for their cruelty—but during the millennium of Chinese domination, three of them stood out as worthy of gratitude by the Vietnamese. In the first century A.D. Tich Quang was credited with administering his region in conformity with "the rites" and justice. In the same century, Nham Diem taught inhabitants in the regions south of the Red River delta to cultivate the soil and grow crops. Until then, they had been hunters and fishermen. Si Nhiep, the best known of the three, was a governor for forty years in the third century. At the end of the Han dynasty, when China was torn by conflicts, Si Nhiep kept the Viet country safe and peaceful. He

greatly encouraged learning and later on came to be worshipped as a patron
of our scholars. Although a Chinese mandarin, he was posthumously
honored by the Tran dynasty and given the title of Great Prince in the thirteenth century.

But what lay closest to the hearts of our scholar-envoys were the lakes,
palaces, mountains, rivers and cities immortalized by the poems of the
Tang and Sung periods. They knew these poems by heart; in imagination
they already saw those places. Now they were there themselves and could
put brush to paper to emulate ancient Chinese poets:

> Range upon range of mountains surround the citadel of Peng,
> They reach up to the clouds, like a jade screen planted on the horizon.
> The angry current of the Hwang Ho,
> Spills its waves over the banks and rushes down towards the southeast.
> Holding my jade seal, I climb up the Golden Pavillion,
> My fingers follow Su Dong Po's calligraphy, carved on the stone.
> This journey lives up to the dream of a lifetime.

The Sung writer Su Dong Po was revered by the Vietnamese for his
poetic essays. He built the Golden Pavillion in the Peng citadel looking over
the Hwang Ho, or Yellow River. The author of this poem was Pham Su
Manh, the friend whom Le Quat bid farewell in a poem cited earlier. The
jade seal in his hand was a figure of speech to show that he was an envoy.
In olden times, envoys were given a jade seal and a flag made of fur as insignia of their mission.

Vietnamese scholars shared with their Chinese counterparts "the four
elegant pastimes." They played a similar kind of music, enjoyed the same
game of chess, practiced brush painting and wrote poetry in the same
script. Not all scholars were talented at music playing or painting. Few were
really keen chess players. But all were good at composing poems. They had
to be, otherwise they stood no chance of being successful at the examinations. "He speaks not words but poetry" was one of the highest praises that
a scholar could receive. On their journey north, our envoys had plenty of
opportunities to indulge in their favorite pastime of getting together
around a bottle gourd of rice brandy and challenging one another to poetry
writing. Their progression was a leisurely one. A few days at Lake
Tungting, another few days at the Palace of the Golden Crane, the subject
of a famous Tang poem and an inspiration for countless poets since, a stop
in the Pei district where the Han empire started, a visit to the ancient city
of the Yao emperor, who was worshipped by Confucian scholars as a model
of a kind and virtuous king, and so on, there were many breaks along the
way for the visitors to enjoy the sights and be entertained by the cream of
local scholars. From a palace looking out to the mountains, or on a boat
moored in a tranquil lake, guests and hosts sipped rice brandy and talked
of literature and poetry. A scholar improvised a poem to which others

responded with poems on the same theme and using the same rhymes. Then, another theme was taken up, another piece was composed and responded to. Vietnamese and Chinese tested each other's talent; to be unable to respond would mean a serious loss of face. As the envoys thus continued in their unhurried way, their reputation preceded them to Peking. For those who gained the respect of their hosts as scholars and gentlemen, all doors in the Chinese capital would open and they would find court mandarins ready to listen to what they had to say. That was the reason envoys were chosen among men of rich experience and knowledge; often, they were older academicians.

To impress Chinese envoys to Vietnam, our people often resorted to disguising learned doctors into boatmen, helpers, sometimes even placing them as beggars at strategic spots in places visited by the Chinese. There were many anecdotes of boatmen joining the visitors in a poetry contest and surprising them with their literary prowess. "It was bold of me to respond with my unpolished poem," the boatman would say in the manner of an excuse. "You will find in our scholars more worthy interlocutors." One boatman did more than improvise poetry. A Chinese party was enjoying a boat trip down one of our many rivers, drinking brandy and talking among themselves when the envoy broke wind, sonorously. His companions burst out laughing and the envoy, perhaps to hide his discomfiture, bragged: "Thunder rolls over the south!" The south for the Chinese meant our country, just like we meant China when we said the north. The boatman could not let this pass. Stopping his rowing, he went to the bow and, in full view of the party, urinated into the river. "Rain comes to the north!" he said. The Chinese could not help but appreciate the *à propos* of his repartee and this became a celebrated anecdote in the history of our diplomatic relations with China. The Chinese, for their part, tested our envoys' mettle by placing them in impossible situations. Mac Dinh Chi, an ancestor of King Mac Dang Dung, went to China in 1308. An ugly man, he was described in history books as short and small and looking like a monkey. At first, the Chinese made fun of his physical appearance. Soon, they had to bow to his extraordinary literary talent. Still, they threw one challenge after another at him, from which he always came out on top. Once, he was asked to deliver the eulogy at the funeral of an imperial princess. He was given to understand that the eulogy had been written and what was expected of him was only to read it. At the ceremony, before the "hundred mandarins" of the Mongol court and other foreign envoys, he stepped out and was handed the roll containing the eulogy. Opening it, he saw only blank paper with a single horizontal stroke which was the Chinese character for "one." Without changing his expression, Mac Dinh Chi immediately improvised a poem to lament the princess' death, taking "one" as a theme: "A single cloud in the sky . . . the only snow flake . . . a unique flower . . . the moon

over the pond. . . ." His short eulogy moved the assembly more than anything that Chinese officials could have written for their princess. Chinese
history books recorded its full text. This time, the Mongol court was definitively conquered. Something out of the ordinary had to be found to honor
such a talent and the Chinese came up with the title "First Laureate of both
nations."

As a diplomat, I can imagine how my ancestor might have felt as he
approached Peking, the goal of his journey. Even nowadays with modern
means of communication, one does not go on a mission to a foreign country
without a sense of excitement and eager anticipation, as well as some apprehension at facing a new challenge in an unfamiliar environment. How
much more so it must have been four centuries ago. What reception were
he and his fellow envoys going to have in the Chinese capital? How well
would they fare in negotiations with the Ming court? We know that a problem faced by the mission was the confusion regarding its status. At the time,
China did not consider our country as a vassal state, but as a dependency.
In an earlier mission, which took place in 1543, the Mac envoy received the
traditional imperial gifts, but the Ming emperor made the point of not giving him a banquet and of ordering that the number of feasts in his honor
be reduced, to show that he was not treated as a vassal's representative. The
Vietnamese, for their part, did not consider their country as a Chinese dependency. The Mac rulers did accept an inferior title from the Ming
emperor, but they continued to call themselves kings. Their tribute missions were described by historians in the same way as those of earlier dynasties, the titles given to envoys were the same. Protocol and status were
important diplomatic considerations, but in reality, China was content that
the appearance of her supremacy was upheld. Ever since the last century,
when their armies were decisively defeated and their domination brought
to an end, the Ming had been reluctant to get involved again in Vietnam.
Behind a condescending attitude, there was a healthy regard for Vietnamese power of resistance. Thus, although our country was small in comparison with China and, moreover, weakened by internal conflict, I do not
think that our envoys would, in any way, entertain a sense of inferiority as
they presented themselves to the Ming court. On the contrary, they represented a country master of its own destiny and it must have been with
pride and elation that my ancestor and his companions entered the Forbidden City to accomplish their mission.

Nguyen Uyen arrived in Peking in the summer of 1581. The period between 1573 and 1582 was one of great prosperity for China, under a government led by the Grand Secretary Chang Chu Cheng. The Ming emperor
was young and Chang was the country's real ruler during that decade. After
he died in 1582, the dynasty steadily declined until it fell to the Manchus
in 1644. Our ancestor thus saw China in the last splendor of the Ming.

He and his fellow envoys were welcomed thirty *li* from Peking by Chinese officials and taken to the diplomatic residence, where they stayed with envoys from other countries who happened to be visiting the capital. The Ming court received missions from a great many places. Under the reign of the great emperor Yung-lo (1402–1424), these came from neighboring states such as our own, Korea, Japan, the Ryukyu Islands and also countries farther away: Champa, Cambodia, Siam, Java, Sumatra, Borneo, Malacca, and even some Indian states. Yung-lo, who raised the Ming dynasty to the zenith of its power, expanded external relations. He sent several maritime expeditions led by Admiral Cheng Ho to southeast Asia, India and as far as the east coast of Africa. Often, Vietnamese and Korean diplomats were in the Chinese capital at the same time and many stories of our people matching wits and poetry with the Chinese mentioned the presence of a Korean envoy. A strict control was exercised by the Chinese to prevent foreign missions from buying history books, Tibetan silk, weapons, gunpowder and, generally speaking, from learning any trade secret. Also, foreigners were forbidden to take any plant or seed out of China. The Chinese were extremely sensitive about these matters, but some of our envoys still managed to elude their attention and bring home new manufacturing techniques and new varieties of crops. Phung Khac Khoan, the man who presented the Ming emperor with thirty poems, visited Szechwan and memorized the way silk was made there, how it was unwinded from the cocoon and how weaving looms were constructed. On his return, he instructed people in his village and created a thriving silk and gauze cottage industry. He also smuggled out seeds of corn and sesame, which, since the seventeenth century, have become two important crops.

In Peking, the Vietnamese envoys first presented their credentials to the Chinese minister for the Rites and handed over the imperial tribute. Then, they were given an audience by the emperor. A ceremony was organized for them to receive the emperor's gifts to the Vietnamese ruler, which usually consisted of precious products from China such as brocade, embroidered silk and ginseng. Time was spent visiting the capital and attending banquets. But the most important activities of our envoys were contacts and negotiations with the mandarins who governed China. On top of everything, they must have sought to meet with Grand Secretary Chang to acquaint him with the situation in Vietnam and cement Chinese support to the Mac dynasty. Did they obtain a private audience with him and succeed in "winning the heart" of a man considered as being, in effect, the emperor? Judging from the welcome they received back home from their king and from mandarins at the Court, they probably did. Having left Thang Long at the end of the year of the Dragon (1580), the mission arrived back at the border fourteen months later, in the spring of the year of the Horse (1582). The following quote is taken from the *History of Dai Viet*:

On the twenty-sixth day of the second month, year of the Horse, the Mac king ordered the minister of Finance, Count of Vinh Kieu (and three other high officials whose names were given) to the border at Lang Son to welcome back the Luong Phung Than mission.

Mandarins were routinely sent to the border to meet tribute missions on their return, but this time a court minister went and the occasion was considered important enough to be recorded in history books. Only once before under the Mac dynasty did the king send a minister and that was in the very special case of envoy Le Quang Bi, who came back after being kept by the Ming for eighteen years. Moreover, historian Le Quy Don recorded in his book that "on the fifth day of the third month, the minister of Public Service Tran Van Tuyen asked to be allowed to retire, so as to make room for the envoys who had just returned from China. The Mac king rejected his request." Among ministers, the one heading the Public Service was the highest in rank; that he offered to cede his place showed the very high credit enjoyed by the returning envoys. By all accounts, their trip to China was a great success. Yet another indication of this success was the sending of another tribute mission in 1584. Relations with China, which were disrupted for a long time by the Le Quang Bi affair, were again back to normal and the old system of triennal tribute missions was reestablished.

Like many envoys "to the north," Nguyen Uyen must have written a number of poems during his trip. Our family was not able to keep any, but I can readily imagine them, short and concise in the mode of classical Tang poems and subtly expressing emotions and feelings through references to ancient Chinese stories and writings. Some poems written by envoys from his time have been preserved. They are quite difficult to understand, being written in the old scholarly script. As eyewitness accounts of the trip to China, they are of little value. Envoys were also known to have written diaries and memoirs, and these would be of much more historical interest. The splendor of Peking at the time of the Ming, the pomp and ceremony at the Imperial Palace, how I would love to see them through my ancestor's eyes! The negotiations with the Chinese, the diplomatic experience at the court of the Son of Heaven, I am sure that Nguyen Uyen wrote about them, not only in his official report but also for his personal records. Most academicians were prolific writers. Private diaries and memoirs, however, tended to disappear quickly in the incessant turmoil of our country. Families could never keep them for long. Our own family lost all papers left by Nguyen Uyen; worse still, it even forgot the crowning achievement of his career, the tribute mission which I only discovered in the *History of Dai Viet*. I was thrilled, the more so since I myself made a career in diplomacy. But searches in other historical sources provided few other details, for the Mac period was one of the least documented in our history. As a result, to

paint a picture of my ancestor's mission, I had to draw on information that
I could gather from other missions.

It was customary for the Mac, like the Le dynasty before them, to reward returning envoys with the position of deputy minister and the title of
tu, or viscount. We have no records of the positions and titles that Nguyen
Uyen and his colleagues were given. But the *ba* that our family remembered
as being his middle name may very well be the title he received. Other
rewards and honors came to the envoys. An ambassador was granted fifty-
five *mau* of rice fields, a deputy ambassador forty-five *mau,* or sixteen hectares. Like newly-graduated doctors, envoys were triumphantly welcomed
back to their villages and feted as popular heroes. At over seventy years of
age, Nguyen Uyen must have retired soon after his return from China. In
those days, mandarins were often subjected to harsh disciplinary measures
such as reprimands, demotions, dismissals, forced resignations. Just to be
able to retire honorably in old age was a matter of much rejoicing. To be
retained in the king's service until Nguyen Uyen's age and to end a career
on such a high note as a diplomatic mission was a rare achievement indeed.
His friends and colleagues would have organized a sumptuous farewell
banquet, poem after poem of praise would have been written on long silk
hangings and presented to him. On the day he left to return to his village,
there would have been a large crowd to see him off at the gates of the
capital.

Nguyen Uyen died when the Mac were still in power. The court conferred on him the posthumous name On Tinh. These were aptly chosen
words to honor the memory of an envoy, for they stand for moderation and
calm. He married twice. The family chronicle only mentions the name of
his second wife, a lady from the Phung family. She was probably stepmother to his only son who, as we shall see in the next chapter, was born
in 1534 when Nguyen Uyen was in his twenties and therefore, more likely
from his first wife. What could have been the reasons for the name of that
Phung lady to be remembered, while that of his first wife was not?

For a long time, Nguyen Uyen was thought to be our first ancestor.
He still holds a very special place in our family history. Most of the traits
and traditions related to the Nguyen of Kim Bai can be said to have
originated from him: scholarship, public service, a long life, a certain
slowness in reaching the top of one's career and a journey to a faraway place
in uncertain conditions. To those of my own generation he comes across
as a familiar figure, much closer to us than his father, which is natural since
links with the latter were lost for quite a long time, but also closer than
many ancestors who came after him. In its length and variety, his mandarinal career was exceptional. Lasting over half a century, it saw a young
doctor rise to become royal delegate to a region, serve in the Academy, the
national center for scholarship and learning, and finally participate in a

mission to China, the dominant power in our world. Nguyen Uyen did not seem to have reached a very high rank. I do not think that he ever was part of the inner council of the Mac king or even belonged to any faction at the court. I rather picture him as an independent scholar-mandarin in the traditional Confucian mould, who put his versatile talent to whatever function the king wanted him to perform—true to the Master's precept that "a gentleman should not specialize"—while always careful to keep a certain distance vis-à-vis his superiors and the king himself, as a means of safeguarding his integrity and independence of judgment. But his reputation must be such that he was still called upon, in the evening of his life, to undertake a most sensitive mission in which the paramount interests and honor of the state were involved: a diplomatic journey to Peking.

The Mac rule lasted for over six decades. Of our ancestors who served it, Nguyen Uyen was the most fortunate in that he graduated and spent his whole career under the same dynasty. In this way, he was spared the heartbreaking choice that his father had to make when the Le were replaced by the Mac as well as the shame and despair which would be the lot of his son when the Mac were defeated. His was a calm and stable period between two storms. It may be for this reason that, while the traumatic first and third generations came to be forgotten, Nguyen Uyen stayed on in the memory of his descendants. The words *Han Lam*, the Academy, mean "the forest of brushes." Our ancestor must have used his writing brush often. With a life as rich as his, there was a great deal to write about. It was said of our country that from the forest of its ancient literary treasures, only a few trees have been preserved. The same can be said of Vietnamese families. Nguyen Uyen must have written poems, essays, diaries, memoirs, perhaps even contributed to a history of the Mac. But following the fall of that dynasty and the decline of our family, the trees that he left were soon destroyed. Not a single one escaped. His long and full life, including fifty years of public service, are reduced to a mention in the *History of Dai Viet*, a few lines in the two registers of high graduates and a paragraph in our family chronicle.

16. The Tragedy of the Third and Fourth Generations

The next generation was recorded in the chronicle by a few short sentences:

> Our third ancestor's pseudonym was Phuc Ninh. His wife came from the Nguyen family. Her pseudonym was Trinh Khiet. They had to move from place to place. There was no recollection of their tribulations.

Then, in the manner of a postscript, came these cryptic lines:

> The family organized a ceremony to call our foremother's spirit. She was buried where the highway ran, outside the boundary of the Pham family's shrine. Consequently, her grave was lost. The date of her death was also forgotten.

"No recollection of their tribulations," wrote my grandfather. There were, about the ancestors of this generation, many unanswered questions. We know that they fled after the Mac dynasty crumbled. Why did they have to flee? It was thought that the departure was on account of the Nguyen of Kim Bai having served the Mac in prominent positions for several generations. Anti-Trinh feelings were strong in our family and these were attributed to persecution at the hands of the new rulers. Was Phuc Ninh himself a mandarin of the Mac? That would be quite likely, considering what his grandfather and father did under that dynasty. But why did the family not remember anything about him, his diplomas, his career or even his name? Phuc Ninh was only a pseudonym. Furthermore, after a long period of absence, Phuc Ninh's wife was able to return to Kim Bai. She died and was buried there. The purpose of the above ceremony was to find the location of her grave. Did Phuc Ninh return? Why was there no effort to locate his grave, which we know was also lost? From what was written in the chronicle, one could sense something sad and tragic, which elders were reluctant to recall. I can remember vaguely something they said about the third generation, that it was an "ill-fated" generation. When my grandfather translated the chronicle from the old scholarly language into modern Vietnamese for the benefit of the young generations, he omitted the fact that the family "had to move from place to place," in other words to go into

214

hiding. He also left out the ceremony of calling our foremother's soul. It seemed to me that Phuc Ninh's case was similar to that of our first ancestor Nguyen Tue. Later generations came to forget everything about Nguyen Tue, because as a mandarin he transferred his allegiance from the Le to the Mac, an act decried as treason when the Le returned to the throne. Similarly, it is likely that some traumatic event also occured in Phuc Ninh's time, which the family at first tried to conceal and ended up forgetting for good. I consulted history books, but since Phuc Ninh was only a pseudonym, there was no possiblity of doing any meaningful research. To me, that generation was a lost cause until the day I came across the following passage in the *Dai Viet Register of High Graduates*:

> In the year of the Goat, fourth year of the Sung Khuong era under the Mac, seventeen candidates were awarded the doctorate diploma.... First among the doctors of the second class was Nguyen Hoang, hailing from the village of Kim Bai, prefecture of Thanh Oai. He graduated at thirty-eight years of age. He rallied [to the Le] and became second deputy-minister of Justice, with the title of count.

The fourth year of the Sung Khuong era corresponded to 1571 in the western calendar. Nguyen Hoang was then thirty-eight, which means that he was born thirty-seven years before as we have to take into account the Vietnamese custom of giving an extra year to every person; when born, a baby is already one year old. Nguyen Hoang was therefore born in 1534; he thus belonged to the generation of Nguyen Uyen's son. Was he the same person as Phuc Ninh? The register of graduates, which so clearly established the family links between our first and second ancestors, failed to provide any clue regarding Nguyen Hoang's parentage. But there were several positive indications. His name is composed of two words, like those of Nguyen Tue, Nguyen Huyen and Nguyen Uyen. Names were made of two words in some Vietnamese families, three words in others. Nguyen Hoang may very well belong to our family, for there could not be several families of Nguyen in Kim Bai with a two-worded name and whose members were scholars with high academic honors to their credit. Nguyen Hoang graduated in a year of the Goat and this is another interesting pointer. Our people attached much importance to the fact that our first and second ancestor were both made doctors in a year of the Goat, at an interval of twenty-four years. In our calendar, the same animal came back every twelve years. As doctorate examinations were held triennially, they were always under the sign of one of the following four animals, the Goat, the Dog, the Buffalo or the Dragon. Among these, the Goat showed itself to be our auspicious animal, for our three doctors Nguyen Huyen, Nguyen Tue and Nguyen Uyen all won their laurels under it. Now, thirty-six years after Nguyen Uyen, Nguyen Hoang also became a "year of the Goat" doctor. Was this just a coincidence, or could it be taken as an indication of direct descendance?

I know that village elders, those in the time of my youth, would surely lean towards the second possibility. They would also invoke the prophecy of the Mountain of the Twins, which said that at any given period, there could only be one family in Kim Bai succeeding at the highest civil service examination.

I discussed my findings with my father. "We can never be sure," he said, "since we do not know Phuc Ninh's real name and the registers of high graduates remained silent on Nguyen Hoang's family links." Nguyen Hoang's surrender to the Le seemed to be at variance with our family recollection, which was that Phuc Ninh suffered tribulations because he had been a mandarin of the Mac. However, my father pointed out that by coming out to work for the victorious Le, Nguyen Hoang would have made it possible for our family to return to Kim Bai. This might also explain why the family had been able to hang on to large landholdings until the seventh generation, as stated in the Cu Hau papers.

Then, I discovered something more about Nguyen Hoang in the *Southern Sky Register of High Graduates*:

> Nguyen Hoang . . . was a doctor of the second class in the year of the Goat. In the Royal Courtyard examination, his papers could have earned him the first class. But he committed the *bach tu* mistake and was downgraded to second class. After the Mac rule ended, he rallied to the Le. He became second deputy-minister of Justice, with the title of count. He was killed by rebel troops.

Such inauspicious happenings as the rallying to the Le and the violent death at the hands of rebel troops would explain on the one hand, why our family had wished to forget about our third ancestor and on the other, why our village had no collective recollection of its most brilliant scholar. The downgrading at the examination would be another tribulation in a life remembered as ill-fated. More and more, Nguyen Hoang and Phuc Ninh became one in my mind.

Nguyen Hoang graduated at the age of thirty-eight. Probably, he had sat for a number of doctorate sessions before getting his name on the "golden board." He must have been talented, but unlike Nguyen Uyen and Nguyen Huyen before him, both of whom won the degree at a young age, luck was obviously not on Nguyen Hoang's side. At thirty-eight, time was running out for him, for few were those over forty who could successfully meet the challenge of a doctorate session. Then, in that year of the Goat, under an animal sign which saw his grandfather, great-uncle and father all graduate, everything seemed to fall into place. Nguyen Hoang went through the four stages of the *Hoi* examinations, attended the Royal Courtyard session and wrote such a good paper that he was deemed worthy of the first class, a rank awarded only to the top three graduates of each session. Would he be given the third title, which carried the poetical name of

Tham Hoa—Searching Among the Blossoms—or the second title of *Bang Nhan,* Eye of the Honors List? Could he win the supreme honor of being made *Trang Nguyen,* or First Laureate of the country? Our family had never had such glorious titles, nor had indeed our village.

But those titles were not given out easily. Quite often examiners, most of whom were doctors of the third class and therefore did not like to see others graduate at a higher rank, tried their best not to award them. They checked the papers again and again for any small mistake and resorted to various rules and regulations to disqualify candidates. Other factors intervened: nepotism, coteries among mandarins, personal dislikes. Many times, it had happened that scholars renowned for their literary talents were not given the highest honors because they were opposed by jealous and powerful mandarins. Nguyen Hoang's papers were found to contain a *bach tu* mistake and, instead of the first class, he was downgraded to the second class. *Bach tu* means that he either miswrote a character or mixed up two characters which were pronounced in the same way but had different meanings. However, it was unlikely that a scholar good enough to obtain a doctorate would make such simple mistakes. Nguyen Hoang was probably a victim of a special interpretation of the *bach tu* rule. As a mark of respect for the reigning dynasty, the names of the king and those of his ancestors were not to be mentioned in public by anyone. Candidates at the civil service examinations had to constantly bear in mind a long list of *huy,* or royal names to be avoided. To write one such taboo word in their papers would mean failure and, in addition, punishment at the hands of the law for what was considered a crime of lèse-majesté. When such a word was to be used, it had to be avoided and a homophone substituted in its place. Vietnamese language, which until the last century was written with Chinese characters, was full of homophonic words. For instance, there were three characters written differently and having different meanings, but pronounced in the same way as *thanh.* One *thanh,* the one in Thanh Oai, the name of our prefecture, means the blue or green color. The second *thanh* was an adjective meaning pure and the third *thanh* was a noun meaning sound. Nguyen Hoang may have used a homophone to replace a royal name, which was not violating any official taboo, but examiners may have disapproved of his choice. In those days, examiners made their own rules. It could very well be that either Nguyen Hoang or his father Academician Uyen had enemies among mandarins of the panel. People may have been jealous of our family, which had already produced three doctors in the space of two generations. We cannot know for sure. Clearly, the mistake was slight, for Nguyen Hoang was still ranked at the head of the second class; in other words, he was made the fourth highest doctor in the country. Doctors of the second class still carried great prestige among the population. In the popular language, they were called *Ong Hoang* or the Golden Ones. But to have come so close to the top, only to fail to reach it! Fate had its own ways with people's lives, some would say. Others would, recalling these lines in the concluding verses of the *Story of Kieu*, express the belief that the Lord in Heaven treated humanity with an even hand, for He:

Would not favour any particular person,
By giving him both talent and good luck in full measure.

Nguyen Hoang, from what we know of his doctorate experience, his having to serve two dynasties and his tragic death, certainly was not blessed with good luck. His career with the Mac had probably started before he obtained his doctorate. But taking from 1571, the year he obtained that diploma, to the fall of the dynasty in 1593, more than two decades had elapsed. As a doctor of the second class, he would have received the lower seventh grade and could be appointed to positions such as reviser at the Academy or head of a small prefecture. From there, a highly-ranked doctor like him could be expected to reach very important government positions twenty years later; yet, history books which I had consulted carried no mention of him. It is true that all history books are notoriously deficient about the Mac dynasty, being written by later historians to whom the Mac were "usurpers" and, therefore, not worthy of much attention. Nguyen Hoang's time was the last part of the Mac period and this was the most cursorily treated, with practically no information given about the government, its policies and the mandarins who served it. The *Mirror of Vietnam's History* did not even allude to the great diplomatic mission of 1580 to China. Like so many other high mandarins of the Mac, Nguyen Hoang may have been simply ignored by historians. But I wonder whether he had a very smooth and successful career. The downgrading at the doctorate session may have marked him as an unlucky man, one on whom shone an inauspicious star, as people would say. A mandarin with a reputation of being "unlucky" often missed out on good appointments because it was feared that his own misfortune would flow on to the people he administered. Moreover, public service in those times was not the stable and secure profession it has become today. Mandarins wielded great authority and power. They were called "father and mother of the common people," but were themselves highly vulnerable to the autocratic judgment of their superiors and the dreaded control of government inspectors and censors. Mistakes were heavily penalized. Not only could one be deprived of promotion or sent to a faraway and insalubrious place; demotion and even dismissal were often meted out. Demotion, in particular, was a scourge which few mandarins could escape in their careers. One may even lose all one's grades if given the radical penalty of *cach tuot,* or demotion right down to the bottom line. The soldier-poet Nguyen Cong Tru, who lived in the first half of the nineteenth century, was perhaps the most celebrated example of the ups and downs in public service. A scholar turned military commander, he led many armies and won many battles, but also could not avoid being the victim of frequent demotions. He always came back. Towards the end of his career, he reached the office of minister for the Army only to be demoted, this time to a foot soldier. He climbed back again, but could only come up to the fifth grade when he retired at the age of seventy-one. Nguyen Hoang, the unlucky scholar, may very well have had a checkered career. His highest rank, as stated in the registers of high graduates, was that of second deputy minister under the restored Le dynasty. At the end of the Mac regime, he might or might not have reached that rank. Although that would put him among the very high officials at the court, one could expect to see him even further up, considering his diploma and length of service. As a comparison, among those who graduated in the same year as he was one Hoa Huu Mo, who only obtained the doctorate third class to Hoang's second class. Yet, history books mentioned that when taken prisoner by the Trinh army in 1593, Mo was already a first deputy minister. Like his father Nguyen Uyen, Hoang was probably an independent mandarin who kept away from court factions and their maneuvers. Consequently, rapid promotions might not have been for him. Certainly, he was not close to the Mac family; otherwise, the Le king would not have accepted his submission and given him rank and title.

"He rallied and became a second deputy minister...." This sentence in the *Dai Viet Register of High Graduates* led me to think, at first, that Nguyen Hoang was not our third ancestor. I had thought that our family had suffered at the hands of the Le following the defeat of the Mac. But if Hoang had rallied, then reached a high office under the Le dynasty, why were his descendants so traumatized that they could not even remember his real name? I was also puzzled that my grandfather, who found the links with our first ancestor Nguyen Tue in the *Dai Viet Register of High Graduates*, did not say anything about Nguyen Hoang. Could he have missed what the book contained about the latter? Or did he think that Nguyen Hoang, although hailing from Kim Bai, was not a member of our family?

However, these doubts were dispelled when I found in the *Southern Sky Register of High Graduates* that after rallying to the Le, Nguyen Hoang was killed by "rebel troops," in other words followers of the Mac whom he had once served. What an unfortunate fate! The family trauma could now be understood. My grandfather never saw that second register and never knew, for instance, that our second ancestor went to China or that our first ancestor took the name of a village in our prefecture, Hung Giao, for his title. Had he known of Nguyen Hoang's ill-fated life, would he recognize in it the tragedy of our third generation? As for me, the matter had become clear. The manner of Hoang's death had provided the last piece of the puzzle.

In 1583, just a year after their diplomatic success in China, the tide of the war began to turn against the Mac. Trinh Tung, the overlord in the south, seized the initiative. Every year, he sent his troops north to attack the Red River delta and capture food provisions. The threat moved nearer and nearer each year to the capital Thang Long. In terms of population and territory, the Mac still held a distinct advantage over the south. They were in possession of the delta, the country's granary and its main source of wealth. But since the death of Mac Kinh Dien, the Mac army lacked a leader capable of measuring himself up to Trinh Tung. Mac Hau Hop, the king, had been in power since 1562. He was not a bad king and even historians of the Le could find little to criticize him for, but he was unable to arrest the slide downwards. More and more, his side was forced into the defensive. In 1587, it built a long and continuous defense line consisting of "earthen walls planted with bamboo," to protect the western and southern flanks of the capital. Our village became one of the outposts on that line, which ran along the Hat River. In 1589, the Mac mustered their strength to launch a large attack against the south. They failed in what proved to be their last chance to win the war. Three years later, Trinh Tung started a big offensive aimed at the capital. Heading an army of 50,000, but clamoring that it was 120,000 strong, he moved north through the western mountains. Bypassing our home region to the west, the Trinh forces went further up north before turning east and descending on the delta. They clashed with the main body of the Mac forces in the province of Son Tay, about thirty kilometers to the north of Kim Bai. They won that decisive battle and crossed the Hat. It was then that our village fell into their hands for the first time. The Trinh reached the capital's outskirts on the eve of the most important festival in our calendar, the Tet. The population fled in panic. As recorded in the *History of Dai Viet*: "That night, men and women, young and old, fought to get into boats to cross the Red River in order to escape. Over one thousand people drowned."

Winter nights in the north were extremely cold and those who fell into the freezing water of the river had little chance to come out alive. Trinh Tung stopped for three days to let his troops celebrate the festival, then gave the order for the assault. On the sixth day of the new year, Thang Long was occupied. The Mac forces retreated towards Hai Duong, the home base of the dynasty, situated farther east in the delta.

There followed an unexpected twist. Having taken Thang Long and having his opponent on the run, Trinh Tung called off his campaign and brought his troops home to the south. Many historians considered his decision as surprising, but the fact was that, although they lost a crucial battle, the Mac were still in a strong position. They still possessed large forces, while Trinh Tung's army had been extended far away from its bases. Probably, Trinh Tung himself was surprised by the magnitude of his victory.

His original plan may have been to make just a deep foray in the north to weaken the enemy. Thus, the Mac came back to Thang Long. Again, they were masters of the capital and of the rest of the delta.

However the loss of Thang Long, even if only temporary, had dealt a crushing blow to the Mac morale. The capital was the traditional seat of power. For centuries, whoever owned Thang Long had been regarded as the ruler of the country. Mac Hau Hop returned there a broken man. Instead of seizing the opportunity provided by Trinh Tung's withdrawal to rally his people, he neglected his duties, became more involved in women and alcohol and alienated his commanders and soldiers by treating them badly. To the eyes of many, the sign was clear: the king was going to his ruin, Fate had decided against the Mac. Mac Hau Hop hastened his end by plotting to kill Bui Van Khue, one of his best generals, in order to appropriate his wife. The general defected to the south. Trinh Tung saw his chance. Saying that "Van Khue has come over to our side, Heaven wants me to succeed," he promptly launched his final offensive. The respite for the Mac had lasted for only eight months. The Trinh forces quickly took over our home region. Their main army camped on the beach of Tinh Than on the Hat River, in our prefecture of Thanh Oai. The last battle of the war was fought at the confluence of the Hat and the Red River, both on land and on the river. The victorious Trinh reoccupied Thang Long. The Mac king fled but was captured a short time later and executed. The Mac dynasty had ended.

History books recorded many instances of surrender by high officials, or of their capture, at the fall of the Mac. Often, their fate was told. For many, it was swift justice: "They were beheaded, all of them," wrote the historian of a group. Others were accorded clemency, even given new mandarinal positions. Some stories were related in detail to show the victor's magnanimity and the consideration he gave to a gallant warrior. When Nguyen Quyen, a duke of the Mac holding the title of Great Protector and commanding their southern army, was captured and brought before him, Trinh Tung untied his ropes and greeted him as a guest.

Nguyen Quyen was the scion of one of the foremost scholarly families in our prefecture Thanh Oai. His father and his maternal uncle both won the title of First Laureate. A minister of the Mac, his father rallied to the Le in 1550. As a young man, Quyen showed great aptitude in martial arts and the overlord Trinh Kiem, Trinh Tung's father, was very fond of him. He helped prepare him for a career in the army. But after his father died, Quyen left the Le to go back to the Mac. He fought countless battles against the Trinh. Now Trinh Tung, recalling the affection that his family had for Quyen, indicated that he would not like to have to kill him but would welcome his submission. Quyen, however, was ready to accept his fate. His head down, he said: "A vanquished commander cannot speak out strongly.

Heaven has forsaken the Mac, even heroes would find it difficult to show their talents." Trinh Tung, the historian noted, praised these words. He sent Nguyen Quyen to end his days in captivity.

I looked carefully in the *History of Dai Viet* to find when and in what circumstances Nguyen Hoang gave himself up. After Thang Long fell for the second time to the Trinh, seventeen Mac mandarins led by Do Uong, the minister for Public Service, and Nhu Tong, the minister for the Rites, came to Trinh Tung's command post to surrender. The dukes, ministers, deputy ministers, royal delegates and other officials who formed that group rallied early to the victors, in fact, even before the last Mac king was captured. Trinh Tung treated them kindly. He had for them words of consolation and sent a message to the Le king proposing that they be allowed to retain their ranks and titles. Both Do Uong and Nhu Tong were no strangers to our family. They took part in the same mission to China as our second ancestor Nguyen Uyen, although belonging to a younger generation. Nguyen Hoang must have known them well. He would have joined them, had he wanted to change camp at that time. But he was not in the group. The *Southern Sky Register* made clear that he only rallied to the Le, "after the Mac rule had ended."

Following Mac Hau Hop's death, a son of the legendary general Mac Kinh Dien took over the mantle of the fallen dynasty. Mac Kinh Chi proclaimed himself king and immediately rallied the people of Hai Duong around him. "Members of the Mac family, former mandarins and commanders of the Mac," wrote the author of the *History of Dai Viet*, "called on each other to join Kinh Chi. He set up his headquarters and issued proclamations calling on the population to enlist. The prefectures responded and, in no time, his army swelled to be seventy thousand strong." Mac Kinh Chi defeated the generals sent by Trinh Tung to fight him. His control soon extended over the eastern half of the Delta. But when Trinh Tung's main army arrived, his newly-recruited troops proved to be no match for it. Kinh Chi's reign lasted for no more than a few months. He and fifteen princes, dukes, marquesses and other members of the Mac family were captured and beheaded. More than fifty mandarins were made prisoners, from the top ministers and head of the Censorate, to academicians and officials of other ranks. The *History of Dai Viet* listed all their names. Nguyen Hoang's was not there.

What happened then to Nguyen Hoang, since he neither surrendered nor was captured at the end of the Mac dynasty? Our chronicle says that he "had to move from place to place," clearly to escape from falling into the hands of the new regime. Not being a follower of a Mac prince, or a member of a faction, he was left on his own when the regime collapsed. He and his family must have fled from the capital. The first place that a Vietnamese would go to, in times of danger, was his village. But Kim Bai had already come under Trinh control, even before the capital did. Trinh troops were present in great strength in our region to secure their main road link between Thang Long and their home base in the south. They may be stationed in Kim Bai itself, for ours was a large village lying next to the highway. When the Le king moved his court to Thang Long a few months after the victory over the Mac, his party passed through Kim Bai and camped some kilometers farther north, at the seat of Thanh Oai prefecture. There, the overlord Trinh Tung greeted the king and escorted the royal party into the capital. Since Kim Bai was a village of scholars and many families had relatives working in the Mac administration, most people had something to fear from the wrath of the victors. Descendants of the second branch of our family, that of ancestor Nguyen Huyen, would have left at that time too. Most villagers took refuge in the foothills of the western mountains, not too far away, there to wait for the situation to settle down. But Nguyen Hoang, as a mandarin of the Mac, would have to find a more distant and safer place of refuge. In the confused situation prevailing after the Mac defeat, it was not difficult to stay out of reach of the new rulers. Numerous Mac princes and army commanders held sway over many areas in the highlands and mountains, as well as in the delta. Thai Nguyen, for instance, where our second ancestor stayed as a royal delegate and where our family must still have had many ties, remained out of government control for years. Apparently, Nguyen Hoang did not rally to the Le before several years. The war between the north and the south had lasted for half a century. Attitudes were hardened by the long conflict, during which each side claimed sole legitimacy and treated the other as rebel. Ours was a family of conservative and rather rigid Confucian scholars, who had served the Mac dynasty for three generations. Time must elapse before Nguyen Hoang could bring himself to take such a difficult decision as to renounce his loyalty. There must also have been compelling reasons, or some extraordinary combination of circumstances, for he was already in his early sixties. At that age, a scholar had started thinking of the cottage and garden in his native village, where he would retire to await the end of his days. Ambitions for high offices did not drive him so much anymore, nor did the dreams of "making one's name known to the rivers and mountains," which a poet once said lay deep in the heart of every Vietnamese. For Nguyen Hoang, such dreams had already been shattered by the defeat of the Mac.

After the flush of victory, the restored Le monarchy had to come to grips with governing a newly-conquered territory. It needed the services of northern scholars, in particular those coming from old families which for many generations had produced graduates and servants of the state. The new regime started seeking out former Mac mandarins who were still taking refuge in areas outside its control, offering them honors and positions to come over to the Le. Colleagues who had rallied earlier could have served as intermediaries for Nguyen Hoang. Several names come to mind; in the first instance, those of Do Uong and Nhu Tong, who went with Hoang's father to China. They were doing well under the new dynasty. Do Uong was made Finance minister and both he and Nhu Tong were sent by the Le king to the border to negotiate with the Chinese. Were they instrumental in bringing Nguyen Hoang over to the Le? I doubt that they were. Radical elements in the Le camp would have opposed Nguyen Hoang because of the role played by his grandfather in the overthrow of the Le some sixty years before. New converts like Do Uong and Nhu Tong would not have dared to advance Hoang's name lest they be accused of sympathy towards a descendant of a "traitor." Someone else must have been involved, one whose commitment and service to the Le were such that no one could question his loyalty.

Our chronicle hints at the identity of such a person. It is said of a Vietnamese that he has not one, but three families: his own, his mother's and his wife's. The traditional "extended family" was, in fact, constituted by all three of them. We cannot trace the families of either Nguyen Hoang's wife or his mother. But we know that his stepmother was a lady from the Phung family. As it happened, the prophet Nguyen Binh Khiem's mother married a second time, to a scholar with the same surname Phung from Son Tay. They had a son named Phung Khac Khoan, who later became a famous statesman under the Le. Khoan was younger than his stepbrother Khiem by as many as thirty-seven years, which made some people think that his relationship with the prophet was just a creation of folklore, but such a big gap was not impossible in those times when girls were married in their early teens. Did Hoang's stepmother belong to the same family? I think it was quite possible as Phung is not a very common family name and furthermore, Son Tay is a neighboring province of ours. I have even hazarded the guess that the prophet may have had a hand in the lady Phung's marriage to his fellow graduate—and our second ancestor—Nguyen Uyen. If that was the case Nguyen Hoang would have had ties, through his stepmother, with Phung Khac Khoan.

Khoan studied under his stepbrother the prophet, then a duke of the Mac. When a young man, he was told by him to go south and serve the Le. This looked like taking an insurance with both sides of the conflict; but later historians explained that the prophet did so because he could foresee that the Le would win the mandate of Heaven and gain final victory. He would have gone himself, they commented, but for an old mother to care for in the north. A compromise had to be made between his conflicting duties to the country and to the family. Phung Khac Khoan left for the south in the end of the 1540s, obtained his doctorate there and became a trusted adviser to the Trinh overlord. Forty years later, he returned to the north in victory. With the rank of deputy minister, he was entrusted with the important task of winning over the population in the newly occupied territories and calling on refugees to reintegrate their villages. Khoan must have been older than Nguyen Hoang. As he left the north at a young age, the two of them may not have known each other. Even if they had, many decades had passed during which they served in opposing camps. Now they were separated by the abyss between winner and loser in a long and bitter civil war. Being on the losing side, Hoang had lost everything except his pride; he would not be the one to make the first move towards establishing contact. Khoan, the winner, would. Moreover, to get good and respected former mandarins to rally to the new regime was one of the best ways to pacify the country which was still in the grip of widespread unrest. But there could be no question of him imposing himself on a scholar and a peer of his. In the event, links would have been established between the two by the women in the family, who often played a bridging role in such situations. On Hoang's side, his stepmother Phung or his wife Trinh Khiet would have prepared the ground for a reconciliation. Then, at an appropriate time, Khoan would have offered to Hoang an opportunity to be again of service to the country by rallying to the Le king. The role played by the lady Phung at that juncture could have been the reason for her name being preserved in the chronicle, while following generations had forgotten that of Nguyen Uyen's first wife and Hoang's mother.

At the top of his career, Khoan was made a duke and given the title of Great Guardian, the second highest mandarinal title. One of the most trusted servants of the Le, he was chosen to lead the first diplomatic mission of the restored dynasty to Peking. His position would have allowed him to sponsor Hoang's return, in spite of what Hoang's grandfather did when the Le lost their throne. Khoan was a man of strong convictions, and very outspoken. Few mandarins would have liked to cross his path. Only the Trinh overlord could have overruled him in this case, but obviously he did not, and Hoang was eventually appointed to a high position at the Le court. Khoan sometimes was outspoken to the point of recklessness. Once, he contradicted the king in public and was demoted to a subaltern provincial post. In the 1597 diplomatic mission to China, he fearlessly protested to the Ming emperor at the full imperial audience. The aims of his mission were to resume the sending of tributes to China and to get the Chinese to again recognize the restored Le king as King of An Nam. During the Mac period, the Vietnamese king only received from Peking the inferior title of Supreme Military Commander of An Nam. The Ming court agreed to the resumption of tribute missions but not to the second request. True to his character, when he was handed over the decree conferring on his king the title of Supreme Military Commander of An Nam at the imperial audience, Khoan refused to accept it. He submitted to the Ming emperor that the decree had put the legitimate Le king on a par with the Mac "usurper." The emperor who, let it be recalled, had high regard for Khoan and conferred on him the title of First Laureate of Both Countries, reacted in a friendly manner. He said that he did not want to compare the Le with the Mac, but "since your king has just reconquered the country, it is to be feared that the people's minds were not yet at rest. You should accept the decree now. At a later date, a higher title will be conferred and it will not be too late. You should go along with this." Perhaps to soothe his feelings, the emperor gave Khoan a gold coin engraved with the symbols of his dynastic title, and to Khoan's deputy, a silver coin. When they were back at their diplomatic residence, Khoan threw his coin to the ground in anger. His deputy was shocked. This could easily be taken as a crime of lèse-majesté. Quickly, he picked the coin up: "Are you mad?" he asked Khoan. "Suppose the Chinese staff report this to the court. Do you want to spend the rest of your life in Peking? Do you not remember Le Quang Bi?" He was referring to the envoy who said something that the Chinese objected to and was kept as their "guest" in China for eighteen years.

"The emperor showed contempt for our king by not recognizing him as King of An Nam," Khoan said. "I do not want to keep his coin."

"The Ming are still favorable to the Mac, there would be hostilities if we oppose them," his deputy replied, adding: "If you do not like to keep yours, I will."

Khoan said, "I do not want to have anything to do with that coin. But if you want to keep both as souvenirs, you can."

Khoan's trip to Peking started in the spring of 1597. It lasted for one year and four months. Probably, Hoang came back to work for the Le before Khoan left. To serve two dynasties had been the lot of many a Vietnamese in the tormented history of our nation. Whatever the reasons for it, it always carried a mark of indignity, so strongly entrenched in our culture was the Confucian rule that "a faithful servant does not have two masters." Nguyen Hoang must have gone through torture and agony before making up his mind. His grandfather before him was faced with a similar choice and it was a quirk of fate that Nguyen Tue opted for the Mac against the Le, while his grandson did the opposite and returned to serve the restored Le dynasty. Their situations, however, were quite different. Nguyen Tue was among a group of mandarins who took the revolutionary step of siding with Mac Dang Dung and deposing the Le king. He was an active participant in events which changed the course of our history. Nguyen Hoang, on the contrary, was a victim of events. Whatever course of action he took, he would have felt a prisoner of forces beyond his control. Loyalty to the former dynasty and to the memory of his father and grandfather, both servants of the Mac state, must have weighed heavily in his mind and it would not be surprising to see him suffer the Mac defeat and spend the rest of his life in exile. But he finally decided otherwise.

After Mac Kinh Chi's gallant but brief episode, followers of the Mac dispersed. The *History of Dai Viet* noted that "remnants of the Mac family split into twenty or so groups and held different areas." Trinh Tung's army could only deal with one or two groups at any one time and many areas remained out of control of the government. But no group posed a serious threat to the new regime. As time passed, it must have become increasingly clear to Nguyen Hoang that there would be no Mac restoration. His choice was between continuing the life of a fugitive and accepting Khoan's offer to be again of service to the country at the cost, however, of swallowing his pride and giving himself up. He might have found it easier to do so in view of the special place that the Le continued to hold in the hearts of the Vietnamese. Years of decline made them lose the throne to the Mac, but although the latter were not bad kings, people never forgot the former dynasty. The memory of past Le kings continued to be revered, in particular Le Loi, the founder of the dynasty who liberated the country from the yoke of the Ming in 1427, and the enlightened King Le Thanh Ton (1460–1497), who gave to Vietnam an era of glory and prosperity such as had never been known before. The people's affection was the main reason why the Trinh overlord, who held all powers, still had to recognize the Le as legitimate king. Other considerations may have played a part in Nguyen Hoang's decision. While fighting continued in the country, a great drought caused the harvest to fail in 1595 and again in 1596. The result was a calamity seldom seen in our history. Starvation and epidemics killed "more than half of the population," according to the *History of Dai Viet*. Bandits and robbers, "in groups of a few hundreds or more," terrorized the whole countryside. Only in the capital and large towns could people live in security under the protection of the army. Nguyen Hoang may have had to return to the capital because there was no other safe place for his family to stay. Also, he knew that if he remained an outlawed Mac "rebel," his descendants would be barred from the civil service examinations. Without diplomas and mandarinal positions, a family of scholars would decline and even drop out of the scholarly class. Perhaps also, as he approached old age—he was then in his early sixties—Nguyen Hoang had felt more intensely the need to go back to Kim Bai, there to lie down in the land of his forebears, when his time would come. Many motives and reasons could explain his action. Perhaps it was simply the hand of Fate which guided Nguyen Hoang towards the final part of his life.

He was given back his rank and title by the Le court, but the promotion to the post of deputy minister at the Justice ministry would have only come later, after he had given sufficient proof of his loyalty and ability. The ministry of Justice was responsible for the administration of criminal law. It ordered the apprehension of criminals, supervised the prison system and acted as a high court of appeal for serious crimes. The Justice minister was assisted by two deputies, a first deputy called "of the left" and a second deputy called "of the right." Nguyen Hoang was deputy minister of the right, the junior of the two, although both deputies were on the same lower third mandarinal grade. Like his grandfather, he held the title of *ba*, or count. But in the troubled situation following the restoration, where the government did not control much of the countryside, he might just have been *ba* in name and did not receive the large land grants which traditionally went with the title. Meanwhile, conditions worsened in 1597, for drought in that year was followed by floods. The Le historian noted that the delta population, harassed furthermore by local officials, "could not stand it anymore. Many joined the ranks of the rebels." People's minds turned back to the "good times" under the Mac. The situation led to a strong Mac revival and much unrest in the countryside. As a rallied mandarin, Hoang might not have considered it safe to return to Kim Bai. Meanwhile, troubles were brewing at the Le court in Thang Long. Mandarins who rallied were given important positions in the government. Do Uong, their leader, was made Duke of Thong and Finance minister. In 1598, he received the grand title of Great Protector of the Second Rank. As deputy minister of Justice, Nguyen Hoang was holding a difficult and sensitive appointment. But in spite of honors and high positions, the former Mac mandarins held little power. The master of the country was the overlord Trinh Tung and he relied on a corps of mandarins who served the Southern court since the days of the civil war, most of whom came from the southern provinces of Thanh Hoa and Nghe An, his power base. Trinh Tung needed northern scholars to govern the north, but did not trust them. The scholars, for their part, felt deceived for they surrendered to the restored Le king only to find that their real master was the Trinh overlord. However, of greater concern to Trinh Tung was the attitude of former commanders of the Mac who rallied. These resented his arrogance and excessive powers, and they had troops under their command. Their simmering opposition was encouraged by Trinh Tung's maternal uncle Nguyen Hoang, a namesake of our ancestor and a duke of the Le.

After King Le The Ton died in 1599. Trinh Tung refused to install the crown prince on the throne, on the pretext that he "was not intelligent." Instead, he chose a younger brother of the latter, aged only twelve. Clearly, the Le monarchy was under his thumb. The following year, opposition against him broke out into the open. Three former Mac commanders, all of them now dukes of the Le and including Bui Van Khue, the general whose defection prompted Trinh Tung to launch his final offensive against the Mac in 1593, rebelled. They joined forces with supporters of the Mac and seized several provinces in the delta. Duke Nguyen Hoang volunteered to go and fight the rebels, but that was just a ploy to allow him to take all his troops with him out of Thang Long and of Trinh Tung's control. He brought them down deep into the south of the country, where he set himself up on his own. The stage was set for Vietnam's next civil war. From their bases in the northern mountains, Mac troops moved towards the capital. Weakened by defections and internal dissension, Trinh Tung decided to abandon the capital and the delta. In the fifth lunar month of the year of the Rat (1600), he escorted the king back to the safety of his home base in Thanh Hoa, or the Western Capital. His move was made secretly and in great haste. Only his original followers were allowed to join in the withdrawal. Rallied Mac mandarins were left behind. Their opposition to him had been growing and the overlord may very well have used the opportunity to get rid of them. The *Dai Viet Register of High Graduates* wrote of the fate of Do Uong, the highest ranking northern mandarin:

> He did not join the king's party to return [to the Western Capital] and was killed. It was not known for sure by whom, but according to the book "A sequel to the national history," when the king's party sought to withdraw, he was killed by rebel troops.

But nineteenth century author Pham Dinh Ho, in his book *Essays Written in Rainy Days*, gave a different account of Uong's death:

> Mac troops were on the rise again and the delta became insecure. The Trinh overlord wanted to bring the Le king back to the south. Do Uong tried hard to dissuade him, arguing that he should stay to defend the capital. The Trinh overlord became suspicious of Uong's motives. Seizing his gold-plated lance, he killed Uong.

Ho was an author much respected for the accuracy of his writings. Do Uong may be the only one to be informed by Trinh Tung of the withdrawal because of his high rank. Nguyen Hoang and many other mandarins had no time to flee as Mac troops returned to Thang Long on the heels of the withdrawing Trinh army. A deputy minister of Justice, whose responsibility was to order the apprehension of criminals and opponents to the regime, could not expect to survive in the hands of rebel forces. Nguyen Hoang must have been killed in the first days of the Mac return. He was then sixty-seven.

Thus, life ended tragically for a talented but unlucky man. Nguyen Hoang's story reminds me of Kieu, the heroine of our celebrated literary work. Kieu was a beautiful and thoughtful girl from a well-to-do family. She was talented in poetry, music, painting and chess playing, the four traditional scholarly pastimes. She fell in love with a young scholar. The two exchanged promises of marriage and looked destined to a happy life together. Then, one tragedy came after another to Kieu. Her father was imprisoned on a trumped-up charge and, in an act of filial piety, she sold herself to a house of prostitution to obtain his release. Later on, a kind man fell for her and bought her out of prostitution. She became his concubine, but could not endure the wrath of his jealous wife and escaped. Again a prostitute, she met a gallant warrior and rebel leader. It was love at first sight for both. He conquered and ruled over a vast region. She was now his official lady, respected and adulated. But he fell into a trap sprung by the king's men and was killed. The victors gave her to a subaltern officer as his concubine. She sought to end her life by jumping into the river, but was rescued by a Buddhist nun. Through no fault of her own, the life of that talented woman was just a series of woes. It was only at the end of her life that she was reunited with the people she loved and could enjoy some happiness. Under the pen of its author, Nguyen Du, this rather melodramatic story became the most beautiful poem in our language. Every Vietnamese, whether educated or not, knows the *Story of Kieu* and can recite by heart at least some of its 3254 verses. In reality, through Kieu, it was the tragedy of his own life that Nguyen Du wanted to express. Just as Kieu could not remain faithful to her first love, Nguyen Du could not stay loyal to the first dynasty he served. Like our ancestor Nguyen Hoang, he was a mandarin unfortunate enough to have to renounce his original oath of loyalty. Nguyen Du first served the Le towards the end of the eighteenth century. When the Tay Son replaced the Le in 1788, he refused to submit to the new dynasty and abandoned his career. In 1802, the Tay Son were defeated by the Nguyen. The new regime sought out Nguyen Du and offered him the responsibility of a junior prefecture. He accepted and later rose to high positions, but all his life would carry the shame of having been disloyal to the Le. He wrote the *Story of Kieu* to justify himself. Although a victim of circumstances, like Kieu, he was afraid that later generations would not understand him and would judge him harshly. Once, he wrote in a poem:

> Over three hundred years from now,
> I wonder whether there would be anyone
> Who would shed a tear for To Nhu.

To Nhu was his pen name. Nguyen Hoang himself could have written those lines, I think, if he was also a poet. I cannot help feeling that he suffered greatly from being disloyal to the Mac and wished that later generations would understand why he acted the way he did. Over three hundred years after his death, at least a descendant of his has now rediscovered the links with him and he can shed a tear over his ancestor's tragic life.

It is quite possible that, due to the circumstances of his death, our family was not able to bury Nguyen Hoang and did not even know where his grave was. The thought of him lying somewhere in an unmarked and untended grave must have tormented our people for a long time, as much perhaps as the violent manner with which he met his death. It must have been after that event that his wife Trinh Khiet decided to make the move back to Kim Bai. A family in exile was like a tree separated from its roots. Already when it grew in the original soil of our village, our tree had remained singularly vulnerable because lateral branches often did not appear. Sons had been few and late in coming. Many generations had been obsessed with the fear that the line would not be able to reproduce itself. Family elders talked wistfully of the centenary *si* tree which stood near the village gate, barring the way to evil spirits. With a dense canopy of leaves and countless roots hanging down from its branches, the tree looked like a large house. In the summer, men working in the fields repaired to the coolness of its shade to eat a light lunch and enjoy a siesta before getting back to work. When the winter drizzle came down and the icy northern wind blew, weary travellers on the highway broke their journey and headed under it for cover. "With the merit accumulated by many generations, one day our tree will expand and develop branches in all directions, like the *si* tree," elders said. But for most of the time, the tree which represented best the succeeding generations of our family was the areca nut palm. With only a straight trunk and a crown of leaves, it shot high up into the air, as high as the bamboo of the village enclosure. One feared that it might never withstand the storms of the monsoon, as it swayed violently and there was nothing to support its slender trunk. But it did. Although in no way resembling a *si* tree, our tree had survived over the generations because it was well suited to the soil of Kim Bai. For countless centuries, its roots had grown deep into it. Taken away from it, how long could it last? Transplanted in another land, would it not wither and die? Later generations would credit Trinh Khiet with returning our family to the place of its roots. Besides, the capital must have become for her and her children forever associated with the ruling Trinh's treachery and Hoang's pitiful death.

The Mac reestablished their rule in Thang Long with Mac Kinh Cung, a brother of Kinh Chi, on the throne and Mac Hau Hop's mother holding the title of mother of the nation. But Trinh Tung's withdrawal was a clever move to draw his opponents out and force them to defend Thang Long, instead of being on the attack at many different places. A few months later, he brought his army back and crushed the Mac. Mac Hau Hop's mother was captured. Kinh Cung escaped and fled to Cao Bang on the Chinese border. That was the last burst of the Mac. They would continue to stay for a long time in Cao Bang, but any chance for them to reconquer the country had gone. Gradually, security returned to the countryside and our people could finally go back to Kim Bai. As their absence, according to family recollection, had lasted about a decade since the end of the Mac dynasty in 1593, they should have been back sometime in the early 1600s, or a few years after Nguyen Hoang's death. Not only were they back, Trinh Khiet also succeeded in resuming possession of the family's landholdings.

Nguyen Hoang's memory would be lost to later generations, but not that of Trinh Khiet. We know that she came from a Nguyen family but, unlike the name Phung in the case of Hoang's stepmother, the name Nguyen was common to so many Vietnamese families that it tells us really nothing. We can only surmise that hers was a scholarly and mandarinal family like our own, for marriages were arranged affairs between families belonging to the same social stratum. Trinh Khiet survived her husband for many years during which she played the role of a matriarch to the family. She was reported as having great courage and strength of character. Now that the story of Nguyen Hoang's tragic life has been rediscovered, we can see that without such qualities, it would have been difficult for her to keep the family together and overcome the shock of Hoang's death. Long after she was gone, her spirit remained "powerful" and often manifested itself to her descendants in their dreams. It was probably following one of those appearances that the ceremony of "calling her spirit" was performed, sometime in the 1860s, or more than two centuries after her death.

As already quoted from the chronicle:

> The family organized a ceremony to call our foremother's spirit. She was buried where the highway ran, outside the boundary of the Pham family's shrine. Consequently, her grave was lost.

My grandfather used such a condensed style that, at places, the meaning of what he wrote was quite obscure. In the eighteenth century, our family went through a critical period of decline and many ancestral graves could not be looked after. When it recovered in the next century, efforts were made to find Trinh Khiet's grave but they brought no result. It was thought that its location was mentioned in the Cu Hau papers but, when these were found in 1861, they only contained information on ancestral graves going back as far as the fourth generation, the one which came after Trinh Khiet's. A meeting of the extended family took place in 1862 and it was probably then that members decided to make another search for her burial place, with the help of a medium. Ceremonies to "call the spirit" of a departed parent were quite frequently held in the country, up until recent times. The medium was usually a woman. After offerings were made and prayers sung, she entered into a trance and family members could see by the way she talked that the parent's spirit had taken hold of her and was expressing itself through her voice. They would then go into a conversation with the spirit. Would it need anything in the other world, such as money, house or servants? These could be sent over in the form of paper representations to be burned at the ceremony. The real object of the exercise came next; it was to invoke the spirit's help in a matter of particular concern to the family. In this instance, Trinh Khiet might have expressed displeasure in her descendants' dreams that her grave was left untended; so the spirit

was asked to show where her burial place was. As far as I can understand
my grandfather's account, the family was told by the medium that Trinh
Khiet "was buried where the highway ran," which means that at some later
date a highway was built passing over her grave and consequently it was
now definitively lost. Whether that was true or not, no one can say, but at
least the family got an answer to a problem which had been of great concern
to it and was satisfied that nothing more could be done. Following that
"discovery," I am sure that Buddhist priests were called to our ancestral
home for a special prayer service to Trinh Khiet's spirit. For several days
and nights, they prayed there and went to pray next to the highway, outside
the shrine of the Pham family, where her original grave was thought to be,
so that Trinh Khiet's spirit could finally detach itself from this world and
find rest in the realm of immortal peace.

In Nguyen Hoang's time and after three successive generations of high
mandarins, our family must have owned a vast amount of land in Kim Bai
and adjoining villages. In addition, our ancestors were given by the Mac
king, in conjunction with their ranks and titles, sizeable grants of land in
villages further away but still within our prefecture. After the defeat of the
Mac, the grants were of course rescinded, but our private land continued
to be exploited by tenants while the family was absent. It did not seem to
have been confiscated by the new authorities, or if it was, it had been restored
to Nguyen Hoang after he came out of exile to work for the Le. Hoang,
however, never came back to Kim Bai. Only after his death did Trinh Khiet
return to claim the land and as the wife of a mandarin who died for the Le,
she must have been given support by the court. Ten years, however, was
a long time to be absent and out of possession. Furthermore, even the
king's writ stopped at the village gate. Inside the bamboo enclosure, what
mattered was the attitude of other villagers to our family.

Because of its proximity to the capital Thang Long, in a war, our village usually belonged to the side which held power there. The Hat River
formed a natural line of defense to the southwest of the capital and Kim
Bai was located right behind that line. Once an enemy crossed the Hat, no
other natural obstacle stood between him and Thang Long. During the
long war between the Mac and the Le, Kim Bai was threatened only twice.
The first time was in 1559–1560, when Trinh Khiem launched from the
south a vast ouflanking move against the Red River delta. His troops went
north through the hills and mountains west of the Hat but they did not
cross the river and Kim Bai was not taken. The second time occured more
than twenty years later. In 1585, the Trinh forces pushed up from the south
towards our home region. They came closer and closer but were turned
back before reaching it. Kim Bai remained in the Mac camp until the very
last stage of the conflict. Our region fell into Trinh hands following the big
battle near the Hat River which heralded the end of the Mac.

Many in Kim Bai were scholars and civil servants. Under the Mac, some reached the highest offices while others served in the middle and lower ranks of the bureaucracy. All through the war, our village was not affected by a divided loyalty and when the war ended, it did not suffer from the tragedy of internecine fighting. There was no revenge, no settling of scores against people who worked for the fallen dynasty. On the contrary, all in Kim Bai found themselves in the same boat, with something to fear from the victorious Le. As for our family, in three successive generations of prominent mandarins, it must have made important contributions to the welfare of the community. As a matter of fact, the Mac period was one of the most prosperous in our village's history. The legendary brothers Nguyen Tue and Nguyen Huyen were the first citizens of Kim Bai ever to gain the coveted doctorate title. Their success inspired other students and the old tradition of scholarship flowered. Both men opted to serve Mac Dang Dung and were given top positions by the new king. Village solidarity meant that they naturally gave a helping hand to fellow villagers and the number of Kim Bai people in the civil service must have increased. Nguyen Tue was made a count and Kim Bai became a seat of power. It must have expanded greatly, for later documents showed it as being formed by an agglomeration of three villages. In the next generations, the brothers' leadership roles were passed down to Nguyen Tue's son and grandson. Academician Nguyen Uyen, in particular, must have done a great deal for his village during his long mandarinal career. Those ancestors of ours had certainly earned the respect and gratitude of their fellow villagers. Their names and deeds would be recorded in village documents and, in peaceful and stable times, these would be kept for all future generations to see. But after the dynasty which they served was defeated, their memory was officially banned, documents about them were destroyed and they passed into oblivion. Centuries later, villagers continued to talk of the Mountain of the Twins and sing the praise of the Nguyen Brothers without remembering what the Twins stood for and who the brothers were.

The restored Le did not look kindly upon a village with so many people in the Mac civil service. But Kim Bai appeared to have escaped serious retribution. Things would have been difficult had there been Mac military commanders among its people. As civil servants could not survive for long without work, after a decent interval those in Kim Bai came out of hiding to join the new administration. Nguyen Hoang's act of submission to the Le was not out of step with the rest of the villagers. On the contrary, it may have persuaded others to do the same. Our village had survived all the civil wars and changes of dynasty because it knew when to acquiesce to the regime in power in Thang Long. In a way, Nguyen Hoang's agonizing transfer of loyalty was a problem faced by the whole community, only in his case it was magnified because of his position as Kim Bai's highest scholar and mandarin. So when his widow returned, Kim Bai's people readily accepted her back.

Our ancestral home and shrine must have been looked after by relatives and I do not think that there was any difficulty for Trinh Khiet retaking possession of them. But it was another problem with our rice fields, mulberry fields, ponds and other land left in the charge of tenants. Could any tenant be happy to see a landlord return after an absence of ten years to claim the fields he had been cultivating, during all the time, for himself? Village authorities may have been ordered by the court to help Trinh Khiet reestablish our family ownership, but that would have been the wrong way for her to go about getting back the land. Our return should be accepted by other villagers, not imposed on them. Trinh Khiet was well aware that the position of power and influence held by our family under the Mac had gone. In the end, I believe that it was through negotiation with the tenants that she succeeded in making them recognize our ownership. In return, they must have received a part of the land as their reward for having taken care of it when we were away. Animosity and bitterness were avoided. It was said of Trinh Khiet that, since the time her husband was a mandarin, she had always maintained a very close relationship with her fellow villagers. I imagine her not unlike my own grandmother who used to say that while in society she was the wife of a mandarin, in Kim Bai she was "a villager like others." When her husband was a powerful official, respected and probably held in awe by the villagers, Trinh Khiet would have remained friendly and approachable. People who wanted to obtain help or favor from him would have gone through her. They did not forget her kindness and on returning from exile, she was able to draw from a vast reservoir of good will towards her. Thus, our family came through the upheaval of a change of dynasty, still wealthy landowners.

In our custom, the head of a generation returned to live in the ancestral home when he retired. After he died, his widow continued to stay there. While younger generations may be dispersed to the four corners of the country and coming back only for festivals and death anniversaries, the two old parents were the link between the family and its ancestral land. Most of the time, it was only the matriarch as our foremothers usually survived their husbands for a very long time. So, when Trinh Khiet came home, the link was resumed. She was to remain in Kim Bai until she died. For many years, insecurity continued to prevail in our region. History books recorded that, as late as in 1613, twenty years after the war had ended, refugees were still fearful to return to their native places. Although living in safety among Kim Bai's community and shielded from the outside world by its bamboo enclosure, our family had to exercise great caution. Rebels favorable to the Mac could still descend on the village and, therefore, real names were hidden. Nguyen Hoang must have been referred to only by his pseudonym

Phuc Ninh. His son's real name was also not used, with the result that he is also now known to us only by his pseudonym. As for Trinh Khiet, that was not a name used during her lifetime, but chosen by her son at her death for the purpose of invoking her spirit in prayers and ceremonies of worship. In normal times, she would be called by her husband's mandarinal position—as wife of the deputy minister—or in association with his diploma— as wife of the doctor—but since both these appellations had to be avoided, she may have been called simply by her position in the family, as *Ba Ca,* or wife of the head of the branch. She went on to live until a ripe old age. Her influence was still felt centuries after her death, as we saw in the ceremony to invoke her spirit. Among our ancestors, the academician-envoy Nguyen Uyen has long been considered as our "first" ancestor, not only because he was the earliest one in memory, but also because he stood first in the affection and veneration of later generations. Among our foremothers, Trinh Khiet was not the earliest known, but she was certainly the "first" to her descendants, who remembered with gratitude the role she played in the most somber period of their family history.

When the Mac dynasty fell in 1592, Trinh Khiet's son—our fourth ancestor—was probably in his early twenties and studying for the state examinations. Phuc Thien was not remembered for having obtained any diploma, but just to make sure that we have not forgotten another ancestor with high academic qualifications and a distinguished career, I carefully checked the records of all doctorate sessions in the last part of the Mac rule and the first period of the restored Le dynasty, when Phuc Thien was likely to have sat for the examinations. No one hailing from Kim Bai graduated from those sessions. But even without a degree, a mandarinal career was open to Phuc Thien. As the son of a mandarin, he would have qualified to study at one of three colleges attached to the Academy, for example the Chieu Van Quan or College for the Advancement of Literature, which was opened to sons and eldest grandsons of dukes, marquesses and counts as well as to eldest sons of mandarins from the second to the eighth grades. The rules of admission to that college stipulated that the sons and grandsons must be "intelligent, keen on studies and still at a young age." Every three years, a number of students were selected by college teachers to be tested in dictation, Confucian Books and Confucian Canons. Those who passed the tests became civil servants.

Most sons and grandsons of the great families of the regime came to the mandarinate by way of the colleges. Then while working, they tried their luck at the triennial examinations as a means of furthering their careers. Phuc Thien's father probably did so and had been working for many years before he obtained his doctorate, at close to forty. As for Phuc Thien, whatever college he went to, his future looked assured. Descendants of mandarins usually took the lion's share at the state examinations. Once in the civil service, they were promoted ahead of others and put in key positions. The regime naturally gave a preferential treatment to families which had served it well, and our ancestors had been high mandarins of the Mac for no less than three generations. Then in 1592, Phuc Thien's world tumbled. The end of the Mac came swiftly and unexpectedly. Three years before, it was they who sought victory by attacking the south. But, under the attacks of Trinh Tung's army, the dynasty collapsed. All of a sudden for the young scholar, it was defeat and flight. When his father decided to surrender to the Le, how did Phuc Thien feel? The agony and shame were perhaps no less for him, but whatever his own feelings, he was bound by filial piety and family solidarity to support his father's decision. He came back to Thang Long with the rest of the family and was probably given a junior post in the Le administration. Then came his father's death. In the chain of events which started with the Mac defeat and led to tragic events in our family, the young man's future, his hopes and expectations, were just swept away like those pieces of wood and other debris that one could see carried by the waters of the Red River during the monsoon season.

In the next episode, his mother returned to Kim Bai and claimed back our land, but Phuc Thien's role in this important endeavor was not known. According to family recollection, he stayed absent for a very long time. In fact, his generation was also considered as ill-fated, like that of his father. What tragic events affected Phuc Thien's life? I had thought that the bitterness towards the Trinh in our family stemmed from the fact that our ancestors had suffered persecution at their hands, being followers of the defeated Mac dynasty. But now that the story of Nguyen Hoang's life has come to light, we can see a little more clearly about his son. Trinh Tung's treacherous withdrawal, which left a great number of mandarins stranded and exposed to the terrible revenge of the Mac, was deeply resented. The old established families in the north intensified their opposition to his rule. They had left the Mac to pledge allegiance to the Le king, not to the Trinh overlord. Trinh Tung, for his part, after he had crushed the Mac revival and returned to Thang Long, set out to cut down the scholars' influence even further. Their cooperation was needed at the beginning to establish his hold over the north, but now his regime had been made more secure. Externally, it had gained recognition from China. In the country, its Mac opponents were soon to be confined to the small valley of Cao Bang in the northern mountains. The future Nguyen overlord, who defied Trinh orders and left for the southern province of Quang Nam, stayed quiet in his fief. Trinh Tung started imposing a strict control on recruitment and promotions. The number of graduates at the civil service examinations dropped sharply. Under the Mac, an average of between forty and fifty new doctors were chosen at each triennial session. The average fell to seven doctors in the first ten sessions following the restoration. The regime wanted only those who were loyal to the house of Trinh. Families like our own stood little chance of having their members succeed at the examinations.

Phuc Thien must have held the overlord responsible for his father's death. Did he enter into opposition to the Trinh? I think he did. Mandarins usually protested in a passive manner by resigning from public service and returning to their villages to teach. Phuc Thien may have had recourse to a more active form of opposiiton and been involved in one of the groups which worked to restore power to the legitimate Le king. For his long absence from Kim Bai looked very much like a form of banishment. Only in his old age could he go back there. The barren life of an exile and the desperate longing for the ancestral land which had marked our family psyche may have come from his generation and not, as I had first thought, from the previous one. The one among our ancestors who stood alone "by the side of the pond," for whom "the fish had gone deep under the water and the stars in the sky were dim," was thus Phuc Thien! His life was even more unfortunate than that of his father, I feel, for at least the latter was able to gain recognition for his talents and put them to use. Like his great-grand-father Nguyen Tue, who took part in the overthrow of a dynasty, Phuc Thien may have had in him the boldness of character to stand up to the might of the Trinh. He would not have flinched from such a formidable challenge. But what could a scholar with his writing brush do? The predictable result was for him banishment, making his life a string of wasted years.

Perhaps he could find some comfort in the thought that, in the tormented history of Vietnam, many good and worthy men before him had been given no chance to be of service to the country just because they were not on the "right" side. Ours had been a nation so often divided within itself. Less than forty years after the Mac-Le war, a new war was developing between the Trinh and the Nguyen. Once again, the country had come to a turning point. Perhaps, the following poem written by a scholar-warrior, who fought against domination by the Chinese in the beginning of the fifteenth century but met with failure, was often in Phuc Thien's mind, as he watched from his place of exile our history unfold its tortuous course:

> The game is still being played, why do I have to grow old.
> This great wide world! All in a drunkard's song!
> When their time comes, good-for-nothings find success easy to get,
> While good men can only swallow their sorrow, after fortune passed them by.

Trinh Tung retained the Le monarchy, still the symbol of legitimacy in the eyes of many Vietnamese, but he was an arrogant man who showed scant regard for the king. He called himself *vuong,* a title very close to king in its meaning. Like the Shogun in Japan, the Vietnamese overlord became a hereditary ruler. The Le king was given a royal guard of five thousand men and as income the taxes from one thousand villages. His role was purely a ceremonial one. He presided over court functions and received foreign envoys. But all state powers rested with the overlord. King Le Kinh Tong, the twelve-year-old who was put on the throne by Trinh Tung, played the role set for him for twenty years. He grew tired of it and in 1619, plotted with one of Trinh Tung's sons to assassinate the overlord. The plot failed and the king was allowed to commit suicide by "self-strangulation" with a length of silk, a euphemism to preserve the king's honor, for actually two aides were there to garrote him. Trinh Tung chose as successor the king's eldest son, who was also his grandson for the queen was his daughter. Cracks had begun to show in Trinh Tung's rule. He must be now in his seventies. When he fell ill four years later, in 1623, two of his sons fought for power. Trinh Tung killed the younger one before he himself died, but troubles developed in the capital. In a repeat of the events of 1600 which saw our third ancestor meet his death, Trinh Tung's eldest son and successor, Trinh Trang, left Thang Long and retreated with the Le king to his home base of Thanh Hoa in the south. Descendants of the Mac, holed up in Cao Bang, seized their chance once again and came down from the mountains. But this time, the Mac did not reach the capital. Trinh Trang quickly recovered and restored the situation. He was back in control, but taking advantage of Trinh Tung's death and the resulting confusion, descendants of duke Nguyen Hoang in Quang Nam entered into open revolt. They refused to pay taxes to the Trinh government and built walls and fortresses to defend their territory. The Nguyen proclaimed their loyalty to the Le king and vowed to rid the country of the Trinh. Their battle banner read: "To support the Le and destroy the Trinh." In 1627, Trinh Trang launched his first offensive. Another civil war had started.

It would be around that time that Phuc Thien was allowed to return to his village. He would be close to sixty. His banishment may have lasted a long time, but in other respects our family did not seem to have been treated too harshly by the authorities. Had Phuc Thien been considered a "rebel," his wife, children and properties would have been seized for the state. But such was not the case, thanks probably to the fact that his father had died for the cause of the Le. He married late. In those times, the custom was for a man to marry and establish a family in his early twenties, or even before twenty. Parents started quite early to look around for possible brides to their sons. Young scholars were allowed to stay single a little longer, so that they were not bothered by wife and children and could concentrate on their studies. Thirty, however, was the limit according to Confucian teaching. "At thirty, I stood on my own," said the Master. His words were interpreted as meaning that by that age, a gentleman should be married and head a separate family unit. In our family, the men were expected to marry young, even though they were scholars, in the hope that an heir would soon come to continue the lineage. From the earliest generations, our people had been worried that sons were so few. But in spite of such expectation, most of our ancestors only married in their thirties. Delays usually occurred, caused by war, insecurity, family bereavement or simply because it took time to find a bride of the same social standing. If it was not one reason, it was another. So much so that our people came to believe they must be under the influence of a certain star, which stood in the way of early marriages. Because of his father's death and his own troubles with the authorities, Phuc Thien would not have married before his late thirties. His wife came from the village of Van Quan in our prefecture. We know her family name Nguyen and a pseudonym My Hanh. Her own given name, like that of her husband, was not recorded. They had one son.

My Hanh helped her mother-in-law in administering family properties and dealing with tenants. She took over the responsibility when Trinh Khiet died. Like her mother-in-law, My Hanh was much younger than her husband and survived him for many years. She brought into our family a strong Buddhist faith and her influence would make itself felt in the next generations. Both she and her husband were buried in the vicinity of our village, but descendants were dispersed during the long period of insecurity which affected our region in the eighteenth century. Survivors who came back could not remember where Phuc Thien and My Hanh were buried. Fortunately, the Cu Hau papers were found to contain the location of their graves as well as the anniversaries of their death. They are the earliest ancestors about whom we possess such information. Phuc Thien's death occurred a few days before the Tet, on "the twenty-seventh day of the twelfth month of the lunar year," a rather inauspicious time for it cast a pall over the New Year festival and, consequently, over the family's fortunes for the whole of the coming year. My Hanh died on "the eighteenth day of the second month." The years were unfortunately not given as the papers were only intended to remind Cu Hau of the days and months on which to celebrate the ancestors' death anniversaries. Cu Hau used the geomantic features of the terrain to describe the graves' locations. He noted that Phuc Thien's grave lay "in the area called Ma Dai, in the middle of a geomantic feature bearing the description of a tree." My Hanh's grave also lay in the Ma Dai area. Our ancestors were traditionally buried in family land, but as a Buddhist, My Hanh wished to be buried in temple land. In her lifetime, a place of burial was earmarked for her and the rice field where it was located donated by our family to the Buddhist temple of Van Quan, her native village. When she died, she was laid to rest there.

17. Recluse Scholars

Few scholarly families could continue to have high graduates and stay at the top for very long. Success usually lasted for one or two generations. Instances of sons following in their fathers' footsteps and gaining a doctorate were rare enough to rate a special mention in the registers of high graduates. To have three generations of doctors—as in the case of our family—was exceptional. Then, the cycle of change started to operate and decline set in. Some families were able to climb up again after a few generations. Others were not and they eventually dropped out of the scholarly class. The run of academic successes in our family ended with Phuc Thien. Our fortunes sank further in the next two generations. Phuc Thien was a civil servant, although his career was cut short. His son and grandson did not reach that status. But while Phuc Thien had an unhappy and unfulfilled life, the following generations were characterized by a strong Buddhist faith and an attitude described in Vietnamese by the term *an phan,* or peaceful acceptance of one's lot.

Our fifth ancestor was named Nguyen Luan. His son's name has been forgotten and the chronicle referred to him by his pen name Khanh Thien. The years of their birth and death are not recorded, but as the average length of a generation in our family is about forty years, we can roughly estimate that Nguyen Luan was born sometime in the 1610s. Given our ancestors' gift for longevity, he would have seen the better part of the seventeenth century. His son Khanh Thien would have been born during the 1650s and have died sometime in the first two decades of the eighteenth century.

Nguyen Luan lived in a time of war. Fighting between the Trinh and the Nguyen started in 1627 and went on for half a century. Six times during that period, the Trinh launched large scale offensives against the south. The Nguyen, who were kept mostly on the defensive, only attacked the north once. Both sides maintained vast armies and navies. According to Christian missionaries staying in the country at the time, including the Jesuit A. de Rhodes, who along with other priests invented the present-day Vietnamese script, the Trinh's army had up to one hundred thousand men and five hundred elephants trained to accompany the troops into battle. Their navy counted five hundred large gunboats. The Nguyen could deploy forty thousand troops and two hundred gunboats in the defense of their territory. Most of the fighting took place in the two provinces of Ha Tinh and Quang Binh, a little to the north of the seventeenth parallel which would become the dividing line between South and North Vietnam in our present century. There, the country was a narrow stretch of plain flanked in the west by mountains and in the east by the sea. Taking advantage of the land configuration, the Nguyen fought behind a series of fortified walls, built by Dao Duy Tu, a scholar whom war had turned into a great military engineer and strategist. In spite of their numerical superiority, the Trinh failed in one offensive after another to get through these walls, vestiges of which still remain today. Our home region in the Red River delta was situated far from the battlefield, but war meant conscription and heavy taxes for the population. Local officials were given increased power and they were often petty and corrupt. Our family suffered from their exactions as well as from the tax burden. But neither Nguyen Luan nor his son was conscripted into the army, being both without any male siblings. The law exempted families with only one son from the draft, so that the ancestors' worship would not be interrupted by the son's absence. Otherwise, the rule applicable was for one male citizen out of every five to be called up. But even if called, one could get out by paying a tax. In those times of war, many conscripts, even if they survived the fighting in the south, had to stay in the army for life. Old and weak soldiers should be sent home, the rules said, but corrupt practices resulted in many dying of old age away from home. Scholarly families of Kim Bai, even if they were poor, did their best to pay the tax instead of allowing their sons to be conscripted.

1672 saw the last Trinh campaign against the south. After it failed, hostilities petered out and the two sides settled into a de facto division of the country. The Trinh held the richer and more populous north. The Nguyen's territory was smaller and consisted of a few poor provinces in the south, some of which had been seized from the Champa kingdom not so long ago. Now free from the burden of fratricidal war, both the Trinh and Nguyen regimes could devote their energies to more constructive endeavors. The Nguyen extended the country's southern borders and led our people's advance towards the Mekong River delta. The Trinh strengthened their regime by reorganizing the administration and introducing a whole range of reforms in taxation, education and the legal system. In 1667, they finally put an end to the Mac by seizing Cao Bang, their last stronghold. Good relations were obtained with the new Ching dynasty in China which recognized in 1667 the Le king as King of An Nam. For several decades, the north enjoyed peace and good government. Our sixth generation, that of Khanh Thien, lived in what proved to be the best period of Trinh rule.

Nguyen Luan and his son were scholars but both were barred from the public service examinations. Our family had long thought that that was because they were "descendants of Mac followers." But now we know that Nguyen Hoang, the third ancestor, had submitted to the Le king, received from him title and position and finally died in his service. Surely, Hoang had paid a high enough price to atone for the role played by his forebears under the Mac dynasty. Why then was our family still penalized in such a severe manner? To deprive a scholarly family of its chance at the examinations was nothing less than to force it out of its class. The likely reason was Phuc Thien's banishment. This could explain not only the exclusion from the examinations, but also another puzzle concerning Nguyen Hoang. Hoang's death at the hands of Mac troops should have made him a martyr to the cause of the Le. Do Uong, the leader of the northern mandarins, became a martyr after he was killed. The king made him a *Phuc Than,* or Benevolent Spirit, and ordered that a temple be erected to worship his memory. The title of Benevolent Spirit was the highest recognition that a king could give posthumously to a subject. It was awarded only to mandarins who gave exceptional services to the nation. Nguyen Hoang did not hold as high a mandarinal rank as Do Uong but there was no doubt that he, like Do Uong, died in the service of the Le king. However, as far as can be ascertained, no posthumous honors were given to him. Usually, such honors were not given soon after death, but many years and possibly decades later. It was clear that, in the meantime, Hoang's son had gone into opposition to the Trinh overlord; consequently, there was no more question of royal recognition for his father's sacrifice.

Our family plight may have been made worse by the actions of local officials, many of whom were tyrannical and corrupt. History books wrote of the population being "harassed" by them and fearful to return to their villages, even decades after the war had ended. A report made by the Assistant Chief Censor in 1612 blasted those who "did everything they could to torment the population; being in charge of a prefecture they made its population suffer, being in charge of a village they made its population suffer." In the matter of examinations, local officials held wide discretionary powers. Aspirant candidates must obtain from them a certificate of good character to be allowed to sit. The law stated that the officials were entitled to refuse the certificate to "those who have violated the code of moral behavior, have acted contrary to filial piety and to harmony within the family, have committed adultery or incest, have propagated lies to sow troubles, etc. . . ." In addition to these general and wide-ranging exclusions, there were specific interdictions against "travelling actors and singers, traitors, rebels and people with a bad reputation; they, their children and grandchildren are not allowed to sit for the examinations." The mention of actors and singers alongside traitors, rebels and other persons of bad reputation may appear strange nowadays. Those were men and women who travelled together from place to place giving musical and operatic performances on the occasion of village festivals. The exclusion here applied, of course, only to the men; women had no place in examinations and civil service, whatever their social background. The travelling artists were strongly discriminated against, the same way gypsies were in Europe, although in our country race was not involved. Confucian morality looked down on their profession and way of living as immoral and encouraging promiscuity. It was feared that their songs and music would have a pernicious influence on the people and lead them away from the right path. In practice however, their performances were very much sought after and many villages had their own opera group. One descendant of musicians became famous in the Trinh Nguyen conflict. He was Dao Duy Tu, the builder of the walls which played such a decisive role in the war. Tu left the north and put his considerable talents to the service of the Nguyen because people like him were barred from the examinations.

With such a high profile under the Mac, now in decline but still wealthy, our family was an obvious target for greedy and corrupt officials. Perhaps it was not pliable enough to their demands so the certificate of good character was not issued. Nguyen Hoang's submission to the Le king could be conveniently ignored, while Phuc Thien's banishment and the role played many decades ago by our ancestor Nguyen Tue in the overthrow of the Le were stressed. An injustice was not easily redressed for a family on its way down. Our people would not have kept many friends in high places, especially when they were in the bad books of the Trinh overlord.

Unable to try for a career in the civil service, our ancestors went into teaching. Nguyen Luan ran a school in Kim Bai, in our ancestral compound. His son continued after him. In those times, most villages had at least one school; those with a tradition of learning like Kim Bai had several. Retired mandarins, doctors and lesser graduates, scholars without degrees, all who wanted could teach. The system was quite liberal and allowed even mandarins dismissed from service or opponents of the regime to have their own schools. Nguyen Luan's school was a small one of perhaps from a dozen to twenty students. Since our ancestors were not graduates, they could only teach up to what would be now the junior secondary level. Youngsters usually started school at seven or eight, but many families waited until they were older. A village school was like a big family with the teacher at its head. The students waited upon him. They prepared his tea, lighted his water pipe and tended his flower garden. They came to give a hand whenever the teacher needed them. Only families which could afford them paid fees; otherwise, teachers were presented with gifts in kind. Being wealthy landowners, our ancestors were in a fortunate position of not teaching as a means of livelihood. They taught to have an occupation and also, in the tradition of Confucian scholars, out of a sense of duty towards the young generations.

Although their academic success was a thing of the past, the Nguyen of Kim Bai continued to enjoy a great amount of prestige among scholarly circles. The name of academician Nguyen Uyen was still a byword in our region. People had not forgotten that under the Mac dynasty, ours was one of the most outstanding scholarly families in the country. Our ancestors' school attracted promising students in Kim Bai and neighboring villages. Some of those students went on to higher studies and became mandarins. It was probably thanks to their intervention that the authorities finally stopped treating our people as "Mac followers" and examinations were again opened to them, in the next generation.

As well as teachers, Nguyen Luan and his son were known as writers. Nguyen Luan wrote under the pen name of Quang Tru—Upholder of Family Tradition. His son had as pen name Khanh Thien—Rejoicing in Goodness, a name reflecting his strong Buddhist convictions as Khanh Thien are terms often used in Buddhist preachings. A writer in those days was someone who composed poems, essays and other forms of rhythmic prose for his own enjoyment and that of his friends. His works did not need to be published; generally they were just circulated within his literary group. Very few people wrote novels, which was not considered a respectable literary form. A gentleman-scholar would only write poems or essays. Over a cup of perfumed tea or around a tray of food and wine, he would recite them for his friends begging them to comment and criticize. If they really liked his poem, they would improvise other poems on the same theme and using the same rhymes. All scholars wrote poems, but to be called a writer one must have at least produced a collection of poems and these must of course be considered good enough among the literary circles of the day. The collection usually had the pen name as title. *Khanh Thien Thi Tap*—Collections of Poems by Khanh Thien—would be the title of our sixth ancestor's book. Unfortunately, our family was not able to keep any of our ancestors' writings, which were all lost in the great calamity of the eighteenth century.

Our ancestor-scholars all had several names, at least two and for some up to four. At birth, a person was given a name—for instance Luan in the case of our fifth ancestor—which, added to the family name Nguyen became his personal or real name. It appeared on his birth certificate and in all official papers concerning him. The given name, however, was rarely used within the family circle or in social intercourse. As a matter of fact, it is called in Vietnamese *ten huy*, or "name to be avoided." Out of respect for others, one should avoid mentioning their given names. Children, in particular, were not to utter the names of their parents or family elders. The same rule was observed in society with regard to older people or those holding a higher social position. Naturally, ancestors' names were not to be pronounced. When a boy, I used to read aloud newspapers to my grandfather. My great-grandfather, who died at the beginning of this century, was named *Dat*, a word meaning "to achieve." Whenever that word came up in an article, it had to be pronounced as *dot*, as if it was spelled with an "o" instead of an "a." If I did not make the change, my grandfather would correct me. Eventually, I got it right without prompting and it became a habit. Sometimes at school, I changed *dat* into *dot* too, to the annoyance of my teacher. Fortunately, my grandfather did not extend the avoidance rule to generations before that of his father. Newspaper reading would have been impossible if I had to change the names of all past ancestors.

A scholar was generally called by his pseudonym, a name he chose for himself. In fact, anyone who wanted it could take a pseudonym and be referred to in society by that name. A pseudonym usually expressed a person's beliefs and aspirations. Most of our ancestors had pseudonyms starting with the word *phuc*, a key word in our traditional system of values meaning "happiness achieved by benevolent action." *Phuc* was quite popular among scholars as the first word of a pseudonym. Our sixth ancestor called himself Phuc Kiem—Good Action and Frugality. In his lifetime, he was known as Mr. Phuc Kiem, or him being a teacher as Teacher Phuc Kiem. He could also be called by his pen name as Mr. Khanh Thien. Our foremothers also had pseudonyms which, unlike the men, they did not choose themselves. Before a mother died, her eldest son would whisper in her ear the pseudonym he had chosen for her and by which she would be referred to by her descendants, instead of her real name. Nearly all our foremothers had pseudonyms starting with the word *tu*, "compassion." Thus, our fifth foremother was Tu Tai—In the Abode of Compassion—and our sixth, Tu Toan—Absolute Compassion. *Tu*, a term of reverence used when referring to one's mother, appeared in female pseudonyms of most families. It is interesting to note, given the way that their pseudonyms were chosen, that the women became known to later generations by names which they did not have in their lifetime. In our family and for all early generations, we only remember of our foremothers the surnames and pseudonyms; the personal names have been forgotten as one generation after another avoided mentioning them. Only from the nineteenth century did our chronicle record in full the surnames, personal names and pseudonyms of the women.

Those of our ancestors who were writers had a third name, the pen name. Finally, some had a fourth name bestowed posthumously on them by the court as a mark of appreciation for the services they rendered as mandarins.

A traditional hierarchy existed among scholars, who were considered as belonging to one of three categories. Ranked in the first place were those who passed the examinations and put their talents to the service of their king and country. They were called *hien nho,* or "eminent scholars." Public service was the ultimate aim of Confucian teaching and the way was laid down to all students in the very first of the Four Books, the *Great Learning*:

> From the Son of Heaven to the common people, all must consider the cultivation of their person as the root of everything.... Your person being cultivated, you can then regulate the life of your family. Your family life being regulated, you can then rightly govern your state. Your state being rightly governed, you can then make the whole kingdom tranquil and happy.

Most eminent among the "eminent scholars" were the high mandarins. They possessed power and wealth and rose above all others in society. Our first three ancestors were such scholars, and perhaps more important to them than power, honors and wealth was the opportunity to play a part in the nation's affairs and to leave a name behind. "Having been born to this land, I must make my name known to its rivers and mountains," said a renowned scholar-poet. That fame, Nguyen Tue, Nguyen Uyen and Nguyen Hoang all achieved in some measure. Their names were recorded in history books. Centuries after their death, descendants could still rediscover forgotten links with them and reconstruct some aspects of their lives and careers.

An nho, or "recluse scholars" came next. They were people regarded as being well-endowed with talents who, however, did not take the path of public service. Living a simple life, they devoted themselves to learning the "way" of ancient saints and sages. Some scholars just chose to become recluse, but many others did so because they were dissatisfied with the political situation or were on the wrong side of the regime in power, as in the case of our fifth and sixth ancestors. Some recluse scholars became famous as teachers or writers. Others were content to stay back in their villages and "tender their gardens." The most "recluse" of them abandoned society completely to go up the mountains and live as hermits, in a lonely quest for Truth. As one of them wrote:

Humming to myself, I enjoy being in the far mountains,
Where apricot trees are dear friends and cranes old acquaintances.

One of the most celebrated recluse scholars in our history was the prophet Nguyen Binh Khiem. For several decades in the first half of the sixteenth century, he chose to keep away from examinations and public service because those were troubled and disorderly times. Only under the good king Mac Dang Doanh did he finally come out of reclusion to win the title of First Laureate in 1535. Immediately, he was given high office but, after only eight years as an "eminent scholar," he resigned to return to his village. He spent the rest of his life teaching, writing, wandering in the mountains to visit Buddhist temples and engaging in religious discourse with the monks. Here are some lines he wrote:

> I am stupid, I seek a place out of the way,
> While clever people go where the bustle is.
> Coming to the foot of a tree, I will sip my wine,
> And look upon wealth and position as only a dream.

Finally, there were scholars who failed the examinations and could not become mandarins. Without a diploma, they could only teach, or go into a minor profession such as village scribe, astrologer or geomancer. Many were poor and lived a life of privation. They were called "impoverished scholars," or to use the literal translation of the Vietnamese term *han nho*, "shivering scholars" who lacked clothes to keep them warm in winter. Still, they kept up the pursuit of scholarship and upheld "the way of Confucius and the ancient sages," and in so doing, commanded the respect of society. It would be the lot of some later generations of ours to know poverty and to shiver as the year came to its end and the cold wind returned from the north.

Most recluse scholars were inspired by the mystical appeal of Taoism, but our recluse ancestors leaned towards Buddhism. In their time, the religion had lost the privileged position and royal patronage it enjoyed under the former dynasties of the Ly (1010–1225) and the Tran (1225–1400). The Ly kings were devout Buddhists who built more than three hundred temples. "Wherever there is a site of great beauty, there is a temple," an inscription from that period reads. Buddhist priests held important positions at the court. In the following Tran dynasty, several kings abdicated to devote their time to religion. But Buddhism started losing the support of the monarchy and the scholars' class at the end of the Tran. It fell further under the Le (1428–1527), when Confucianism gained pre-eminence and became the national "teaching." In the time of our first three ancestors, knowledge of Confucian texts, and them only, was required for the civil service examinations. Taoism was not taught at school and it was left to the scholars to learn for themselves the works of Lao Tzu and Chuang Tzu. As for Buddhism, it was shunned and openly criticized by officialdom, as shown in the following comments made by the official historian of the Le in the *History of the Dai Viet*. Writing about Tran Thanh Ton, a king of the former dynasty who ruled the country for twenty stable and peaceful years, the historian duly praised him for "having regard for the wise and respect for the learned ... [thus] strengthening the foundations of the House of Tran." He then added this disparaging remark: "But he became obsessed with the religion of liberation [Buddhism], which was not a good way for a king to govern."

However, Buddhism remained strong in the country among the common people and particularly the women. In our family, it was the women who went to the temples to make offerings and to pray. Our scholar-mandarins did not practice the religion, but unlike the historian quoted above, they would have shown it due respect as being one of the "three traditional teachings" and out of the consideration for their mothers', wives' and sisters' beliefs.

My Hanh, the wife of our fourth ancestor, came into a family which had been struck by misfortune and tragedy. After Nguyen Hoang's death and Phuc Thien's tribulations with the Trinh, the Nguyen of Kim Bai had lost their mandarinal status. She brought with her a strong Buddhist faith and her religious attitude would have a profound impact on our next generations. My Hanh was a "religious at home," meaning that she followed Buddha's teachings without having to become a nun and to leave home and family. Lord Buddha was once asked whether lay men and women leading a normal family life could attain high spiritual states. He replied in the affirmative. Not only one or two persons or a few hundreds could do so, but many, many more, he stressed. Buddhism gave to every adept the possibility to realize Nirvana. Traditionally, a practicing Buddhist was one who took the Three Gems—the Buddha, his Teaching and the Order of Monks—as "refuges" and daily observed the Five Abstinences—not to destroy life, not to steal, not to commit adultery, not to tell lies and use indecent language, not to take intoxicating drinks. With the Three Refuges and Five Abstinences, a Buddhist could go into a personal quest for liberation in the privacy of his or her home. The practice was quite common in Vietnam and has continued to this day. Popular wisdom considered it as even more praiseworthy than retiring from life and entering a religious order. A proverb says:

Firstly, are those who practice their religion at home.
Secondly, are those who practice it in the market place.
Thirdly, are those who practice it in a temple.

One can follow Buddha's teaching everywhere. To do so in the noise and among the crowd of a market place is more difficult than in the calm atmosphere of a temple. Moreover, to do so in one's own home, without either support or supervision, requires the highest degree of self-discipline and commitment.

My Hanh's commitment to her faith lasted throughout her life. As we know, it was her wish to be buried in temple land instead of family land. She lived to an advanced age and exercised a strong influence over the religious beliefs of both her son and grandson, the next two generations of our family. Like her, Nguyen Luan and Khanh Thien were "religious at home." The path they chose was Zen. Daily, they recited Buddhist sutras, meditated and sought to understand the Four Noble Truths of Buddha's teaching. Our family had gone from prosperity to decline, but instead of rebelling against an adverse fate, as the last generation did, their attitude was one of peaceful acceptance. As good Buddhists, they endeavored not to attach themselves to worldly things but to live in the present time, with no regret for a past that was gone and no expectation for a future that was yet to exist. Zen or Meditation was probably the Buddhist discipline best suited to the training of a Confucian scholar. Zen aimed at cultivating one's mind for the search for Truth. It stood very close to the central Confucian precept of cultivating one's person by "extending one's knowledge, keeping one's thoughts sincere and rectifying one's heart." A Confucian scholar must constantly seek to learn and to improve himself. Likewise, a Zen disciple needed to constantly train and develop his mind. Confucius told his students to "make themselves new, each and every day." This could equally apply to those who followed Zen.

Our ancestors would not have necessarily belonged to a Zen school. A Zen priest may have given them guidance on the techniques of meditation, but theirs could have been essentially a personal and independent quest. Anyone could choose his or her own way of search for Truth in Zen. There was no requirement to subscribe to a particular dogma or set of rules. Nguyen Luan and Khanh Thien remained Confucian scholars and continued their occupation as teachers, while practicing Zen. They learned by reading Buddhist sermons and, especially, by drawing from the treasure trove of writings left by ancient Zen priests. These were often poets. One does not need to be a Zen follower to appreciate the beauty of Zen poems, such as this one by Van Hanh who died in 1018. Van Hanh was not only a renowned priest. His advice on political matters was eagerly sought by two dynasties of kings. He lived through a change of dynasty, saw the rise and fall of families and witnessed the same kind of upheaval which would befall our own family some centuries later. I think that this poem must find a particular echo in the minds of our Zen ancestors. It was a lesson that Van Hanh gave to his disciples on the subject of impermanence:

> Our life is like a flash of lightning; it is here, it has gone.
> All plants flourish in spring, to dry out with autumn.
> Fate may bring us rise or decline, do not be afraid,
> For rise and decline are dew drops shining on the blade of grass.

In the Zen tradition, a master taught his disciple not by a long discourse but by engaging into a dialogue with him. The disciple ask questions. The master gave answers. These were usually very short and designed not to explain but to shock the disciple into realising that the real answer to his questions lay within himself. No master could give it to him. Truth dwelt in everyone of us and in everything that we could see. Many Zen dialogues are famous and have been pondered by generations of followers, in particular "religious at home" who, like our ancestors, were engaged in a long and lonely quest to reach for an "insight" into the nature of things. A story is told of King Ly Thai Tong (1028–1054) who visited a temple one day. He met an old priest whose name was not known and who was only remembered as The Old Zen Man. The king asked him where he came from and how did he become a Zen priest. The old man replied with two verses:

> Suffice to know the time and day of now,
> Why recall past springs and autumns!

The king was puzzled. Seeing this, the old man continued with a few more verses:

> The green bamboo and yellow chrysanthemums,
> Their reality is not outside me.
> The silver clouds and bright full moon,
> Reveal to me the whole Truth.

As the king still did not seem to understand, the old man ended the conversation by exclaiming: "What is the point of using words!" Suddenly, the king understood and was enlightened, so the story says.

Our ancestors were recalled to be writers but none of their writings survived the wars and upheavals in our country. I believe that they were not major writers, but only members of a small literary group. Being followers of Zen, they would get inspiration from Zen masters and, I imagine, take their style as a model. Vietnamese Zen writers came into prominence under the Ly dynasty (1010–1225), which saw the first blossoming of our literature and poetry. Many Zen poems of that early period could rival in melody and beauty of expression the best poems written during the Tang dynasty, the golden age of Chinese poetry. In addition, Zen poems have that indefinable quality which is called "Zen spirit." A discerning reader can recognize it at once. Zen masters were people who, after years of meditation and rigorous training, had conquered their doubts and come to terms with themselves and the world. Their spirit shone through their works. Among the best-loved poems of the Ly period was the following from Man Giac, a Zen priest living in the eleventh century. He died at forty-five. He wrote this poem to let his disciples know that he was ill and had not much longer to live:

> When spring leaves, a hundred flowers will fall,
> When spring arrives, a hundred flowers will bloom.
> Life rushes past before our eyes,
> Old age comes, starting from the top of our head.
> But do not say that all flowers will fall when spring fades away,
> For last night, in my front yard, I saw a branch of apricot flowers.

Zen spirit sustained our people when their fortunes were down, and set to stay down. Nguyen Luan and Khanh Thien were condemned to be scholars without titles. With examinations and public office out of bounds for them, there was no way that they could move up in society. One would expect them to be affected by a mood of despondency, even despair. Yet, these two generations were remembered as a period of calm and contentment. Our ancestors found happiness and peace of mind in the pursuit of religion. Thus, in the aftermath of the change of dynasty, two women played decisive roles in our family. Trinh Khiet, the wife of our third ancestor, led the way back to our roots in Kim Bai and recovered our land. Her daughter-in-law My Hanh armed her descendants with a strong Buddhist faith and helped them cope with a long period of decline.

It has been so in our history. The men won diplomas and mandarinal positions. A phase of prosperity was started. As the family moved up, the women stayed in their husband's shadow. But when fortunes turned and rise gave way to decline, often our rigid scholars failed to adapt to changing circumstances. Then, our foremothers rose to the occasion and were instrumental in guiding the family through difficult times. Their leadership role did not fit in with Confucian teaching, which said that a woman must "defer to" or "follow" her father when a daughter at home, her husband when married and her son when a widow. But it was in character with the ancient culture existing in Vietnam before our country fell under Chinese domination in 111 B.C. Then, men and women had equal rights. Their responsibilities were also equal, a situation which showed itself most clearly in the army where soldiers and commanders came from both sexes. The Trung sisters, who died in the Hat River near our village, led our first national movement of resistance against the Chinese. They were not the only women to do so. In A.D. 248, Trieu Au sought to break the foreign yoke at the head of an army she raised herself. Family members tried to dissuade her from going into a perilous campaign, but she said: "I want to ride the big storm, break the angry waves, kill the mighty whales in the eastern sea, sweep our country clean to save the people from the quagmire. I do not wish to imitate others who stooped to become a man's concubine and servant." Confucianism spread to Vietnam during the thousand years of Chinese rule, along with Taoism and Buddhism. Eventually, it became the dominant "teaching," in particular among the scholars. However, it never succeeded in eradicating the ancient equality from our society and the role of the Vietnamese woman has never been just "to follow."

Our scholars were strict Confucians who ruled their family in a rigid and authoritarian manner, in conformity with precepts laid down a long time ago by the Master and his disciples. Discipline was strict, especially for sons, for upon their success would depend the family's future. Relations between father and son were formal and rather similar to those between a stern teacher and his pupil. In fact, many generations of our family used the term *thay*, or teacher, as an appellation for father. Fortunately, our foremothers had a more understanding attitude and were more responsive to the needs of the young. Often, their influence over the latter was the dominant one. In our chronicle, the women remained in the background. Unlike the men's diplomas and careers, their activities were hardly mentioned. But interestingly, later generations would continue to talk about the roles played by Trinh Khiet and My Hanh, while most of the achievements of the mandarins of the first generations came to be forgotten. Even the existence of Nguyen Tue and Nguyen Hoang was lost to their descendants, for a very long time.

Nguyen Luan and his son were said to have written important chapters of the old family chronicle which was destroyed by bandits in the eighteenth century. All generations of our family had a duty to add a chapter to the chronicle which was deposited in the Ancestral Shrine. As a rule, a generation did not write about itself, but about the ones that preceded it. A scholar must not record his own life and career, however successful they may be. He should leave that task to his son. As for him, his responsibility was to make sure that the achievements of his father, and those of more distant ancestors, would be known to his descendants. He must search into his ancestry and "throw light on the past," as my grandfather wrote in the chronicle. In normal circumstances, our second ancestor Nguyen Uyen would write about his father Nguyen Tue and his son Nguyen Hoang would write about him. Then, it would be the turn of Phuc Thien to do so for Nguyen Hoang, Nguyen Luan for Phuc Thien and Khanh Thien for Nguyen Luan. However following the collapse of the Mac, it was probable that neither Nguyen Hoang before he died nor Phuc Thien in his troubled existence, contributed much to the chronicle. Nguyen Luan and his son would have to fill the gap left by them and put on record the times and lives of Nguyen Hoang and Phuc Thien. Apparently, they also wrote about our first two generations, for family tradition recalls that they were the chroniclers of our "golden period" of doctor-mandarins. Whatever the case, they must have been able to give a fairly complete account of that period, being close to it. With their writing talents, this must also have been a very readable account, for later generations would keep talking about it long after it had been destroyed and its contents mostly forgotten.

Nguyen Luan's wife came from a family whose name could be either Le or Nguyen. The chronicle is not clear on this point. She was one of the very few among our foremothers to have left a personal name. The chronicle recorded it as Thang, which is an unusual and rather interesting name for a woman. *Thang* means "to win" in the common language and is more often chosen as a name for a male. It has also an archaic and little-known sense of hair ornament. In ancient times, women made artificial flowers out of colored papers to put on their hair, those flowers were called *thang*. Some scholarly families gave that name to their daughters, for that reason. Finally, Buddhist vocabulary has an important expression *thang nghia*, which means "the right and winning path." Our foremother's name may have come from there, in which case it would denote a strong Buddhist faith in her family. The meaning of names is a fascinating field of study. Vietnamese parents, especially scholars in the old times, used to take great care in choosing their children's names. These could reveal much of a family's background, its attitudes and beliefs. It is such a pity that so many of our ancestors' names have been lost. By her name, we can surmise that Nguyen Luan's wife came from a scholarly family following the path of Buddhism; in other words, a family very much like our own. Probably, she was also a "religious at home," like her husband and mother-in-law.

As with the four generations before it, this one had only one male descendant. An added source of anxiety for Nguyen Luan and his wife was that their son was not born until many years after their marriage. For a time, there was real fear that the line might end with them. Our foremother went to numerous temples, pagodas and shrines to pray for a son. She was a regular worshipper at Kim Bai's own Snake Temple, whose Spirit had been kind to many a childless couple. Her husband sought the help of geomancers. On their advice, our ancestral home was given a new orientation. Such a change of orientation had happened before and for the same reason. Our men did not go to temples in search for a descendant. They considered what the women did as popular superstition, but were ready to listen to practitioners of geomancy. This was a field of knowledge which, like astrology, enjoyed the respect of scholars. The practitioners were themselves scholars who specialized in the difficult study of the Book of Changes and other learned treatises on the configuration of the land and the way it influenced human affairs. Those acclaimed as master geomancers were said to have gained an insight into mysterious forces that ruled people's lives. It may have been in this generation that the episode of the Chinese geomancer called in to move our ancestral tombs, which has been recounted earlier, took place. Finally, a son was born when Nguyen Luan was in his forties. The danger had passed, but the underlying fear remained. For more than a century our lineage had been preserved by a single branch. Without new branches appearing, how much longer could it last?

Our sixth ancestor Khanh Thien was married to a woman of the Nguyen family. Here again, we know very little about her except that being a Nguyen, she was probably not from our village. There were in Kim Bai several Nguyen families which were not related to one another. But village customs frowned upon marriages between people with the same family name, perhaps on the premise that they belonged to the same original stock. Unlike his father, Khanh Thien had an heir at an early age. That was a good omen and hopes were raised that this generation would see the end of the "drought" in male descendants. But then no other son came, or if they did, they could not survive their infancy. The years passed by. It looked as if the one-son pattern was there to stay. Khanh Thien and his wife were in their middle age when another son was born. A full twenty years separated him from his elder brother. The parents' joy could be imagined. At last, the old pattern was broken. Nearly a century had passed since the trauma of the change of dynasty. Difficult times had been with our family long enough; indeed as long as the three generations mentioned in the proverb. It was time for the wheel of fortune to turn and this could be the signal.

18. The Great Calamity

Khanh Thien's first son was named Nguyen Duc Y. His younger brother's name is not recorded in the chronicle. We only know his pseudonym Thuan Can. As we can see, Nguyen Duc Y is a three-word name. Until the last generation, all our people had names composed of only two words, the family name Nguyen followed by a personal name, as for instance Nguyen Tue in the case of our first ancestor and Nguyen Uyen in the case of the second. The three-word name that Khanh Thien gave to his son was a departure from family tradition. He would not have taken such a decision lightly. The name transmitted down the generations by our ancestors had a symbolic, almost sacred, character. I think that Khanh Thien acted in the hope that a new name would usher in a new phase in the life of our family. That may have been his way to conjure Fate, so that the things that had kept us down would be done away with: the ban from the civil service examinations and the scarcity of male descendants. Besides, he was following a general trend in the country. From the early periods until about the seventeenth century, most scholars listed in the registers of high graduates had names of only two words. Then, as the population increased and it became difficult to avoid having the same combinations of words, especially for people sharing prevalent family names such as Nguyen, Tran or Le, more and more families opted for the longer name. Eventually, the majority of graduates in the registers had three-word names. The movement was gradual and operated over a great many generations. Our family opted for the change early on, which was surprising, for we have always been conservative. Khanh Thien must have felt a pressing need to do something to change our luck.

Soon enough, things started to look up. Duc Y, who was born sometime in the 1670s, showed good promise as a student. A younger brother was born. Then, the interdiction with regard to the examinations was lifted, probably under the rule of overlord Trinh Can (1682–1709). Prior to that, our relations with local authorities had improved, through the good offices of former students of Nguyen Luan and Khanh Thien. Under Trinh Tac, Trinh Can's predecessor, hostilities with the Nguyen in the south abated and the regime could devote more attention to education and the training of talents to serve in the administration. Scholarship was encouraged. In

1662, Trinh Tac ordered the renovation of the national university, which had fallen into disrepair. Fortnightly meetings were again held there for students to receive tuition. Civil service examinations had been taking place, but malpractices were common. People brought their textbooks with them into the examination enclosure, some hired others to sit for them. The standard of graduates fell well below that at the time of the Mac. The situation became so bad that, in 1664, all those made bachelors during the past ten years were ordered to sit again. More than half of them were failed. In the same year, doctorate examinations were reorganized. In 1678, a new system of regional examinations was put in place. Local authorities were instructed to list all persons with learning, so that no one would be passed over when examintaions were held. In these circumstances, it was perhaps only natural that families like ours, which were kept out for political reasons going back to many generations ago, would have their situation revised. Duc Y was allowed to take part in the examinations.

He did not obtain the license which would have opened for him a mandarinal career. But he became a successful teacher who presided over a revival in our family's fortunes. Although the chronicle does not mention it, I believe that he held a bachelor degree for he prepared students for the regional competitions, the equivalent of today's university examinations. Such a high level of tuition was seldom given by untitled scholars. Duc Y ran his own school and taught under the pseudonym Dinh Thuyen. *Dinh* was the royal courtyard, an allusion to the royal courtyard examinations in which our earlier ancestors took part and where Duc Y must have dreamed he could go. *Thuyen* means to choose good and wise men to serve as mandarins. Thus, after two generations of Zen Buddhists, the name Dinh Thuyen announced the return to purely Confucian values. Many generations of young scholars studied under Duc Y in their quest for "the golden board." He remained their "teacher" long after they had left his school and it was said that even those who became high and powerful mandarins continued to regard themselves as "students" in his presence. For the family, Duc Y's success signalled the end of a long period of stagnation. Confidence was rebuilt and the younger generation, which included not only his children but also a brother who was twenty years his junior, was encouraged to study and prepare itself for better times ahead. Duc Y provided strong leadership. As a mark of gratitude for the role he played, the family later on adopted the first word in his pseudonym, Dinh, as its middle name. Descendants of his branch and of the junior branch all took the same middle name. In time, we became known in Kim Bai as the Nguyen Dinh—or the Nguyen of the Royal Courtyard Examination—to differentiate us from other Nguyens in the village.

We are not descended from Duc Y, but from his younger brother who was thus our seventh ancestor. His real name was not recorded in the chronicle. We know his pseudonym Thuan Can, which means Gentleness and Caution, two of the qualities often praised by Confucian writers in a gentleman. Thuan Can was born sometime in the 1690s. His life was spent very much in the shadow of his elder brother who, considering their difference in age, must have been like a father figure to him. He followed in Duc Y's footsteps, with however much less success. He was good enough a scholar to pass the test held at the prefecture level to choose candidates for the regional examinations, but got no diploma at these examinations. He taught in his brother's school, but his teaching career earned him nothing like the reputation that his brother had.

During the last three generations, the land owned by the Nguyen had been gradually reduced in size. Part of it went into the hands of corrupt officials who took advantage of Phuc Thien's opposition to the Trinh to prey on our family. Then, our recluse scholars had no regular livelihood other than the rice fields they inherited and had to dispose of a number of them. Still, at the start of this generation, our landholdings remained extensive. We had rice fields, mulberry fields and ponds in several villages in Thanh Oai prefecture, besides our own village. The dreaded one-son pattern at least had a good side to it; it prevented our assets from being divided. But that situation was going to change. Two branches appeared and the inheritance was split. Most of it went to Duc Y. As the eldest son, he received firstly the ancestral home and a large amount of land to be used for the worship of ancestors, then his own share. Thuan Can only received his share. This still gave him a comfortable existence, but he could not afford to be like his father and grandfather and not worry about earning a livelihood. Teaching and getting an income became for him a necessity.

Thuan Can's wife was a Nguyen and, therefore, probably from a family outside Kim Bai. She managed the reduced family holdings and engaged in trading activities at the market to bring in an additional income. The couple had two sons, of whom the younger one was our eighth ancestor. His name was Nguyen Dinh Binh, Dinh being the newly adopted middle name common to the whole family and Binh his own given name.

For his part, Duc Y had three sons, the eldest of whom would be in the same age group as his uncle Thuan Can. The new generation grew up under the rule of overlord Trinh Cuong (1709–1729), the last good period of the Trinh before a great agrarian rebellion engulfed the country. The two decades of his rule saw a further improvement in our family's fortunes. Duc Y's heir, Nguyen Du, obtained the license at the regional examinations and entered the mandarinate, the first in five generations of our family to do so. He reached the positon of senior prefect of Gia Hung, a senior prefecture in the province of Hung Hoa, in the northwest of the country. A senior prefect held the lower sixth mandarinal grade, just one grade away from the *dai phu* or high mandarins. His importance could be seen from the fact that the number of senior prefectures in the country was then fifty-two and he was in charge of everything in his prefecture, except for the preservation of public order. Gia Hung was in size probably the largest of all senior prefectures, larger even than many of the country's provinces. It bordered on China and Laos and only had a sparse population composed of Vietnamese, Chinese and mountain peoples of the Thai and Meo races. The area was poor and mostly covered with forest. Its climate was insalubrious. In the hierarchy of prefectures, Gia Hung stood below most others, but Nguyen Du did not have a doctorate and he already had done well to become a senior prefect.

Nguyen Du's two brothers were unsuccessful at the examinations. One of them was Cu Hau, the ancestor who left the papers mentioned in previous chapters. Cu Hau looked after our Ancestral Shrine and managed the extensive cult land belonging to it. In this generation, our family was still well-off and the Ancestral Shrine continued to receive donations from the branches. Cu Hau himself was a man of means who had donated land to Kim Bai's Association of Literati. Land donors were usually people without descendants; they gave land in order that the association perform the ceremonies of worship for their spirits after they died. Cu Hau, however, had descendants and he did so to support the association's activities in favor of young scholars in the village.

At about the same time as Nguyen Du broke the drought for our family by going into the mandarinate, success came to other scholarly families in Kim Bai. More students qualified to take part in the regional examinations. More gained degrees. Then, one claimed the high prize of a doctorate diploma. As recorded in the *Dai Viet Register of High Graduates*, Nguyen Huy Thuc hailing from Kim Bai was made a doctor in 1739, at the young age of twenty-four. He worked in the Censorate, the body which kept watch over the actions of mandarins and saw to it that they were in conformity with the laws and customs of the country. Nguyen Huy Thuc was one of the thirteen censors assigned to oversee a province. Although also a Nguyen, he was in all probability not related to us, for our chronicle says nothing about him. Besides, our family had by then become the Nguyen Dinh, a name easily distinguishable from that of Nguyen Huy.

Nguyen Du's success naturally made him the leader of our extended family. He took over that position from his father Duc Y. In our chronicle, which is that of the younger branch, my grandfather did not expand on their roles. He merely noted that the history of their lives was kept by the heir to the eldest branch. Those two ancestors had started our revival and hopes were raised high in the family. It had taken us two generations since the first harbinger of better times appeared with our tree spreading out into two branches. Talents had been rewarded. Duc Y was a respected teacher. His son rejuvenated with our tradition of public service. Progress had been slow and gradual, but that had always been the case with our family. Our way up the Mountain of the Twins had been through a long and tortuous path. As the generational cycle kept turning, the young generations would continue to forge ahead and reach higher peaks of success.

But there followed a great calamity, the result of which was that, instead of pursuing its revival, our family sank deeper into decline.

Already under Trinh Cuong, there were early signs of a deteriorating situation in the countryside. The overlord had to take measures to prohibit public officials from abusing their position and buying land in areas under their jurisdiction. He ordered that court procedure be speeded up to settle the claims of peasants whose land had been grabbed by mandarins and big landlords. His son Trinh Giang succeeded him in 1729. A violent and bloodthirsty man, Trinh Giang murdered King Le Duy Phuong and killed several good and loyal mandarins who had served his father well. His spendthrift ways caused heavy taxes to be imposed on the population. To bring more money in, he put administrative offices up for sale. Anyone could become prefect by paying the Treasury 1,800 *quan* and senior prefect by paying 2,800 *quan*. Mandarins could go up one grade with a contribution of 600 *quan*. This measure destroyed the reputation of the mandarinal corps and increased corruption, for those who paid for their offices would recover their money—and take more—from the people. Resentment became widespread. Rebellions broke out nearly everywhere, supported by the peasantry. The rebels all proclaimed to fight the Trinh rule in order to restore the Le monarchy to real power. Historian Tran Trong Kim wrote that peasants in the Red River delta

> took their harrows and sticks to join the rebels. Big movements counted up to tens of thousands men, smaller ones a few thousands or a few hundreds. Villages were attacked and pillaged. Towns were surrounded. The army was unable to quell the insurgents.

Roads were cut. The authorities had to build guard towers on high ground to observe the movement of rebel groups and light fires to warn of their approach. As the situation threatened to get out of hand, the high mandarins got together to depose Trinh Giang, in 1740. His brother Trinh Doanh succeeded him. By then, big and small rebellions were taking place all over the country. History books mentioned up to a dozen large movements which the Trinh could only put down after more than ten years of fighting. The whole of Trinh Doanh's rule (1740–1767) was taken up by military campaigns to pacify the country.

Author Pham Dinh Ho, who was born in 1768, gave a chilling account of what he heard of the calamity which descended in 1740 on his province of Hai Duong, southeast of the delta. One can read in his *Essays Written in Rainy Days*:

Our province suffered from the hostilities for up to eighteen years. Wild dogs and pigs multiplied in the fields. People who survived had to peel tree bark and catch field rats to eat. A *mau* [about 3,600 square meters] of ricefield could only sell for the price of a small cake. In my canton, there was an old and wealthy widow who had silver coins piled up like a mountain [sic]. That year, her household ran out of paddy. She took with her five bags of silver to exchange for paddy, but could not find any and was found dead of hunger. Our village was abandoned and vegetation grew over it. When hostilities ended, villagers followed one another to return from the capital. Cutting down thatch and clearing grass, they looked for the foundations of their old homes. They gathered the bones of family members to bury.... The fields had to be burnt to clear them. It was not yet possible to build accommodation, so everyone assembled around the high foundations of the Communal Hall.

From the above, we can have an idea of what the people in our own region went through during those dark years. There were periods when Kim Bai and neighboring villages too had to be abandoned and their fields left to "wild dogs and pigs." Our area lay at the mercy of bands of insurgents who operated from their dens in a marshy area to the south and in the western foothills across the Hat River. They came to plunder and destroy at will, time and again. Whether they were political rebels, poor peasants revolting against their condition or simply bandits taking advantage of the absence of law and order, no one was sure. Those bands did not seem to belong to any of the big rebellions mentioned in history books. Kim Bai people recalled that period as "the great upheaval" or "the great calamity," and referred to the insurgents as "rebels" or "bandits." The population fled, then returned to work the fields, but their harvest would be taken. There were years when no one returned.

By then, in the two decades of the 1740s and 1750s, our seventh generation had developed into five branches and some of the elder ones had sub-branches. Our family tree had started looking more like the *si* tree at the entrance of Kim Bai. But the upheaval made the branches disperse and their ties weakened. All branches suffered from the calamity. Lives were lost. Family members sought the safety of provincial towns or fled to the capital. Some found work in the lower echelons of the bureaucracy. Others more humbly eked out a living teaching children or offering their services as scribes to write out letters, documents or pleas to the authorities for illiterate people. Some moved out of the scholars' class and became shopkeepers or petty traders. All became impoverished and many tried to come back to Kim Bai to hold on to their land, but often had to leave again as the bandits reappeared. Our own branch stayed away from Kim Bai for long periods. Our eighth ancestor Dinh Binh was a young man when the trouble started. He was trained to become a scholar, but did not manage to get any diploma. He earned his living "rapping on young heads," as the activities of those who taught children were often derisively portrayed.

Even though a scholar, he was at the bottom of his class, among the mass of those not so talented who remained untitled and therefore had to "suffer from the cold." The memories of privation and hardship that were imprinted in our familial mind could be traced back to his generation and the one following it.

Dinh Binh married a woman of the Nguyen family. They had five children, three sons and two daughters. Our chronicle noted that "the first and third sons died without descendants." One wonders whether they had died during the years of turmoil. One daughter married into the Chu family, whose ancestral compound was situated in the Middle Hamlet, quite close to ours. That was the beginning of a series of marriages between the Chu and the Nguyen Dinh, occurring over several generations. The other daughter died young. As can be seen, daughters have appeared for the first time in the chronicle and we are given some information about them. The second son, named Nguyen Dinh Phuong, became our ninth ancestor. Although three sons were born to them, Dinh Binh and his wife ended up with only one male descendant. The old fear was reawakened. Was the one-son pattern back to haunt us again?

In the 1760s, security was finally reestablished in the countryside. People could reintegrate back into their villages. Sometime after the return, our family members got together to build a new Ancestral Shrine upon the foundation of the old one. But this time, it was just a small thatched cottage. Then, each branch went its own way. Everyone was occupied with their own survival. There was no one to play a leadership role and keep the branches together. The eldest branch, which used to be wealthier and more talented than the rest, and had produced such leaders as Duc Y and Nguyen Du, was now as destitute as the others. The Shrine used to own a great deal of cult land, which was the common property of the family. That land had disappeared, yet no one seemed to know or be concerned about it. Ceremonies at the Shrine dedicated to the memory of common ancestors were held a few times, then they stopped. A new chronicle was written and deposited at the Shrine. But based purely on the recollection of the survivors, it contained wide gaps. Among the early ancestors, only Nguyen Uyen was remembered. Ancestral graves were lost. Death anniversaries were missing. Yet, no one sought to fill in those gaps.

Our ninth ancestor was born sometime in the 1760s. Although the family had fallen into hard times, the young continued to be given a scholar's education. Nguyen Dinh Phuong was sent to study under good teachers in town, while his father, mother and sisters all worked to make ends meet, the women adding the proceeds of their market activities to the meager income of a teacher. "Pages were torn, but the spine of the book must be kept intact," as my grandfather said. Dinh Phuong grew up in a calmer and more orderly period. The new overlord Trinh Sam (1767–1782) completed the pacification work of his father and strengthened the Trinh rule. With the north safely under control, Trinh Sam set his sights on the south where the Nguyen regime was in the hands of a mandarin usurper and, moreover, confronted with an important revolt from the Tay Son brothers in the highlands. In 1774, he resumed the hostilities which had remained dormant for a century. His army quickly broke through the lines of walls defending the south and occupied the Nguyen capital Phu Xuan, now called Hue. The Nguyen descendants fled to the newly gained and still sparsely populated Mekong River delta. Their challenge to the Trinh seemed to have ended. The leaders of the Tay Son revolt made their submission to Trinh Sam, who looked poised to extend his rule over the whole country. Who could then have imagined that the Trinh were to be defeated and totally disappear from the national scene, only a decade later?

Success went to Trinh Sam's head. Breaking with a tradition that had seen the Trinh keep power in their hands for nearly two centuries while the Le king remained a figurehead, Trinh Sam wanted to become king himself. To take over the throne would be an easy matter for him, but for the fact that the Le king was a vassal of the Chinese emperor and the consent of the latter was needed for a peaceful change of dynasty. Trinh Sam sent a diplomatic mission to Peking to plead with the emperor to bestow the title of king on him, because—as his argument ran—there were no more descendants of the Le worthy of sitting on the throne of Vietnam. As head of the mission, he chose Vu Tran Thieu, a scholar-mandarin with the rank of deputy minister. His own trusted men were placed within the delegation, with large quantities of gold and silver to bribe the Ching mandarins. The mission broke its journey at Lake Tung Ting, the place where all Vietnamese envoys used to stop and rest for some time, before moving on to the Chinese capital. There, perhaps recalling the achievements of former envoys who upheld the honor and integrity of our country at the court of the Son of Heaven, and pondering over how history would judge him, Vu Tran Thieu burned the submission entrusted to him by Trinh Sam, then drank poison to kill himself. He must have been convinced that the people's will still favored the Le over the Trinh. The mission was aborted. Trinh Sam had to drop the idea of becoming king.

Trinh Sam's decision regarding his own succession then threw the Trinh into a grave crisis. He had a young consort named Dang Thi Hue, of whom he grew very fond. She came from the village of Phu Dong in Bac Ninh, the seat of the mythical Heavenly Prince, who transformed himself from child into warrior and saved the country from the rebels, in a legendary past. My grandmother came from the same village and the same family, five or six generations after the Dang lady. History books mentioned that the latter was a "commoner" who was recruited as a maidservant to one of the ladies at the Trinh palace. She caught the eyes of the overlord and became his favorite. The mandarins, eunuchs and other followers at the palace first thought that she was just "a woman with a pretty face," who did not even come from a scholarly family. There was nothing to be concerned about her, they believed. They were soon proved wrong. Dang Thi Hue bore the overlord a son, named Trinh Can, and such was her hold over him that he made Trinh Can his official heir, instead of his elder son Trinh Khai. Dang Thi Hue gathered around her a circle of supporters and the palace became divided into two camps, one following her and the other following Trinh Khai. A few years later, Trinh Sam died of illness. His testament made Trinh Can, then only six, the new overlord. The elder son, Trinh Khai, allied himself with the Palatial Guard. Two months later the guards revolted. They killed the regent appointed by Trinh Sam and arrested Dang Thi Hue and her son. Trinh Khai became overlord, but he could not control the guards, who held sway in the capital and elsewhere, killing, pillaging and plunging the country into anarchy. Dang Thi Hue was imprisoned and tortured, but she refused to beg for forgiveness for her "crimes." At the anniversary of Trinh Sam's death, she committed suicide. Her dignified end was praised by scholars and won her public sympathy. Popular belief also had it that the Trinh rule, which had never won the affection of the people, was destroyed by her. In fact, although she did cause it to weaken, the two hundred–year Trinh rule was brought to an end by an irresistible movement originating from the central highlands, the Tay Son.

Trinh Khai's overlordship began in 1783. As he and his mandarins tried to keep the guards in check, the Tay Son, who earlier had made their submission to Trinh Sam, consolidated their hold over the highlands. Further south, in the Mekong River delta, a seventeen-year-old descendant of the Nguyen overlord, Nguyen Anh, was husbanding his forces to make a comeback. The scene was set for the most turbulent period of our history. In the next two decades, the country would go through a succession of regimes. A military intervention by China would be defeated. Our history would turn a corner; having done so, it would then turn again, and again. The Tay Son were people "wearing rough cloth," meaning they were poor, from the village of Tay Son in the province of Qui Nhon, hence their name. Three brothers led the movement, with the eldest bearing the title of king. Nguyen Hue was the youngest brother. Sometimes in the history of a nation, there appears an exceptional leader who conquers everything before him. In a very short time, he rises to the greatest heights of glory and makes an indelible imprint in the minds of his countrymen. Nguyen Hue was such a leader. His reign was short. When he disappeared, he left behind him no dynasty worthy of that name. But he was revered by posterity like few dynasties could ever be. History books described him as having "immense physical strength," a commander who "disposed his troops and directed his generals as if gifted with a supernatural genius." He relied on the speed with which he moved his troops. In the words of an opponent, these "whirred past you ... one cannot hit them and it was futile to chase them." His most feared weapon was his elephants. In a big battle, he would bring with him up to two hundred well-trained elephants and hurl them against his opponent's rear at a critical moment, sowing panic. Nguyen Hue fought in the south against the Nguyen overlord, capturing Gia Dinh—where Saigon now stands—several times. In 1783, the Siamese king sent in a strong force to help the Nguyen overlord. Nguyen Hue destroyed it in one battle. In 1786, taking advantage of the troubled situation in the north, he attacked Phu Xuan, the former capital of the Nguyen in the south, now in Trinh hands. In the space of a few days, he seized Phu Xuan and came right up to the old dividing line between the Trinh and the Nguyen during their long civil war. Then, he marched north. The mighty Trinh military machine, undermined by the revolt of the guards, crumbled before him. In less than a month, his forces were at the outskirts of Thang Long. Trinh Khai lost the battle to defend the capital and killed himself. The Trinh rule had ended.

The north was his. But, like the Trinh before him, Nguyen Hue refrained from doing away with the Le monarchy. He kept the Le king who conferred on him a dukedom and gave him his daughter in marriage. Dissension appeared within the Tay Son camp. Suspecting his brother of establishing a power base in the north, the Tay Son king rushed to the Le capital and brought Nguyen Hue back to the south. Power was left in the hands of the Le, but neither the king nor his court was able to keep it. A confused period ensued, in which descendants of the Trinh and lieutenants sent out by Nguyen Hue fought and tried to grab power for themselves. Eventually, Le Chieu Thong, the Le king, fled from the capital. The queen and queen mother went to China to ask for help to recover the throne. Emperor Qian Long of the Ching had designs over our country, he readily responded to the request and sent in a two hundred thousand strong army under the command of Sun Shi Yi, the governor of the two Guang provinces bordering Vietnam. In 1788, the Chinese occupied Thang Long and put Le Chieu Thong back on the throne. From his headquarters in the south, Nguyen Hue saw the imminent danger of the Chinese domination. He decided to take matters into his own hands. Before the assembled troops, he proclaimed himself Emperor Quang Trung, thus rejecting both the Le monarchy and his own brother the Tay Son king. Then, he led the troops north.

In a masterly campaign lasting just six days, he annihilated the vast Chinese army. Sun Shi Yi escaped from Thang Long in the middle of the night without having time to saddle his horse and wear his armor. After his victory, Quang Trung immediately set about making peace with the

Chinese. He told his aides that China being ten times bigger than our country, it would be dangerous if, having lost a battle, she planned a revenge. "I need time to make our country strong," he said. Quang Trung was as successful in diplomacy as in war. The Chinese accepted his peace moves, recognized him as King of An Nam and asked him to appear before the emperor in Peking. Not a man short of stratagems, Quang Trung dispatched a man looking like him. The old Emperor Qian Long, although his army was beaten, or perhaps because of that, had great consideration for Quang Trung. He received the "false king" like a father would his prodigal son, entertained him in his private chambers and had him meet members of the imperial family. Before he left, the emperor had a portrait of him made for his keeping. The "king" was false, but he proved to be an excellent actor and diplomat.

The Le king fled to China hoping that with Chinese help he would be able to get back to his throne. But the Chinese had changed their policy and the young king met with one rebuff after another from his hosts. He died in shame and despair in 1793 at only twenty-eight. How extraordinary was the fate of the Le family! No other dynasty had been able to hold our people's affection the way they did, and over such a long time. In 1428, they liberated the country from Chinese domination and ruled for one hundred years. They lost to the Mac, but after more than sixty years of Mac rule, the population continued to be attached to them. The Trinh defeated the Mac, but had to be content with being the de facto ruler, while the Le were restored to the throne. From 1592 to 1786, the Le were deprived of all powers. Successive Le kings were proclaimed and deposed at will by the overlord. The Le were marionettes in the hands of the Trinh, yet people persisted in looking up to them. They became the symbol of "legitimacy." All rebels and challengers to the Trinh claimed to fight in support of the Le. Even a man like Nguyen Hue had to, at first, go along with popular feeling and keep them as monarch. Then, the Le made the mistake of calling on the Chinese to intervene in Vietnam. More than a mistake, that was treachery. "To carry pickaback a snake home, so that it can eat your own chicken," was how our people sneered at and condemned those who sought the support of the Chinese for their own political ends, without regard for the greater interests of the country. But even such an action did not turn public opinion against the Le. On the contrary, people felt sorry for the last Le king and the ill-treatment he received from the Chinese. Many mourned his death. In 1802, under the new Nguyen dynasty, his remains were dug up to be brought back to Vietnam. It was said that when the coffin was opened, his body had decomposed except for a "red heart" which remained intact. Can such a story be true? The fact is that the king's heart became, in popular folklore, the proof of his indestructible love for his country.

Quang Trung only reigned for four years. His territory extended over

the north and most of the central part of the country. Further south was
the territory of his eldest brother, the Tay Son king. Quang Trung was a
conqueror. He looked north, west, and south. He sent his troops west to
Laos to exact tribute and to take their elephants which had played an important role in his battlefield tactics. He conducted a census of the population and increased conscription in preparation for an attack on China. His
brother was unable to contain the Nguyen overlord in the south, so he also
laid plans for an expedition there. In 1792, he sent a mission to China to
ask for a Chinese princess in marriage and to request the "return of the two
provinces of Guangdong and Guangxi" to Vietnam. Ancient history books
had it that back in the third century B.C., our border lay in the Wu Ling
mountains north of the two Guang and now Quang Trung wanted these
provinces back. Did he really intend to take on our giant neighbor, or was
it just a feint to keep China guessing while he went to the south to deal with
the Nguyen overlord? Who can say where lay the horizon of a warrior who
had acquired a reputation of "fighting a hundred battles and winning a
hundred victories," and whom Western travellers in Asia at the time had
dubbed "the new Attila?" The fact is that Quang Trung had been recruiting
Chinese rebels and pirates and sending them to China to harass the Ching
authorities. But his immediate concern was the south, where with the help
of the French, Nguyen Anh was pushing back the Tay Son forces under his
brother. Quang Trung had readied his forces. He had issued a proclamation to the people of the south prior to the start of his campaign. But he
died suddenly, on September 16, 1792, aged forty. His son Quang Toan,
a ten-year-old child, succeeded him. Ten years later, Nguyen Anh vanquished the Tay Son and unified the country under his rule. Nearly three
centuries of internal conflict had ended. He founded the Nguyen dynasty
which would last until 1945.

While all those momentous events were pressing upon one another on
the national scene, our family stayed back in our village. A proverb says: "A
man makes his opportunities in times of upheaval." It is a measure of our
deep decline that our ninth ancestor Dinh Phuong was not able even to move
away from the bamboo enclosure of Kim Bai. True, the time was for rough
and tough warriors, not for pen-holding scholars. "Can you write a poem
to chase the bandits away?" a general under Nguyen Hue asked a civilian
adviser as hundreds of thousands Chinese troops swarmed over Vietnam.
"As for us," he went on, "we only know how to draw our swords out of their
sheaths." A scholar's path passed through the examinations, but none were
held between 1782 and 1788, when Dinh Phuong would be in his twenties
and at an age to sit for them. After Quang Trung came to the throne, he
wanted to encourage the popular language, which was the expression of our
national character, to the expense of the scholarly language inherited from
China. Popular language became the administrative language and

examinations rules were changed to accommodate the new policy. Candidates trained in the study of Chinese classics, like those in our family, found themselves at a disadvantage. Mandarinal families in the north resented the move, which they considered as a way by the Tay Son regime to keep them away from public offices. As a matter of fact, among northern mandarins, many remained loyal to the Le. They retired or went into hiding in the mountains, so as not to serve the new emperor.

When examinations were resumed, it appears that Dinh Phuong did sit for them, but without success. He spent his life as a village teacher. He married the only daughter of the Pham, a family of fellow villagers. The Pham had no male descendant. As recorded in our chronicle, they "treated Dinh Phuong like their own son and entrusted him with their land and properties." The support given by his in-laws made life easier, although both Dinh Phuong and his wife had to work hard to bring up four children. In gratitude, he gave as middle name to his son the word Quang, taken from Quang Thanh, his father-in-law's pseudonym, instead of the customary word Dinh. Our tenth ancestor was thus named Nguyen Quang So, meaning Place of Light. At the death of the Pham, the heritage went to Dinh Phuong and it fell to him to celebrate the worship of their spirits. It was then that a second altar was set up in our ancestral home, devoted to the cult of ancestors on the maternal side.

Of Dinh Phuong's four children, three were daughters. The one-son pattern had returned, adding its gloom to the life of an unsuccessful and impoverished scholar. The eldest daughter married into the Chu family in Kim Bai, already allied to ours in the last generation. She had two sons and a daughter. The second child, also a girl, became another daughter-in-law of the Chu and had two sons. The third born was a son who became our tenth ancestor. It will be seen that his wife also was a Chu, though from a different branch living in a neighboring village. The youngest daughter died in childhood. Ties between the Nguyen Dinh and the Chu would continue right up to the twentieth century, for my great-grandmother again was a Chu. The two families would become preeminant in Kim Bai and would stay so until the communist revolution in 1945.

Academic success and social position eluded Dinh Phuong, but his memory was later honored by the Nguyen dynasty. His great-grandson, my grandfather, rose high in his career and in 1940, Dinh Phuong was bestowed posthumous rank and title by the court of Hue. His title of Lecturer at the Academy and his lower fourth grade put him in the higher echelons of the mandarinate. His wife was made a posthumous *Cung Nhan,* "Lady at the Palace," a title accorded to the spouse of a fourth grade mandarin. The merits that those ancestors had gathered during their obscure and humble lives were thus recognized by the court to have played a part in the achievements of their descendant, and duly rewarded.

19. The Businessman

My great-great-grandfather was born in 1792, the year Emperor Quang Trung died. He was ten and had started schooling when the Tay Son dynasty was defeated and the Nguyen overlord became emperor with the dynastic title of Gia Long. Our national history had changed its path once again, this time to go into a period of stability and consolidation. The long series of civil wars had come to an end. For the first time in nearly three hundred years, in fact since King Mac Dang Doanh under whom our first ancestor served, a single dynasty ruled over the whole country. In the sixteenth century, Vietnam's southern borders stopped at the extremity of Quang Nam province, or a little farther south than where the town of Da Nang stands today. In the next centuries, our people conquered the kingdom of Champa, then the Mekong River delta. Under Gia Long, the country extended from the pass of Nam Quan on the Chinese border to the point of Ca Mau jutting out into the Gulf of Thailand. Vietnam had reached its present day's boundaries. Gia Long's career, in contrast to that of Quang Trung, was painstakingly slow. He was a scion of the House of Nguyen Phuc, the overlord in the south. Under the attacks of the Trinh and the Tay Son, the Nguyen Phuc were chased away from their capital and pursued into their last refuges in the newly-settled land of the south. Gia Long, then Nguyen Phuc Anh, was only seventeen when he took up the banner of a house close to extinction. For nearly twenty-five years he fought, often "lying down over thorns and tasting the bitterness of defeat." At one time, he was reduced to lead the life of an exile in Siam. At other times, all the territory he had left was some forgotten island away from the coast. But he was always able to return to the newly colonized land of the south and resume the fight, for it was under the House of Nguyen Phuc that the settlers had gone there to build a new life and they remained loyal to his family. Moreover, much more so than his opponents, Nguyen Phuc Anh was aware of the superiority of Western technology. He sought to obtain it from France, sending his son there in 1787 to conclude a treaty with the French government. The treaty was never implemented, but through a French Catholic priest, Monseigneur Pigneau de Behaine, private assistance in terms of arms, equipment and some twenty technicians were sent to Nguyen Phuc Anh, giving him a decided advantage over the Tay Son. For this, left-wing historians would later attack him as having "carried picka-back a snake home," using the line reserved to those Vietnamese in receipt of Chinese help. They forgot that the French never gained any influence under him; in fact, he was a master who used Western arms and the service of Frenchmen for his own ends. Later on in 1817, the French government sent a vessel in to claim the benefits of the 1787 treaty. Emperor Gia Long replied that it had been inoperative and therefore he refused to recognize it. It was not he, but his descendants who failed to rise to the challenge of French colonialism, when it came in the second half of the century.

Traditional scholarship suffered an eclipse during the Tay Son period. It came back to the fore under the new dynasty. One of Gia Long's first edicts was to appeal to the many mandarins and graduates who had refused to work for the Tay Son to come out. "I will give public service positions to the best of you," the new emperor said, "so that you can make yourself useful to the country and help reduce my load of sovereign." The training of young talents to serve the state was treated as a matter of priority. New school curriculums were established. Graduated scholars were appointed in the provinces and prefectures to oversee the schools, which were in private hands, and to encourage learning. Examinations to recruit public servants, abandoned in the years of hostilities, were resumed in 1807. Nguyen Quang So, my ancestor, was then fifteen. His training was that of a traditional scholar, through the study of Confucian Classics. Family expectation for him was high; certainly prospects were better for his generation than they were for his father's.

But Quang So, who liked poetry and even wrote some, was not one to spend long hours memorizing ancient texts and pondering over commentaries made by ancient authors. He was an adolescent eager for action. "Like an arrow ready to be dispatched to the four corners of the world," later generations would often quote this popular saying when they recalled him. Quang So could not wait to be on his own and move out of the bamboo enclosure of his village. Physically tall and strong, adept at martial arts, his real vocation may have been a career in the army. He grew up in a time of war, where heroes and those holding the highest positions in society were warriors. Then, the ambition of young men was to fight for their king and gain fame on the battlefield.

> Putting down my brush and ink-slab,
> I prepared myself for the business of war....
> On the walls of the citadel, the sound of drums made the moon shake.
> The smokes of war rose to hide the clouds above.
> I was ushered into the king's chambers to be given my sword of command.
> At midnight, a proclamation was read to the troops. The date for their
>   departure had been decided.

These are extracts of the *Song of a Warrior's Wife*, a long poem in popular language by Doan Thi Diem, a celebrated poetess living in the first half of the eighteenth century. Long poems, as a genre, were much prized by Vietnamese authors. This piece totalling 412 verses expressed the feelings of longing and loneliness of a wife whose husband was called up and who lived for the day he would return home, his task done. In the continuing climate of war, it was quickly adopted by the public and was so well-liked that many people could memorize it from beginning to end. It was ranked as one of our most beautiful and melodious literary works, until the *Story of Kieu* appeared at the beginning of the nineteenth century and became the accepted masterpiece of its genre. The *Warrior's Wife* was my great-great-grandfather's favorite poem. He was fond of reciting its verses in a chanting voice and never failed to do so when friends came to share with him a pot of tea. If he was born a generation earlier, when leaders like Quang Trung and Gia Long were fighting for the control of the country, I think that Quang So would be glad to drop his brush and ink slab for a sword and a bow. He would have been the first one to part with the family tradition of being scholars. But his time was one of return to peace and unified rule. Eventually, he would still break with tradition and strike out in an entirely new direction. He would hold a very special place in our family history, although not as a warrior.

For the time being, however, Quang So was staying within the family path and studying for a career in letters. He got through the preliminary test held in our prefecture to select candidates for the regional examinations. At these, which at that time took place only once every six years, he failed twice. Clearly, he was not cut out for academic success. He could work as a teacher like his father, or join the subordinate ranks of the public service as a clerk, but did not want either of these. In his late twenties, he left home and village to make a fortune in business. He went to Thang Long, then no longer the capital—the Nguyen emperor ruling from present-day Hue—but still the principal commercial and cultural center of the country.

Quang So belonged to the tenth generation of our extended family and its youngest branch. In the last hundred years, the other branches had quickly multiplied. Elder ones had reached the eleventh, some even the twelfth, generation. Ours was singularly slow and unprolific. Ancestors in our branch stubbornly tried to cling to the old conception of scholarship. They went for the state examinations to become public servants; failing that, they would settle for a teaching career and nothing else. In the other branches, however, members had gone into a wide range of occupations. Thus, we had a practician of eastern medicine reputed for treating bone fractures with a dressing made of herbs, chicken bones and other products. The formula of his dressing was a trade secret known only to his descendants.

A geomancer relative of ours was often called to other villages on consultation; yet within his own family he was no prophet. When the need was felt to change the orientation of our ancestral home, it was a Chinese geomancer who was called instead. There were also astrologers among our people. Parents came to them to be told the future of their children, sons in particular, through the stars which governed their lives. Before a marriage could be agreed upon, the families must consult an astrologer to see whether the stars and age of the young man were suited to those of the girl. The astrologer would also decide on an auspicious date and time for the wedding. Other Nguyen Dinh had left Kim Bai to work as clerks or scribes in public administration. All the above occupations, although they did not enjoy the same status as the mandarinate or teaching, were still considered as fitting for a scholar. Village hierarchy put a clerk or eastern physician above the peasants, artisans and traders. Those who learned from books and worked "with their brain" stood apart from the mass of people who had to sweat and toil for a living.

By then, there were also members of our extended family who had dropped out of their class. Some stayed in Kim Bai to work on their fields as peasants, but most left to "go into business in town," a vague expression which could mean anything from owning a shop or a stall in the market to hawking one's produce in the streets. To leave one's village and cease being a scholar was a sad happening; no one would think of asking them for details about their "business." If successful, they would one day come back to tell their stories. If not, the family would be unlikely to see them again. In the past, going away meant moving to one of the many towns in the populous Red River delta. The more adventurous, or more desperate, would go farther north, into the mountainous country next to China. There, rebels and brigands maintained a chronic insecurity and in the insalubrious climate one risked a life cut short by illness. But land in the valleys was fertile and trade with the Chinese was always a ready source of income. Few of Kim Bai's people had ever migrated to the south. For nearly two centuries, the country had been divided between the Trinh and the Nguyen. The great Vietnamese advance towards the Mekong River took place under the Nguyen, ruler of the south. That advance changed the balance of forces between north and south. The new land, fertilized by the Mekong River and its tributaries, was scarcely populated and hardly put to use before the Vietnamese came; in terms of exploitation, it was as new as the Canadian prairie. Its acquisition increased manyfold the wealth of the south while providing an outlet for its expanding population. The masses of the north, for their part, had nowhere to go for although the two halves of the country were not totally cut off from each other—people could still cross the dividing line—the Trinh Nguyen conflict made it impossible for any sizeable movement of population to take place. Population pressure, combined with maladministration and corruption, exploded into rebellions and jacqueries, the culmination of which was "the great calamity" of the eighteenth century. Moreover, the south was young and vital, not bound by such rigid tradition as the division of society into four classes. Leaders there proved themselves by the deeds they performed in war or in colonizing the new lands, not by the diplomas that they may have. The House of Tay Son and their followers, for instance, were "people wearing rough cloth," traders, descendants of colons sent into the highlands, hill tribesmen, descendants of the Chams whose country was taken over not so long ago by the Vietnamese, Chinese migrants, outlaws, all of whom would rank at the bottom of the traditional society. A revealing incident was told about Emperor Quang Trung when he went north and met a scholar holding the title of Searching Among the Blossoms, a title given to the third-ranked doctor at a triennial session. No one in the north could ignore what that title meant and such a graduate was destined for the highest positions in government. Yet Quang Trung asked him: "What does Searching Among the Blossoms mean? Can you administer a group of villages?"

Those may have been the reasons why victory in successive conflicts went to the side which held the south. Firstly, the Tay Son army marched north to destroy the Trinh. Then, it was the turn of the future emperor Gia Long to lead his troops from the south to vanquish the Tay Son. Reunification under Gia Long opened the Mekong delta to migrants from the north. There was vacant land everywhere in the south for the taking. Tales of miraculous wealth were told by the conquering troops. Fields yielded up to ten times as much as those in the north, so it was said. Only later did it become known that Marshall Le Van Duyet, the legendary governor of the south, had instructed all those going north to multiply the yield of their fields by ten, in order to attract more population to the new land. Other information that circulated about the country bathed by the Mekong—in Vietnamese *Cuu Long* or the Nine Dragons, the dragon being a symbol of power and fecundity and nine a most auspicious number—were true, however. Rice culture was easier as there was no need to transplant the young rice plants for them to bear grain. The soil was so rich that rice seeds had only to be sown; the plants would grow fast, faster even than the speed with which the waters rose in the monsoon season. There, instead of land being parcelled into small plots as in the Red River delta, a man could own wide-opened fields, over which "the egret could fly until it got tired." The south, where the climate was warm all year round, was our Eldorado and our Wild West.

Some in our family, as well as other villagers, quickly seized their chance. They took the risk of venturing thousands of kilometers away, to places they had only heard of and where "looking into the four directions, one would not be able to see a familiar face." They were young and animated with a pioneering spirit which cast them apart from those who also left their village but stayed within the traditional limits of the north. Mostly, they were younger sons who did not have the responsibility of celebrating the ancestors' cult and looking after ancestral graves. Thus, of the five original branches of the Nguyen Dinh which came out of the seventh generation, some ended up with only one descendant remaining in Kim Bai. Our chronicle had a brief comment on those who went south. "Their trace was lost," it said. Indeed, members who left for other parts of the north would send word home, or return occasionally. But the family would not hear from their sons who migrated south. Whether they made good their new life or not was not known. The nineteenth century marked a turning point for our family. Until then, our people were attached to their native place to such a point that war, persecution, even calamitous events like those of the last century, could not sever their ties with it. They always tried to return and live within its bamboo enclosure. Now, many among them were prepared to go to distant lands in search for a better life. The Nguyen Dinh had grown out of their village.

In leaving home and village to "go into business," my ancestor Quang So was thus doing something that many of his relatives had done before him. Still, his decision was most distressing to his parents. They were proud that for many generations and in spite of adverse circumstances, our family had been able to keep "the spine of the book" intact. Now their only son was doing away with his books and writing brush to become a trader.

The four classes of scholars, farmers, artisans and traders reflected social attitudes more than any legal or economic reality. Thus, the peasantry came second but the lot of farmers was often better than that of impoverished scholars, as expressed in this piece of popular wisdom:

> The scholar ranks first and the farmer second.
> But when you run out of rice
> And roam about everywhere to get it,
> It is the farmer first and the scholar second.

Life would have been easier for our impoverished forebears had they cultivated themselves the land they owned. Yet, they continued to farm it out to tenants while pursuing their teaching career. As for traders, who ranked last in the social scale, they could be wealthier than most people. "One cannot become rich without being a trader," a proverb said. Early European travellers were impressed with the high level of trading in the country. In the seventeenth century, the Jesuit Alexandre de Rhodes wrote:

> Thanks to the convenience and great number of ports, the country's traders worked so actively and advantageously for profit that they doubled their capital two or three times a year without running the risks going elsewhere with maritime trade. Along the country's coastline, which extended to more than

three hundred and fifty French leagues, there were up to fifty ports to which flowed quantities of rivers, so that those who sailed could stay every night in one of those ports.

But there was never a strong class of traders. Vietnamese were mostly involved in small trade and someone with a few boats to ferry goods from one region to another was already considered a big businessman. Whole-sale trade, in particular the important trade with China, was in the hands of the Chinese. Even though trade may have been highly profitable, there were few families with a strong trading tradition. The scholar's class had such prestige and held such an unchallenged position in society that a suc-cessful trader would want his sons to study, sit for the examinations and become mandarins instead of following on his footsteps.

In our family, the women had been involved in petty trade at local markets. Like other women in Kim Bai, they had been selling rice, cloth and other things that village folks needed. Their activities earned the family a complement of income, often a very useful one, for their teacher-husbands were not paid much. The men, however, were not involved in such activities; so when Quang So decided to make trade his profession, op-position to his move was strong. The more so as he was not only an only son, but also the only descendant in our branch. The tradition established by our teachers and scholar-mandarins would be lost to the branch. But Quang So's mind was made up and his parents finally had to give their con-sent. He went to Thang Long. The beginnings of his endeavor seemed to be difficult. He came back from time to time and said little about his business. The family only knew that he had travelled widely, for he brought home gifts from many places, including Laos which was then a sort of pro-tectorate of Vietnam. He also had a great many tales to tell relatives and village folks, being an excellent raconteur. At each of his visits home, it was recalled that his mother tried to talk him into taking a wife and settling down. He was approaching thirty. His parents were getting old. They wanted their only son to give them a grandchild before they died. A number of possible matches had been lined up. It only depended on him to indicate his choice and marriage proceedings could start immediately. But Quang So always had good excuses for delay. He only married after both his parents had died.

The time was right for our ancestor to go into trade. Peace and a unified regime had brought an upsurge of economic activity. For the first time, people and goods could move freely between the populous delta of the north and the rich new land of the south. Vast opportunities offered themselves and, as usual, the Chinese were the first to take advantage of them. "Almost all trade [in the south] was in the hands of the Chinese," wrote J.B. Chaigneau, a Frenchman who served Emperor Gia Long for many years and became a high mandarin. "Nothing can equal the activity of these traders. It is only since very recently that one could see some [local people] go into that field." Chaigneau noted that in the 1810s, "about three hundred Chinese ships, with a capacity varying from 100 to 600 tons, entered each year into the ports of the south." Merchant ships from Europe had been coming to our shores since the last century or so. They were few and far between. But now France and England took a more concrete interest in commercial relations. When he returned to France in 1820, Chaigneau was asked to make for the French government a report on Cochinchina, the name that Europeans called the south. He detailed the possibilities for trade and stressed the immense potential: "Cochinchina, fertile in all its areas, has no more than 5% of its soil exploited. . . . What that country can already produce in sugar, areca, pepper, silk, etc. . . . is little compared to what it would if commerce was developed." In 1822 John Crawford, the governor of Singapore, visited Hue. French shipowners reported in 1820 that their ships were well-received in Cochinchina and allowed to bring in goods, as well as buying out produce, "without any kind of duties." The shipowners pressed the French government to move into the market, because "the nation that this prince [Emperor Gia Long] dreads is the empire of the English in the East Indies. France is the only nation that he loves and held in high esteem, in gratitude for the services that she had been willing to provide him," an allusion to the assistance given by the French when Gia Long was fighting against the Tay Son.

Quang So had no experience or training in commerce, yet he went boldly into it. Not for him the small retail shop. From the beginning, he aimed for wholesale trade and travelled, buying things in one region and selling them in another. It took him many years to establish himself. He made frequent trips to the northern highlands, probably bringing to settlers tucked away in valleys the products that they missed from the delta, such as silk from our province Ha Dong, high quality *nuoc mam* or fish sauce and other foodstuffs. In return, he would take down to the delta tea and precious medicinal products of the mountain such as cinnamon, ginseng, young antler and tiger-bone jelly. Every Tet he came home with bulbs of rock narcissi from the mountains. Their flowers, when they came out with the new year, were unequalled in beauty and fragrance by anything that could be bought at the local markets. His trips to the highlands caused great anxiety to the family, as malaria incurred there was often fatal or otherwise could make a man suffer for life; but Quang So was blessed with a strong constitution. He went to the regions bordering China and to Laos without his health being adversely affected.

The next stage of his business saw Quang So become a timber merchant, probably operating with a group of partners, for the timber trade required a great deal of capital and manpower. Timber was bought in the highlands of Vietnam and Laos, assembled in rafts and floated downstream to their destinations in the delta. Our ancestor dealt in precious hardwood of the types which could not be attacked by termites and which, once seasoned, would not warp. Such wood was used for making house pillars and beams, furniture and also coffins which, traditionally, wealthy people bought on approaching old age and kept ready for their final journey. Labelled "iron wood" because they were as hard as iron, four were singled out for being the most valuable: *dinh, lim, sen, tau*. Dark red *Lim* wood, in particular, could be seen standing as tall and proud pillars in temples, communal halls and the homes of the wealthy. Quang So went up the highland to buy the timber and accompanied it on its way down. It was a dangerous and high risk business. The rafts had to negotiate rapids and strong currents. Losses were frequent. Of course, during the monsoon when every river became a torrent, no transport was possible. Moreover, although a single emperor reigned over the whole country, the highlands next to the borders remained far from secure. Rebellions continued to oppose the central government; in the 1830s, several movements were taking place there, one of which was led by a descendant of the Le trying to restore the old monarchy fifty years after it had ended. As for bandits, whether Vietnamese, Chinese or from the mountain tribes, they were a chronic threat. There were times when business had to stop, as the danger of going to the border area was too great. Still, it was a profitable line and our ancestor would keep doing it later, in between his trips to the south of the country.

His business developed and several men of Kim Bai worked for him. One of them named Khau went with him in all his trips. Khau's son was in his sixties when I stayed in Kim Bai as a boy. His house was next to our compound and he often came to talk to us in our front yard on summer evenings, after the brick surface had been watered to take away the heat of the day and we all sat there waiting for the southern breeze to rise. He told us stories about bandits, tigers, ghosts and spirits of the mountains. A tiger there was not just called a tiger but respectfully as "Mr. Tiger." Tigers often killed and ate their victims. They caused a lot of harm but those who went out to destroy them saw strange things happening to themselves. Thus, a man thought he had killed a tiger but in fact only injured it; the same animal returned after many years to kill him. A group was attacked by a tiger who only went at one man while sparing all others; it was found out later that his father had killed tigers years ago. So the stories went. "Mr. Tiger" was vested with human, even supernatural, faculties. Local people lived in fear of him and wished that they would not cross his path. Of the cruelty of bandits, we were told how innocent people were killed by them and thrown into the river, and how the corpses kept floating alongside the timber rafts until the traders had to stop and find a place to bury them. Many women were kidnapped and sold to the Chinese. In some Chinese towns across the border, most of the women were, in fact, kidnapped Vietnamese. Traders could operate and come out of the area alive only if they had an arrangement with the bandits. That was not so difficult, for the bandits were willing to let the traders and their goods pass through their territory, provided that the right amount of money was paid.

The most exciting stories that we heard from the old man were those of ghosts and spirits. Spirits inhabited every part of the mountains. They were in temples dug deep in marble caves or suspended high between the summits and the clouds, where Buddhist monks and Taoist recluses died after spending their lives in the pursuit of Truth. Time and again in our history, Vietnamese warriors were called to the border to fight off Chinese aggression. Their spirits continued to guard the passes where they laid down their lives, and where gates and temples were erected for their worship. Lesser spirits ruled over special geographical features such as river, mountain, lake or even a particular stretch of road and waterway. Before their boats crossed a dangerous rapid, for instance, the traders never failed to make offerings at the small shrine on the bank and pray to the local spirit for a safe passage. Included in the offerings were incense, fruits, flowers, quantities of gold and silver monies in paper reproduction, and also a live cock which was sacrificed at the ceremony.

People living in the northern mountains had to contend with all kinds and manners of ghosts. All those known to delta people were found there, and some more. Traders who came down the river on boats or rafts had to be wary of the water ghost. Lying in wait at the bottom of the river, that ghost extended its enormously long arms to seize the legs of a swimmer and pulled him down. The ghost's grip could not be shaken off, however hard the swimmer tried. Just before drowning, he suddenly found himself released to the surface. For ghosts did not normally kill people; they only frightened them, then let them go back to tell their tales. An effective way of dealing with the water ghost was to do what the forefathers of our race did in prehistoric times, when they went out to sea to fish and were continually attacked by strange creatures there. They tattooed their body to make the creatures think that they were also fish living in water, not land-based humans. Khau's son said that his father had tattoos on his chest and was never troubled by the ghost. I wonder whether my ancestor had tattoos also. If he had, that would be very unusual, for I have never heard of scholars tattooing their body. Certainly, men in our family were not known to do so. Some mountain ghosts were particularly feared because they could take possession of your body and turn you into a ghost. The *ma ca rong*, or *ca rong* ghost, only existed in the northern highland. It seized its victims, made them into ghosts, then sent them out in the night to attack people and suck their blood. It was the Vietnamese version of the vampire. Those possessed by the *ca rong* ghost often lost their minds or committed suicide. Another ghost of ill repute came from the border provinces of Lang Son and Cao Bang. It appeared under the unlikely form of a cock. If it took possession of you, you became yourself a cock to terrorize people and make them fall ill. However, I found it difficult to understand how anyone could be frightened of a cock. As a boy, I raised chicks in the backyard of our house in Hanoi. I remember the thrill of waking up in the early morning and hearing the first crow of young cocks I had had since they were just newly hatched chicks. A full-grown cock was one of the most majestic and beautiful creatures I knew. How could it become a feared ghost? Khau's son did not give any satisfactory explanation. He only asserted that the cock ghost struck deep fears among mountain peoples.

Quang So's activities brought him in contact with Chinese merchants who were in control of most of the country's trade as well as its exchanges with China. That was the start of a successful association. As noted in the chronicle: "Our ancestor entered into partnership with the Chinese and operated in that way for several years. He became known as a wealthy businessman."

The Chinese had been trading in Vietnam for as long as one could remember, but rarely had they and the Vietnamese joined hands in business ventures. Solidarity was the Chinese's strength. Migrants from the same region of China, and even more so from the same prefecture or the same village, stuck together and supported one another in their commercial enterprises. The typical Chinese hawker in my young days was the seller of grilled peanuts. He did not speak Vietnamese but was popular because he always gave a good serving and his peanuts had the flavor of spices not found anywhere else. He was certainly new to the country and had probably arrived penniless from faraway Guangdong or Yunnan. Immediately, he was taken under the wings of his countrymen. They gave him a loan to start his business, with no other guarantee than that he came from the same place than they and therefore was to be trusted. They told him a few things about local conditions and there he went, selling peanuts to schoolboys. With perseverance, hard work and financial support from his compatriots, in a few years' time he would not need to hawk his product in the streets but would sell from a small shop. From there, he would continue to progress to better things. Chinese traders were closely-knit, unlike the more individualistic Vietnamese. They formed solid partnerships, while Vietnamese were less inclined to trust one another and could not stay together in partnership for long. This advantage, coupled with a good business acumen, put the Chinese on top of our trade. Those *khach* or "guests"—the term we called the Chinese to make clear their position of migrants vis-à-vis us, the hosts and original inhabitants of the country—did not even need Vietnamese as interpreters or local guides. They could always rely on their own community which had settled in Vietnam for generations. A mixed partnership, like the one Quang So had with them, was very unusual indeed. It tells us much about our ancestor. To start with, he must have had the temperament of a pioneer, unafraid to go into new fields. Then, he must have had an open and flexible mind to overcome the cultural and behavioral differences between us and our "guests." He gained the respect and affection of his Chinese partners, as would be seen later when he died in the south. He must also have spoken Chinese, probably the Cantonese dialect. He would have been at a disadvantage if he did not, for he was apparently the only Vietnamese in the group and among his partners there were certainly people able to speak both languages. Finally, the Chinese must have seen in him qualities of a good businessman and a gentleman whom they could trust.

We were then in the early 1830s. Quang So moved away from the northern region where he had been doing most of his trade, to go into a new field: plying the sea between the Red River delta and the Chinese province of Guangdong. It was just as well that he did so, for soon that region would be the theatre of an important rebellion which the government took the best part of two years to quell. During that time, few traders could venture there. The partnership thus came at a good time for our ancestor. It owned a number of junks which came to pick up their shipments at Hung Yen, a river port southeast of Thang Long (Hanoi) and about forty kilometers from our village. Hung Yen, by its previous name Pho Hien, had been an important commercial center since the times when the king resided in Thang Long. Chinese, Dutch, English and other European vessels which came for trade in the seventeenth century were allowed to sail up the Red River as far as Pho Hien, but not to the capital which lay farther upstream. From Hung Yen, the junks belonging to Quang So and his partners started the voyage down the river until the South China Sea. There, they turned north for the short run to Guangdong, all the time hugging to the coast. Quang So made several trips to China and I could imagine the exciting stories he told the people at home on his returns. He must have been familiar with the Bay of Ha Long, hailed by European travellers as one of the marvels of the world, with its myriad of rock islands thrusting out of the sea. At that time though, the Bay was no tourist attraction. From the mouth of the Red River to the Chinese border lay a series of bays well-sheltered behind a profusion of big and small islands. Traders usually went through the bays instead of braving the high sea, although they risked falling into the hands of pirates who hid in island caves and suddenly appeared to attack their boats. Danger lurked at many places, but a successful trip could mean for the trader and his family financial security for several years. Of the many products transacted between Vietnam and Guangdong, Quang So and the Chinese dealt mostly in textiles. They exported the natural silk of Ha Dong, our own province, and a shiny black silk called *linh* which was used to make trousers for women. The Chinese were very fond of *linh*. Early European traders in China had noticed that material and praised its softness and attractive look. From Guangdong, the junks brought back brocade, an embroidered material sought by mandarins and wealthy people for their formal dress, high quality tea, a traditional import from China, and fine china which could not be produced in our country. A good source of supply and a safe sea journey were all that was required for a successful venture. Once the junks were back in Hung Yen, a well-organized network of distributors set up by the Chinese took over. Selling the goods was not a problem, although they were expensive. After three decades of political stability and with the new land of the south acting as a spur to the economy, the country was getting more prosperous. "People were waiting to buy all the brocade, tea, china and other Chinese products that could be brought in," old folks said.

When Quang So went into partnership with the Chinese, he was already an established trader with years of experience as a travelling salesman and timber merchant. He must have also built up a good financial base. However, the funds put into the partnership were said to be not only his, but also his wife's. She was a daughter of the Chu family, from a neighboring village. Her given name was Che. Like the Chu of Kim Bai to whom they were related, Quang So's in-laws were rather well-to-do landowners which, in those times, meant having one or two hectares of rice fields. They had two sons and two daughters. Both sons died young, leaving no heir. Quang So married the eldest daughter and, as recorded in our chronicle, "after his father-in-law died, the responsibility of celebrating the ancestors' worship in the Chu family fell to him." Did he inherit valuable assets which could then be used for the business? Quang So's father, it can be recalled, had inherited house, garden, pond and rice fields from his in-laws. But for his part, Quang So may have received only some land for the purpose of celebrating the cult, as he was survived by his mother-in-law who would have remained in possession of the rest of the Chu family's properties. Thus, the money for the partnership did not come from inheritance but must have belonged to his wife. She had a previous marriage and may have been left with some wealth after her first husband died. In any case, the fact was that she contributed financially to Quang So's business and did so at a crucial time, when he was embarking on his most ambitious commercial venture.

They were both in their thirties when they married. She had two children of her own, a boy and a girl. It was not an arranged marriage. Quang So was not one to let his life be ruled by the family or by rigid traditions. He resisted parental pressure to start a family early so as to ensure continuity of our line, turning a deaf ear to all prospects put to him by his parents and elder sisters. Eventually, when well past thirty, he took for wife a woman of his choice, a widow with two children. How an old-fashioned family reacted to that union can easily be imagined. Were his parents still alive, in particular his strict teacher-father, one may wonder whether Quang So would have gone ahead with his marriage. They were gone, but he still had to contend with opposition from his two sisters, in spite of the fact that both were married into the Chu family of Kim Bai and, therefore, related to the woman he wanted to marry. Quang So, however, was by then a mature man who had travelled widely and had become well-established in his profession. Once his mind was made up, the sisters could only fall in line. After the marriage, our foremother Che moved with her two children into the family's ancestral home. A woman of character, she quickly settled into her position as wife of the family head and made everyone else accept her as such. The chronicle added that "our ancestor adopted his two stepchildren and considered them as his own. When they came of marriageable age, he found a wife for the son and a husband for the daughter." The term "adopted" is not to be taken here in a legal sense, for the children were not given the surname Nguyen. They continued to keep their father's name Le.

Quang So's business prospered. Most of the time, he was away from Kim Bai. When he came back, it was to supervise some building work. Our ancestral home was a thatched house set up by his grandfather in a corner of the Nguyen ancestral compound. Quang So extended our plot by buying adjacent land from cousins and other neighbors. On a new emplacement, he built a new house with the timber he chose himself in a trip to the Laotian border. Instead of a straw roof like the old one, the new home was covered in latania leaves. Then, a smaller house was built in the compound to entertain his business relations. Next would come a project very close to our ancestor's heart, about which he often spoke to his family: a new shrine to worship the memory of common ancestors of the Nguyen Dinh.

An endearing side of his character was the pride he took in his roots. My grandfather wrote: "He sought to bring into prominence the achievements and virtues of our forefathers. He cleared a path for descendants to follow." In his time, the memory of count Nguyen Tue was forgotten. He only knew as far back as what is now known as the generation of academician Nguyen Uyen. Even so, he felt that the existing shrine, a humble cottage, did not befit a mandarin who served his king and country with distinction and laid the foundation for a long line of scholars to follow. The original shrine, destroyed in the last century, was still very much present in our people's mind. They kept talking about its imposing size and the wealth of its cult instruments. Quang So had no ambition of building a similar shrine. His project was on a modest scale, but it represented something very important to him, something akin to a goal in his life. He had bought timber from the mountains and had it stored on the Hat River while waiting for construction to start. He had composed parallel sentences and poems dedicated to the spirit of our forefathers and had them carved in commemorative boards. Alas, as written in the chronicle, "the new shrine never came off the ground. That year—it was not remembered which year—he went to Dong Nai in the Gia Dinh province of the south, contracted an illness and died. Heaven did not allow his wish to be fulfilled."

Four generations before Quang So, our ancestors were Zen Buddhists. Confucian teachers followed them. In this generation, the pendulum swung back to Buddhism. Quang So's faith owed much to his mother and maternal grandparents, who were devout worshippers. They used to bring him along with them to temple service when he was a child. He grew up to become a believer. He chose to be known as Chan Nguyen, meaning The True Source, a pseudonym very much Buddhist in character. In doing so, he parted with family tradition for, as we know, most of our scholar-ancestors favored including in their pseudonyms the Confucian word *Phuc*, or Happiness. Chan Nguyen, in fact, was the name of a Zen master in the seventeenth century who led a revival of the Buddhist Truc Lam sect. Quang So attended temple assiduously, a rare occurrence among male members of our family. Temple worship had been an activity reserved mainly to our women. The men, even when they broke away from a strict Confucian tradition to become Buddhist followers, had shown a peculiar reluctance to it. Our fifth and sixth ancestors studied and practiced Zen, but did so "at home." Of the three Refuges that Buddhism offered to its faithfuls—the Buddha, his Teachings and the Assembly of Monks—the last one had proved to be most difficult for our people to seek. When Buddhism was at its apogee and treated like a state religion, under the Ly and Tran dynasties, monks held a high position in society. Many were accomplished scholars. Their sermons were listened to by kings and mandarins. But since the fifteenth century, Confucianism had gained a complete ascendancy in the state and Buddhism had been reduced to being a religion of the common people. Monks ranked well below scholars and were in no position to preach to them. Mandarins did not go to temples; they called the monks to their residences to perform religious services whenever they needed them. Of course, at all epochs, there were monks whom the most erudite scholars and highest mandarins would readily recognize as their spiritual masters. These monks, however, did not go out among the faithfuls. They retired to the mountains to meditate and teach a few selected disciples. Few laymen could hope to meet with them. Perhaps it was for the above reasons that those of our ancestors who sought to find a path in Zen did not have a guide or teacher. Their only "refuges" were the faith they had in Lord Buddha and whatever they could understand from their own reading of his Teachings.

Quang So was neither a Zen follower, nor did he spend much time

meditating or studying Buddhism. He was a believer in the popular sense
of the term, one who went to temples to make offerings, worship and listen
to the priests' sermons. Few scholars were seen there, but that did not matter to him. By becoming a trader, he had shown how little regard he had
for conventions. Every year, he made a pilgrimage to the Huong Son Temple, one of the most famous in the north. Dedicated to Phat Ba Quan Am,
the Lady of Mercy, the temple was built in a grotto some distance away
from our village, south along the Hat River. According to legend, it was in
that grotto that the Lady of Mercy attained enlightenment. Pilgrims flocked
to Huong Son during the festive season which took place in the first two
months of the lunar calendar. Actually, Huong Son was not one but a
group of temples set in a formation of limestone hills. Some temples were
built in grottoes, others on hilltops. A small river winding its way through
apricot orchards linked the temples together. Boats punted by young village
women carried the pilgrims amidst a fairy-like scenery, especially when the
trees were blossoming. In the fifteenth century, the great king Le Thanh
Ton visited the temple of the Lady of Mercy. Moved by its beauty and
sacred character, he wrote a few words in large calligraphy to praise it as
"the first grotto under southern skies." Monks carved the characters on an
overhanging rock at the entrance of the grotto. They can still be seen today.
Our ancestor used to bring his family to the temple some weeks after Tet,
just when the apricot blossoms were coming out. They stayed there for
several days, making offerings and worshipping at every temple. Only once
this religious duty was over, would Quang So get ready to leave his village
and resume his business activities.

While our family improved its lot, other branches of the Nguyen Dinh
stayed in decline. Many relatives had left Kim Bai. Family ties loosened.
Sometime around the turn of the nineteenth century, a grave event occurred. The cult land belonging to our Ancestral Shrine was taken over
by others without our kinsmen doing anything about it. Did they not know,
or were they powerless to stop it and had to keep silent? A generation later,
the existence of our extensive cult land had been forgotten. Quang So certainly had no inkling of it. A man proud of his ancestry and with wealth
at his disposal, he would have done something to recover the land, had he
known. He did, however, know about the Cu Hau papers and had often
expressed regret over the fact that our family had lost all written evidence
of its ancestry. A strong belief of his was that the Cu Hau papers contained
the full history of our family and that, when found, it would reveal a golden
period of our past. He was told that the old Ancestral Shrine was built like
a temple and adorned with magnificent cult instruments. "That shrine
must have been built by wealthy and powerful men," he said. "Wars and
changes of dynasties have made us forget our most illustrious forebears."
In his time, only Nguyen Uyen was remembered among our ancestors, and

it was not even known that he was sent by the king on a diplomatic mission to China. We know that Quang So spent time searching for the papers. In particular, he sought during his business travels to reestablish contact with those of Cu Hau's descendants, who had gone away from Kim Bai. He never found the papers. But he might have left some clues which would help his son, later on, to trace them. That would explain the sentence in our chronicle which says that he "cleared a path for descendants to follow."

Quang So stayed on the Guangdong route for several years, then directed his activities elsewhere. The route was a very profitable one. Did he stop because of losses at the hand of pirates around the bay of Ha Long? Or was it because the danger was always there and he had an intimation that his luck with the pirates may be running out? Our ancestor was a superstitious man. Before taking up any business project or making an important trip, he always sought the advice of astrologers or fortune-tellers. At every place he visited, he looked out for good ones to consult. His superstition extended to even trivial things such as, for instance, the cry of a crow in the garden early in the morning. For him, that bird with its inauspicious color and ugly sound was a messenger of bad tidings. He would refrain from entering into any business commitment, at least during that day. Perhaps also, his natural bent was that of a pioneer drawn towards new challenges and he could not stay in the same activity for very long. Within the country, trade between the north and the south had been developing at a fast pace. The Chinese had been reaping their profits from it. It was bound to attract a man like Quang So. He made his first expedition to the Mekong delta in the fall of 1835. The timing was rather risky, for the south had just come out of a large rebellion, the first that had ever occurred there against the Nguyen monarchy. Le Van Duyet was a eunuch general in Gia Long's victorious army. For his role in helping his emperor gain the throne of Vietnam, he was made Marshall of the Left, one of the three highest military titles along with those of Marshalls of the Center and the Right. A hero to the populace, he however antagonized many officials on account of his extensive powers and rough manners of a warrior. After he died, his enemies trumped up charges of usurpation against him and persecuted his family. His adopted son Le Van Khoi revolted, seized the six provinces of the Mekong delta and was only defeated after nearly three years of warfare. Le Van Duyet was condemned posthumously, but later on his memory was rehabilitated and the people of the south worshipped him as a protector spirit. All those who have been to Saigon know the Temple of the Marshall of the Left. On the last night of the year, it becomes a sea of pilgrims who come to invoke the Marshall's blessings and to pray for a new year of happiness and prosperity.

By the fall of 1835, the last remnants of the rebels had been crushed.

Government control was reestablished and traders could resume their normal activities. Quang So's expedition was a success. He returned home full of optimism. He had seen for himself the great empty spaces of the south, its rich land, its young population constantly reinforced by migration. How different it was from the north, where masses of people were concentrated in a small delta, on a land exhausted by millenniums of cultivation. How complementary too were the new and old parts of the country. The south was a natural supplier of agricultural products to the north, while being on the receiving end for manufactured goods. Trade opportunities between the two were almost limitless. But it was not just a question of trade. Quang So felt strongly attracted to the new land. Having been there, he knew that he would not go anywhere else. "The south is my country," he said. "Why should I go and trade in another country!"

He continued to be associated with the Chinese and to operate within their network, but was now more on his own. His own junks sailed south to the Mekong delta. That was a long run of over one thousand kilometers, but quite an easy one during the dry months. Numerous ports, harbors and well-protected coves could be used by the junks to stay the nights or in case of emergencies. Pirates were here and there, but the route was usually safe. The Nguyen monarchy maintained a particularly strong navy to guard the capital Hue and many large towns built along the coast. The long and narrow region which formed the center of the country contained some of its most impressive sceneries. An uninterrupted chain of mountains—called Truong Son or the Long Cordillera—ran from north to south close to the sea. Its foothills came at intervals right down to the water. Between them were small valleys where rivers flowed out and townships were established. "Poets sang the beauty of our country, they described our rivers and mountains as clothed in brocade and the most precious silk; now I know what they meant," Quang So told his family of the view from the mountain passes over the lowlands and the sea. On reaching the south, his junks went up the river to "the town of Dong Nai in Gia Dinh province," as recorded in the chronicle, a place which is now Bien Hoa some thirty kilometers to the northeast of Saigon. Dong Nai had received Chinese settlers since the seventeenth century. Refugees from South China fleeing before the Manchu invasion came to Vietnam and were sent there by the Nguyen overlord to populate the land newly acquired from the kingdom of Champa. By the end of that century, Dong Nai had become a flourishing place, where traders from Japan, India and the West lived side by side with Vietnamese and Chinese.

Quang So had his quarters in the Chinese settlement. The shipments he brought in contained textiles, which remained his preferred line of trade, paper, china, cooking utensils in copper as well as other products that Chinese associates ordered from him. Once these were sold, he set out for the heartland of the delta, where the Mekong, its tributaries and canals criss-crossed the rich and flat land. There he loaded his junks with rice, sugar, dried fish, fish sauce and other foodstuffs for the return trip. He was back in Kim Bai before the Tet of that year. Although travelling almost con-tinually, he always celebrated the new year in his ancestral home. In the spring of 1836, he set sail again for the south. This time, it was a prolonged stay, not only because he wanted to find ways to expand his business but also, I believe, because he loved the life there. The south was a young and vital place. Soldiers and peasants had opened the way there together, the soldiers establishing their outposts and providing security while the peas-ants cleared and cultivated the land. Others followed them, poor people searching for a better life, adventurers, banished criminals, Chinese refugees. For everyone, it was a new start. Criminals were given a chance to make good and live as normal citizens. Chinese could buy land and take roots in the country, unlike in the north where they were forever "guests," forbid-den to own land and only allowed to earn a living in commerce. The old class system and its rigid conventions were left behind. A man with a pioneering spirit and an unconventional mind like Quang So must have found life in the south more congenial. In spite of his success as a businessman, our ancestor was still a failed scholar in the eyes of northern society. I think that he would have gone south to live, if he had not been the only descendant left in his branch and so much attached to his roots.

Quang So's fortune was quickly made from profitable ventures and he spent generously. He lived well, enjoyed good food, wine and the company of friends. In particular, he was fond of listening to the *a dao,* or song-stresses. The custom then was for a host to entertain his guests by calling in a troupe of *a dao* to sing their repertoire of poems. Sometimes musicians were also called, sometimes only the singers. A guest would beat a cadence on a small drum and a songstress would then sing to the beat of the drum, in the same way as a singer would follow the baton of her conductor in Western music. The drum must correctly announce the mood of the poem which was going to be sung. Often, a poem expressed a succession of moods and therefore, the beat must quicken or slow down accordingly. During the evening, host and guests took turns to beat the drum. All engaged in a bit of competition to show who could bring out the best renditions from the beautiful songstresses. To be good at the drum was something of a hall-mark of a man of the world. Quang So had such a reputation and it was said that many a renowned songstress in the capital had sung to the beat of his drum. He was generous with his family. The weddings of his two stepchildren were lavish affairs. Much of his money was put in the building of a new ancestral home and a guest house. In other words, our ancestor did not save much. When he died in the south and the capital he brought there with him was lost, the family fell into hard times again.

His wife Che was a lady of strong will and independent mind. They were both proud and assertive people, perhaps a reason why their marriage had more than its fair share of stormy periods. Quang So was often away from home on account of his trading activities, but the family believed his absence was also for another purpose, to avoid having frequent clashes with his wife. While he kept himself occupied elsewhere with his business, she stayed in Kim Bai and ruled the household. He refrained from interfering in her domain. When the houses were built, he had the timber and other materials brought in, started construction and stayed on for some time. Then, he was on the move again, leaving it to his wife to see that the work was finished. Two daughters were born to their union and as she reached her mid-forties, it looked as if they would not have any more children. Would the absence of a male heir, dreaded by so many generations, become a reality? Quang So, however, did not seem to be concerned by such a possibility. His wife went to the Snake Temple to pray for a son. He did not. He doted on his daughters and appeared ready to accept whatever situation Fate had in store for him. Then in 1836, his wife gave birth to a son, when forty-four. That year, his activities expanded in the south. He came back home early to celebrate the Tet. Everything was going well, he should be a happy and contented man. Yet, a drama was soon going to unfold, even before the old year was over.

My mother told me that when she came into our family, people still referred quite frequently to Quang So, who died almost a century before. His wife, who survived him for thirty years, was remembered as a matriarch with a fiery temper. "There was a sad love story in his life," my mother said. "I learned it from my grandmother-in-law, who was a young girl in the village when that happened." My mother has an excellent memory and quite a talent as raconteur. This, in her own words, was what made Quang So rush into his last trip to the south:

> He was linked with a woman in the village. She was extremely beautiful, as her name Nu Son, or Vermillion Bud, showed. She lived next to our central hamlet, in the hamlet near the dike. Our ancestor wanted to marry her as his secondary wife, following a custom which was quite common then. Nu Son's family was poor but of a good lineage. Like many other girls in Kim Bai, she worked on the weaving looms, made paddy into rice and sold rice and cloth at markets for a living. To toil all day in the fields was not her lot, so she kept her figure slender and her complexion fair. Moreover, she was not shy and could hold a conversation with a lot of charm. Our ancestor in his forties was twenty years older than her, but he was a well-built and handsome man, looking very young for his age and known for his good manners and generous character. In fact, he remained very much a scholar while conducting a successful business. Nu Son was agreeable to marrying him, be it as a secondary wife.
>
> Our ancestor was engaged, among other activities, in the timber trade. Timber purchased in the highlands and in Laos was tied together in large rafts,

then floated down river to towns in the delta. The old ancestral home and guest house next to it were built with the timber he sent home on the Hat River. That year, in the tenth month, he returned from one of his business trips and decided to spend a few months at home. He would celebrate the Tet before leaving again. This was special because he led a busy life and was generally not home for long. He brought back with him six rafts of timber. He ordered that three rafts be tied securely to stakes planted in the river bed. They were to be kept in the water until work could start on a new Ancestral Shrine. He said nothing about the other three rafts. So rumour spread quickly in the village that he was going to marry Nu Son and the timber was intended as a present to her.

That brought matters to a head within the family. Our foremother was deeply hurt. Her money helped launch her husband's business. Having achieved wealth, he wanted to get a secondary wife, at a time when she just gave him a son and heir! By the way, most women in those times would accept that their husbands have secondary wives, and concubines as well. But our foremother was different. A proud and strong-willed lady, she could not control her anger when the Nu Son rumour broke out. Every morning, she took issue with her husband and clashed with him. Every morning, she went to the gate of our house to shout aloud her misfortune and called upon villagers to witness it. It became a scandal. Relatives and friends came to pacify her, to no avail. Her mother, who lived in a village not far away, rushed to Kim Bai. "You bore him only one son," she tried to reason with her, "if he takes a secondary wife at one of those places he goes for his business, how are you to prevent it? Is it not better that he takes someone in the village? Nu Son is a girl of good character from a good family. The only thing against her, from your own point of view, is her beauty, but could you not accept it?" Our foremother refused to listen. She continued with her verbal attacks, day after day. So much so that her husband could not bear it any more. One day near the end of the year, he packed up and left for the south, accompanied by Chu Khau, his faithful companion. He did not stay to celebrate the New Year with the family, as he had planned to do. To start such an important trip when, as our people say, "the year was dying out" was a bad omen. Our ancestor would have never done so in normal circumstances. He would have consulted astrologers for an auspicious date, once the new year had begun. In that fateful year, he also missed his traditional pilgrimage to the temple of Our Lady of Mercy in the Huong mountains. He always went there to pray for her blessings on his business endeavours. He stayed away for a long time. Whether that was because of business commitments, or the wounds had not been healed yet, we do not know. Eventually, Chu Khau came back to bring the news of his death.

Our foremother courageously took up the role of family support. Her husband did not leave any money. All his business in the south was lost. The family had a few acres of ricefields handed down from previous generations; in his lifetime, our ancestor did not acquire any land other than the additions to the family compound. Of course, there were the newly-built ancestral home and guest house, but these and the land of the compound, our foremother was determined not to part with, in however straitened circumstances the family would find itself. She was nearly fifty when the bad news reached home. Life had been easy for her and she was looking forward to a leisurely old age. But now she got down to work, without uttering a complaint. Every day, she carried her baskets to the market, to earn a meagre income from petty trade. By herself, she brought up three young children. Then, with the help of her two grown-up daughters, she toiled until old age to give to her son a scholar's education. As the years passed, the memory of her jealous outburst faded, to be replaced by the love and respect that she owed to her husband. When her son became a young man, she sent him to the south to bring his remains home. She very much hoped that he could finally rest in the land of his birth and his tomb could be well looked after, but that was not to be. The last years of her life were miserable. She was ill, could not move and suffered constantly. Her daughter-in-law had to spoon-feed her at every meal. She died close to eighty.

"I could not help thinking," my mother concluded, "that our ancestor attached too much importance to beauty. As for our foremother, how could she expect to keep a husband by talking and behaving in that way. Too much jealousy can break up homes."

That ends the story about our ancestor, but that of Nu Son continues:

At that time, our village was frequently attacked by a group of bandits. Their leader was a huge man who painted his face to make him look even more ferocious. People called him Ong Ba Bi, or Mr. Bogey. Sometimes, villagers succeeded in keeping the bandits out; sometimes, they did not and the village was ransacked. The threat was constant, like a sword posed above the villagers' necks. Mr. Bogey, however, also fell for Nu Son. He did not force his way into the village to kidnap her, the way bandits do. Instead, he sent emissaries in to ask for her hands, promising that in return, Kim Bai would be spared from further attacks. Nu Son refused at first, but villages intervened to ask her to reconsider her decision. Those bandits attacks had gone on for too long and caused too much suffering. Kim Bai folks longed to live and work in peace. She finally agreed, on the condition that Mr. Bogey return to the life of a law-abiding citizen. In accordance with her wish, the villagers promised that Mr. Bogey would be allowed to come to Kim Bai to settle. The wedding took place and Nu Son became Ba Ba Bi, or Mrs. Bogey. The nickname stuck to her too. Soon after, the couple slipped out of Kim Bai and never reappeared. Perhaps, they did not feel at ease in spite of the promise made by the villagers. Perhaps, they wanted to make a clean break and go somewhere where no one would call them Bogey. Years later, people still recalled Nu Son, her beauty and the action she took for the sake of her village.

Quang So left just before the Tet of that year, or some time in January 1837. "He died in the south when his son was only three," noted the chronicle. His son was born in 1836. Taking into account the custom of considering a newly-born child as a one-year-old, he became three in 1838. Quang So, therefore, died in that year, at the age of forty-six. Chu Khau, who accompanied him to the south, stayed on for one hundred days to tend his grave and perform daily ceremonies of worship, as required by our religious custom. He set out for home afterwards. But, either he took a junk which stopped at too many places or he followed the long and difficult land route, he did not arrive until more than a year later. It was only then that our family got the news. Clearly shaken by his ordeal, Chu Khau could not say exactly on which day our ancestor died. He thus failed to provide an essential piece of information, for yearly ceremonies of worship must be performed on the anniversary of our ancestor's death. Chu Khau only remembered that it happened during the rainy season, which means between May and November 1838. Quang So's final stay in the south thus lasted for about a year and a half. He was maintaining in good health, according to Chu Khau, when he suddenly became ill and no amount of medicine could save him. The onset of the rainy season was notorious for its bad effects on health. In any case, not knowing the day, our family had to fall back on an ancient custom which applied to missing travellers or soldiers who went missing in war. Their spirits were worshipped on the anniversary of the day they left home. For Quang So, that was the twelfth day of the twelfth lunar month.

Chu Khau also could not explain why Quang So stayed so long in Dong Nai. Since his business was trading between the north and the south, why did he make no return trip for more than a year? Why was nothing left of his business after he died? I suspect that things did not go well on that last trip. He may have incurred losses. There may not have been enough money to finance a trip back. A superstitious man, our ancestor must have been affected by the unfortunate circumstances of his departure. Maybe the drive and self-confidence that made him a successful trader had deserted him on that last venture. But Chu Khau was able to provide a description of the funeral, which brought some comfort to our family. "The Chinese in Dong Nai," he said, "bought magnificent cult instruments for his funeral. All proper rites were observed at the procession and the burial. He rested in the Chinese settlement in Dong Nai. A tombstone bearing his name was erected." In his last moments, Quang So the traveller turned his thoughts towards home. "I want my old bones to return to Kim Bai," he told Chu Khau, "to be buried in the land of my forebears and be looked after by my children."

Our ancestor was remembered as a generous man who did much for the family and could have done more, had fate not taken him away when only in his forties. He was a pioneer, the first person in the family to have made his mark in trade, the first to have gone into joint ventures with Chinese merchants, the first to have taken advantage of the vast opportunities for commerce in the south. He was also the only one to break with family tradition and earn a living in business. After he died and his fortune was lost, his wife raised their infant son to become a scholar. Three decades later, when she died at the age of seventy-seven, the son had gained a fine reputation in letters and was vying for academic honors. The family had gone back to the path of learning. Tradition had reasserted itself.

Our chronicle recorded that "in 1936, our ancestor was posthumously made an Academy Lecturer and his wife a *Cung Nhan*, or spouse of a mandarin of the fourth grade. In 1940, he received a higher honor and became a Director of the Imperial Carriages. His wife was made a *Lenh Nhan*, or spouse of a mandarin of the third grade. The court also honored our ancestor with the posthumous name of On Tinh Tien Sinh." Thus, a century after his death, official honors came to Quang So and his wife as their grandson rose to be a high mandarin. Imperial certificates were delivered in great pomp in Kim Bai and placed on our Ancestral Altar. Quang So, who chose to become a trader occupying the lowest position among the four classes, never cared much about social conventions. Honors, therefore, may not mean much to him. But he was proud of his roots and I think that the position of Academy Lecturer would appeal to him because our second ancestor Nguyen Uyen was a member of that august body, back in the sixteenth century. Moreover, the posthumous name On Tinh Tien Sinh, meaning Moderation and Calm, must be very close to his heart for it was the same that the Mac king gave to Nguyen Uyen to highlight the qualities that he displayed as a diplomat in China.

20. The Hermit of the Mountain of the Twins

The only portrait on the altar of our ancestral home was that of my great-grandfather, our eleventh ancestor. Normally it was stored inside the red and gold tabernacle standing at the end of the altar. On the anniversary of his death and the eve of the Tet festival, my grandfather took it out. Reverently, he dusted it and placed it in front of the tabernacle for the ceremony of worship. I cannot recall whether it was a photograph or a painting; if a photograph it must be among the very early ones taken in Vietnam, since great-grandfather died in 1909. He was shown wearing the traditional black turban and a black dress in thin gauze. His face was square with regular features, "square like a rice field," as people used to say when they wished to praise a man's face. There was a certain sadness in his expression, which reflected a life dogged by failure and misfortune, but his eyes retained a proud and piercing look. From all accounts, he was a strict and difficult man.

He was born in the year of the Monkey (1836) and died at the age of seventy-three in the year of the Rooster (1909). His full name was Nguyen Dinh Dat, Nguyen Dinh being common to all our extended family and Dat his personal name. Dat means "the achiever." He took as pen name Hy Tu, an unassuming expression which can be translated as "wishing to receive in some small measure." For a pseudonym, he chose to be known as Song Son Dat Dan, or the "Hermit of the Mountain of the Twins." His posthumous name was Kiem Thien, or "full goodness." My great-grandmother was his second wife. She came from the Chu family in Kim Bai. Her name Uyen means both "graceful" and "harmonious." She was born in 1854 and died in 1949 at the age of ninety-five. It will be noted that she had no pseudonym, unlike the foremothers of earlier generations. In 1949 when she died, the old scholarly society had largely disappeared. A war was going on and most of north Vietnam was under communist rule. The old custom of using a pseudonym because it was taboo to mention the real name of ancestors had ceased to be observed.

Nguyen Dinh Dat never knew his father, who left when he was only a few months old. He did not know the comfortable life enjoyed by the family in his father's lifetime. He grew up not exactly in poverty, for our people still owned some land, but his mother had to work hard to raise him and his two sisters. When she grew old, the sisters took over the role of family provider. Thanks to the three women, he could devote himself to his studies. His life could have come straight out of a book of folklore stories, where the most popular story ran something like this:

> A family became impoverished after the father died. The mother and elder daughters toiled to eke out a living and to send the young son to school. They cheerfully accepted sacrifices so that he could receive a good education and successfully compete for the king's service. Their love and dedication were recognized by the Lord in Heaven. The son grew up to be a brilliant scholar, who passed all examinations with flying colours and became a mandarin. He brought prosperity and renown to his family. Thus, the women's efforts were duly rewarded and in the abode of the spirits, the departed father would have been also gratified.

That was how folklore stories went. Life, however, was not a folklore story. In Dinh Dat's case, the beginning looked so auspiciously like one. He showed great promsie as a student. Even before he started sitting for the regional examinations, his brilliance at writing poems and essays was already well-known. His name would be seen on the golden board at the Royal Courtyard examination, people said. For a long time, our village had had no doctor; surely he would be the one to renew with its glorious past. But, as a proverb says: "Talents at learning are shown during studies, success at examinations depends on fate." Dinh Dat's fate was to fail at one session, then at another. With great determination, he kept on studying and presenting himself at each triennial session, until his hair became sprinkled with white dew. But he never obtained an academic degree.

As a child, Dinh Dat knew that it would be his duty, one day, to go south and bring his father's remains home. Every evening, his mother used to light incense on the ancestral altar and remind herself and the children of her husband's last wish. After hearing the news of Quang So's death, the family had to wait, in the first place because in our religious custom, a grave must not be disturbed in the first three years. Then, the exhumation should be performed by a descendant of the deceased, preferably a son, and this meant a further wait for many more years, since Dinh Dat was only two when his father died. As time passed, his mother became more and more concerned that she may never see the day when her husband's last wish would be fulfilled. Chu Khau, the servant who went with him to the south, also was growing old and he alone knew the place in Dong Nai where Quang So was buried. An increasing sense of urgency was attached to the trip south. Dinh Dat undertook it when he was very young, only sixteen or seventeen. The year would be 1852 or 1853. He had not started sitting for the examinations; the idea was perhaps to have the trip over and done with, so that upon his return he would be free to concentrate on his studies. Chu Khau went with him. He was then in his fifties. The sea journey in a trader's junk was thought to be too risky for the only son of the family, so the two took the more time-consuming land route. They had gone for more than a month, passed through the imperial capital Hue and were somewhere south of it when Chu Khau was taken ill. The journey was interrupted so he could receive treatment. A few weeks later, he died. What a shattering experience for young Dinh Dat! Left to himself, he had to organize Chu Khau's burial, turn back—for there was no way that he could go to the south without a guide—and find his way home. The long-awaited trip had failed and he was deeply affected, as revealed in this brief passage of the chronicle: "After more than a month, the two had not reached Dong Nai when Chu Khau died. O Lord in Heaven! Why did you make it so! This is recorded so that later generations would know."

A shocked family was thankful that at least Dinh Dat was back safe and sound. Worse may have happened. At such a young age, he should never have gone on such a long and difficult journey accompanied by Chu Khau alone. His mother was so scared that she did not mention again about going to the south. But with typical obstinacy, Dinh Dat returned to his task several years later, when in his early twenties. He went to Hanoi, Pho Hien and other places in the north where Chinese merchants plying the trade with the south had their warehouses and staging posts to look for people who knew his father. None could be found, but he obtained a clear idea of the Chinese settlement where his father was buried and decided to make another try. Chu Khau had described the grave to him many times; built in bricks and with a tombstone bearing his father's name, it should be easily found. His mother's health was failing. He wished to give her the satisfaction of seeing her husband's remains brought home at last. Preparations were being made for the journey, when news came that the French had invaded and occupied the port of Da Nang, south of Hue. That was in 1858. The next year, the French turned their attacks on the south and took possession of Gia Dinh. With a war being fought there, no hope of going could be entertained any more. Dinh Dat must be resigned to the fact that his father would, forever, rest in a faraway land.

A part of the south had been lost to the foreign invader, but the Nguyen dynasty was unable to face up to the realities of the situation. Isolated in the capital Hue, away from the populated deltas of the Red River and the Mekong—the two vital centers of the country and its "baskets" of wealth, it was undecided whether to negotiate or to fight to recover the lost territory. The very survival of Vietnam as an independent nation was threatened, yet nothing was done to mobilize the population. In the north, life went on as before. Examinations continued to be held and scholars continued to pursue their dreams of golden board and mandarinal position.

Dinh Dat concentrated on his books. He started sitting for the examinations when in his early twenties. His first tries were failures, but this was not taken as a cause for alarm. The selection system was so restrictive that even the best scholars may taste defeat before succeeding. He also began earning a living as a teacher. Meanwhile, his mother was busy looking for a wife for him. A descendant from a long line of mandarins and teachers, himself a talented scholar, Dinh Dat had a bright future. Moreover, he enjoyed the reputation of being a dutiful son who deferred to his mother's wishes and gave her loving care in her old age. Confucian ethics placed filial piety at the very top of moral virtues. A dutiful son could not help but be a gentleman; certainly he would make a good husband. Several wealthy families in our region with daughters of marriageable age had sent word that they would welcome an approach from our family. They had done so, it was noted, in spite of the fact that our matriarch was known to be of stern character and to have a short temper. She would be a difficult mother-in-law to please.

Dinh Dat got married in his mid-twenties, at a younger age than was customary in our family. His wife turned out to be the girl next door, and not wealthy. She was a daughter of the Chu, a family allied to ours in many instances before. A few years younger than her husband, she was no stranger to our house and knew that she would have to conform to the ways of an authoritarian and demanding mother-in-law. But a remarkable transformation took place following the wedding. Saying that her task was done now that her son had taken a wife, the matriarch gave her daughter-in-law the keys of the house and put her in charge of everything. As for herself, she had earned the right to spend the rest of her time in leisure. Although in her seventies, she started making trips away from home, visiting relatives or going on pilgrimage to Buddhist temples, in particular those that her late husband had visited. Thus, the young couple started their married life very much on their own. The bride worked assiduously on her weaving loom and constantly reminded her scholar-husband to busy himself with his books. The folklore tale that seemed to be Dinh Dat's life continued:

> Midnight has passed. I put the house in order,
> Before sitting down in front of my loom.
> A few hours' sleep and soon dawn will break.
> Softly I call on my husband
> To wake up and not to sleep any more.
> For the king will soon order that examinations be held.
> On the golden board shining in the sun, your name will be written.
> You will repay the efforts of your parents,
> Who toiled away to buy brush and ink-slab and to provide for your studies.

Dinh Dat sought to improve his chances at the examinations by going to Hanoi and studying under well-known teachers. The couple had brief occasions to stay together when she brought him, at intervals, his provision of rice and other produce from home. She would make the thirty kilometers or so trip from Kim Bai, carrying two heavy baskets at the ends of a pole over her shoulder. Starting early in the morning, she would arrive at dusk in the maze of streets, lanes and paths of the large city, and have great difficulty in finding the place where he stayed. When seeing him, she would be happy, but shy and hesitant because they had not been married for very long. Such was life for many young couples when the husband was a scholar vying for academic honors. The image of a young wife carrying rice to town for her scholar-husband was depicted in many a folk poem. Here is one:

> Both my parents are old.
> I married you, a talented scholar,
> So that my future could safely be in your hands.
> Whether it is summer or winter,
> The produce of each session is ready for you to take, when you go away.
> When you send words that rice had run out, I carry it to you.
> Asking people to direct me to where you are staying for your studies,
> Finally I find the right lane and come to your place.
> Putting my baskets down, I can only find these words to greet you: "Dear
>   husband!"

But in spite of his talents, Dinh Dat kept failing at the examinations. Bad luck dogged him. Sessions were held only once every three years, but on those crucial days, either he was caught in poor health or something happened so that he could not put four good papers together to cover the required examination subjects. A turn for the worse came when his mother fell ill and became almost paralyzed. Most of the time, she was confined to her bed. It was a difficult period for the couple. Dinh Dat was busy tutoring younger students, while pursuing his own studies. His wife continued to make cloth and sell at the market, but she also had to nurse an ailing mother-in-law, washing her, giving her food and medicine, keeping her company. The old lady was crippled with pain, but stoically she remained cheerful and never complained. In the last years of her life, the quick temper and severity of her character disappeared. Like her late husband, she sought refuge in the Buddhist religion and her attitude became one of quiet acceptance. To her son, who had grown increasingly despondent and impatient because of his lack of success at the examinations, she talked of the need to follow one's fate. Talent, she told him, rarely came hand in hand with good fortune. Success may come late to a brilliant scholar, or it may not come at all; we were all bound by our karma. Happiness would come with our readiness to accept what was in store for us, according to Lord Buddha's teachings. When she died after several years of debilitating illness, her mind was at peace. As a pseudonym for her, Dinh Dat chose Tu

Thuan. *Tu,* or Compassion, was the usual first word for a mother's name. The second word was the virtue by which he wanted to remember her for, and that was *Thuan,* meaning Acquiescence. The *Thuan* here was taken from a passage written by the Taoist philosopher Chuang Tzu about his Master, Lao Tzu. It said: "When the Master came to this world, it was at a proper time. When he left it, he readily accepted that it was also at a proper time. Quietly acquiescing to whatever happens leaves no room for grief or for joy."

Dinh Dat was devoted to his mother. He often told the family that his father's death and the loss of the family's fortune in the south could have meant poverty and irremediable decline, were it not for the sacrifices made by his mother. Her role was praised in the chronicle in these terms:

> Dinh Dat's father died in the south when he was only three. He was brought up by his mother who toiled to send him to school and give him a future. Thanks to her, he became a scholar who soon acquired a fine reputation in letters.

During her long illness, he and his wife cared for her in the most dutiful manner. More than anything else, he had hoped to be able to graduate and give her the satisfaction of seeing her efforts rewarded. But when she died, he was still just a plain scholar, at the age of thirty-three. Dinh Dat also owed much to his two elder sisters who, since their teens, had worked on the weaving loom and gone to the market with their mother. When she grew old, they became the family's mainstay. The chronicle put on record Dinh Dat's debt towards them: "His sisters Tu Loan and Tu Hao kept themselves busy in petty trade so as to provide him with an income. Thanks to them, he could go on with his studies."

The two were married to fellow villagers, one to a gentleman of the Pham family, the other to a cousin of Dinh Dat's wife. They continued to help their brother financially until he established himself as a teacher. Later on, when tragedy befell him, they would be there again to give him a supporting hand.

Some time after his mother's death, Dinh Dat opened his own school inside the family compound, using for that purpose the guest house built by his father. He could have anything up to a dozen students, of different ages and levels. A stern master, he drove his pupils hard and used the rod liberally. In those times, parents would see in the rod the mark of a good teacher. "You love them, you give them the rod; you don't and you let them play," a proverb said. Dinh Dat's reputation grew. He not only taught in Kim Bai but, as reported in the chronicle, "was a visiting teacher at several places." Villages without their own teachers secured his services for a few months each year. He did not have much of an income. It was accepted custom that children from poor families receive free tuition. Presents of rice, cake, fowl or fruit was all that he received from most of his students. It was a strenuous life moving from one place to another, but there were compensations. In his own village, which was traditionally one of scholars, Dinh Dat was ranked behind all those who held diplomas and mandarinal offices. But a visiting teacher was often the top scholar at the place where he stayed. Dinh Dat was an honored guest at communal festivals or family celebrations. Moreover, he functioned also as a scribe, a calligrapher and writer of parallel sentences that people liked to hang in their homes. Our family still owned some land. Dinh Dat's wife contributed with the proceeds of her weaving and market activities. All things put together provided for a frugal living.

Academic titles continued to elude our ancestor, but at least his family life was coming along well. In 1871, when he was thirty-five, the couple had a son. Two years later, a daughter was born. Fate, however, was waiting to show its hand. The next year, it struck. His wife of more than ten years, who after a long period of caring for an invalid mother-in-law had finally settled into the life of a wife and mother, died. Then, as misfortune never happened just once, his five-year-old son died too. All that was left of his family was a baby daughter. At forty, his aspiration to become a graduate and mandarin had, for all practical purposes, gone for at that age he had not even obtained the bachelor's degree.

One can understand why he wanted to look elsewhere than the conformist ideals of Confucianism for an answer to a life afflicted by adversity. He could have sought refuge in the Buddhist religion, as did his parents and his forebears of some generations ago. The roots of Zen in our family were still there, waiting to grow to the surface again. Instead, Dinh Dat turned to the mystical doctrine of Taoism. He was a keen student of the works of Chuang Tzu, the renowned Taoist philosopher who lived in the third century B.C., some two centuries after Lao Tzu, the founder of Taoism. Chuang Tzu was a great exponent of that doctrine and he, more than Lao Tzu, was responsible for propagating it and making it into one of the three mainstays of Chinese culture. He was also a great writer. His book, consisting of philosophical discourses, tales, fables and parables is one of the best-loved works of Chinese literature, although in many passages one of the most difficult to understand. I remember being introduced to Chuang Tzu through the *Story of Kieu*. I was reading the *Story* to my grandfather when we came to a verse with a reference to Chuang Tzu's celebrated puzzle about himself and a butterfly. Grandfather took out the book of Chuang Tzu writings, wrote that passage down—for me to copy for I was then also learning calligraphy—and explained it to me. Once Chuang Tzu dreamed that he was a butterfly, fluttering about and enjoying itself. When he woke up, he did not know whether it had been him dreaming that he was a butterfly or it was now a butterfly dreaming that it was Chuang Tzu. Grandfather taught me a number of easy passages from the book. What a refreshing change from the study of the Confucian classics! Chuang Tzu wrote in such a lively and witty way that one is not quite sure whether he was seriously engaged in a profound discourse, or just enjoying himself and letting his imagination run. This, for instance, is how he dealt with the subject of death. A man was dying. His family was wailing with grief. A friend came and told him: "What is the Creator going to do with you? Is he making you into the liver of a rat, or the wings of an insect?" To which the dying man replied: "I am like a son, wherever his parents tell him to go, east, west, south, or north, he would obey." In another passage, Chuang Tzu wrote: "How am I to know that my love of life is not a delusion? and my fear of death is not like that of a child who had lost his way and did not know that he was going home?" I tried to read Chuang Tzu in the Chinese text by myself, but without the guidance of a teacher could not make any progress. Only much later in life did my knowledge of Chinese improve enough to allow me to approach that task, and I still needed to have with me two translations, one in popular Vietnamese, the other in English.

It was when he was around forty that Dinh Dat took up the pseudonym of Song Son Dat Dan, or Hermit of the Mountain of the Twins. For the rest of his life, he would be known by that name. To me, it evokes a scene often depicted in old paintings. The hermit is a tiny figure standing alone next to a pine tree. In front of him are mighty peaks surrounded by misty clouds. He has left his cares and ambitions with the world below. In the calm of the mountain, he searches for Tao, or "the way." Chuang Tzu often represented his *Chan Nhan*, or True Men, as hermits or recluses of the mountain. True Men were those who "knew the part that Heaven played and the part that man played"; in other words, who had reached an understanding of the fundamental harmony that lay behind all things. That harmony was the Tao. Chuang Tzu's hermits were old men "whose complexion was that of a child," and who behaved rather crazily. One of them was always rambling about, slapping his buttocks and hopping like a bird. Yet, kings, princes, philosophers, scholars, the mighty and the learned of this world, all came to them in the hope of gleaning something of their wisdom. It was not easy to find a hermit in the mountain though, and he would not say much at the first meeting. One had to come back again and again before he would consent to talk. Dinh Dat must have dreamed of going up the western mountains, the cradle of our race which from his village he could see turn purple in the light of the setting sun, there to devote himself to his quest. But family and work tied him down to Kim Bai. His Mountain of the Twins was never anything but a mythical place.

Among the many tales told by Chuang Tzu, I found one which seemed particularly relevant to Dinh Dat and all those scholars like him who failed at the examinations and had to spend their lives teaching in some obscure village school. With their talents unrecognized, they may feel useless. Chuang Tzu told of a useless tree which, however, was destined to quite a different fate. A carpenter came to a place where stood a tree used as an altar for the spirits of the land. The tree was so large that it could shelter a thousand buffaloes. It measured a hundred spans around and rose high before throwing out branches, tens of which were big enough to be made into boats. So many people came to see it that the scene under its canopy was like that of a market. Yet, the carpenter did not turn his head to look at it and went on his way without stopping. An apprentice of his, however, was filled with admiration and ran after him, saying: "Since I followed you with my axe and bill, Sir, I have never seen such a beautiful timber. Why did you not look at it, but went on without stopping?" The carpenter said: "I did look, but it is useless wood. A boat made from it would sink, a coffin would quickly rot, an article of furniture would quickly decay, a door would be covered with sap, a pillar would be attacked by insects. Its wood is useless, that is why it has grown into such an old tree." The apprentice listened, but the next day he returned to that problem: "Sir, that useless tree, how is it that it became an altar for the spirits of the land?" The carpenter replied: "It is a secret. That tree happened to be there. People who do not know think that it is useless. If not used as an altar, would it not be in danger of being cut down?"

Among scholars of his days, Dinh Dat was well-respected for his literary talents. If his poems or writings in prose were kept, I am sure that we would find in them a Taoist inspiration and the yearning for a life in harmony with nature that the pseudonym he chose expressed so well. But scholars of the old days did not write with an eye for posterity, only to enjoy themselves. They would like nothing more than to exchange poems with their friends over a cup of perfumed tea or sweet wine, singing the poem aloud, commenting upon them, composing variations on given themes and rhymes. Few would seek to make themselves known to a wider public and that was another reason why so much of our literary treasure had been lost. Up to the beginning of this century, when the country finally had a publishing industry, literary magazines, museums and public libraries, the survival of a literary work was often a matter of luck more than anything else. A writer would gain a good reputation, his poems would be learned by heart and circulated outside his circle of friends. One day, some scholar of renown would judge them good enough to be included in his literary anthology and in this way, their author would stand a chance to leave his name to later generations. Most of our ancient literature was preserved in anthologies, which by some quirk of fate had survived while the original works had disappeared. Our ancestor Dinh Dat was known to scholars of his region, but never won the kind of fame that would put his name in anthologies. When he died, his poetry died with him. Some scholars would not even want their poems to survive after them. For them, poems were like personal papers, to be shared only with friends. That they could be read by unknown persons was an unaccceptable invasion of privacy. Back in the fourteenth century, a king put the seal of royalty over the radical practice of destroying one's literary and artistic creations. Tran Anh Ton (1293–1314) presided over the destiny of the nation in the period following its glorious victories over the Mongol army of Kublai Khan. The Mongols came to subjugate our people. They were defeated once, came back and were defeated again. The Vietnamese forced them to accept peaceful relations. Our national pride rose to its peak. "A grasshopper taking on a chariot," so the saying went, but in this case the Vietnamese grasshopper succeeded in knocking the Mongol chariot off its wheels. It would have been easy for a Vietnamese king in the circumstances to entertain illusions of grandeur. However, Tran Anh Ton remained a humble and modest man, intent on keeping the peace and giving the country a good administration. He relaxed by painting and writing poetry; probably most of his works were a combination of both, with a poem written over a corner of a landscape painting. We have no means of judging his talents as painter, but the few poems of his which are preserved in anthologies show him as a gifted and sensitive poet. Anyway, there must have been no dearth of courtesans and high mandarins to praise his poems and paintings and to tell him that they deserved to be kept for the enlightenment of thousands of generations to come. Before he died, however, the king told his chamberlain to bring him the entire collection of his works, entitled "Letting my brush wander along the water and with the clouds." Then, he ordered him to burn them to ashes before his eyes.

My great-grandfather did not go to the extreme of destroying what he had written. As a follower of Chuang Tzu who once said that the writings left by ancient sages were just "the dregs they left behind ... when they died, they took with them thoughts that could never be transmitted," I do not think that it mattered in the very least to him that his poems were preserved or not. One day, I discovered two wooden cabinets lying under the altar of our ancestral home. I had to crawl on my hands and knees to reach them in the dark. On them were old padlocks of the kind formerly used in our country which could easily be opened with any narrow and flat piece of metal. Inside were piles of old handwritten books. I was then learning the old scholarly script and was excited to discover another set of books to test my newly-acquired skill. So I took a few out to examine them at leisure. They were all written in a cursive style so strange that I could only decipher a few characters here and there. The rest made no sense to me. Great damage had been done by bookworms which had made furrows in most pages. The cabinets were placed in a damp place never reached by sunlight. My grandmother happened to pass by and asked me what those books were. When told where I took them from, her expression changed. "They were your great-grandfather's books," she said. "Put them back at once! Your grandfather would not be pleased if he knew that they were taken out." Her attitude seemed to imply that these relics left by great-grandfather had something of a sacred character. I should not have touched them, let alone taken them out and risking to lose them. I believe that the cabinets contained mostly textbooks used for teaching. Printed books were few and expensive in those days, so scholars used to copy them in a fast and cursive style of writing which was highly personal and very difficult to read for anyone else than themselves. Great-grandfather's personal papers and any prose or poetry that he wrote must be in there too. The books were stored in a hallowed place right under the altar, but no care was taken to preserve them from insects and dampness. Even without a war and a revolution, they would be soon destroyed.

I cannot recall my grandfather mentioning any piece written by his father. Presumably, that was because none if his children knew the old scholarly script and I was the only grandchild to whom he taught it. Dinh Dat only composed in that script; if he had also written in the popular script which became the national language at the beginning of this century, we may still have had some of his poems today. Moreover, his poems in scholarly script were probably composed in the manner of the old school and laden with learned references to ancient Chinese texts. They would be very difficult to understand to the uninitiated. What would be the point for grandfather to read them to us, who went to French schools and were more familiar with the language of Molière than with the script used by our forebears! Even if he would translate the words of a poem, its melody and evocative quality would be lost. Truly that would be, to use a popular expression, like "playing music to a buffalo's ears."

Wherever he went to teach, his literary talent made Dinh Dat a kind of resident scholar and poet. People came to ask him to compose complimentary poems and parallel sentences for such auspicious occasions as the building of a new house, a mandarinal promotion or a seventieth birthday. Most of the time, he would take out his brush and write something down right away. Good scholars had that capacity to make instant verses; as people said: "They only have to open their mouth, and words will come out in verses!" But if it was for a close acquaintance or a respected scholarly family, he would take time to think of something special. His sentences and poems were carved on heavy boards which were then lacquered in a combination of red, gold and black colors and hung on walls as decorations. Made of precious wood, the boards could stay in good condition for many generations. Had peace and stability prevailed, some of Dinh Dat's boards would still adorn traditional homes in our region and, through them, we would still be able to get some idea of his style and inspiration. But since his time, there were the French war of conquest of the 1870s and 1880s, the communist revolution and another war with the French. When the Geneva Agreements were signed in 1954, all that our family had left in Kim Bai was the empty shell of an ancestral home. All furniture and decorative boards had gone, after just one war. The boards were not appropriated by other people; they were too heavy to carry and did not have any other purpose than decoration, a luxury that one could hardly afford in a time of war. But they were a ready source of fuel to a soldiery which could not care less about culture and history. Dinh Dat's boards would have had to survive two wars. It would be a miracle if any of them were left.

Overshadowing the problems besetting Dinh Dat's personal life was the gloom which descended upon our country. Since the tenth century and except for a brief period of Chinese domination (1414–1427), the Vietnamese had been masters in their own country. The only threat to their survival as a nation came from China and it may be said that after millenniums of living next to the Chinese, the Vietnamese have learned the way to deal with them. But now they were faced with a new challenge originating from the West. European traders and missionaries came to Vietnam in the beginning of the seventeenth century, but relations were kept at a low level until the end of the next century, when a crucial development took place. As we saw earlier, political and military links were established between the Vietnamese and the French. The overlord Nguyen Anh obtained French arms and the services of French experts. He won the war against the Tay Son and founded the Nguyen dynasty. Thus, we had a leader who saw the superiority of the West in military art and technology long before the Japanese were convinced of the same and opened their country to modernization. As Emperor Gia Long, Nguyen Anh ruled for seventeen years, from 1802 to 1819. Had he continued to learn from the West and to make the necessary changes in the country, we would have stood a good chance of joining the modern world as a strong and independent nation. But no more French experts were brought in. Young Vietnamese were not sent abroad to study Western technology, the way that Japan would do so successfully later. Neither Nguyen Anh nor his successors had the foresight of a Japanese Meiji. His successors, in particular, paid little attention to developments in the rest of the world and resolutely pursued a policy of going back to classical Confucian teachings. Catholicism was forbidden; its followers were persecuted. The country closed its doors to Europeans. French initiatives to establish trade and consular relations were rejected. In retrospect, it appeared that the opportunity was then lost and Vietnam's history took the course it did. Historian Tran Trong Kim wrote of that period: "Our people did not understand the changing times. We kept priding ourselves that we were more civilised than others, instead of trying to learn new ways like them and to follow the way of progress."

Western imperialism appeared off the coast of Vietnam in 1847 in the form of French warships. The French demanded that the persecution of Catholics be stopped, sank a number of Vietnamese ships in a show of strength, then left. That action could have served as a salutary warning to Vietnam, in the same way as the American "black ships" would do for Japan in 1853. But it was not the case. The emperor and his court neither took the necessary steps to bolster our defense, nor made any move to open relations with the West. Nine years later, French ships came back to bombard the port of Da Nang, just south of the imperial capital Hue, then left again. Again, the warning went unheeded. Finally in 1858, a Franco-Spanish armada of fourteen ships and three thousand troops launched the invasion, under the pretext of saving the Catholics from persecution. French priests has assured the leaders of the expedition that Catholics in the country would rise up in their support. To meet such a force, the Vietnamese had a navy consisting of small boats, an infantry equipped with swords, scimitars, lances and a few muskets and an artillery still using cannons dating from Nguyen Anh's time which were loaded from the mouth of the gun. Da Nang was attacked and quickly occupied. The French sought to advance north towards the capital, but a large force under Marshall Nguyen Tri Phuong succeeded in stopping them. A few months of stalemate followed. As the expected Catholic uprising did not materialize and their troops suffered heavy losses due to cholera, the French decided that the rich Mekong delta in the south would be an easier target. Leaving an occupying force behind in Da Nang, they moved their ships south and attacked Gia Dinh, nowadays Saigon. Their conquest of Vietnam started from there. It was a drawn out process, taking place over as many as twenty-five years and alternating between military campaigns and phases of negotiation. Our country was taken bit by bit, very much like a mulberry leaf being eaten by a silkworm. During all that time, the Vietnamese court was like a paralyzed body, unable to find effective ways to oppose French arms or to seize the opportunities that arose to make peace.

My great-grandfather Dinh Dat was twenty-two and preparing to go south to search for his father's grave when the French launched their aggression against Da Nang in 1858. His trip had to be abandoned. He followed closely the events there, unlike many people in the north who had little concern for what happened in the distant land of the south. The war situation did not look too bad in the first two or three years. The French took the citadel of Gia Dinh at the beginning of 1859, after two days of fighting. They seized a vast amount of arms, ammunition, money and food. The defeated commander, Vu Duy Ninh, committed suicide. The loss of Gia Dinh was a serious blow. But French occupation was still confined to two enclaves, Da Nang and Gia Dinh. In 1860, the French withdrew their troops from Da Nang. France and England were then engaged in a war with

China and reinforcements needed to be sent there. But the Vietnamese took the withdrawal as a sign of French weakness. The court proclaimed victory and Marshall Nguyen Tri Phuong was despatched to attack the remaining French in Gia Dinh. Expectations rose that France would soon be forced to leave the country. Dinh Dat was thinking again of going south, once peace had returned. But by the end of 1860, China had been defeated and the French came back in force to Gia Dinh. Following a series of hard-fought battles, they extended their hold over neighboring provinces. However, the citadel of Bien Hoa, which commanded the access to Gia Dinh from the northeast, remained in Vietnamese hands. As long as Bien Hoa could hold, hope was not lost that reinforcements sent from Hue could mount a counterattack to regain Gia Dinh. Bien Hoa lay close to our family's heart. It was there that Dinh Dat's father was buried. When it fell in December 1861, the fate of Gia Dinh was sealed and any lingering hope that Dinh Dat may still have had of finding his father's grave also disappeared. In 1862, Vietnam was forced to sign a treaty ceding Gia Dinh and the eastern part of the south to the invader. By the same treaty, it also pledged to respect the freedom of religion and to open three ports for trade with France.

As the country came under the attacks of a mighty European power, its leaders were men who held fast to the ways of the past. Under the Nguyen dynasty, Vietnam had become a power to be reckoned with in the region. It had enjoyed peaceful relations with China, while exerting a considerable influence over its smaller neighbors. Its national territory had grown larger than ever before. The high mandarins in Hue prided themselves on governing according to precepts laid down millenniums ago by Confucius and the ancient masters. The world had changed. Industrialized countries in the West had spread their tentacles to Asia. For years, the threat from France had been looming. But the mandarins continued to think of their world as safe and secure. Historian Tran Trong Kim gave of them this critical assessment:

> Since the nineteenth century, life and education abroad had progressed greatly, competition among countries had intensified. Yet, those holding political responsibility in our country were only keen on pursuing their literary education and improving their writing skills. When discussing national affairs, they knew only to refer to emperors in golden ages several thousand years ago, as examples for the present times to follow. From their high pedestal, they thought of themselves as superior to other people and treated foreigners as barbarians.

The scholars' class in the country was the image of its political leaders, conservative and parochial. Our ancestor Dinh Dat, however, belonged to a younger generation of men who reached their thirties in the critical decade of the 1860s. He had travelled widely in the country, firstly to look for people who had been to the south with his father and who may give him some information about his grave, and then to find relatives who had left Kim Bai and taken with them the Cu Hau papers. He had visited many trading towns on the coast, talked to Chinese and Vietnamese traders, and maybe even came into contact with European travellers. Thus, he was better aware of the problems facing the country than the majority of scholars, for whom knowledge was to be found in classical books.

The shock created by events in the south gave rise to a reformist current. Dinh Dat was among those who realized that Western methods and techniques would have to be adopted if Vietnam was to stand a chance of overcoming the French challenge. In 1865, envoys sent to France and Spain to negotiate the return of the southern provinces came home to report on the wealth and power of European countries. In their submissions to the court, they advocated a series of measures such as teaching foreign languages, developing the mining industries and establishing a school on maritime transport. The following year Nguyen Truong To, a scholar converted to Christianity, went to Rome and Paris. On his return, he drew up a comprehensive plan to reform the education system, strengthen the army, develop industry and urbanism. Other scholars and mandarins who stayed back at home petitioned that the army be modernized, Vietnamese be encouraged to go into commerce and industry and a number of ports be opened to international trade. The submissions and petitions were examined by the court which rejected them all, some for "not being adapted to the times (sic)" others more seriously for being harmful to law and order. The high mandarins did not want Vietnamese to have contact with foreigners, which was rather understandable in the climate of xenophobia created by the French invasion, but they also opposed suggestions such as the development of commerce and industry. In the 1860s these were revolutionary ideas. Vietnamese society was then composed of four classes: the scholars, farmers, artisans and traders. It had no equivalent of the Western bourgeoisie. The principal source of wealth in the country was agriculture. There were no industries except artisanal ones. Mining was a state monopoly and scarcely developed. Trade was mainly in the hands of the Chinese, who were "guests" with no role to play in the nation's political or social life. Vietnamese traders ranked last in the social scale. To encourage the Vietnamese to go into commerce and industry would be to strengthen the ranks of artisans and traders, thus disrupting the traditional order. The mandarins were fearful that they would not be able to control the activities of businessmen, especially if trade with foreigners were to be allowed. They knew well that economic changes would necessarily lead to other changes in the social and political system.

But faced with a deteriorating situation in the south, the court eventually had to take some reformist measures. Vietnamese priests were called to the capital to translate French books, students were encouraged to learn the French language. A few interesting moves were made in 1866 when the authorities picked a number of bright students and good artisans, paid them well and sent them to Gia Dinh under French occupation. Their mission was to find out what they could about French technology. At the same time, mandarins were sent to France to buy textbooks and to recruit professors and scientists; a school was going to be established for them, until events in the south claimed all the attention of the court and nothing more was heard of the project. Other initiatives were taken, but all in a piecemeal fashion, without any central purpose or direction. In the end, those measures made no difference to the course of events.

The Nguyen emperors ruling from Hue were never very popular with the people of the north, many of whom were still attached to the Le dynasty which lost the throne in 1788. Indeed, the north was still referred to as "the traditional land of the Le." Real or imaginary descendants of that dynasty were often able to rally supporters and foment rebellions there. Several such rebellions broke out in the 1860s, when the south was being invaded by France. Among northern scholars, in particular those who failed at the examinations and were dissatisfied with their lot, nostalgia remained strong for the Le times when Thang Long was the capital and cultural center of the country. Dinh Dat was an unsuccessful scholar, but he never shared that attachment for a long-gone dynasty. He greatly admired Tu Duc, the Nguyen emperor who ruled from 1847 to 1883, and whose misfortune it was to preside over the loss of our national independence. He was eleven when Tu Duc became emperor, at the age of eighteen. They belonged to the same generation. Confucianism was then at its most influential period and in the king Dinh Dat could admire an elder and a Confucian gentleman. Tu Duc was a learned scholar. His knowledge of history and the classics was regarded with awe by his advisers, who counted among the most erudite doctors in the country. His passion for learning was well-known. He read all the papers submitted to him by his ministers and annotated them at length, often his comments took more place than the paper itself. Everyday after official duties were over, he spent long hours with his books, reading well into the night. A conscientious and hard-working sovereign, Tu Duc held court almost daily, starting just after dawn. Mandarins had to get up and eat their breakfast when it was still dark, so that they could be at the Palace on time. It became customary during his reign that houses in the mandarins' quarter were lighted up and buzzing with activity even before the cocks started crowing.

Loyalty and filial piety were two prime virtues required of a Confucian gentleman. Tu Duc was a most obedient son, a quality highly appreciated by Dinh Dat, who was himself very much attached to his mother. Tu Duc never let his responsibilities as a king interfere with his filial duties. He visited his mother regularly, to enquire about her well-being and to talk about his and the nation's problems. The advice she gave him was carefully recorded in a book entitled *Teachings of a Mother*. As a king, Tu Duc owed loyalty to nobody, but Dinh Dat saw in him a fervent patriot who suffered greatly for having lost part of the country to the aggressor. The story went round the nation that after the 1862 treaty, the emperor's hair became white as dew in a matter of days. He was only in his early thirties. And never again would he smile, since that fateful event.

Like many reformists, Dinh Dat placed his hopes for change in the emperor. He blamed the failure to adopt reforms on the high mandarins. These were old men unable to adapt to the new situation, but Tu Duc was believed to be well aware of the need for change. He had read all the petitions, including those made by the Catholics, whose religion was proscribed by a series of royal edicts. His kindness to Nguyen Truong To, the Catholic scholar who on returning from Europe had submitted to him his ideas on modernizing the country, was well known. The few measures taken by the court to encourage the learning of languages and sciences were seen by the reformists as signs that the emperor was gradually overcoming the opposition of the old guard. Dinh Dat, for one, was convinced that the sovereign would eventually lead the country towards reforms and salvation.

The 1862 peace treaty was followed by a five-year pause in the fighting. Diplomacy took over during that period. Phan Thanh Gian—a mandarin in his seventies and one of the highest ranking ministers in the government—was appointed to lead a delegation to France, with the unrealistic task of "buying back" the lost provinces in the south. He returned empty-handed but convinced that the country was not in a position to fight a war with France and that, therefore, it should seek peace and take the path of modernization. The French also sent a delegation to Hue to discuss a new peace treaty. Meanwhile, they consolidated their occupation. The Vietnamese, for their part, were unable to take advantage of the lull in the fighting. The court was fully engaged in putting down a series of rebellions in the north fomented by the Catholics and followers of the Le. In the capital Hue itself, an uprising by soldiers aimed at killing the emperor and replacing him with another member of the royal family was crushed. Religious antagonism intensified in the country following the invasion. Popular suspicion grew against the Catholic converts, especially as French priests in the south openly called on their flocks to cooperate with the occupying forces. In 1867, the French set out to conquer the rest of the south. The Royal Delegate there was Phan Thanh Gian, the envoy who advocated peace. He offered no resistance, believing it to be futile and only causing death and destruction to the population. But he drank poison to take his own life. "My duty as a subject is to die," he wrote in a last petition to the emperor, ". . . [but if] Your Majesty would make the appropriate changes, our strength would still allow us to succeed." Tu Duc was furious at the loss of the last southern provinces without a fight. Phan Thanh Gian was tried posthumously and condemned. But many in the country understood the reason of his action. If a man like him, who had faithfully served three kings and was renowned for his integrity, chose to kill himself rather than fight, then the situation must be truly desperate. They reckoned that Phan Thanh Gian had wanted to jolt the country into doing something to save itself, before it was too late.

By then, Dinh Dat had reached his thirties. He was among a small number of scholars in the north who supported the call for reforms, but without a diploma he did not have a voice. Nor was he in a position to send petitions; coming from an untitled scholar, they would be unceremoniously dismissed by the mandarins. Only with success at the examination could he aspire to play an active role. Although time had started to run out on him, at each new session he set out to try again. For scholars of his caliber, little stood in reality between failure and success. If he got through the regional examinations and obtained there a licentiate degree, he would qualify to go to the capital Hue in the following year to sit for a doctorate. If successful, and he would join the elite of the nation. In the space of just over a year, an obscure village teacher could become someone whose opinions on modernization and reforms would carry weight with the high mandarins and with the emperor himself. For this to happen, Dinh Dat knew that he needed only a small measure of luck.

At the beginning of the 1870s, word came that Japan under a new emperor had embarked on a policy of modernization. The Japanese army and navy were reorganized according to the Western model; industry and transport were developed; the education system was reformed. Students were sent abroad to learn and teachers were recruited from Europe and America. A whole nation had taken down the barriers in an effort to catch up with the West. The news thrilled Dinh Dat. He was sure the Japanese example would have an impact on his country. Here was an Asian ruler leading his people in a revolutionary transformation; if Emperor Tu Duc was still hesitant about reforms, this should convince him. But Dinh Dat was wrong. No attempt was made by the court of Hue to follow Japan's lead.

Having taken over the rest of the south in 1867, the French made another pause. Again, the Vietnamese were given a breathing space in which to implement reforms and strengthen the country's defenses. But for much of the time, the attention of the court was again taken up by the situation in the north, where remnants of a Chinese rebellion against the Ching dynasty had crossed the border and taken control of several provinces. Their two main groups were called the Black Flags and the Yellow Flags, from the colors of their banners. Between 1868 and 1871, a succession of campaigns by government troops failed to dislodge them. Thus, the Vietnamese were no better prepared to meet the next phase of the French advance when it took place in 1873. From the south, the French had been casting their eyes over the north, which they saw as a door to the vast market of China. When a dispute arose between the authorities there and a French trader, and the Vietnamese court made the mistake of asking them to help settle it, they immediately seized upon the opportunity. Navy Lieutenant F. Garnier was despatched to Hanoi with a small force of 170 soldiers and some gunboats. The Vietnamese were not unduly worried by F. Garnier's mission. Hanoi, the old capital, was defended by seven thousand troops under the command of a celebrated commander, Marshall Nguyen Tri Phuong. The French intention was probably only to establish a presence in the north, but once in Hanoi, F. Garnier decided that he could take the town by a bold raid. Under the cover fire of his gunboats, he attacked the citadel, which fell after an hour of fighting. Taken prisoner, Nguyen Tri Phuong fasted to death. Like the Gia Dinh defender and Phan Thanh Gian before him, he could only find in death the way to eradicate his shame and pay his debt to the country.

The fall of Hanoi brought home to the population of the north the specter of domination by the white man. Resistance of it would later develop, but for the moment, the feeling was one of utter despair and helplessness. Hanoi, the ancient seat of Vietnamese dynasties and through the centuries a proud symbol of our nationhood, could not be defended against a few hundred Frenchmen. What hope therefore was left? In a matter of weeks, French forces captured several other towns in the Red River delta. Vietnamese troops had no answer to the superior French weapons, from the rifles used by infantrymen to the cannons which reduced fortifications to rubble in the first minutes of an attack. In desperation, the government enlisted the services of the Chinese Black Flags. The Yellow Flags, for their part, worked as mercenaries for the French. From the northern mountains, the Black Flags came down to the delta through the province of Son Tay which lay next to our province. They engaged French troops in the vicinity of Hanoi and won an important victory. F. Garnier, the leader of the French expedition, was killed. With so few troops, the French could not hope to hold the north, but their lightning attack had produced its effect. The Vietnamese court sued for peace. Under a treaty signed in 1874, Vietnam ceded the whole of the south to France. For its part, France returned the towns it had seized and withdrew its troops from the north, except for two small garrisons in Hanoi and in the port of Haiphong.

From their village, the Kim Bai people could hear the sound of the battle in Hanoi. But neither the French troops, nor their Chinese Yellow Flag mercenaries, ventured to our region. The Black Flags, however, stayed in

Vietnam for several years, long after the French had withdrawn. They were fighting on our side. Their chief was given the rank of a Vietnamese general following their success against the enemy, but the Black Flags were an undisciplined lot. When I was a boy, stories of killing, rape and destruction by the "pig-tailed bandits," as the Black Flags were called after the pigtail hairstyle worn by Chinese men, were still being told by villagers. Several generations had passed, yet the fear of those bandits remained very much alive.

Eighteen hundred and seventy-four was the blackest year in Dinh Dat's life, the year when his wife died. With his family life in tatters and his country's independence all but lost, the scholar underwent a personal crisis. Like the emperor he admired, his hair soon turned white like that of an old man. More and more, his mind turned away from the Confucian ideal of public service to move towards the mystical world of Taoism. When his young son died too, he left his village. If the country had been at peace, I think that he would have gone very far away, perhaps to the south like his father. But there could be no question of him doing so, now that the south was under foreign occupation. Dinh Dat went to Hanoi, where he hoped to continue his teaching activities. In the troubled period following the French attack and with bands of Black Flags roaming our region, not much work occupied him in Kim Bai. He stayed in the former capital for some length of time, but could not make a living and returned home. Fortunately, his two sisters were there to help him in his crisis. They reared his daughter and looked after the ancestral home while he was away. Three years after his wife died, they found a bride for him and Dinh Dat remarried. The new spouse came from the same Chu family in Kim Bai; she was a niece of his first wife. Seventeen years younger than her husband—she was twenty-four and he forty-one when they married—she brought him a new reason for living, and more. For the couple would lay the foundations for the family to grow and expand into the many branches that we know today.

When regional examinations were resumed after the hostilities, Dinh Dat sat for them a few more times. He was pursuing a dream rather than aiming for a mandarinal career. His white hair made him stand out in the crowd of candidates. People thought that he must be one of the oldest to go after the golden board. In fact, he was only in his mid-forties, while other candidates could be found in their fifties, some even in their sixties. In 1879, a son arrived in the family. He was my grandfather. As Dinh Dat's life was rebuilt, success returned to his work. His school flourished and other villages again invited him to come and hold classes. The white-haired scholar of Kim Bai was kept busy teaching and was constantly on the move, staying for a few months at one place, then on to another village and another group of students.

The events of 1873–74 shook Dinh Dat's faith in Tu Duc, the emperor whom he so much admired. Until then, he was inclined to blame the mandarins for failing to modernize the army, mobilize the population, adopt the necessary reforms. For him, the emperor stood above reproach. With Tu Duc at the helm, Dinh Dat believed that, somehow, our country would be safe and would survive the aggression. But the speed and ease with which the French took Hanoi and other towns showed how hopeless our situation had become. Vietnamese troops used to fight better at the beginning of the war; now they were demoralized and leaderless. Nguyen Tri Phuong was the same commander who stopped the French advance towards the imperial capital Hue in 1858. Three years later, in the defense of the Ky Hoa fortress in the south, he engaged the enemy forces in fierce fighting and inflicted on them heavy losses. In Hanoi, he suffered a humiliating defeat that ended his life. Since the invasion started some fifteen years ago, the country had been on a downward slope. With the tricolor flag flying over the old capital, Dinh Dat felt that all was lost.

But then, the 1874 treaty was concluded and French troops withdrew. Government control resumed over the north. Confidence returned to the population. Some people thought that the French had been defeated, others that they were compelled to leave because China threatened that she would intervene to help Vietnam. They seemed to forget that the enemy had already reaped the benefits of its action with the treaty which ceded all the south to France and that, in any case, its small force could only make a raid against the north but not occupy it. Still, another breathing space was given to the Vietnamese. This would prove to be their last. The reformists again pleaded for change, but theirs remained a minority voice in the country. The mass of scholars continued to be against it. At the triennial examinations in Hue in 1876, candidates were asked to write a paper on the policy of opening and modernization initiated by Emperor Meiji in Japan. Was it beneficial to Japan? Most gave a negative appraisal. As for Dinh Dat, he again placed his faith in Emperor Tu Duc as the only authority who could override the immobility of the mandarins. By the late 1870s, the court did show a more favorable disposition towards reforms. A small number of students were sent to France, Spain and to British schools in Hong Kong to learn western technology. Important changes were made in the civil service: people with knowledge of foreign languages, experts in ship building, mining, arms manufacturing, military training, etc. . . . were given degrees and recruited as mandarins. Diplomatic missions were sent to Hong Kong and Siam to try and establish relations with other countries. An unofficial envoy visited Washington and obtained an audience with the American president. He pleaded for American help against French colonialism. However, all those measures proved to be too little and too late. Emperor Tu Duc showed that he was well aware of the urgency of the situation, but he had to deal with a recalcitrant bureaucracy which, even at that late hour, still could not bring itself to accept change. In 1881, a member of the Academy submitted another proposal for modernizing commerce and industry. The high mandarins again rejected it. A despondent emperor remonstrated with them. "As old servants of the state concerned with its well-being," he told them, "you never fail to examine carefully each problem, but you should bear in mind the need for making progress, for not to progress means to move backwards."

The country continued to be plagued by disorder and rebellion. After the French withdrew from the north, massacres took place against the Catholics who were accused of having cooperated with the enemy. In the central provinces of Nghe An and Ha Tinh, scholars rose up in arms to protest against negotiation with France. Their mobs went on rampage, burning and destroying Catholic villages. Loyalists of the former Le dynasty, who fought on the side of the French when they attacked the north, kept on harassing several provinces. Chinese bands were in control of large areas of the northern mountains. Government troops succeeded in killing the leader of the Yellow Flags in 1875, but the fight against other bands went on for years. The court had its hands full dealing with internal emergencies; thus, the breathing space once again proved to be of no benefit. The French sat back for nearly a decade after the 1874 treaty. Then in 1882, they made their final move. What was going to happen was a strange case of history repeating itself. As in 1873, a dispute involving their traders in the north gave the French a pretext. They despatched a small force of some three hundred troops to Hanoi, under the command of Colonel H. Rivière. This time, the Vietnamese were on their guard, but just as F. Garnier did before him, H. Rivière launched an attack against the citadel of Hanoi. He took it after a battle lasting a few hours. The Vietnamese governor, Hoang Dieu, chose to die by hanging himself. The Black Flags who, after 1874, had been persuaded to return to their bases in the northern mountains, were again asked to come to fight the French and they repeated the success they achieved ten years before by killing the leader of the French expedition. The court thought that the French could again be persuaded to withdraw. But there ended the similarities with events in 1873. The French now intended to stay. From the south, they sent in reinforcements. The parliament in France voted for a massive increase of money to the Indochinese venture. The Vietnamese sought help from China and Chinese troops intervened. As the twenty-five-year conflict move toward its climax, Emperor Tu Duc died.

For many Vietnamese his passing marked the end, not just of a reign, but of an era. They saw in it the portent of a great calamity that would descend upon their country. The war would soon be lost and Vietnam placed under foreign rule. Dinh Dat mourned a king whom, in his youth, he had seen as a model of a Confucian scholar. He had hoped to gain diplomas and serve under him. When Vietnam fell victim of French aggression, he had trusted that Tu Duc would save the country with a policy of bold reforms. Now with the emperor gone, Dinh Dat felt that he was mourning at the same time the sad fate of the nation and his own lost opportunities. In a period of peace and stability, Tu Duc the Confucian scholar would have made a good king. But the nineteenth century was the time when Western imperialism spread to Asia. What Vietnam needed was a leader who could keep it at bay while leading his country into the modern world. Tu Duc proved himself woefully ill-adapted to be such a leader. He was not really committed to reforms. Petitions were referred by him to mandarins who found various reasons for rejecting them. Instead of imposing his authority, Tu Duc let the matter pass. He ruled over a divided nation. Partisans of the old Le dynasty, Catholics and other opponents were in rebellion. Tu Duc was never able to unify his people against the French invader. In particular, he failed to deal effectively with the Catholic problem and let it become the pretext for French aggression as well as a festering division among the Vietnamese.

The emperor's death immediately sparked trouble at the court. Two high mandarins nominated by Tu Duc as regents usurped power and put on the throne, not his chosen heir, but a young prince more to their liking. A month later, in August 1883, a French naval force attacked the fortifications defending the imperial capital. The capital itself was going to be bombarded when the mandarins capitulated. By the Peace Treaty of 1883, French rule was extended over the whole of Vietnam, with the south—Cochinchina—being a French colony, while the rest of the country—Tonkin and Annam—were placed under a regime of protectorate. Vietnam had ceaseed to be independent. In his village, now constantly exposed to sorties by French troops, Dinh Dat received the news with resignation. The nationalist and monarchist in him suffered. Not only had his country lost its sovereignty, Dinh Dat found it hard to accept that the emperor could remain on the throne and serve a foreign power. In the long history of our country, it had never happened that way. If a king was defeated, he died and his dynasty died with him. Dinh Dat knew that it was the regents who signed the treaty establishing the protectorate and that Tu Duc's successor was only a tool in their hands. That made him even more bitter about those regents who had, firstly, violated their emperor's trust and accumulated power to themselves at a time when defeat was staring the nation in the face. Then they capitulated to the enemy, bringing dishonor to the king and the nation. "Emperor Tu Duc was the pillar," he said. "When it fell down, the entire house and everything else came down with it, the country's independence, the moral principles, the duty of loyalty owed by mandarins to their king." His white hair became, if anything, even whiter. When he did not wear a turban and it was just tied loosely in a chignon at the back of his head, he was the picture of a Taoist recluse in the mountain. Some people called him *ong tien,* or an immortal, one who had through the study of Taoist texts and meditation found the secret of long life. But when teaching a class, dressed in a black tunic with a large black turban wrapped around his head, he looked a dozen years younger. By now, he had built a strong following of students, some with examination success to their credit.

A period of great confusion followed the treaty of 1883. Among Vietnamese commanders and mandarins some did not recognize it and kept up the fight. Others laid down their arms and went home. Still others stayed on to cooperate with the former enemy. Chinese forces and the Black Flags continued to engage the French. Patriots recruited their own troops, called *nghia dung* or "the faithful and the brave," to defend the honor of the country. At the same time bad elements, outlaws and highwaymen, took advantage of the situation to rob and plunder. Old scores were settled. Vietnamese were killing one another while their country came under the yoke of colonialism. At the court in Hue, the two mandarins usurpers made and unmade kings. As soon as a young sovereign showed some sign of independence, he was killed and another one put in his place. In less than a year, three kings followed one another on the throne. The region around our village of Kim Bai remained for a long time under the control of Vietnamese forces and the Black Flags, even though Hanoi had been under the French since April 1882. A number of Dinh Dat's students joined the ranks of patriots who defended the citadel of Son Tay, some thirty kilometers to the northwest of Kim Bai. In December 1883, the French launched their attack against Son Tay and the battle which took place there was one of the fiercest of the war. The Vietnamese army, the patriots, the Black Flags and Chinese regular troops fought against some six thousand French troops for several days and inflicted on them heavy losses. But they were unable to sustain the intense shelling by French artillery and had to withdraw into the northern mountains. Few of Dinh Dat's students came back. Many were killed in the battle. Others eventually retreated to China where they lived as exiles, hoping that one day they could return to their country and fight the French again.

The students were like members of his family and the news from the battle of Son Tay was a hard blow to Dinh Dat. Some months later, he fell ill. He was forty-nine. The family was greatly concerned because the forty-ninth year—and also the fifty-third—in a person's life were believed to be years of ill omen. According to astrologers, the configuration of stars was especially harmful to health in those years. That was the reason why most middle-aged people were not be able to survive one or the other of those two years. Many families took the precaution of consulting astrologers and holding prayer ceremonies to invoke the protection of the spirits when a member turned forty-nine, even though no untoward signs had been detected and he or she was keeping in perfectly good health. In Dinh Dat's case however, he had been depressed and his health had been failing since the previous year, when the fall of Hanoi and the treaty of 1883 did away with our independence. Then, in his forty-ninth year, he was struck by a grave illness. Medicines and prayer ceremonies did not lead to any improvement in his condition. The signs were ominous and the family thought that he was going to die. But he was saved by a Taoist priest, an acquaintance of his who led a lonely existence up in the purple mountains. That man was renowned for the medicine made from herbs he picked himself in the wild. On hearing that Dinh Dat was dying, he came down to visit him. He took his pulse and in true Chuang Tsu tradition, burst out laughing. "The white-haired teacher is not ready to change into a bird yet! He is still too heavy to fly!" he said, referring to the Taoist and Buddhist belief in reincarnation to another form of life. "I am giving you this bag of herbs which will help you get over the forty-ninth year and, moreover, will leave you with enough strength to overcome the barrier of the fifty-third. After that, you will gingerly get to the landmark of seventy." Thus saying, the priest returned to his temple in the mountain.

True enough, Dinh Dat recovered and soon could resume his teaching. In 1885, his spirit rose. Imperial forces in Hue reopened the hostilities with an attack against the French garrison. The attack failed and Emperor Ham Nghi fled the capital. From a base in the countryside, the young emperor called on the population to rally to him in the fight to recover independence. Dinh Dat had been waiting for this act of defiance. It rekindled his faith in the monarchy. Since the shock of capitulation, many in the country had been waiting for it too. The response to the emperor's call was a vast movement of resistance. Bands of "faithful and brave" patriots, most of them a few hundred strong but some reaching into the thousands, appeared nearly everywhere displaying the banner of *Can Vuong,* or Loyalty to the King. Under the command of scholars calling themselves "commanders," "generals" and "marshalls," they seized prefectures, at some places even provinces. In reality, it was not the young king, but the two regents who made the decision to attack the French. These regents soon showed their true colors. One promptly surrendered to the French when their move failed. The other fled to China with the professed purpose of seeking Chinese help. Emperor Ham Nghi was left in a perilous situation, but with the support of loyal mandarins he rose magnificently to the occasion. From jungle bases north of Hue next to the Laotian border, he gave inspiration and unity of purpose to the hundreds of resistance movements generated by his appeal. Our region was too close to Hanoi for resorting to armed insurrection, but young scholars went to join groups of patriots operating in the mountains, while older people like Dinh Dat kept up the morale of villagers and collected money and food for the fighters. However by 1885, the French had extended their hold over the country. Their repression took some time to come, but when it did the armies of patriots led by scholars with no battlefield experience proved no match for French troops. Also at many places, the insurrection turned into indiscriminate killing of people suspected of being pro–French and especially of Catholics, thus pushing them over to the side of the protectorate. The patriots were fighting a losing battle. Emperor Ham Nghi stayed to the bitter end, ignoring all the offers of reconciliation and appointment made by the new king who was put in his place by the French. In 1888, three years after he left Hue to start the resistance, he was betrayed, captured and delivered to the enemy. The young king—he was then eighteen—was an example of dignity in defeat. He suffered in silence, not uttering a single word to the Westerners who were now the masters of his country. He remained silent as he left Vietnam's shores to spend the rest of his life in exile in Algeria.

That was the final episode of the war. Although some movements deep in the mountains continued to defy the French well into the next decade, the Red River delta was pacified even before the king's exile. Dinh Dat resigned himself to the fact that defeat was now irreversible. "My generation has failed," he told his students. But his mind was at peace. He felt that Emperor Ham Nghi, by behaving in the way a king should, had saved the honor of the monarchy and the nation. "This game of chess has ended and we have lost. It is now your turn to prepare for the next game." The students asked his advice about joining the new schools established by the French. He encouraged them to do so. "Our young people who fled abroad are trying to learn from the Chinese and from the Japanese, so that one day they may return and fight more effectively against the French," he said. "We who stay back in the country should be prepared to learn from the former enemy, for that is the only way we could progress."

Triennial examinations were held again as the new French regime went out of its way to gain the scholars' support. Among Dinh Dat's friends, some were serving the protectorate. They pressed him to sit for the examinations, assuring him that his talents would be properly recognized. He declined, saying that at over fifty he was already an old man. "At fifty a man should understand the decrees of Heaven," he quoted the *Analects* of Confucius. "I know now that I am only good to be a village teacher and that diplomas and public offices are beyond me." He continued until a ripe old age, teaching students and his own children. With his second wife he had three sons, the last one born when he was fifty-four. My grandfather said that he drove his students hard and his sons even harder. "Back in the sixteenth century, our ancestor Nguyen Uyen won the highest diploma, but since then and for many long generations our family has not been able to obtain much success at the examinations," he told his sons. "You owe it to the books from which you learn and the lamp by which you study to succeed," he said quoting an old saying. One can imagine his joy when his eldest son graduated. My grandfather wrote in the chronicle: "When the good news arrived, he [Dinh Dat] was already in his old years but still strong and lucid. He expressed great satisfaction that a son taught by him had finally paid the family's debt to lamp and books."

A few years later, he joined the ranks of "the few since antiquity" who reached the age of seventy, an occasion for great rejoicing and celebration. But Dinh Dat's unlucky star was still following him and even such an occasion was for him tinged with sadness. His youngest son, then sixteen, wanted to leave the country and flee to China "to work for the revolution," in other terms, to fight for the overthrow of the French protectorate. The young man's spirit made him proud and Dinh Dat gave him permission to go. But he knew that the life of a revolutionary was one of hardship and sacrifice. His son may never come back. At any rate, at his age, Dinh Dat would not live to see him again. Thus, the birthday celebration was also a farewell party, although this had to be kept hidden from the eyes of the secret police and for the other relatives and guests. The young man was just going to town to further his studies.

My father was born in 1907. Dinh Dat waited impatiently to see his first grandson, for the custom was for a daughter to leave her in-laws' place and go back to her own parents' to give birth to her first child. There she would stay for several months until the child was strong enough to travel. Many generations of our family had been obsessed with the fear of not having an heir. Both Dinh Dat's father and grandfather only had one son, at a late stage of their lives. Dinh Dat himself had thought at one time, after his first wife and son had died, that he would not leave a male descendant. But his second wife gave him three sons and now a grandson had come. At last, the grandchild was brought to him and the old man could hold him in his arms. With three generations living together under the same roof, the Taoist recluse appeared happy and reconciled with the world.

Like his father, Dinh Dat spent time and effort researching the family history. In his time, the missing piece in the puzzle was thought to be the Cu Hau papers. To his credit, the papers were found and although they did not contain anything about the early generations, they did show the large amount of land owned by our family up to at least four generations following that of academician Nguyen Uyen, who is now known as our second ancestor. How could an academician, remembered by his descendants as having reached only the position of inspector-delegate to a province, own as large an amount of land as that of an ennobled high mandarin? Nguyen Uyen served under the Mac dynasty which lost its throne to the forces fighting for the restoration of the Le, after a long civil war. But the Cu Hau papers made it clear that our family was able to retain most of its land after the change of dynasty. How did it manage to do so? These were questions to which Dinh Dat found no answer, but they would lead his descendants on to new and fruitful avenues for research. What Dinh Dat was able to do immediately was to restore the ties between the different branches of the Nguyen Dinh, then on the brink of disappearing as an extended family. He called a plenary meeting of all its members in 1862, which resulted in a decision to resume the yearly ceremony of worship at the Ancestral Shrine and to write a new family chronicle. In all this, Dinh Dat's role was one of leadership, although he belonged to the youngest branch of the Nguyen Dinh and was then only in his twenties.

Dinh Dat did not know that the brothers Nguyen Huyen and Nguyen Tue of the village legend, who graduated at the same doctorate session, were his own ancestors. Nor did he realize the link between the prophecy about the Mountain of the Twins and his family. Yet, he must have sensed something in his subconscious mind to take the mountain's name as his pseudonym and call himself Song Son Dat Dan, or The Hermit of the Mountain of the Twins. In doing so, he appropriated the village prophecy and it was a measure of the respect he enjoyed among the scholars of Kim Bai that they did not criticize his choice as being misplaced or pretentious. Indeed, he was known mostly by that name, either as a teacher or as a writer, in preference to his pen name of Hy Tu.

Dinh Dat died in 1909 when seventy-four, according to the traditional way of calculating his age. In actual fact he was born in 1836 and was thus only seventy-three. But our old custom gave an extra year to everyone. When I was young, I also heard elders saying that Dinh Dat died at the age of seventy-five, in deference to another custom which said that when a person was born, he received a year from Heaven and when he died, Mother Earth gave him another extra year. The number of years that a person accumulated was a good indication of the virtues and good fortune that his family was blessed with. Dinh Dat's father was a wealthy man; under his son, the family would again enjoy a prosperous living; but he remained throughout his life a poor scholar. My grandfather often regretted that he was not able to provide more fully for his father in his old years. As he wrote in the chronicle:

> His eldest son Ba Tiep won a bachelor degree, then a licentiate degree three years later, when Dinh Dat was already in his late sixties. After three more years of study at the School of Administration, his son was appointed as Educational Officer to a prefecture. Although a mandarinal position, it was a junior one. Salary and allowances were very small. In 1909, Dinh Dat joined our ancestors. After taking leave for a year to perform his duty towards his departed father, his son returned to his career. Gradually moving up the scale,

he attained the higher ranks of the mandarinate. Dinh Dat was posthumously awarded the lower fifth mandarinal rank, elevated to the lower fourth, then to the third, finally to the second rank. Four times, he was a recipient of favours bestowed by the Imperial Court. In the abode of the Spirits, he may have derived some glory and pride, but his son's wish to serve and care for him for one single more day will never be fulfilled.

The one-year leave on the death of one's parents was common administrative practice in those days. It was considered so essential in our Confucian culture that it took precedence over even the most important affairs of state. Even the highest mandarins laid down their seals of office during the period of mourning. Scholars in mourning were not allowed to sit for the examinations.

Dinh Dat was buried in a field owned by our family in an area called Lung Dinh, or Raised Platform. The land in that area was higher than the fields around it, only a few meters but enough to make it safe from floods. Geomancers could see there plenty of auspicious features where an ancestor's grave would be of benefit to his family. Here was a dragon, there a phoenix, they would point out. They could even see a rhinoceros watching the moon at one place and a group of immortals having a drink together at another, all special features to look for when choosing a place for burial. Later on, my grandfather converted the plot containing Dinh Dat's grave into a family tomb, intending it for use for his parents' and his own generation. The tomb was quite close to the Si Gate, just on the other side of the highway. It had a low brick wall painted in cream color and decorated in all its length with green pieces of ceramic carrying representations of flowers and auspicious Chinese characters such as Longevity and Good Fortune. Unlike other tombs, it had no garden. Dinh Dat's grave sat in the middle of a square patch of lawn. It was not in brick or stone, but only a mound of earth several times the size of an average grave and covered with a mat of green grass. There was no headstone over the grave, no altar or shrine next to it. Grandfather had wanted the family tomb to be very simply laid out. In fact, except for the patch of grass around the grave, the land inside the tomb continued to be cultivated with rice and other cereals, depending on the season. The only special feature in the tomb was pine trees, planted in rows along the four walls.

When we stayed in Kim Bai during the summer, our group of boys and girls in their early teens used to go out of the village and its barrier of bamboo to catch the evening breeze in the open countryside. We had the choice of either going up the dike on one side of the village and enjoying the sight of the Lichee Field over a backdrop of purple mountains, or going to the tomb on the other side. There, the scenery was one of flat land typical of the Red River delta. Rice fields extended as far as the eyes could see, interrupted only here and there by great clumps of bamboo which were villages.

There were very few trees besides the pine trees of the tomb. Only one or two solitary banyans could be found, which gave some shade to farmers working in the fields during the day. No houses could be seen, except for some tea huts strung along the highway. On days when a light wind was blowing, we liked to go to the tomb to listen to the song of pine trees. These belonged to a species called *phi lao,* with long and soft needles which swayed and sang at the faintest breeze. In our cultural tradition, a pine tree is the image of freedom from the shackles of time and of human worries. Popular folklore has this poem, which has inspired many a poet:

> In the next life may it please Heaven,
> Not to make me a human,
> But a pine tree standing tall in the sky
> And singing with the wind.

There was another reason for the planting of pine trees around our family tomb. Dinh Dat was a Taoist scholar dreaming to lead the life of a recluse in the mountain. Taoist mythology used a number of symbols, one of which was the pine tree. The great Chinese poet Li Po of the Tang period once described in a poem his visit to a Taoist sage up the mountain. There, he saw:

> Next to flowers blossoming in the warm air,
> Green buffaloes lay resting.
> High on the pine trees,
> White cranes were sleeping.

That was a classical Taoist scene. While buffaloes were plentiful in our region, the only bird remotely close to the crane, by its color, was the white egret which sometimes could be seen perched on our pine trees.

There used to be no pine trees around our family tomb. During one of his terms of office, my grandfather had a beach bungalow amidst a forest of pine in Dong Chau, not far from the mouth of the Red River. He liked their shape and sound and, in memory of his father's Taoist aspirations, had seedlings planted in the family tomb. They took roots well and in a few years had grown into tall and beautiful trees.

Dinh Dat's second wife, my great-grandmother, survived him for forty years. She came from the Chu, a family of middle landowners in Kim Bai. They played a leading part in village affairs, with several of their members becoming mayors or holding positions of responsibility in the village council. But I do not think that they ever had any graduate at the civil service examinations and, therefore, could not be regarded as a family of scholars. My great-grandmother was much younger than her husband. She married an impoverished scholar, a widower down on his luck who, at over forty, did not have much time left to realize his aspirations of academic title and mandarinal position. The beginning of her married life could hardly be called auspicious and indeed for her, it was work at the weaving looms at night and selling at the market in the day to supplement her husband's meager income and bring up four children, three sons of her own and a daughter from her husband's previous marriage. But she was from Kim Bai, a village known for the resourcefulness of its women and so, besides raising silkworms and working on the weaving looms, she also made paddy into rice, prepared cakes to sell at markets and engaged in the petty trade of haberdashery. In the tradition of Vietnamese women, she accepted her fate and worked without complaining, often by herself as her husband travelled from place to place to teach. She continued in that manner until her eldest son graduated and obtained his first official appointment. Only then could she afford to slow down, as financial conditions in the family improved. The improvement, however, was gradual, for her son's career took a very long time to take off. From my grandfather's own account, it was only much later that he felt he could provide for his mother in the way he wanted. She was then past seventy.

In the last part of her life, great-grandmother presided over a pros-perous family, with a large number of grandchildren and great-grandchildren. From the Imperial court, she received the award *Tiet Hanh Kha Phong,* which was given to widows who stayed single and devoted themselves to their families and whose sons became distinguished servants of the state. The words of the award meant that her devotion and good con-duct deserved to be recognized by the court. Four times, her husband and herself were recipients of honorary mandarinal ranks, but while for her hus-band they were bestowed posthumously, she was there in person to receive the imperial honors, in special ceremonies taking place in our ancestral home in Kim Bai. My mother attended all these ceremonies. She said that strict rules of protocol were to be observed in the presence of the Imperial Messenger and because great-grandmother was already in her seventies, it was feared that she might forget what she was expected to do. My mother's role was to stay next to her and remind her when to kneel down, how many times to bow, when to get up, and so on. However, great-grandmother was still blessed with a very good memory and not once, my mother said, did she need her help. It was the old lady who told her many of the stories of past generations, in particular those relating to Dinh Dat and his father Quang So. My recollection of great-grandmother was of a frail old lady, hard of hearing and with failing eyesight, but still able to go about by herself within our family compound. She was then too old to tell long stories, although from time to time she would call one of us youngsters to come by her side and pluck some of the curly hairs that made her head itch, while she recounted some happenings in our childhood. To me, she said: "When you were born, your great-uncle had a look at you and exclaimed: 'He will not be as bright as his elder brother, because he does not have the same high forehead!' Yet you did not do too badly at school, did you?" She smiled and continued: "You are lucky to be alive. You were so weak and so often sick in your first years that I thought you would not be able to make it."

In 1937, my grandfather was appointed governor of Thai Binh, a large province in the delta on the mouth of the Red River. Thai Binh was grandfather's last appointment before retirement. After he had assumed office, a day was set for the new governor to welcome his mother to his province. Under the old mandarinate system, parents of a high official were greeted with great pomp on their first visit. After all, his achievement was attributed as much to their "virtues and merits" as to his own talents. That morning, we started from Kim Bai. With great-grandmother were grandmother, her youngest son and myself. All generations of our family were thus represented to accompany great-grandmother on that occasion. My uncle and I were both seven at the time. We were driven in a brand new blue Peugeot 402, a French car which had come only recently to the local market. The large car could just get through under the Si Gate of the village. The four of us had plenty of room on the back seat. On the front seat were the driver, an aide to help him in case of tire puncture on the way and a servant to look after our food and drink. Thai Binh was about a hundred kilometers away, through entirely flat country. On the two sides of the road was a continuous carpet of green rice fields. We were in the middle of the Red River delta, the granary of the north. Great-grandmother was in high spirits and kept leaning forward to look through the car window, although she was told that she might feel sick if she did not sit back. We crossed many groups of peasants going to the market and each time, she tried to see what the women were carrying in their baskets to sell. Perhaps they reminded her of herself many years before. The wife of an impoverished scholar, she worked like them then. Now as the mother of a governor, she was on her way to visit his province.

The car made its way slowly for the day was hot and great-grandmother soon felt tired. Often we had to stop, switch off the engine and open wide all the doors so that the smell of petrol would not disturb her. We passed the town of Ha Nam where grandfather was governor three years before, then Nam Dinh, the third largest town in the north. There, we had another stop for rest and refreshment. Nam Dinh was next to Thai Binh and soon after, we arrived at the river which formed the boundary between the two provinces. A ferry boat was waiting for us at a crossing place called Tan De. The car drove down onto the ferry, which was just large enough to hold one car. Two men using long bamboo poles pushed the ferry slowly across the wide river. On the other bank, we saw a crowd of people and soldiers waiting. Right next to the ferry dock was the seat of the prefecture of Thu Tri and its prefect was the first official to greet great-grandmother on Thai Binh soil. It happened that the prefect was married to a great-niece of great-grandmother. He was Duong Cu Tam, the poet at our New Year party in Kim Bai. Combining official and family duties, he led us into his residence where we had lunch followed by a long siesta. It was mid-afternoon when we left Thu Tri. The township of Thai Binh was only some fifteen kilometers away, but before reaching it we crossed the territory of another prefecture. There again, the local mandarin was waiting to present to great-grandmother his respects and to invite us in for tea. At last, we arrived in Thai Binh as the sun had just set. Instead of a bright heat, the town with its cream-colored houses was bathed in a soft and pinkish light. One could already sense the faint cool breeze of the evening. It was the most prized moment of a summer day, made more precious because it was so short. In no time, darkness would fall. The car entered the gate of the governor's mansion guarded by soldiers who presented arms. It followed a driveway between flowered gardens and stopped at the foot of the stairs leading to the governor's office. My grandfather, in a black gauze dress, and all the town mandarins were standing there waiting to greet great-grandmother. One could easily imagine her feelings as she stepped out of the car to greet her son.

In our Confucian culture, a woman's role was to help her husband and sons gain success and honors in society, while she herself remained within the circle of home and family. Their achievements were her rewards. As a wife and mother, the only social recognition she could expect to receive was that which flowed from the men's achievements. Great-grandmother bore a son who graduated at the examinations, his career brought him to high positions. Now, he was welcoming her into his governor's mansion at the head of the town's dignitaries. What a shining moment in her life this must have been.

Among the few old photographs still in our family's keeping is one taken in Kim Bai in 1936, probably when great-grandmother was awarded one of her honorary mandarinal ranks. She was seated in a carved wooden armchair, under the porch of our altar house. Her turban, tunic, trousers and shoes were all black. But her face was brightened by the hair which came out from under the turban onto her forehead and shone like snow. On her right side stood my grandfather in a dark brocade dress, the color of which did not show in the black and white photograph but which must have been blue. On her left side stood my father in a similar dress of a lighter shade. In front of my father was my elder brother, then aged nine. He was dressed in an European sailor suit which was then quite fashionable for children to wear. The photograph showed "four generations under the same roof," a traditional symbol of familial happiness. Not many families could claim such happiness. Certainly in the past, our own had seldom been blessed with it. Many generations were composed only of father and son. Some, like that

"Four generations under one roof" — *(left to right)* my grandfather, great-grandmother, father and elder brother (circa 1936).

of Dinh Dat, had three generations living together, but elders could not
quite recall when was the last time that a branch of the Nguyen Dinh had
reached the threshold of four generations. Yet, that was not the ultimate.
Exceptionally, some families could boast of "five generations under one
roof" and the New Year wishes that our family received all contained that
consecrated formula. In an era of peace and social stability, that may well
have been within our reach, for great-grandmother lived until 1949, when
my elder brother was twenty-two.

But while Heaven was kind to great-grandmother in her old age, the
last chapter of her life was one of sorrow and suffering. All her three sons
died before her. The youngest left the country while an adolescent to
engage in activities aimed at overthrowing the French colonial regime. The
last news he sent home was more than forty years before. In 1947 her second
son died, a few weeks after the Tet. Then, in the eighth lunar month, as
the monsoon ended and the year went into autumn, it was the turn of her
eldest son, my grandfather. That morning, we all knew that the end was
near. Grandfather was lying in the room next to the ancestors' altar, in the
house which he built twenty years ago. The entire family was there, except

for my father and elder brother who were captured by French troops and taken away many months before. The time had come to perform our last act of obeisance to our patriarch. In turn, each of us went into the room, knelt down and touched the soil with our forehead twice. Grandfather was lying in his bed, accepting our expression of gratitude without any reaction, seemingly unconscious. But when we had finished, he motioned us to make him sit up and put pillows behind his back. He called for his black tunic and turban and had them put on. Then, he begged his mother to come in, so that he could show obeisance to her and at the same time ask her for forgiveness. He would not be able to survive her and perform the last rites for her; therefore, as a son, he had failed in his filial duty. His remaining strength did not allow him to kneel, so he could only sit and bow, his hands joined together in front of his forehead. He bowed not twice, as called for by custom, but many times. His face had already taken on the color of death, but his eyes were still alive and they were the picture of suffering. Great-grandmother sat on the edge of the bed; one wondered to what extent her withered old heart could still suffer. She did not cry, only repeated in a low voice: "Governor, you do not have to do that." She always addressed him and referred to him as governor. She never used the term son, or called him by his name. It was the same with my great-uncle whom she called "Mr. Two," after his rank in the family.

In the same year, her two remaining sons had died. A few months later she fell, broke a leg and became paralyzed. My grandmother had to feed and care for her daily. As attacks by French troops grew more frequent, the rest of the family had to leave the village. Only one or two faithful servants stayed back. Each time the French approached, a servant had to carry great-grandmother on his back and flee down to the Lichee Field, returning home only after the danger had passed. The last year of her life was a wretched period. She was in pain and no medicine was available. When death came, it was a merciful deliverance. Only grandmother was at her side. What a difference from the prosperity and the "multitude of descendants" that she had known! We Vietnamese believe in reincarnation and in the law of causality. People like her are thought to carry a "heavy karma." In preceding lives, she must have tried hard to lighten her load and, as a result of good deeds performed and of virtues gathered, she was able in this life to enjoy good fortune and happiness. She had been given much. The wife of a poor and untitled scholar, she became the mother of a high mandarin and presided over a family of four generations. But her karma was still "heavy with debts" so that, at the end of her life, she still had to suffer. One cannot avoid one's karma. Every action, whether good or bad, will bring its results just as a tree will always produce its fruit and a fruit will always carry its seed. The results will appear, if not in this life, then in the following lives. Causality is an iron law. That is why the teachings of Lord

Buddha are that we should endeavor to lead a virtuous life and perform good deeds. We should not worry as to what will happen to us, for it will inevitably happen. As expressed in the ending verses of the *Story of Kieu*:

> Our karma is linked with ourselves
> So, let us not complain that Heaven
> Is too close or too far from us.
> Instead, let us tend the roots of goodness
> That lie within our heart.

21. The Governor

I spent most of my childhood living with my grandparents. I followed my grandfather in all his appointments to different provinces, while my own family stayed in Hanoi where my father worked. When I joined my parents, brothers and sisters, it was like a special holiday which was always too short. Not that I was unhappy living with my grandparents, but I missed my close family and the special warmth it provided. Of all my siblings I was the only one to grow up in this way, away from home. The reason for it was that my uncle and I were of the same age and it was thought that it would be good for the two of us to stay together and go to the same school. Also, I was a weak and delicate child. Small provincial towns where my grandparents stayed in mansions with large gardens were better for my health than the small house in which my parents lived, in one of the busiest areas of Hanoi.

My grandfather was born in 1879 and died in 1947, aged sixty-eight. His name was Nguyen Ba Tiep. *Tiep* means quick in the sense of quick-witted. *Ba* means elder and is often used as a middle name for the eldest son. His pseudonym was Kim Dam, or Golden Pond. The word *Kim*—golden—indicates the association with our village Kim Bai. Scholars cherished the image of a pond. My maternal grandfather also took it for his pseudonym, although he used *Tri*, another word for pond. His name was Dong Tri, or Eastern Pond. All three doctrines of Confucianism, Taoism and Buddhism made the pond, or lake, the symbol of quietness and reflection. As its tranquil surface unruffled by waves reflected the sky, so too would a mind, free of subjective thoughts and clear as a mirror, become one with nature and the universe. Some scholars went for *Ho,* or lake, as a pseudonym. Other more modestly opted for the pond.

Grandfather died when I was seventeen. He was of stern and undemonstrative character. That was the image I have kept of him, although my mother said that in his younger days, he was quite different: jovial, playful and with a keen sense of humor. He was very close to his children, she said, often making them laugh with his jokes. But I only knew him as a grandfather, old and aloof. I spent a lot of time with him and it was said that he considered me his favorite grandchild. He taught me the scholarly script; I read aloud books and newspapers to him. Sometimes, when he was interrupted in a game of *to tom* cards, he called me to temporarily take his place, an honor and a show of confidence in my young talents. I was a teenager sharing a game with elders, some as old as grandfather himself! But still, I felt respect and awe for him more than love. Maybe I was too shy to come nearer to him. Maybe in our traditional culture, a gap of two generations was too large to bridge. In the end, he remained to me a distant figure. An episode when I was twelve or thirteen stayed vivid in my mind. It happened in Kim Bai during the summer. After lunch was taken, my uncle prepared to leave for Ha Dong on his bicycle. The sun was beating down mercilessly. I had a white "colonial" hat, made of cork and cloth which offered good protection against the heat but was a bit old-fashioned. Young people did not like to wear it. Indeed, the trend among us was not to wear any hat, going bare-headed in the full heat of a summer day was the "in" thing. Grandfather told me to let my uncle use the hat, which I was quite willing to do. But my uncle did not want it. Our solution was for him to leave the house wearing the hat and me to accompany him to the village gate, then take the hat home. To my bad luck, by the time I returned, grandfather had already had his siesta and was sitting in the altar house drinking tea. The white hat was bulky and could not be hidden away. He went into a furor and scolded me for being selfish and not wanting to lend the hat. I protested but he would not listen. Grandmother was sitting opposite him, but while normally she would try to calm things down, that time she did not say anything, perhaps because she saw that grandfather was really worked up. That made me feel forsaken. Later that afternoon, I was reading in my room when grandfather came in. He wandered around the room, wanted to know what I was reading and talked to me about this and that. I can still see me sitting at my desk and him standing beside me in his cream silk casual clothes. In his hand was a large paper fan. In summer, each of us had such a fan, made of brown paper, to help fight the heat and chase flies and mosquitoes away. Ours was plain, but his was beautifully decorated with cuttings of flowers and birds. He was ostensibly fanning himself, but in fact doing it for me. After a while, he left the room. The matter of the hat was not touched upon, although I knew that it was his way of making up.

My grandmother came from the Dang Tran family of the village of Phu Dong. She was born in 1885 and died in 1965, at the age of eighty. Phu Dong was the land of the Heavenly Prince of ancient legend and the hallowed site of many Buddhist temples. It was a much larger village than Kim Bai, being composed of as many as ten hamlets. The Dang Tran was the largest extended family in Phu Dong and belonged to the Western Hamlet. Grandmother was the daughter of a scholar who came first in the test held in his province to select candidates for the regional examinations, but did not get any diploma. Her family was known more for its wealth than for academic success. I was very close to grandmother. To me, she was like a second mother. I took leave of her in 1950 to go to France for my university studies. When the country was partitioned four years later, she stayed back in North Vietnam while my parents went to live in the south. She died in the north.

Grandmother was very fussy about my health. I remember that even up to the age of ten, if I had a cold or some other illness, she would move me to sleep in her bed in order to keep an eye on me. In the family, I belonged to the same age group as my uncle and elder brother. As the eldest grandson and heir to his generation, my brother's position was unique. My uncle was my grandparents' youngest son and he was, of course, higher in rank compared to me. In everything, it was they who went first. Once, when about twelve, I complained of being treated as *nua ong nua thang,* or half as a sir, half as a nobody. This was reported to my grandfather. He pondered for a while then nodded his head in approval, saying: "He had a point there." Knowing this trait of mine, grandmother always paid a special attention to me. She often said how proud she was that I was such a good student: "You are following on your grandfather's footsteps," she told me in encouragement. Like the women of her time, she never went to school. She could only read some scholarly characters and knew a little of the new alphabet, but had a quite positive attitude towards change and progress. She was never afraid to look ahead. When I went to France, she was very happy that her grandson had an opportunity to study higher and widen his experience. The only counsel she gave me was: "Family and lineage are matters of fundamental importance. When you go abroad, there is no preventing you from enjoying life. But remember that for the family's sake, I wish that your wife be Vietnamese." At dawn that day, as I said farewell to her at Hanoi's Gia Lam airport, I wondered whether I would see her again when coming back to the country. She, however, was full of joy and optimism, exclaiming: "A young man should spread his wings!"

My grandfather Ba Tiep was born into a family of scholars. As in previous generations, all hopes were placed on the sons to study well and obtain academic titles. He and his younger brothers learned under a man renowned in the region as a fine teacher and a stern master, their own father. Theirs was not a childhood full of fun and play. After the other pupils had left at the end of the afternoon, the brothers were urged to go on studying late into the night. Without a proper lamp since the family was poor, they had to make do with a saucer filled with oil in which was dipped a wick providing a flickering flame. In winter, they had no warm clothing and, as grandfather sometimes told us, he had difficulty in keeping his writing brush still, so shaky was his hand from the cold. From a young age, Ba Tiep showed signs of intelligence and promise. Kim Bai, being a land of graduates, had developed a tradition of encouraging and supporting its

My grandfather Nguyen Ba Tiep in formal dress of blue brocade with white trousers and black turban. On the right side of his chest, a plaque showed his mandarinal rank. *(Right)* My grandmother Dang Thi Duyet formally dressed in black tunic, trousers and turban (circa 1942).

bright prospects. An association of scholars gave them financial help. People promoted their talents. Stories were circulated about their "accomplished writings and fine calligraphy." After some time, a sort of lore was created around a promising student who found himself carrying the hopes of a whole community. Such was the case for young Ba Tiep. Village folks liked hearing his voice reading aloud from classical books or chanting poems in the night. Such a full and rich voice heralded a bright future, they said. Older graduates posed difficult riddles to test his knowledge of the classics. They challenged him to compose poems on rhymes set by them. His responses showed the depth of his learning as well as his strength of character. At seventeen, he had already made a reputation for himself and was invited to tutor in neighboring villages. One day as he returned from a tutoring session in our prefecture of Thanh Oai, he found an old scholar barring him the entrance of the Si Gate. The scholar said some verses to which he must reply on the spot with verses of his own. His must balance the scholar's verses, both in meaning and in rhyme. If the scholar was happy about his reply, he would let him in; if not, the young tutor would have to enter his village by another gate and his reputation would suffer. Here are the scholar's verses:

> Young man, you came back from tutoring at the prefecture.
> Pray, tell me, the offices, the mandarin's mansion, the town's landscape,
> How do they look like now?

The old man was playing himself down and pretending that he was a simple villager, who had not even ventured in recent times up to the prefecture located just a few kilometers from Kim Bai. In fact, in his younger days, he had gone to Hue, the capital, to sit for the doctorate examination in the royal courtyard. This is the tutor's reply:

> Honourable sir, you went to the imperial capital for the examinations.
> Please talk to us about the palaces, the king's courtyard, the capital's marvels,
> How beautiful they must be!

The scholar was pleased with the reply. He told grandfather: "Young man, one day you will be at the top of the village hierarchy."

In 1900, when he was twenty-one, Ba Tiep sat for the regional competition, called the *Huong* examinations, in Hanoi and obtained the degree of bachelor. At the next session in 1903, he became a licentiate. The *Huong* examinations had a total of four subjects, including interpretation of the classics, dissertation on public policy and test on literary knowledge. The last subject was a supplementary test on all the above three subjects. A candidate who successfully passed the first three subjects became a bachelor. He was made a licentiate if he passed all four subjects. Bright students could obtain the latter diploma on their first try. Grandfather did not. His progress was gradual, first the baccalaureate, then the licence. Like many others in our family, he did not have the gift of moving fast and leaping over intermediary stages. After his first success, his old father called him in. He was pleased, but what counted in the *Huong* examinations was the four-subject degree of licence. Only that higher degree opened the door to the mandarinate. Moreover, without it one could not go on to try for a doctorate degree. "I have taught you all that I know," he told his son. "You will have to go to another teacher." He sent him not to Hanoi, the cultural center of the north and so close to our village, but a hundred kilometers farther away to the town of Nam Dinh. There, grandfather studied under a widely respected scholar known as the Headmaster of Son Nong. Students of the Headmaster had gained many an academic honor. Grandfather stayed in his school for two years and made many friendships that would remain with him for life. One of his friends of that period was to become my maternal grandfather.

In a book published in France in 1981 and entitled *Quand les Français Découvraient L'Indochine* (*When the French Discovered Indochina*), one can see a series of photographs taken at the *Huong* examinations in Nam Dinh in 1897. The scene at the examination in Hanoi where grandfather participated three years later would not be different. Under the eyes of officials perched in a high watchtower, candidates were seen going to their appointed places in the examination camp, which was a vast expanse of flat terrain, where they would set up their small tents. They were dressed in long black tunics and white trousers, with a turban on their heads, black for most and white for those who were in mourning. Some had shoes, others went barefooted. Most looked in their late twenties or thirties. At twenty-one, grandfather would be on the youngish side of such a crowd. The next photographs showed the ceremony of "calling out the names" of successful candidates. Examiners dominated the crowd from their high chairs shaded by parasols. The names were called out by soldiers holding long loudspeakers looking like trumpets. Parents, friends and well-wishers were in their thousands; in such a crowd, the mayor of Kim Bai really made a spectacle of himself when he dropped his trousers jumping for joy as he heard grandfather's name. The series of pictures continued with one showing the new graduates kneeling before the Temple of Literature dedicated to the memory of Confucius. They were now dressed in formal attire provided by the authorities and consisting of a wide-sleeved tunic made of light blue gauze, white trousers and large black boots. On their heads was the traditional scholar's black hat. Next, the graduates were seen kneeling again, this time in the courtyard of the governor's mansion, before the governor and other representatives of the emperor. Then came the banquet given by the governor, where the graduates sat on wooden platforms, four men to each tray of food. They all looked serious and rather self-conscious, perhaps not able yet to make the transition from simple scholars to being part of the nation's elite. Finally, they were seen on their way home, each followed by an aide carrying a parasol, their new symbol of authority.

Grandfather received excellent marks at the *Huong* examinations and he confidently looked forward to sitting for a doctorate in the following year. The doctorate, or *Hoi*, examinations were held triennially in the imperial capital Hue. All licentiates, as well as those bachelors who had graduated with very high marks, were allowed to take part. The new licentiate Ba Tiep made the long trip to Hue, close to one thousand kilometers away from our village. The world had changed and the country had lost its independence. It was believed that soon the protectorate would establish a new education system and the old examinations would be done away with; yet scholars still pursued their dream of winning the highest possible academic prize. Centuries of tradition were behind them. Whatever the future may hold, they knew that nothing could be taken away from their success. Their fame would spread to the whole country. Their names would be carved in stone and placed in the hallowed grounds of the Temple of Literature where they would stay for all time, alongside the names of doctors of past generations. Ba Tiep spent several months in Hue in preparation for the examination. But he failed to emulate his forebears of four centuries ago. He did not try again. Only a few more sessions would follow his, before all examinations based on the scholarly script were abandoned in the 1910s.

The time had now come for Ba Tiep to choose a career. He enrolled in the School of Administration to train for the mandarinate. For a graduated scholar to become a mandarin was a most natural progress, but those were special times and our licentiate only made up his mind after a great deal of soul-searching. The scholars' class, in its great majority, remained opposed to the protectorate. In 1885, when Emperor Ham Nghi called upon the population to join the resistance, patriots from all parts of the country rallied to him. Ba Tiep was then a child. He saw his elders put aside their writing brushes to take up arms against the French. The scholars fought bravely but their scattered and ill-organized groups were no match for the troops of the protectorate. After the emperor was defeated and sent into exile, other armed movements appeared to fight in his name. Some were led by scholars, others received their support. All, however, proved short-lived. Ba Tiep grew up and did his schooling in an atmosphere where discouragement following the crushing of a revolt in one region would soon be replaced by hope coming with a new revolt flaring up in another. The most important one was that launched by Phan Dinh Phung in the mountains of Ha Tinh, in the center of the country. Phan Dinh Phung was a former mandarin and renowned scholar. He came first in a doctorate session back in the times of emperor Tu Duc when Vietnam was still free. He started his movement in 1888, when already close to sixty. Unlike other scholars who thought they could turn overnight into military leaders, Phan Dinh Phung retired to the mountains to patiently prepare his campaign. He sent people to China and Siam to learn the manufacturing of guns and ammunition. He took time to train his troops in the manner of a modern army. These were armed with rifles copied from the French infantry rifle and made in factories installed in the mountains. In 1893, Phan Dinh Phung hoisted the banner of insurrection. He fought for two years, but failed. He died even before his movement collapsed.

The end of Phan Dinh Phung marked a watershed in the history of opposition to French rule. Although there would be other movements to continue on the path of armed struggle, more and more people had come to realize the futility of using force to overthrow the protectorate. The end of the nineteenth century was a time of reappraisal. When Ba Tiep had reached the age to sit for the examinations, radical elements among the scholars still refused to have anything to do with them, but they had been reduced to a minority. Examinations were the very *raison d'être* of a scholar and it was pointed out that they were run by mandarins appointed by the emperor, not by the French. In any case, what did those French "devils" know about the scholarly script and our culture to intervene? Once again, candidates flocked to the triennial sessions. For Ba Tiep, the advice given him by his father was clear: "Whatever you want to do later, you have to gain public recognition first," said the old man, who had not been able to have any public role in his life, being a plain untitled scholar. "That recognition will come from you gaining diplomas."

After they graduated, the scholars had to decide whether to join the public service—and be seen as collaborating with the protectorate—or to mark their opposition by staying away. Ba Tiep and his friends were divided. As armed struggle had failed, they all believed that the "national spirit" and "inner strength" of the country must be built up before one could talk of doing away with the French. In particular, educational standards must be raised and the people must be made more aware of their responsibilities and the choices facing the nation. Within the group, however, some chose to stay in their private capacity and serve the community as teachers and educators. Licentiate Duong, one of Ba Tiep's closest friends, was a leading advocate of that view. Others, including Ba Tiep, opted for the mandarinate. In spite of the special circumstances created by the protectorate, they still considered that the primary duty of scholars was to serve the people. Their position rested on the teachings of Mencius according to which the people should come first, even before the king. Besides, if all scholars refused to come out, the court would have to rely on people without learning and qualifications or worse still, the French would have a pretext to impose a regime of direct administration. In becoming mandarins, however, they made clear that they were servants of the emperor, not of the French. It has to be added here that although hostility against French rule continued to run strong, the new generation of scholars had acquired a different perception of France than their elders. Ba Tiep and his contemporaries had read about the French Revolution and come across the works of authors such as Montesquieu and Rousseau, not in their original versions but through translations made by the Chinese. They had discovered another face of France, besides that of a hated colonial power. Their contact with French philosophy and literature was new and superficial—the influence of Western ideas would be fully apparent only in the next generation—but that was enough for them to see that there were also "scholars" among

Frenchmen, with whom they could engage in a dialogue and, maybe even talk about political reforms. Thus, Ba Tiep started his training for a mandarinal career. In doing so, he still stayed very close to those of his friends who took the other path. That was perhaps one reason why his career was never a smooth and easy one.

Ba Tiep married early, for the first time when only a student. Of his first wife, little is known. My mother said she heard that she was a kind and gentle person; however, the marriage fell apart after a few years because the couple had no children. One day, a dispute arose about the loss of some valuables, the result of which was that she was disowned by her husband's family and left. After grandfather obtained his degrees, numerous friends and acquaintances were willing to act as matchmaker for him. One of them was Licentiate Duong. He told grandfather that he had in mind a young lady from the village of Phu Dong. "Her family is one of the wealthiest of the region," he said, adding: "She came from the Dang family who, several generations ago, produced a lady who held the fate of the house of Trinh in the palm of her hand." He was referring to Dang Thi Hue, the consort of Overlord Trinh Sam who ruled from 1767 to 1782. But what grandfather wanted to know was how old the lady was and how beautiful she looked. "She is twenty and in praise of her beauty, I can only say that it is easy for people to mistake her for Heaven's younger sister," replied Licentiate Duong, who was a poet. Grandfather was impressed. He looked for an opportunity to meet her and found it at the festival which each year celebrated the Heavenly Prince's victory. Among the crowd, he saw her and had a glimpse or two of her face under the conical hat which she pulled down low over her head, aware that a pretender was following her.

The Dang family was willing to give their daughter in marriage since the bridegroom-to-be stood as a good scholar with a bright future, although it was pointed out that he "was not good-looking." When grandmother told me that, I objected. I always found grandfather elegant and handsome, particularly in his old age with silvery white hair and a long beard flowing down to his chest. One morning, the family was shocked to see him coming out of the bathroom with the beard shaved off. Only the moustache was left. He did not tell anyone in advance. We later found out that at a dinner party some days before, some ladies convinced him that he would look younger without the beard. Grandmother never minded telling people that her husband was "skinny and not good-looking" when young. I myself was very skinny and angular as a child and she used to console me, saying that "even your grandfather could find a beautiful wife; what matters is to be a successful scholar." Often, she repeated for me in a modulated voice this proverb: "In your books, you will find a girl with pearl-like beauty." Once the Dang had agreed to the union, a problem remained to be solved. Social custom called for the bride's family to "challenge" the groom's for the provision of wedding presents. These must be shown to all relatives and guests at the wedding to prove that the bride was married into a family of comparable wealth and social standing. But our family was in no position to supply the required presents. After much toing and froing, a secret understanding was arrived at. In the red round lacquer boxes used to carry the wedding presents, only the top layer would consist of expensive items. It was up to the groom's family to put whatever things it liked underneath to make up for space and weight.

On the wedding day, the groom's party came with a dozen servants carrying the red lacquer boxes on their heads. The boxes were opened and showed around. All the guests were impressed with the brocade, silk, tafetta and personal jewelry displayed. Quickly, the bride's family asked servants to put the boxes away as the ceremony must proceed and the bride must leave her home at the time designated by astrologers. No one saw the stratagem and everything went right. But after that, our family enjoyed a rather flattering reputation of being very wealthy, when in fact it was not.

The wedding took place in 1905, when grandfather was a student at the School of Administration. His family life had now settled and his career path was also clearly drawn. The same year, my great-grandfather celebrated his seventieth birthday. Things appeared to be going well, but in the same year his younger brother had left home and a crisis was impending.

Grandfather's two younger brothers were brought up like him as scholars. However, they did less well in their studies. Both were active in subversive activities against the French occupants, in particular the youngest whose name was Nguyen Tam Tiep. *Tiep,* written like his brother's name but carrying a different tone, means "to continue." *Tam* means third, thus *Tam Tiep* was the third son who continued the line. Tam Tiep joined at a very young age secret organizations in which former students of his father were involved. After Phan Dinh Phung's movement was crushed in 1895, other armed rebellions which broke out in the Red River delta suffered the same fate. Only in the northern mountains could the revolt led by Hoang Hoa Tham continue to hold out against the French. Many revolutionaries fled to China to fight another day. Secret organizations sent young people out of the country to join them. In 1903, scholars under the leadership of Phan Boi Chau formed the Movement of the Restoration of Vietnam, with at its head Cuong De, Marquess of Ky Ngoai, a member of the royal family. The movement planned to recover independence by mobilizing the population into a vast national movement. It sent emissaries to all parts of the country to enlist patriots.

Meanwhile, events in Asia forged ahead. Russia was defeated by Japan in Manchuria. In the naval battle of the Tsuchima Straits, the Russian fleet was decimated. For the first time in contemporary history, an Asian country emerged victorious against a European power. The news resounded all over the continent. To our revolutionaries, it brought a lesson: they must follow Japan's lead and get help from that country. In a book relating his revolutionary life, Cuong De was reported to have said:

> The news (of the Japanese victory) came to warm the heart of so many Vietnamese. We believed that if we asked Japan for help, it would be readily given, for the Japanese and the Vietnamese share the same culture and are both Asian.

In 1905, Phan Boi Chau escaped from Vietnam. He went to China and Japan to solicit aid. Soon, Cuong De was to join him there. That was the situation when my great-uncle Tam Tiep decided to leave home. The appendix to the chronicle written by my father stated that he "went abroad when sixteen years of age." It did not specify the year when Tam Tiep left, but as he was born in 1889 and by my father's generation, the custom of giving everyone an extra year had been dropped, that year should have been 1905. He made the escape along with Nguyen Hai Than, who later became the leader of the Quoc Dan Dang, or Nationalist Party, and was Ho Chi Minh's opponent in a bitter struggle for power in 1945. Nguyen Hai Than, a scholar holding a bachelor degree, was about ten years older than Tam Tiep. They were among the very early self-exiles and Tam Tiep at sixteen was probably the youngest of them. Historical documents confirmed that Nguyen Hai Than left the country at that date. When Phan Boi Chau was in Japan in 1905, he wrote a propaganda booklet entitled "Encouraging the Young to Study Abroad" and wanted to send it to Vietnam to be distributed. Author Phan Khoang, in his book *History of Vietnam under French Domination 1884–1945*, wrote: "Nguyen Hai Than, then newly arrived in Japan, volunteered to finance the cost of disseminating that document." Whether Tam Tiep also went to Japan with him was not known. It was also not clear whether the two belonged to Phan Boi Chau's movement or to some other revolutionary group.

Tam Tiep left well before the "Go East" movement of Vietnamese students to Japan, which was started by Phan Boi Chau some years later. His departure was a severe blow to the family, firstly because he was so young. At sixteen, he looked a mere boy. Secondly, although he was one of three brothers, our family had been through so many generations with only one heir that it was still obsessed with the fear of losing the lineage. At the time, my grandfather had just remarried—his first marriage was childless—and the second brother was still single. But many of Dinh Dat's students were in China and their presence there was an assurance for the old man that his son would be well looked after. Also, it was still rather easy then for revolutionaries to make return trips as French security forces were not yet able to impose a strict control over the comings and goings of the population. Thus, Tam Tiep was not going into the completely unknown, with no promise of return. Yet, risks and dangers were evident in such an enterprise. It was a hard decision to make for his parents. Our scholarly tradition, however, was based on the notion of service and service to the country was of paramount importance. There was no question of them denying Tam Tiep the opportunity to respond to the call of the fatherland.

Things went right for a time. "Tam Tiep was able to send news home at the beginning," wrote my father in the chronicle, "but security control became tighter and tighter. After a while, the news ceased to arrive." In fact, Dinh Dat's former students brought home not only news, but also letters and even photographs of young Tam Tiep taken in China. They could visit their teacher without creating suspicion. Security services were not even aware of Tam Tiep's absence. To everyone else in the village, he was pursuing his studies in town. Nguyen Hai Than, who left with Tam Tiep, actually returned to the country and involved himself in political agitation for several years before leaving again for China. Then, one of the messengers was caught. Under torture, he disclosed everything about Tam Tiep. Officials and soldiers descended on our house in Kim Bai. Fortunately, warning was received just in time for all of Tam Tiep's letters to be burned. But his mother could not part with the photographs, so they were hidden over the beams of the roof, in between the latania leaves. My grandfather was then in Nam Dinh at the School of Administration, but his second brother was home. He fled. Dinh Dat and his wife remained to bear the wrath of officials and to see the soldiery put their house upside down searching for evidence that would incriminate the family. Nothing was found. Their line of defense was that Tam Tiep was not a good student and he had left home to look for work. Since then, he had not been in touch. The search party was preparing to leave when someone said that the roof had not been looked into. Dinh Dat's wife looked at him in horror. But it was not easy to find something under a roof made of latania leaves, unless it was taken down. The officials were not prepared to do this. Dinh Dat was a retired teacher and widely respected. So, they just did a perfunctory search of the roof and left.

The above happened sometime in 1906. Grandfather was preparing for his examinations to get into the mandarinate. The security services interviewed him in Nam Dinh. He and his second brother were considered to be mainly responsible for Tam Tiep's subversive activities, for their father was then an old man in his seventies. But grandfather was not arrested. A licentiate soon to become a mandarin, he was already a personality among northern scholars. The French thought it unwise to arrest him and create a stir in public opinion. So he was allowed to sit for the examinations. But the crisis must have affected his performance, or it could have been the long arm of the secret service, for he came out of the School of Administration at a very low rank. While many of his friends were immediately appointed to lead a prefecture, he was sent to a small prefecture to work as *Huan Dao,* or Education Officer. For the next ten years, he would languish in a teaching position.

The second brother Nguyen Thuc Phan was hunted by the regime. He managed to elude the police dragnet for several months before being caught. But no evidence could be produced against him. He was released, then rearrested an released again. His studies were interrupted and although he sat for the examinations, he never gained any diploma. The police continued to dog him. In 1909, a marriage was arranged for him and was due to take place when the security services arrested him again. The families, however, agreed to proceed with the ceremony and so it turned out that only the bride was present, while the groom spent his night of nights in jail.

As grandfather started his mandarinate career under the protectorate, he had a brother among the revolutionary ranks abroad and another one under surveillance by the security services. The brothers were engaged in different, one could even say opposite, paths. They seemed to be divided on political lines, but only apparently so. To grandfather, the eldest son, fell the responsibility of providing for the parents and assuring the survival of the family. A basic Confucian teaching, enunciated in the very first pages of the *Great Learning*, was that those who wished to do well in administering their states should first try to order well their families. If one's own family could not be maintained as a vital unit, how could one expect to successfully serve one's country? Ours was a nationalist family and, like his brothers, grandfather suffered to see Vietnam under foreign domination. He, however, realized that it could not be opposed by force. Our country was too weak. It needed to be strengthened through economic development, social reforms, and the raising of the level of education among the population. Accepting that we could not get rid of the protectorate, ways should be found under that regime to achieve those goals. As for grandfather's brothers, they could throw themselves fully into their activities against the French, knowing that he was there to look after their old parents. Outsiders looking in may see a contradiction in their attitudes, but our family remained fundamentally united. In any case, political attitudes have never affected the loyalty and solidarity among its members, either then or half a century later when Vietnam would become divided between nationalists and communists. As it turned out, revolutionary activities in the beginning of the century proved ineffective against the French domination. People like Tam Tiep only succeeded to keep up the flame of resistance. Meanwhile, it was grandfather who was the mainstay of our family and who laid the foundations for its new prosperity.

The second brother Nguyen Thuc Phan, whom I called Great-uncle Two, settled down in business. He did so as a form of political opposition. He followed a movement started by scholars who, while they stayed out of the public service sought to develop the nation's potential by going into popular education for some and into commerce, industry or agriculture for others. The time was when people with academic titles could be seen opening shops and textile factories, exploiting mines, cultivating rice fields and exhorting the population to use local products instead of those imported from France. The aim was to create in the country a strong bourgeoisie like that in Western countries, which could then give effective financial support to those fighting for independence. With their activities, the scholars also wanted to bring in social changes and do away with the traditional four-class society in which the mandarins sat enthroned at the top. Great-uncle Two married a city girl and together they opened a shop on Sugar Street in Hanoi. The center of Hanoi—its City—was from olden times composed of thirty-six streets, each specialized in the trade of a product. The names remained: Sugar Street, Silver Street, Hemp Street, Fan Street ... although the specialization had gone and shops now sold a variety of products. Sugar Street was one of the main thoroughfares in the City. The unique tram line in Hanoi ran along it. The couple's shop bore the name of *Vinh Dong*, meaning Forever Together. It retailed textile materials such as linen, cotton and silk. The family was excited with the move made by Thuc Phan, which brought back to mind the success enjoyed in trade by his grandfather Quang So. He succeeded better than many a scholar turned shopkeeper by conviction, and the shop provided him with the means to raise a large family. But of the caliber of Quang So, who went to the northern highlands, the Mekong River delta and south China, and who built up a business enterprise on a par with those of Chinese merchants, Thuc Phan was not. He and his wife were devoted to each other. True to the name they gave to their shop, they would stay together in their shop all their lives. They had ten surviving children, two sons and eight daughters. With such a numerous progeniture, life must have been difficult. I can only recall few occasions when we went to my great-uncle's place for a meal.

Thuc Phan was a brilliant conversationalist with a rather wicked sense of humor. He ridiculed people's foibles mercilessly. Whenever he came to visit, everyone would rally around to listen to him commenting on the way the world was going. He used words in a bold manner, swearing freely. *Cho dai*, dogs for breeding, or *ngua dai*, horses for breeding, were the names he called us young boys. He knew some French and some of the swear words he often used in that language were positively scandalous: *salaud, con, couillon;* so much that one day his son had to bring a big Larousse dictionary and explain in detail to him their crude meaning. "Father, you used these words so frequently," he told him. "You only got away with them because the people you talk to do not understand French!" Until old age, Great-uncle Two remained intensely nationalistic. In 1945, after both the French rule and Japanese occupation came to an end in Vietnam, he gave full expression to his joy and excitement. He came to see my parents—we were then living in a house in Quan Thanh street, close to Hanoi's Western Lake—and quickly climbed the steps to the first floor lounge, although he was then close to sixty and not keeping in good health. As my mother served tea and my parents enquired about his health, he took off his turban and was in high spirits. "I can still fight to keep the independence of our country," he said. He called my elder brother and me to stand in front of him and addressed us, not in his usual mocking style but very solemnly:

> Our country is now independent. We are no longer servants of foreigners. Our people are free to trade and work as they like for a living. Do you young-sters feel happy? Can you realize how lucky you are growing up in a sovereign country?

In opposition to French rule, he had chosen not to try for a position in the civil service and had gone instead into commerce. Although he did reasonably well with his shop, it was an obscure and hard life, made even harder at times such as the Great Depression of the 1930s. He could not afford to buy a parcel of land in his village on which to retire, the dream of any Vietnamese. The western house in our compound which belonged to him was given him by my grandfather. Compared to the latter, he was always the brother who had dropped behind. One could sense in him a certain bitterness and discontent at the life that fate had laid out for him.

When a child, I was nicknamed *Ong Nhieu,* or Mr. *Nhieu. Nhieu* in the old village system was an appellation given to persons who were exempted from unpaid labour imposed by the authorities. Villagers who could afford it bought the exemption. Mr. *Nhieu* stood above the lowest category of citizens in the village, but that was the only precedence he enjoyed. He ranked below all other village officials. That nickname was given me by Great-uncle Two. It was not complimentary at all, but our custom wanted children to be called by rather deprecatory or ugly-sounding nicknames. For parents to boast about their children was poor taste. Great-uncle Two, so my mother told me, liked to carry me in his arms while he walked around reciting in a modulating voice the following folk poem:

> Before the New Year, people planted ceremonial poles to celebrate the Tet.
> He waited until the seventh day of the New Year, when festivities had ended, to plant his.
> Early in the morning of the first day of the year, scholars took out their ink slab and writing brush to write their first poem.
> He wrote his when afternoon was drawing to an end.
> Everyone wanted to find a rich wife. His was poor.
> He went to school for studies, but the only title he earned was Mr. *Nhieu.*

Clearly Mr. *Nhieu* did not fit into his time and place. In giving that nickname to his great-nephew, perhaps Great-uncle Two was thinking in the first instance of himself and his own destiny.

His wife died in 1940 of tuberculosis. I do not recall much about her, except that she was an educated lady who was good at writing poetry, in particular satirical poems. Some of these I could still recite by heart. Her eldest son Nguyen Duc Ung was also a poet in his spare time and wrote a number of pieces under the title "Collection of Duc Ung's Poems." Great-uncle Two had two sons both of whom had only daughters. Thus after one generation, his branch had ceased to have male descendants.

Great-uncle Three, Tam Tiep, threw himself into revolutionary activities at a very young age. He chose the radical path of leaving home and country in order to fight against French rule. In the period under the French, self-exiles like him were heroes worshipped by the young generations. Few people knew what the exiles were doing abroad. Mystery and imagination entertained the hopes placed in them. Away from the reach of the French secret police, helped by Chinese friends and sympathizers, they were setting up secret armies with modern arms not yet seen in this country. Thus, the rumors went. In time, they would come back to liberate us from the colonial yoke. We would be free, independent and strong again. Did Tam Tiep set out to go to China or Japan? We only knew that he "went abroad." After the lines of communication with him were broken up by the police, our house in Kim Bai was placed under constant surveillance. Former students of Dinh Dat, even if they were still able to assure the liaison with China, would not have dared to show up. Forty years passed. In our family, Great-uncle Three was not mentioned anymore in conversation. But in the mind of a great-nephew who did not know him, being born long after he had left, he remained very much present. To me, he was wrapped in an aura of prestige like a hero of legend. For he symbolized the pure spirit of youth as well as the daring of a pioneer; most of all, he loved his country and did not falter from going into a life unknown in a place foreign in order to fight for it.

In 1945, Japan surrendered to the Allies. Vietnam proclaimed its independence. Chinese troops came to the north of the country to disarm the Japanese forces. The revolutionaries returned from China. Nguyen Hai Than, with whom Tam Tiep went abroad, was now at the head of the nationalist party Kuomingtang, the second most powerful organization in the north behind the communists. Our family hopes were rekindled. Great-uncle Three may be coming back! But days went by and the good news failed to materialize. Contact was made with some revolutionaries who could not give us any information about Tam Tiep. The man to ask was Nguyen Hai Than himself, but he was now a leader of a party engaged in a death struggle with the communists to decide political supremacy over the country. It was not easy to get in touch with him as he was heavily guarded by his own troops and by the Chinese. Finally, my maternal grandfather was able to meet him to renew their friendship of decades ago. Nguyen Hai Than agreed to come to his place for lunch, one of the very few times that he left the safety of his headquarters. As the two reminisced over a cup of wine, while nationalist militants swarmed around the house and in adjoining streets to guard their leader, my maternal grandfather enquired about Tam Tiep. The old revolutionary, now over sixty, found it hard to recall events of forty years go. After a while, he said: "I do remember that eager young man from my home town," alluding to the fact that both he and Tam Tiep came from villages within the province of Ha Dong. "But I was with a group of several people and after arriving in China, I handed them over to the organization. The idea was for the young people to learn Chinese, then go into military schools or universities to become military or political leaders." Nguyen Hai Than then branched into another topic of conversation and my grandfather thought that was all he would say about Tam Tiep. But he returned to the subject afterwards. "In the 1910s, after the Japanese joined hands with the French and expelled all Vietnamese revolutionaries from their country, the Chinese also grew less supportive of us. Financial sources of help dried up and our young people had to abandon their studies to earn a living. The organization could not help them anymore. It was everyone for himself. Our people dispersed in all directions. China is a vast country. It was impossible to keep track of them." Nguyen Hai Than continued:

> I do not know what Tam Tiep did for a living or where he went. Most of our first wave of revolutionaries must have died. They did not live to see the end of French rule. They were not able to say to themselves that their sacrifices were not in vain.

Thus, Nguyen Hai Than implied that Tam Tiep had died. I remembered that when the news was relayed to him, my (paternal) grandfather took it stoically. He must have guessed that much, for nothing that the family had heard had given it any hope that Tam Tiep was still alive. But his brother was sceptical. "That Nguyen Hai Than is old and maybe his memory is not that good," he said. Politically, he did not agree with the Kuomingtang, his views being more to the left. "We must continue to ask," he insisted. Later on, grandfather also managed to see Nguyen Hai Than. He was hoping that the previous meeting had jogged the latter's memory about Tam Tiep. But he could not obtain any new information. In 1945, if he was still alive, Tam Tiep would have been fifty-six. He was younger than most of those who left for China at the start of this century. Besides Nguyen Hai Than, our family was unable to meet with anyone who belonged to that "first wave of revolutionaries" and who could give us a firsthand account of Tam Tiep.

Our further enquiries proved fruitless until a person told us that he did not know Tam Tiep personally, but had known of him. He heard that Tam Tiep married a Chinese woman and had children before dying, a long time ago. If that was true, there would be a branch of the Nguyen Dinh now living in China. Who knows? I might find cousins of mine in China some day.

From Nguyen Hai Than's account and from documents published since 1945, we now know how difficult and precarious life was for those revolutionaries abroad. Instead of setting up vast armies to fight the French, as we tended to believe in our dreams, they were struggling to get a living. Only the lucky ones could gain a scholarship into the Military Academy or could find a Chinese benefactor to finance their studies. At first, secret collections of money were made in Vietnam and sent out. They never amounted to much. In 1906, the Movement for the Restoration of Vietnam devised a plan to call on the public to buy shares in trading companies serving as fronts for the revolution. The plan proved a failure. After that, the only hopes rested with China's or Japan's willingness to help a fellow Asian nation. There, the revolutionaries soon discovered that, as the Marquess Cuong De had commented bitterly, foreign policies were based not on sentiment but on concrete national interests. They could never rely on assurances of help given either by the Chinese or the Japanese. It all depended on the policy of the government of the day. There were "good times" when the Vietnamese were assisted with money, arms, military training and scholarships to go into universities. But help, when available, was always given in small amounts, drop by drop. There were "bad times" when nothing came, not even a word of moral support. The worst blow that ever fell on the Vietnamese exiles was in 1909 in Japan when, following an agreement with France, the Japanese government expelled all of them, from one day to the next. All nationalist parties struggling for independence abroad were placed in that vulnerable situation. They could never really build themselves up into powerful organizations. The only group of revolutionaries who could rely on regular help and guidance from a foreign power were the communists, their struggle for Vietnam's independence being a stage in a world proletarian revolution directed from Moscow. Consequently, they held a decisive advantage over the nationalist groups when the Second World War ended and Japan left. As the French had been kicked out by the Japanese a few months before, Vietnam was there for the taking and the communists, being the best organized force, took it.

Our family being poor, Tam Tiep could not have taken much money with him. At sixteen, to struggle for a living in a foreign environment must have been extremely hard. I have often wondered whether circumstances had allowed him to work for the revolution the way he hoped to. Was his wish to serve the country fulfilled? Or did he not, when evening fell at his place of exile, sometimes regret his decison to leave home and say to him-self: "If only I could play this game all over again!" I believe that he had died years before 1945, when the French were still well entrenched in Viet-nam and no one could have forecast the cascade of events that would come with the end of the world war. Yet, I hope that in his heart, that patriot had found some consolation and peace as he closed his eyes for the last time, away from his homeland.

Grandfather started his mandarinal career in a prefecture called Truc Ninh, which was part of the province of Nam Dinh, a rich and populous province in the delta, southeast of Hanoi. The township of Nam Dinh was the third largest in the north, after Hanoi and the port of Hai Phong. It was an important cultural center, with schools of high reputation like that of Headmaster Son Nong, where grandfather studied. Triennial examina-tions to select bachelors and licentiates were held there as well as in Hanoi and the Nam Dinh center often attracted more candidates. Truc Ninh, however, was only a prefecture and not among the large ones in Nam Dinh. A position of education officer there was perhaps one of the lowest that a licentiate could get on graduating from the School of Administration. Out of a scale of nine mandarinal grades—which was in fact eighteen as each grade was composed of two subgrades called upper and lower—an educa-tion officer occupied the upper eighth grade, or only three steps above the lowest grade which was the lower ninth. By comparison, colleagues of grandfather who were appointed as prefects held the lower sixth grade. For him, this could hardly be called an auspicious start.

Certainly, it looked as if grandfather was shunted aside by the regime, but when a delegation of young mandarins was picked to go to France on a study trip, he was chosen. An album of the trip was kept with his personal papers in Ha Dong until everything was burned down in 1946, at the start of the war. I could still visualize the photographs in the brownish-red color typical of prints in that early period. Grandfather was among twenty or so Vietnamese gentlemen, looking somewhat rigid and awkward in their new European suits, each sporting a new Parisian felt hat. Many of them had grown beard and moustache in the style fashionable in France at that time. I cannot remember if grandfather had them; probably he had not. But I am sure that the one who would become my maternal grandfather appeared with a very well-groomed moustache. The group was shown on the docks of Marseilles, in front of the Eiffel Tower, in the Luxembourg gardens and at other scenic spots. The delegation was a product of French policy aimed at exposing members of the Vietnamese elite to the culture and civilization of France. At the same time, it was a countermeasure to the "go east" movement promoted by revolutionary leaders calling on young people to go and study in Japan. The only person I could recognize in the group other than grandfather was Hoang Huan Trung, a close friend of his. They were

Hoang Huan Trung, my maternal grandfather, in full Court uniform of a Governor (circa 1934).

classmates under Headmaster Son Nong. They graduated at the same 1903 *Huong* session and studied together at the School of Administration. A year before they left for France; their wives gave birth to a girl and a boy and they happily promised to each other that their children would become husband and wife.

The French trip lasted nine months. It was thought that on returning from it, grandfather's career would take a turn for the better. But he was back to the same teaching job in Truc Ninh, where he stayed for another year. Then his father died and, following the custom of that time, he took leave and went into mourning for a year. In 1910, he was reappointed as an education officer, although to a larger prefecture, that of Thu Tri in Thai Binh. Thu Tri was the prefecture on the banks of the Red River, where a ferry linked the province of Nam Dinh with that of Thai Binh. After spending two years there, grandfather became a teacher at the Model School in Thai Binh. As its name indicated, that was a school whose teaching methods were meant to be taken by others as models. Only the cream of teachers was appointed to its staff. It was a prestigious establishment, but grandfather still ranked below the prefects and he knew that as far as career path was concerned, unless he reached that rank of prefect, there was no way he could move to the higher echelons of the mandarinate. He stayed at the Model School for an inordinately long time, from 1911 to 1917, while mandarins usually did not remain in the same job for more than two or three years. Either he was considered too good a teacher to do something else, or the powers-that-be had decided that he should stay there and go no further.

A good teacher grandfather was. He descended from a long line of teachers. Teaching ran in his blood and he enjoyed doing it. During those six years in Thai Binh, he trained a whole generation of students who were caught between the old education system based on the scholarly script and the Confucian classics and a new system based on the popular script, the French language and the sciences. It was a difficult period of transition for teachers and students alike. Grandfather, a licentiate of the old school who had gone to France, was eminently qualified and some of his students would later on reach high positions, even national prominence. Author Duong Quang Ham, for instance, the grammarian and literary historian who, incidentally, was a brother of his good friend Licentiate Duong, studied under him. Numerous former students from those days continued to visit him in Kim Bai in the 1940s, after he had retired. Many kept attending every year the anniversary of his father's death. His long stay there made Thai Binh a second home town for him.

For the moment however, his career was at a standstill. Already, he was under suspicion because of his brothers' activities. In 1907, another anti–French campaign broke out and his standing in the eyes of the regime took a further blow. "Modernist" scholars, whose aim was to strengthen the national spirit and to oppose the French by legal means, opened in Hanoi a school named Dong Kinh Nghia Thuc, or Righteous School of the Eastern Capital. *Dong Kinh*, the Eastern Capital, was an ancient name for Hanoi. It was also the Vietnamese translation of Tokyo, the capital of

Japan. The scholars who established the school took their inspiration from a school in Tokyo which had been a training ground for reformist leaders in Japan, a country then looked up to as the standard-bearer for an independent Asia. The new school was opened to both male and female students, a revolutionary step in our male-dominated Confucian society. Tuition was entirely free of charge. Public lectures were organized in which speakers discussed the need for economic and social reforms and called upon the Vietnamese to find strength within themselves. People crowded at the lectures in a festive atmosphere. The school was such a success that, nine months after it started, it was closed down by the French. Its leaders were arrested, among them several of grandfather's friends and classmates, in particular Licentiate Duong. Grandfather was then teaching in a far-away prefecture; as a civil servant he could not have been involved with the school. But he must have been sympathetic to his friends' endeavors. Most scholars agreed with the aims of the school and, as an educationist, grandfather must have been thrilled to see new concepts being tried such as those of a mixed and open school. Anyway, he stayed in touch with his scholar friends and aroused official suspicion against him. In those circumstances, it was rather surprising that the French still included him in the delegation going to France in the following year. Perhaps, they had thought it worth their while to go to some length to bring someone like him over to their side.

Grandfather was a royalist, although not with the same degree of fervor as his father Dinh Dat. The country had fallen under French protectorate and the emperor had lost much of his powers and prestige, but for many mandarins the distinction between the Imperial court and the protectorate was a capital one. They resented the many encroachments perpetrated by the French upon the authority of the court. In 1907, the French deposed Emperor Thanh Thai whom they themselves had chosen for the throne. But he was now judged uncooperative and they sent him into exile. In 1913, they dug up the tomb of Tu Duc, the emperor who fought against them in their long war of conquest of Vietnam. Tu Duc was worshipped by Dinh Dat and that sacrilegious act affected his son deeply. In 1916, the young emperor Duy Tan—Thanh Thai's son—plotted an armed revolt, taking advantage of the fact that France was occupied with fighting a war on her own soil. He tried to carry the nation with him in the way Ham Nghi did thirty years before. But he failed utterly. His plan leaked out. Only one prefecture rose in his support. Even the court mandarins did not follow him. Although France had her hands full with the war in Europe, she maintained an unshakeable hold in Vietnam. Duy Tan was sent to join his father in exile. All those events had a depressing effect on grandfather. He was a proud and rigid man. The court had become little more than a tool in the hands of the French, but he would stubbornly cling to the notion that a Vietnamese mandarin was a servant of his emperor and no one else.

Every year, a commission of high mandarins met to decide whom among the teachers and education officers would be promoted to the rank of prefect. For the junior officers, the commission's decisions would shape their careers. Only if chosen could they move into the senior ranks of the mandarinate. One of the most powerful mandarins in the north in grandfather's time was Hoang Trong Phu. The son of a former viceroy who gained his position pacifying the north for the protectorate, Hoang Trong Phu had the full confidence of the French. He did not like grandfather. Whenever his case came before the commission, Governor Hoang opposed the promotion. "Ba Tiep, that stubborn fellow!" he exclaimed and the other mandarins, either out of respect for his opinions or out of fear of his powers, assented. Year after year, the way was blocked for grandfather. Others placed in his situation would try their best to placate Governor Hoang and win his favors, but grandfather refused to do so. Even his friends told him that was what he should do, but he still refused: "The governor is right," they said, "you are really stubborn." It is interesting to point out that the governor did not criticize grandfather's capabilities; in fact, the marks he received from his superiors were always good. Nor did he say that grandfather was suspected of being a nationalist, which would have put paid to his career. He only considered him a stubborn person and that was enough to keep him out for many years. But grandfather's work in Thai Binh had come to the notice of a high mandarin who had spent most of his career in that town. His name was Pham Van Thu. He was one of those mandarins who reached positions of high influence not because of political patronage or of being pro–French, but because they were respected for their integrity and capability. Pham Van Thu was also a mandarin of the old school who wanted to uphold the prestige of the Imperial court. He was the only one to speak out in favor of grandfather. At first, he could not make Governor Hoang change his mind. But he returned to it in the following year. He kept on for several years until grandfather at last got his promotion. That was in 1917, when he was already thirty-eight. Grandfather always kept in mind the debt he owed Governor Pham. He had the opportunity to repay it twenty years later, long after the governor had died. By then a governor himself, he gave his daughter in marriage to his benefactor's grandson.

His appointment as prefect finally removed a stumbling block in grandfather's career. Realistically, however, he judged that he would advance no further than the middle ranks of the mandarinate. He was close to forty and had just reached a rank that many of his classmates at the School of Administration had held ten years earlier. It could take a prefect something between six and ten years to become a senior prefect. By that time, he would be close to fifty and looking down toward retirement, which was then fixed at fifty-five. He became *Tri Huyen,* or prefect of Tung Thien in the province of Son Tay and stayed there for three years. As head of a prefecture his strength of character and independence of judgment, which in more subaltern positions had made him appear stubborn, could be fully put to use. He gained the reputation of a good administrator, not afraid to take initiatives and quick to respond to emergencies. After Tung Thien, he was transferred to the prefecture of Phuc Tho in the same province. Two years later, he was nominated for the rank of *Tri Phu,* or senior prefect, having under his authority three or four prefectures. This time, Governor Hoang did not oppose his promotion. Thus, in a matter of five years, grandfather had achieved what others would take perhaps twice as long. He now held the lower fifth grade and was given charge of the large prefecture of Quoc Oai, also in Son Tay. I believe that it was during his time in Son Tay that an incident occurred which caught the imagination of the local population. He was placed in a situation of extreme danger, but escaped unhurt. People believed that he was saved because Fate had earmarked him for higher things. Every year, the livelihood of the delta people depended on the dikes holding firm when the rivers swelled in the monsoon season. The threat of flood was particularly serious that year and grandfather spent days and nights touring his prefecture, through which flowed the Red River. Here, he exhorted the population to maintain their vigil on the dikes; there, he gave orders that certain sections must be urgently reinforced and all available hands in neighboring villages be conscripted for that task. He was on a dike observing a group of peasants carrying earth from the fields, when ominous rumbling sounds were heard and cracks appeared not far from where he was standing. The peasants, his aides, all fled for their lives. He continued to stand there. Surely, the raging current was going to smash the dike and carry him away. The cracks came nearer, but then they stopped. The dike was holding. Seeing this, the peasants returned and succeeded in making it safe again.

After two years in Quoc Oai, grandfather moved to Hoai Duc, a prefecture in his home province of Ha Dong. He liked Son Tay and enjoyed its splendid highland scenery, something he could only dream of from his village of Kim Bai and from the flatlands of Thai Binh where he worked as a teacher. But Son Tay was not considered an important place to spend one's career. Lying on the fringe of the delta and next to the highlands, it was a rather poor province with not a lot of population. Ha Dong, on the contrary, was where all mandarins would like to be posted. The township of Ha Dong was so close to the old capital Hanoi that it could be considered one of its suburbs. Although no longer the nation's capital, Hanoi was still the administrative and political center of the north. Moreover, it remained the cultural heart of Vietnam. People continued to refer to it as *dat ngan nam van vat,* "the land where for thousands of years culture and learning have flourished." In former times, to be governor of Hanoi was the highest honor that a mandarin could aspire to. But Hanoi had been ceded to the

French and placed under direct French administration. In the absence of
Hanoi, Ha Dong became the most coveted place for mandarinal appointments. The man instrumental in bringing grandfather to a prefecture in Ha
Dong was Governor Hoang, the same one who for so long had blocked his
career. Ha Dong was his fief. He had been a governor there for years, while
other mandarins were not allowed to stay in the same place for more than
a few years to prevent abuses of power. Grandfather was surprised to be
transferred to Hoai Duc. He did not know that Governor Hoang had his
eyes on him. But he was happy and proud; to be appointed to a place in
one's home province was considered to be a signal honor for a mandarin.
However, it was made clear to him that he was only on trial. Governor
Hoang had heard of the good work he did in Son Tay and wanted to observe him more closely.

Grandfather did not stay long in Hoai Duc. He went there at the beginning of 1923. The same year, he left to become *Thuong Ta* of Ha Dong,
or counsellor to the province governor. The counsellor ranked as the fourth
highest mandarin in the province. He functioned as principal assistant and
head of the chancery to the governor. All matters requiring a decision from
the latter would come first to his desk. It had not taken long for Governor
Hoang to observe and promote the "stubborn fellow" to a highly sensitive
post. The promotion was a clear recognition of grandfather's abilities, but
nevertheless it caused some concern. Hoang Trong Phu was more feared
than liked by the corps of mandarins because he was very close to the
French. Grandfather was one of those who stuck to the belief that, as mandarins, they were servants of the emperor in Hue and not of the French protectorate. Being of an independent character, he would have preferred to
pursue a career away from the patronage of high and powerful men. But
of course, he could not refuse an offer coming from Governor Hoang, who
had become a sort of de facto viceroy of the north. As it turned out, the
move was not such a good one, for he would stay in the same position in
Ha Dong for the next ten years.

He and his family moved into the official bungalow reserved for the
Thuong Ta. By then, he already had five children. His eldest son, my father,
was born in 1907, when he was a teacher in Nam Dinh. Grandmother then
gave birth to three or more children, who all died in infancy. The old fear
came back to the family. Would the line once again have only one male
descendant? Fortunately, we were in the twentieth century and modern
medicine had been introduced into the country. The scourge of infant mor-
tality receded. In 1913, six years after my father, another son was born in
Thai Binh. He survived and the string of misfortunes was broken. Six more
children followed, the last one in 1930 when grandmother was already
forty-five. My parents were married during the time grandfather was
Thuong Ta of Ha Dong. They lived with the rest of the family in the

official bungalow. It was there that my mother gave birth to her first three children.

Grandfather took great care in choosing our names, in particular that of my brother, his eldest grandson and the head of a new generation of the family. A name expresses the hopes and aspirations placed in the child and *Hong,* my brother's name, says much about grandfather himself. It was taken from a slogan adopted by Sun Yat Sen, the father of modern China, to describe the flag of the new Chinese republic which was established in 1912. Transcribed in the Vietnamese language, the slogan read: *"Thanh thien, bach nhat, man dia hong,"* meaning "The sky is blue, the sun is white, the whole earth is red." *Hong,* or red, was the traditional color for loyalty, goodness and good fortune. In the struggle led by Sun Yat Sen to bring China out of feudalism and into the twentieth century, it became associated with courage, defiance and revolutionary fervor. The Chinese leader was greatly admired by Vietnamese nationalists, who saw in his Three People's doctrine of nationalism, democracy and socialism a model for Vietnam's own struggle to recover its sovereignty and develop into a modern nation. The choice of Hong as a name showed grandfather's attachment to the nationalist cause, even though he was working as a mandarin under the protectorate. When I was born, grandfather decided to continue with the red color. He named me *Dan,* meaning the bright red of the cinnabar, a term associated with loyalty and royalty. Thus, *dan tam* is a loyal and faithful heart, while the red royal courtyard was called *dan tri.* For his next grandson, my grandfather chose the name *Dong,* meaning vermilion. When my youngest brother was born, grandfather found that he had run out of red-colored names. There were other Chinese characters for red, but they were not considered auspicious. Just then, a visitor came bearing a gift of freshly picked *dao,* or peaches. This gave grandfather the idea of naming him Dao, for *dao* was also the pink of the peach blossoms, a color close enough to red. Moreover, *dao* was often alluded to as a symbol of filial piety. According to an ancient legend, the fruit that grew in the Peach Paradise made people live their full span of one hundred years. Therefore, pious sons would slip into the Paradise and steal the fruit for their parents, so that the latter may live longer and they—the sons—may continue to serve and care for them.

Grandfather was a good chief of staff. He took over most of the day-to-day administration of Ha Dong, leaving Governor Hoang free to deal with the French authorities who were more and more intent on imposing their direct rule on the north. The arrangement suited the governor; as a result, he kept grandfather in Ha Dong for that inordinately long period of ten years. When the time came for him to be promoted to *An Sat,* or chief judicial officer and the third highest ranking mandarin in a province, grandfather received the new grade, but not the appointment; he remained in the same position in Ha Dong. Four years later, he was promoted to the grade of *Bo Chanh,* or chief executive officer and the second ranking mandarin in a province; yet he went on being *Thuong Ta* of Ha Dong. It was only in 1933 that that situation was brought to an end and he was appointed *Tuan Phu,* or governor, of the province of Bac Giang. Bac Giang was a small province bordering the highlands and *Tuan Phu* a junior rank of governor. Grandfather was then fifty-four. As at that time mandarins retired at fifty-five and as only in special cases would they be retained to serve for a few more years, it looked as if that may well be his last appointment.

In fact, that was the start of the most successful stage of his career. After only a year in Bac Giang, he was promoted to Ha Nam, a larger and wealthier province in the delta. The departing governor of that province was my maternal grandfather Hoang Huan Trung, and so it was that the handing over of office took place between my two grandfathers, who had been close friends since their youth. I have no recollection of it, but my parents say that my brother and I, then seven and four, were at the ceremony. Instead of waiting for his successor on the perron of his office, as prescribed by protocol, the retiring governor led the two of us to the gate of his mansion and waited there, as he would have done if his friend was coming for a visit. After grandfather arrived, the four of us walked toward the office where the town dignitaries were assembled, holding hands and making the official handing over ceremony look very much like a family occasion. I started going to school in Ha Nam. My parents had by then gone to live in Hanoi, but I continued to stay with my grandparents.

I do remember the first day and the small state primary school where my uncle and I went, each carrying a new schoolbag in one hand and a pot of purple ink in the other. I liked school and was a diligent student, to the point that I would not even go and see my parents in Hanoi if it meant that I had to miss class. My grandfather stayed for two years in Ha Nam. Besides school, some memories of that period remained with me, in particular a boat trip on the river. We were in summer, a day of the full moon. Grandfather had invited a group of friends for an evening of music and card games. He took my uncle and me with him. The party boarded a large wooden boat. Musicians and *a dao* were called. The *a dao* were the Vietnamese equivalent of the Japanese geishas. They could sing, recite poetry, keep up a conversation, even discuss rhyme and verse with scholars. While food was served to the guests, I climbed with the singers on the roof of the boat to enjoy the scenery of sky and river in the soft colors of the sunset. The boat had left its moorings and we were in the middle of the vast river. Villages on the two banks seemed very far away. Soon, it was darkness. Everything disappeared from view and our boat was alone between the water and the sky. Then, the magic moment arrived. The full moon rose and the landscape all around us came back, bathed in a golden light. The river itself was a scintillating mass of gold. In days gone by, one of the most refined pleasures in life was to be:

> With singers in a boat,
> Drifting to where the waves would carry you.

In 1936, grandfather became a senior governor. He was appointed to the province of Bac Ninh, his wife's home province. Mandarinal rules would normally prevent such an appointment, for fear that a governor would unduly favor his wife's relations. The rules were stricter for one's own home province. Exceptions were made only for those mandarins known for their integrity and whose services were urgently required. The rules were waived for grandfather, in both instances. While in Ha Nam, he was called upon several times to act as governor of Ha Dong, his home province, when Governor Hoang had to be absent for prolonged periods. Then came his appointment to Bac Ninh, which was a special case. He was sent there after a succession of governors had their careers broken by the French representative. Although the protectorate treaty recognized that Vietnamese authorities were responsible for internal administration, many French officials were all too willing to impose direct French rule. When matters came to a head, the Vietnamese mandarin would have to go. As it turned out, grandfather got on very well with his French counterpart. For one thing, he had been to France and could express himself in French reasonably well. For another, he made clear to the Frenchman in their first meeting that he had passed the official retirement age and fully expected that Bac Ninh would be his last appointment. His message got through. The Frenchman knew that he would be dealing with someone who had nothing to lose.

I continued to live with my grandparents in Bac Ninh, only joining my parents in Hanoi during the holidays. Bac Ninh in the mind of a six-year-old boy was the town with a railway line. The train ran near the governor's mansion, near my school, and near the municipal park where we went to play. Everyday on my way to school, I waited at the level crossing for it to pass. The train stopped at the small station, where some Saturday evenings I eagerly waited for my father to visit me. Then, it left for the mysterious highlands of the north, where non–Vietnamese tribespeople lived. Pushing further, it would arrive at the Chinese border where, so we were told, bandits abounded and kidnapped children—because they went out of their homes by themselves and were drugged by wicked women—and were sold to become slaves in China. But the train also went south to Hanoi and it carried me, at the start of the holidays, home to my family. Before reaching Hanoi, it crossed the mighty Red River on the Doumer bridge, which was several kilometers long and the longest in the country. From the train moving slowly along the narrow bridge, I could observe the many boats going to and fro on the river and, on the next lane, the long line of pedestrians, cyclists and peasants carrying their heavy baskets of produce to the markets of the capital.

Bac Ninh had also an airport, which served as the airport for Hanoi. There were only a few four-wing planes there. Our people called them *chuon chuon*, or dragonfly, because from afar, they looked like that insect. It was in one of those dragonflies that grandfather had his first flight. A French aviator arrived with much fanfare; I believe that he was on a flying trip from France or somewhere far away. Grandfather was invited to fly with him and he accepted, causing dismay to his family. Riding an airplane then was perhaps as adventurous as going in a rocket to outer space nowadays. That morning, all of us went outside to watch. We heard the noise first, growing bigger and bigger before the plane appeared, as it flew quite low. It circled the town several times, so that all the townfolk could see their governor "riding the clouds" next to the pilot. Many people said that he was actually waving at them. I only remember seeing his face, but so clearly that I could distinguish his white beard.

In Bac Ninh, for the first and only time in her life, my grandmother danced at a French ball. The family talked about it for a long time. At evening parties given by French officials, grandfather had sometimes danced with French ladies. We did not find it surprisng for he had been to France. But grandmother had been content just to sit and watch. She spoke no French and her contact with French people was limited to those few social evenings. She told us that she liked the music and admired the grace of the dancers. But the thought had certainly never crossed her mind that she might go on the dance floor herself. Yet, she did. One evening, the mood of the party was particularly jovial and there was an important guest from Hanoi who kept asking her to dance. At the end, she could refuse no longer and got up to dance with him, to the delight of the whole assembly. Afterwards, we often teased her by asking how she could dance without having had any lessons. She smiled and said: "That was not difficult at all. I have been telling you that learning the ways of high living was quite easy!"

Grandfather's stay in Bac Ninh was short. The following year, he moved to Thai Binh, on his last appointment. He was fifty-eight. In the old system, a high mandarin was often given his choice of last appointment. That would not necessarily be the highest post he could aspire to, but one he would be happy to have before he retired. Thai Binh was large and populous, although not among the two or three most important provinces in the Delta. A mandarin of the traditional school, grandfather had always kept his distance from the representatives of the French protectorate who, for their part, had sometimes suspected him of sympathy for the nationalist cause. The very top governorships were not for him. With Thai Binh, he had had a long association. Early in his career, he had spent seven years there as an education officer. A whole generation of Thai Binh scholars had studied under him. His reputation was high. Former students of his went into the public service, education and the arts. Some were already prefects, others had become prominent authors. The scholars' community in Thai Binh would like to have their old teacher back, this time as the head mandarin of the province. When he left Thai Binh, grandfather was a junior mandarin. Two decades later, he had reached the top of his profession and to return there would be a source of particular satisfaction for him, as well as a fitting end to his career. In 1937, the post of Thai Binh became vacant and his wish was granted. When he went there to assume his new functions, it was like a homecoming.

I followed my grandparents to Thai Binh. I was then seven and in my third year of primary school. We lived in a large compound which contained the governor's office, his residence and outbuildings for the staff and servants. In one corner stood a rather lugubrious-looking blockhouse in concrete, with loopholes to shoot from, a reminder of the troubled period of 1929–1930, when nationalist insurrections broke out in many parts of the country. The blockhouse was not manned anymore; instead, it had become a sleeping place for the soldiers who guarded the compound. The front garden with symmetrical flower beds, shrubs and low hedges, had no particular appeal to me. But the back of the office opened into a private garden shaded by big trees, which gave to the compound the character of a rural retreat. The garden led to a pond, where ducks were reared. I very much liked that garden, perhaps because its lawn, flowers, pebbled path, and especially its pond and trees, were all the things that I missed in our ancestral home in Kim Bai. Shrubs grew in profusion on the edge of the pond, as well as several clumps of bamboo. They attracted a great number of birds, small black or yellow-green ones which produced a delightful twitter, and bright-colored kingfishers with shiny green breasts. But the bird I was most interested in was a small water bird, with dark grey feathers. It usually made its appearance around noon, when the sun was very high and hot, and emitted a plaintive call. "Quoc, quoc," it said. The call reverberated over the surface of the pond, and all other birds seemed to fall silent. The only sound one could hear was "quoc, quoc." *Quoc* in Vietnamese means country. The story about that bird was that it was a reincarnation of an ancient king who lost his throne and country, and had to spend the rest of his life in exile. The king longed for his old country. After he died, he became a water bird who kept calling "quoc, quoc." Since then, in the turbulent history of Vietnam, many were those who had to go into exile like the ancient king. Fate had put them on the losing side of civil wars, and their souls continued to cry for their lost country through the bird's sad call. As a young boy, however, I was interested in that bird not so much because of its sad story, but because I never saw it fly. It walked from the shrubs to the waterline, then walked back. I thought I must be able to catch it. My uncle and I would converge from opposite sides on the shrub, ready to pounce on it. Needless to say, it managed to elude us every time.

A pair of peacocks, symbols of wealth and power, roamed free in the garden. They were supposedly tame, but could give a fright to those who approached them too closely. Even the gardeners were sometimes attacked by them. The feathers in their wings were cut to prevent them from flying away, but there were times when they could be seen perched on a high tree branch, and it was quite a problem getting them down and back to their cage in the evening. Among the trees of the garden were two imposing *bang* trees, which were usually found at road intersections and a most welcome sight for travellers in hot summer days. With branches thrusting out horizontally, and leaves as big as a plate, a *bang* tree was an oasis of shade. The traveller would find a tea hut or two under its canopy, where he could sit down and quench his thirst with a hot bowl of strong green tea. Our two *bang* trees were as tall as wide, and we could play under them even in early afternoon, when the sun was at its fiercest. The cream-colored flesh of the *bang* fruit had a sweet smell, but was not edible. We had to break its hard stone open to eat the kernel, which tasted like an almond. There was also a flame tree, as tall and wide as the *bang*, but whose small leaves did not provide much shade. In Vietnamese folklore, the flame tree suggested an image of students going for their examinations as it bloomed in early summer, the examinations season. I remember well my first examination, which took place in Thai Binh. Our tree was then a mass of bright red blossoms.

In Ha Nam and Bac Ninh, I went to the Vietnamese state school. I was quite happy and worked well. Thai Binh, a larger province with a strong minority Catholic population, boasted a French school run by nuns. My grandfather decided to put the two of us, my uncle and myself, there. He wanted us to study under the French system so that, later on, we could go to France. The thought of going to study in France was implanted in my mind ever since I was a small boy. It was my consolation when I missed my parents and wanted to go and live with them. The transfer to the nuns' school was a logical step, but it made me very unhappy. I could not communicate with the nuns, or with the other children who were mostly French. For a long time, I dreaded going to school in the morning. Anyway, although we were no longer in a Vietnamese school, when the end of the academic year came we still sat for the Junior Primary examination, which was opened to anyone who had done three years of primary. That was the first of a series of examinations in the life of a Vietnamese student. After it came the End of Primary examination, then the Junior Secondary, then the End of Secondary or Baccalaureate. I was quite relaxed going to the test, in spite of the fact that for the last several months I had been in a French school and had made no preparation for it. I was eight and had already acquired the reputation of being a bright student. But I flunked all my papers. By the end of the day and without waiting for the results, I knew that I had failed. When the results were announced, and neither my uncle nor I got through, it was quite an event. The whole town talked about it. The son and grandson of the governor, who descended from a long line of scholars, failing at the most junior of all examinations! My grandfather was not too concerned about it. "At least that was a good experience for them," he said. But my grandmother was furious. She fumed against the teachers of the state school who ran the examination. "They purposely set the papers on the topics that they (my uncle and I) did not study," she claimed. She even said that this may have been a way for the teachers to show their displeasure that we had opted for a French school instead of the state school. Looking back over that matter, I felt a lot of admiration for the teachers. It was much easier for them to let us pass than to fail us, thereby causing a loss of face for the family of the new governor. They showed their courage and integrity by treating us just like any other candidates.

Fortunately, our examination system gave a second chance to those who failed at their first try. At the end of the summer vacation, a second session was held for them. Grandmother, after the first reaction of anger, set about to repair the damage. She invited the teachers in, to ask whether they would consent to take my uncle and me as their pupils during the vacation. The teachers happily obliged. Thus, instead of the seaside, we spent the time in Thai Binh. Everyday, we took our books to the empty state school, where the teachers coached us and made sure that, this time, we would not fail.

Parties and banquets were frequent at the governor's residence. The cooks prepared a combination of Vietnamese, Chinese and French food. Even from our study, located on the other side of the garden, we could smell the nice aroma. I often made a dash to the kitchen, careful not to be seen by grandmother. There, I watched the cooks arrange their beautiful displays of food. Carrots, turnips and other vegetables were cut into flowers and leaves of different shapes and colors. Their hands pressed thickened cream out of paper cones, and the drops of cream magically became fruits, flowers, letters and other decorations. The cooks offered me tasty morsels, such as the crunchy skin of a roasted suckling pig, or the heart pulled out from inside a sizzling roast duck. They explained to me why a proverb stated that the parson's nose was the "number one" part of a chicken. Many of the dishes they made cannot be obtained nowadays, because people have no more time to prepare them. For instance, one can still order swallow nest soup in Chinese restaurants. But what one gets is a few shreds of bird nest lost among other ingredients. The original swallow nest soup was made only of swallow nest. To serve such a dish, people had to sit for hours sifting out feathers and other impurities from the very fine noodle-like nest. Swallow nest could come at the beginning of a meal as an appetizer, cooked in clear chicken broth with just a few cubes of chicken meat. Or it could come at the end as a dessert, cooked in a syrup of rock sugar. Often, it was served late in the night as a snack, while the guests played the game of *to tom,* or listened to music and singing performed by a group of songstresses. Another dish which has disappeared is the ice cream made out of a hand-operated mill. It took a long time to prepare. Two men had to take turns to turn the mill. But vanilla ice cream made that way had a freshness, consistency and flavor with which the industrial kind of today cannot be compared.

The office and residence were built in the traditional style, with wide verandahs to keep the heat away from the rooms. The verandahs were lined with potted plants and dwarf trees, many of them camelias and miniature palm trees. My grandfather had a few prized *quynh,* a cactus-like plant with flowers of white petal and yellow stamen. The flowers came rarely and only opened at night to wilt in the morning. Each *quynh* plant coming into bloom was a special occasion. Grandfather invited his friends to come over, some from Hanoi and other provinces. After dinner, there were music, songs and poetry writing while host and guests waited. When the moment arrived, everything stopped and everyone crowded around to admire the delicate flowers which had only a few hours to live. A poet has written these lines about the *quynh*:

> The young moon has risen above the roof. It is past midnight.
> The garden holds a thousand fragrances within its fragile petals.
> The leaves are sleeping and the wind is lost in its dreams.
> As a trail of mist wanders by silently,
> A bashful *quynh* flower reveals her virginal beauty.

Around New Year's time, the white, red and pink camelias started to bloom, and the verandahs received a great many cumquat trees. A pair of cumquat, heavy with fruits, was a traditional present for the Tet festival. The golden fruits were symbols of prosperity. They added color to the verandahs and stayed on the trees all through the season of festivities which followed the Tet. Many of grandfather's scholar friends came to see him during that season. For days, they played card games, challenged one another to poetry writing, and reminisced about old times. One year, grandfather invited all friends who graduated with him in 1903, more than thirty years before, to a reunion. It was a very special reunion. The twenty or so remaining scholars knew that it was their last, for grandfather was the only one among them who had not retired and, because of his position, had the means to organize such a meeting. Grandfather ordered the cooks to prepare the dishes that he knew his friends liked. He brought over a troup of songstresses from the neighboring town of Nam Dinh, a traditional cultural center in the country. Many of the scholars had studied in Nam Dinh, grandfather included. He went to great lengths to make the reunion a success. Since the guests were all Vietnamese and some were close friends of our family—my maternal grandfather was at the party too—I was allowed to go to the reception room and mix with them.

In the reception room were displayed two cumquat trees of a beautiful round shape and with so many fruits that they appeared more golden than green. The trees were placed in antique porcelain pots. The pebbles at their base were so shiny that they looked unreal. In fact, they were pebbles covered with candy. It was the fashion then for candy to be prepared that way, for people to suck, then spit out the small pebble. Normally, these candies were offered to the guests in a tray. But for the special reunion, someone had gotten the idea of placing them around the base of the cumquat trees. I wanted to eat the candies and posted myself near the trees, waiting for the scholars to start. Then, I would follow suit. They came, by groups of two or three, to look firstly at the white porcelain pots and their landscapes painted in blue. Some recited aloud the poems written on them. Then, they admired the shape of the trees and praised the extraordinarily high number of fruits. But no one seemed to notice the candies. Could it be that they thought these were just pebbles, I wondered to myself. Groups came and went. I was getting discouraged, when one came by himself. Like the others, he watched the pots, trees and fruits. Then before moving away, he nonchalantly picked up two candies, put one in his mouth and, with a smile, handed the other one to me.

Grandfather was a mandarin who kept on the move, visiting villages to acquaint himself with the life of the population. His dark blue Peugeot car was a familiar sight on the roads of the province and the prefects knew that it could appear in their areas without warning. My uncle and I often accompanied him. He brought us along on festive occasions such as regional fairs, market openings and sporting events. When he went to areas stricken by drought or floods, we were with him too. Obviously, he wanted us to see for ourselves the harsh conditions that country folk had to face, for we often attended those somber occasions, instead of going to school. The two of us used to walk behind him, at the head of the official party. We saw villages destroyed by cyclones, rice fields transformed into parched land by drought. People who had lost everything were sitting there with a resigned look, waiting for the authorities to provide them with some help. We could hear survivors describe how giant tidal waves come in from the sea to uproot houses and trees, and take away men and beasts. We were, however, only observing the destruction and suffering from our side of the barrier, until an incident occurred to me which drove home the lesson that my grandfather had probably intended me to have. The occasion was a distribution of food and clothing to victims of a drought. It was a particularly hot day and the waiting crowd was particularly large. At one point, it surged forward and submerged the official party. Soldiers let fly with their long whips to push people back. Somehow, I got separated from my uncle and the rest of the party. Several times, I just avoided being lashed by the soldiers. As the crowd retreated, I was drawn farther and farther into its midst. Everyone around me was in tatters. There was a strong smell of dust and poverty. I was terrified. I had never been out on my own before. So many times, I had been told stories of children being kidnapped and sold to the Chinese. But the people around me were friendly and my courage gradually came back. Some talked to me, asking where I came from. When I said that I was the governor's grandson, they did not seem to believe me. After a while, I started looking for my way back to the official party. The food distribution had begun. Everyone was trying to get there. I pushed those in front of me, others behind pushed me. My fear was gone. The misery, smell and dust ceased to affect me. I realized that I was not among strangers, but countrymen who were no different from the folks of my own village. I felt that I was part of the crowd and that feeling gave me strength and self-confidence. It was in a quite different frame of mind that, after a great deal of pushing and jostling, I managed to rejoin the party.

My most cherished memory of Thai Binh was summer at the seaside. We Vietnamese traditionally referred to the sea as *be dong*, or the eastern sea. All our coastline, except only for a small section in the south, duly faced eastwards. To me seashores abroad from which one could not watch the sun and the moon rise, seemed to be lacking in something essential. Our eastern sea brought hope in the morning, as sun rays emerging from it pierced the darkness of the sky. In the evening, the moon rising from under the waves was the bearer of dreams. Dong Chau, Thai Binh's seaside resort, did not have the scenic beauty of so many other beaches in Vietnam where the green mountains descended right next to the blue sea. It was situated near the mouth of the Thai Binh River, a major tributary of the Red River, on absolutely flat land. But it nestled in a forest of pines and the sand beach ran along the coast for miles. The long needles of the pines sang to the lightest breeze. They could also howl like an army of ghosts in the night when a strong wind blew. The resort had only a few bungalows serving as holiday homes for the town mandarins. The fishing village of Dong Chau was some distance away. The governor's bungalow, a wooden construction with a thatched roof, stood right on the beach. It had at the front a covered verandah in the shape of a half moon. In the afternoon, I used to sit there listening to the song of pines and the sound of waves, while the water lapped close to the steps of the bungalow. Some mornings, I woke up to find that all was absolutely silent. The pine trees were immobile. The sea had disappeared. From the verandah, all that I could see was a vast expanse of wet sand. Our group of vacationers had to walk for hundreds of meters, sometimes even more, for our early morning swim. When we finally reached the water and turned back to look, the pine forest and village of Dong Chau were reduced to some blurred lines. The Red River and its tributaries carried a great amount of alluvion to the sea. As a result of their action, land steadily extended out. Large areas of Thai Binh were gained from the sea in the course of the last centuries. From time to time the sea would come back, and newly established villages on the flat land would disappear. Then, the sea would withdraw, and the land would resume its slow expansion. When the monsoon season started, Dong Chau often came in the path of tropical cyclones. We could stay there only in the dry summer months. Some years after we had left Thai Binh, I learned that the area was struck by a violent cyclone. The fishing village was destroyed. Many lives were lost. The bungalows on the beach must have been taken away on that occasion too.

During his term of office, grandfather did much to make the province of Thai Binh better known to the rest of the north, or Tonkin, as it was then called by the French. He organized a highly successful Exposition of Thai Binh, to show the products of its agriculture and industries, as well as the various aspects of its culture and folklore. The Exposition was attended by the highest authorities in Tonkin. It lasted for quite a long time, perhaps several weeks, and attracted large crowds of visitors. The highlight of the closing day was a soccer match pitching the Racing Club of Hanoi, then the undisputed leader of the Tonkinese soccer championship, against a selection of the best players from the other clubs. The prize was the Exhibition Trophy. The French army band came from Hanoi to give more pomp and ceremony to the occasion. It performed before the start of the match, then stayed on the side lines to strike a tune each time a team scored a goal. The Racing Club of Hanoi had only Vietnamese players, although it was sponsored by the largest French department store in Tonkin. The selection opposing it was a mixed French-Vietnamese team, with the French in majority. The Racing was known for its slow start; it was often led in the first half, only to come back strongly in the second half. That afternoon, I was among the crowd, the biggest that the stadium in Thai Binh had ever seen. Naturally, we were all behind the Racing Club and its Vietnamese players. The two teams came onto the field, the Racing in its customary color of all black with only the shirt collar and sleeves lined in yellow. The selection was in white. The French players looked enormous next to their black Vietnamese opponents. As expected, the first half belonged to the selection, which got as many as three goals. Each time, the French army band launched into a vibrant victory tune. At the interval, our confidence in the Racing was rather shaken. It was famed for its staying power, but a three-goal deficit was difficult to make up. The match went into the second half and for a while, there was no sign of the Racing's recovery. Our apprehension was turning into panic when the men in black scored their first goal. Suddenly, the tension was released. There were wild scenes. The band had just finished playing when a second goal came. The floodgates were opened. Goals came so fast that the band did not have time to play a piece in between. Finally, the Racing won the Exposition Trophy with a score of 5–3, and that soccer match has remained the most memorable in my life.

A governor's term of office usually lasted for two years. Grandfather would have retired in 1939, but being a successful governor he was allowed to stay on for another year. He enjoyed working in Thai Binh and was proud to recall that, during his stay there, the "hundred families" under his care were able to go about their daily lives in conditions of peace and security. He would feel much happier had the natural elements been kinder to "his" province, but cyclones, floods, and at other times droughts, were unfortunately frequent occurrences in a low-lying region, many areas of which were newly claimed from the sea. When he left, in 1940, the constituent bodies of Thai Binh wanted to erect a statue or name a street after him. He wisely persuaded them not to. "I was just doing my duty as a public servant," he told them. "A quiet retirement is my reward." In the mandarinal tradition of our country, for a high official to retire in old age, peacefully and honorably, was indeed considered an achievement. Arbitrary rules, factional jealousies, and especially frequent political changes, made a smooth career out of reach for many. A mandarin may succeed in leaving a good name with the people he administered. He must, however, shun all forms of public fame or expression of gratitude, not only out of modesty but because these would be the very things to keep him away from a quiet retirement. "When gold and jade fill the hall, one cannot keep them safe. . . . When the work is done and one's name is becoming distinguished, to withdraw into obscurity is the way of Heaven," was the advice given by Lao Tseu, millenniums ago.

Grandfather retired in the summer of 1940. Momentous changes were looming ahead for the world, and our own country. The year before, France and England had declared war on Germany. In the following months, nothing much happened on the battlefield in what became known as the "funny war." But everyone knew that it would only be a matter of time before the Second World War started in earnest. Nearer to us, the Japanese army was poised on the Chinese border. An ally of Germany, Japan wanted the rice, rubber and coal of French Indochina. It was only waiting, so our people reckoned, for hostilities in Europe to flare up and France's hands to be tied there, to invade. Then in May 1940, Germany launched its blitzkrieg. France collapsed. Within a month, that mighty world power and the largest colonial empire after England, had capitulated. The news came as a profound shock to the Vietnamese, who were convinced that the Japanese troops would now walk over Indochina. French domination would end and a new phase of Vietnam's history would begin. Our people expected Prince Cuong De, a member of the royal family who had been living in exile in Japan, to return home and be given the reins of the country. But we were in for another shock. In September 1940, the Japanese forces crossed the border. Fighting broke out, followed however by an agreement which left in place the colonial regime, while allowing Japanese troops to enter Indochina. Other economic and trade agreements gave to Japan effective control over the resources of the Indochinese countries. Thus, the French managed to stay on as political master in Indochina, after having lost the war in their home country. Japan's conduct was a bitter disappointment to the Vietnamese. Here was an Asian power, which had so often proclaimed that Asia should belong to the Asians, ready to make a deal with the French colonial regime over the heads of fellow Asian people. When the Japanese attacked the French at the border, they were joined by a force of Vietnamese revolutionaries who seized the opportunity to fight for the liberation of their country. Left to themselves after the agreement, the revolutionaries were wiped out by the French.

By the winter of 1940, the excitement was over. The change for our people had only been for the worse. The French regime was still there. In addition, the country was under a Japanese occupation force. After he retired, grandfather went to live in Hanoi. His only brother and most of his children were settled there. Hanoi was close to his hometown and, of course, it was the ancient capital and "the land where culture and learning had flourished since a thousand years." He wanted to be there, to keep in touch with his friends and also with the changing political situation. At first, he rented a house in a well-established suburb on the western side of the city. The house was a few streets away from the Western Lake and the White Bamboo Lake, where Hanoi people liked to go for walks and boat trips on weekends and summer evenings. The narrow path separating the two lakes, bordered on both sides by weeping willows, was an idyllic meeting place for lovers. The sight of country girls paddling their small boats and gathering lotus flowers in the Western Lake had inspired many a painter and poet. When the situation had settled down with the agreement between the French and the Japanese, grandfather bought a plot in a newer part of the town, on the southern side. As his pseudonym indicated, he was very fond of lakes and ponds and he chose a piece of land close to a small lake. In the beginning of 1941, work started on a large three-storeyed house. By the month of June, the house was ready. But grandfather never moved in there. The new building was requisitioned by the Japanese army, and so he had to stay on at his rented place.

He led a quite active life. Since 1917, he was a member of the Khai Tri Tien Duc, an association of scholars of the old school. The association aimed, as its name said, "to develop the mind and advance the scholarly virtues." For many years, it had been working to stop the decline of classical studies and to encourage the young generations to preserve the scholarly language. In the middle 1930s, its Cultural Committee published a Vietnamese dictionary which was the first ever to cover both the scholarly and popular languages. Following retirement, grandfather joined in the activities of that committee. Its chairman was his close friend Hoang Huan Trung, my maternal grandfather. He took part in two projects that the committee was pursuing. The first one was to translate the Confucian Four Books into the popular language and to annotate them for the use of young students whose vehicle of learning was that language. The second was a more ambitious and longer term project: the revision and upgrading of the Vietnamese dictionary published a decade before. Like the French academicians, whose work L'Encyclopédie they took as their model, our scholars went painstakingly through all the words of the vocabulary, hoping to produce a definitive work on our language. Meetings were held weekly. Grandfather attended them regularly. The draft of the new dictionary was believed to be near completion when the communists came to power in 1945 and the association was forced to close down. In the war which broke out in the following year, the product of so many years of patient work by the scholars was unfortunately lost.

Grandfather was also occupied with the Temple of Literature, the place dedicated to the cult of Confucius. Under the French regime, official rites had ceased to be celebrated at the Temple. But worshipping ceremonies continued to be held by an association of scholars, to which grandfather belonged. He dutifully attended all the ceremonies, even after his health had deteriorated. He often expressed concern over the condition of the Temple. The shrines, lecture rooms and library—for the Temple was also the seat of the university—were being run down for lack of maintenance. He observed that even the doctor's names on the stelae, which were chiselled in stone, were becoming difficult to read, for the stelae had been left out in the open and at the mercy of the natural elements for many centuries. Village affairs took some of his time too. For many years, he had held the position of *Tien Chi*, or Head Dignitary of Kim Bai. The position was a purely formal one when he was a mandarin, but grandfather now presided over the important meetings of the village council. He often returned to Kim Bai, making the trip not anymore in his Peugeot car, which had been sold soon after he retired, but by rickshaw. It took him a whole day to get to Kim Bai, only thirty kilometers from Hanoi, for he always made a prolonged stop in Ha Dong where our family owned a small textile factory. There, he had lunch and his customary siesta, before starting on the second leg of the trip in the afternoon. Grandfather and the council sought to develop the Kim Bai market into a shopping center for the region. They had more shops built there and traders, particularly the Chinese, were encouraged to come and set up their businesses.

By the time grandfather retired, he had only a few close friends left. Their favorite pastime was to get together over a meal or a drink to talk about the war and political situation, or to challenge one another in poetry writing. If it was a meal, they would go to a Chinese restaurant. But mostly they would gather at the Jade Mountain Temple, on a small island in the Lake of the Returning Sword, in the very heart of the city. The lake's name dated back to the fifteenth century. At the beginning of that century, Vietnam fell under Chinese domination for the second time in its history. The first time, the Chinese stayed for one thousand years. The second time, the loss of independence was mercifully very much shorter. The Ming rule started in 1414. It ended in 1427. Le Loi hoisted the flag of resistance in 1418. Within ten years, he had liberated the country. Legend had it that at the start of the struggle, he received a divine sword and, with that sword by his side, he went from one victory to another. He established the Le dynasty, with its seat in the Eastern Capital, now Hanoi. One day, the king took a boat trip on the lake. Suddenly, he saw a giant tortoise swimming towards his boat. He pointed his sword towards it, but instead of swimming away, the tortoise jumped forward and took the sword in its mouth. Before disappearing under the water, the tortoise told the startled king: "You were given the sword to rid the country of Chinese intruders. Now that your mission has been accomplished, it must return to its owner."

Thus, the lake acquired the name of *Hoan Kiem,* or Returning Sword. For centuries, it had been the most celebrated landmark in the capital, with the Tortoise Tower in the middle and the Jade Mountain Temple on another island linked with the shore by a wooden arch bridge. Residents of the capital flocked to the temple to pray during the three days of the Tet festival. In the middle of last century, two of the most renowned writers of that time, Nguyen Van Sieu and Cao Ba Quat, used to come with their friends to the temple to discuss poetry. They started a tradition. The temple became a favorite meeting place with scholars, writers and poets. In the calm and contemplative atmosphere of the temple, separated by the lake from the busy life of the city, they listened to one another's writings and commented upon them. Over a cup of wine, they searched for inspiration and tried to emulate famous poets who had come there before them.

A gourmet who liked to eat out at restaurants, grandfather sometimes ate out, even without his friends. He would take my uncle and me with him. In Hanoi, I continued to stay with my grandparents, even though my parents were living in the same city, and their street was not far away. I only returned home for weekends. He always took us to the same restaurant,

in a predominantly Chinese street called Sail Street. Those who knew
Hanoi in the 1940s would remember the name Dong Hung Vien. Through
him, I was introduced to the rich cuisine of southern China. I liked it, but
after a few times there, I wanted a change. Once I made bold to suggest to
him to go somewhere else, a Vietnamese restaurant for instance. "What do
you want to eat there?" he asked. I replied that I had heard of places serving
very good *thang*, a noodle soup with chicken, pork meat pie, omelette,
peanut as well as other ingredients, and also *cha ca*, grilled fish fillets to eat
with rice noodle and green vegetables. *Thang* and *cha ca* were two northern
dishes which usually went together to make a complete meal. They were
eaten not with the usual *nuoc mam*, or fish sauce seasoning, but with a
shrimp paste which smelled even more strongly, to which was added a few
drops of *ca cuong*, or beetle condiment. "The best *thang* and *cha ca* are
cooked by your grandmother," grandfather told me. "Cantonese cuisine is
one of the richest in China. You do not know much of it yet." He was keeping good health and enjoying his retirement, until he fell ill in the winter
of 1942. It was not a sudden or acute illness. He started by losing some
sleep, then some more. His condition worsened. Doctors and practitioners
of oriental medicine could find no explanation for the illness. He did not
respond to drugs. For months, he hardly had any sleep and the family was
prepared for the worst. But as gradually as it came, the illness went away.
Sleep came back to him, little by little. "It was as if I had gone through the
full circle and the illness naturally came to an end," he said. He recovered,
but there was no more question of him continuing his work with the Cultural Committee. Doctors advised him to seek the healthier climate of the
countryside. Meanwhile, Allied forces had started rolling back the Japanese
in the Pacific. The war moved nearer to our country. Air raid sirens
sounded more frequently in Hanoi. He left the capital to return to Kim
Bai.

By then, a villa was being built in Ha Dong. When it was finished, he
moved in there, sharing his time between Ha Dong and the village. His days
were spent quietly "among his fields and gardens," as scholars liked to
describe their lives in retirement. He taught his children and grandchildren,
saw some friends, or otherwise just watched events go their course. The
Second World War was drawing to its climax. It was not long before it
would end and our country would be plunged into a tumultuous phase of
its history. At the Tet festival of 1945, he told the family gathered around
him: "Thanks to the merits acquired by our forebears, I am now going on
into my sixty-seventh year." Recalling his illness, he went on: "Who knows,
I might still be able to walk slowly to my seventieth." That, in our culture,
was the ultimate landmark in a person's life. "Since antiquity," a proverb
said, "few have been those who reached seventy." But grandfather would
only come close to it.

In that fateful year of 1945, events rushed upon our country. In March, the Japanese finally decided to do away with the French regime. In one night of fighting, everything was over. The eighty-year French rule had ended. There was general relief, but no rejoicing. Everyone knew that Japan was going to lose the war and that the new Vietnamese regime it had put into place would not last long. Moreover, the Japanese occupation forces had proved to be no better than the French colonialists and Japan had lost whatever special consideration it had with the Vietnamese as a fellow Asian nation. A few months later Japan capitulated, creating a political and military vacuum. Taking advantage of it, the communists seized power. They took most people by surprise. It was thought that the ones to come back to take power would be revolutionaries in exile in China. In our family, hopes were rekindled that grandfather's brother might be amongst them. A very confused period followed. Chinese troops came to disarm the Japanese. The nationalist party Kuomingtang took over several provinces. A French expeditionary corps was sent to reconquer Vietnam. The communists, who needed time to consolidate their position, accepted French terms. The French army returned to Hanoi. There was an uneasy period of coexistence with the French, while the communists sought to eliminate their Vietnamese opponents. Then in December 1946, war broke out.

After they came to power, the communists abolished the old village administration and replaced it with their own system of village committees. Grandfather lost his position as Head Dignitary. But he continued to enjoy the respect of villagers and for that reason was treated with consideration by the authorities. At village festivals, it was still he who received the best meat portion, and not the committee chairman. Our family's sympathies lay with the Kuomingtang. I remember that when news came that the Kuomingtang's stronghold of Yen Bay had fallen to the communists, grandfather was saddened. "If my brother was still alive, he would have been in the ranks of the Kuomingtang," he said. The last time he visited Hanoi was in September 1946, just three months before the war started. The situation was already very tense in the capital. His health had declined. The short trip by rickshaw from Ha Dong to Hanoi took much out of him. Yet, he insisted on coming to participate in an important ceremony at the Temple of Literature. The old scholars knew that the cult of Confucius was frowned upon by the communists, yet they defiantly went ahead with their celebrations.

Soon after the hostilities started, the villa in Ha Dong was burned down by the communists, in application of their scorched earth policy. Grandfather was distressed by the news, for not only the house but all his books and papers were lost. Three months later, his only surviving brother died. The funeral was barely completed when French troops launched their first operation against our region, and my father and elder brother were taken prisoners by them. Kim Bai was spared in the course of that operation, but the French came back after a few weeks. This time, they entered the village and pillaged our ancestral home. Grandfather had to be evacuated, firstly to a small village in the Lichee Field, then as French pressure increased, to the village of Sao on the other side of the Hat River. He fell ill there. Although Kim Bai was exposed to enemy attacks, the family decided to bring him home so that he could die in the land of his ancestors. We were then in the eighth month, the month of the Moon Festival. The weather had been dry. The early moon which shone brightly in a cloudless sky carried the promise of a beautiful festival. But of course, with the war and grandfather's condition, no one was thinking of celebrating it. All our family had assembled in the ancestral home. The white clothes of mourning had been made ready.

Grandfather died in the morning of the twelfth day. With him, academic success and high public offices returned to our family. His was a prosperous time, indeed the most prosperous that our family had known since the golden period of the doctors under the Le and Mac dynasties, some four hundred years ago. Under him, the family grew and developed into many branches. The old fear of an absence of male descendants had been left behind us. He built a new shrine to honor the Nguyen ancestors and devoted time to search into the family's history. Thanks to him, we now know more about our roots. As a head dignitary of Kim Bai, he contributed greatly to its welfare and development. Looking back over his life, there must be much for him to be thankful for, but I know that there was also regret. He died without having by his side his eldest son and grandson, the heads of the next two generations. Since they were taken prisoners by the French, not much news from them had reached home. With a war raging in the country, when would the family be reunited? Then, a great misfortune was that he had to die before his old mother and thus, could not fulfill his filial duties towards her. He was, moreover, her only surviving son. His friend Hoang Huan Trung referred to this, in a commemorative piece he wrote upon receiving the news of grandfather's death:

> He upheld his family's tradition of academic success, became the highest mandarin that his village Kim Bai has produced. An abundance of descendants, a life close to seventy years, what more can a man expect? Yet, there must be sadness that he was survived by his old mother. Perfection is frowned upon by our Creator. Now as before, it has been always like that.

As soon as the news of his death spread, villagers flocked back to Kim Bai from their places of refuge. In spite of the communist revolution, he remained their Head Dignitary. Old folks told me that when they saw black clouds suddenly gathering on a dry morning and bringing an unexpected shower, they knew what had happened. "When a distinguished man leaves this world, even the sky is saddened," they said. Villagers joined in the preparations for the funeral, including the communist members of the village committee. A notable absence was that of my great-uncle, the former mayor. He was arrested and taken away by the communists at the outset of the war, "as a precautionary measure," as they explained. Had he been in Kim Bai, Great-uncle Mayor would have assumed the responsibility for organizing the funeral. Now the communists were saying that everything should be done well, to show that the absence of the former mayor was of no consequence. Normally, the burial would take place only several days after a person had died. But in the special circumstances of war, grandfather was buried the following day. We were all worried that the French might attack when everyone was back in the village, or that their planes would spot the cortege. It would be a great misfortune if the funeral were to be disrupted. Fortunately, all went well. Nearly the whole village accompanied grandfather on his last journey from our ancestral home to the family tomb. In the next three days, our family could perform all the traditional rites for the newly departed. We felt relieved and immediately prepared to leave for our sanctuary on the other side of the Hat River. Early on the fourth day, the sound of approaching small arms fire woke us up. Quickly, we all fled ahead of the advancing French troops.

Five months after grandfather's death, my family went back to Hanoi where we were reunited with my father and brother. Grandmother and great-grandmother continued to stay in Kim Bai, in spite of the danger of French attacks. My father took steps to bring them to the capital once he succeeded in recovering possession of the house that my grandparents built there. But by then, the old lady was too weak to be moved. She died in 1949. The funeral over, grandmother was preparing to leave for Hanoi when the French attacked. This time, they occupied Kim Bai, making it one of their regional headquarters. Our ancestral home became a barrack. Grandmother had to flee deep into the highlands. Only in the following year could we get in touch with her and arrange for a guide to bring her to Hanoi. We knew that it would be an arduous and dangerous trip. No date of arrival could be given to us, for all depended on when the guide would think it safe to cross the fighting zone.

One late Sunday morning in August, I had just finished escorting my mother back home from her learning sessions of Buddhist canons and was on the balcony, just idly looking out onto the street, when I noticed an old lady. In the very hot weather, she was dressed in a brown tunic and black trousers. Her head was covered by a thick brown scarf. On the burning bitumen, she was going barefooted. She looked so much like an old folk from the countryside and so much smaller and frailer that at first I did not recognize her. But she turned towards the gate of our house and I knew that she was grandmother. She had arrived and she was safe! We were all overcome with joy and gratefulness.

The next four years were a leisurely and happy period in her life. As in the old tradition, she lived with her eldest son and was cared for in her old age by him. All her children and grandchildren in Hanoi were around her, in the same house. With the security situation worsening in the countryside, several of my great-uncle's children came to join her too. A bungalow had to be built in the garden to accommodate everybody. The atmosphere was like that of our ancestral home in years gone by. I still have a photograph of her taken at a Tet festival. She was sitting alone on a carved bed, ready to receive the New Year greetings of her family. Behind her were two silk hangings with large Chinese characters, in praise of two cardinal Confucian virtues: loyalty in a subject and filial piety in a son. The photograph evokes for me images of peaceful and orderly times, when it was good to live and people did not have to fear war, revolution or foreign domination. Grandmother liked to tell me stories of those long gone times, when I was a child. "Doors had no need for locks or bolts . . . no one picked up money found in the street . . . cattle stayed out in the fields at night. . . ," she said. As she told me the stories, her constant preoccupation with work seemed to have left her. Her expression became composed and relaxed and for a while, she was just sitting there, instead of rushing about doing things. That leisurely period in Hanoi was the last in grandmother's life. In 1954, our country was partitioned and the north came under the communists. Our extended family was partitioned too. Of grandmother's eight children, five went to live in the south, while three remained in the north. My father opted for the free regime of South Vietnam. Grandmother would have gone with him, for her place was with the eldest son. But she decided to stay in Hanoi. Her children had all had families of their own, except one, the youngest son who was of the same age as I. Her duty was to be with him, she told my father. He stayed as long as he could with her, and only left Hanoi on the last day, when the city was already being handed over to the communists.

Once in full possesssion of the north, the communists ruthlessly imposed their totalitarian regime. As part of their land reform program, they ordered all villages to stage public trials in which "rich landlords" were tried for their "bourgeois crimes." Grandmother was a victim of such a staged trial. All the land owned by my grandparents were confiscated. The result of my grandfather's lifetime work, they amounted to some thirty acres of rice fields in Kim Bai and the two neighboring villages of Kim Lam and Cat Dong. Our ancestral home was taken over by the communist authorities. Grandmother could not return to live in Kim Bai and look after her husband's grave. In Hanoi, she was given the use of one single room in her own house. At over seventy years of age, she had to work to receive a ration card. In 1956, our family got to know an Indian official in the International Control Commission, the organization in charge of supervising the cease-fire in Vietnam. That man made frequent trips between Saigon and Hanoi. He agreed to go to her house in Hanoi to try and meet her. Posing as a tourist who happened to pass by, he went into the house and saw that she was looking after a group of children in a creche. He could not communicate with her in English and, in any case, was concerned that his visit could cause her problems with the communist police. So, without speaking a word, he just took out his camera. She probably guessed who sent him and let him take a photo of her. Thus, he could bring back to us a rather fuzzy diapositive. Grandmother was sitting on a chair, dressed in a faded brown tunic. She looked weak and tired, with a sad smile on her face. That was the last memento we have of her.

How different life would have been for her, had she accepted to accompany my parents to the south. There, although they had to work hard to resettle, they would have been able to provide for her. She would not have had to toil in her old age. Most of all, she would not have had to suffer the pain and humiliation meted out by an inhuman Marxist regime, intent on sowing hatred among the people and forcing upon them their model of class struggle. I have often thought that grandmother may have had a premonition of what was going to happen to her, ever since those summers that we children spent with her in Kim Bai before the war and revolution. She made us do the work of other villagers, and the proverb that she taught us is still inscribed in my mind:

> It is not difficult,
> To learn the ways of high living.
> But how to live a poor and humble life,
> That is indeed difficult to learn.

"Why should one learn how to live such a life?" I wanted to ask her, but did not. The last photograph of her brought me the answer to that question. I took some comfort in the proverb, for I knew that she was well prepared to meet with the challenge of adversity. She did not fear poverty and never shunned hard work. In the following years, news about her was scarce. We were only told that she was keeping in good health. Then, the war intensified and the news stopped. She died in the summer of 1965. Later on we learned that, because of the American bombings, she was evacuated from Hanoi. She went to stay with a son of her late sister in Nuon, a village close to her own village of Phu Dong in Bac Ninh. She died there. Her wish would have been, I am sure, to be buried next to her husband, in the fields of Kim Bai. But she was laid to rest in Nuon. Her grave, I am told, was built on high ground and the family in Hanoi could make frequent visits, since the place was not far from the capital. I have some recollections of Nuon, as grandmother sometimes took me there when I was a child. The small house in which her sister lived opened into a vast orchard full of orange trees. When these were in bloom, their sweet fragrance pervaded the air. Grandmother was fond of that place. "Nuon is like my own village," she told me, adding that "Our Heavenly Prince of Phu Dong fought the An aggressors all over here and so all this region is part of his legend." Thus, although she could not be returned to Kim Bai, I am glad that grandmother now rests in a place that she loved, near the sacred land of the Heavenly Prince of Phu Dong.

Her life was all work and diligence. I can still see her short and stocky figure constantly on the move in our ancestral home. The wife of a mandarin, she led a simple and laborious existence, going to the market, busily working from dawn to dusk, doing every chore just like any other villager. Her relationship with the people of Kim Bai was especially close and easy going, so it must have been a bitter experience for her, as well as for those villagers who had to "denounce" her at the public trial, for "crimes" that she never committed. In the family, grandmother was a bridge between the generations. She served her mother-in-law in the manner of old—alone among her generation she was able to carry out all filial obligations towards great-grandmother—while staying close to the younger members and sharing their hopes and aspirations. In a traditional Confucian family like ours, each person had a clearly defined position. One must defer to one's elders, but for his part, an elder also had the obligation to give due consideration to the opinion of those below his rank. If need be, he should be prepared to give way to them. The precept said: "Respect your elders, give way to your juniors." As was their wont, our male elders often tended to forget, or to neglect, the second part of the equation. But grandmother was there to see to it that a certain balance was restored and that the wishes of the young were heard. Her kind and loving nature helped temper the rigidity of the Confucian system and maintain in the family an atmosphere of warmth and informality.

Epilogue: Leaving Kim Bai

The war broke out in December 1946. For the first few months, things were not too bad in Kim Bai. We only heard the distant sound of artillery fire. French planes sometimes swooped down to strafe on villages not far away, but ours remained untouched. Refugees from Hanoi and Ha Dong came in great numbers. In our own compound, all the houses were full of people. Even the transversal house was used as a sleeping place, although it had walls only on three sides and we were in the middle of winter. Young people of my age group slept there. We had rather trying nights when the icy northern wind blew. For refugees as well as villagers, the hostilities still seemed somewhat unreal. No one thought that they would last long. Negotiations, it was rumored, were being pursued with the French on a cease-fire. Meanwhile at the market of Kim Bai, tents and huts sprouted on both sides of the highway. Almost overnight, the place became a bazaar where one could buy almost anything: clothes, textiles, Western medicine, even books. I found some novels and collections of poems of the 1930s that, before the evacuation, I could not obtain in any of Hanoi's bookshops. There were several bicycle repair shops, the bicycle being the most convenient and effective means of transport during the war. Eating places were numerous. Some well-known noodle shops in Hanoi had reappeared there. In spite of the hostilities, they still served an excellent *pho*, our national dish of beef noodle soup. People made the trip to Kim Bai for the sole objective of having a bowl of their favorite *pho*. Activity during the day was subdued because of the risk of strafing by enemy planes. But once darkness fell, an extraordinary animation took over the market. I bumped into several school friends. When we said good-bye in Hanoi, we never thought that soon we would meet again over a bowl of *pho* in Kim Bai, exchanging the latest rumors about the war. "You are lucky to take refuge in this bustling place," they told me, "and not in some forsaken little village." My grandfather and the former village council sought to develop Kim Bai into a marketing center. Events proved them right. Kim Bai had that capacity and it quickly became a bustling bazaar in response to the influx of refugees into our region.

The Tet festival in the beginning of 1947 was still celebrated, more or less normally. People still gambled. We youngsters served as guards at the village gates and spent the nights there playing cards. The noodle shops were full, although one wondered about their delicious broth; how did they manage to get ox bones to cook it? Rumor had it that it was not ox bones but field rats which, by the way, were huge and provided an excellent meat. But that Tet was a watershed. As soon as it was over, the war descended on us. Having completed their occupation of Hanoi, the French attacked and took over the town of Ha Dong. In addition to artillery fire, we could hear from Kim Bai the distinct sound of small arms fire. In the quiet of the night, it sounded as if it were coming from the next village. Refugees who came to our village were on their way again, fleeing further away towards the south or the western foothills. One by one, the shops at the market folded up. In the village, people buried their brass urns, candle holders and incense burners, as well as their china and copper cooking pots, everything that could be buried. One day, orders were issued by the communists that dogs had to be disposed of, for their barking would reveal the presence of guerrillas operating at night to the enemy. In a space of two weeks, all dogs were killed. It would be a long time before villagers would have as much meat to eat as during those two weeks. For our family too, the new year brought with it bad tidings. These began with grandfather's villa in Ha Dong being burned down. Then, my father came under threat of arrest. On the surface, relations between him and the communist authorities were correct. They asked him to preside over this and that committee, but that was a way for them to keep an eye on him. His movements were under strict surveillance. He was not allowed to go to other villages, even on official business of his committee, without being accompanied by two or three communist cadres. Soon, he heard that orders for his arrest had been sent out. Luckily, the communist hold on the administrative apparatus was still loose at the time. Friendly officials succeeded in sending the orders to the wrong village. A few months after the Tet, my great-uncle died. French troops launched an operation against our region and my father was captured by them.

Sorties by French troops had moved closer and closer to Kim Bai. Villagers had had a few false alarms, but that morning they knew that it was going to be the real thing. Not only was there the sound of gunfire, they could also hear the creaky noise of tank tracks. People from upper areas ran past, telling us that French tanks were destroying the obstacles erected on the highway and the dike, about five kilometers from our village. Hurriedly, we grabbed our bags and fled across the dike to the Lichee Field. There, the trees offered good cover and the absence of the motorable roads would, we hoped, deter the French from venturing in. My father, as president of the evacuation committee, stayed back to make sure that all villagers were warned to leave. My elder brother, uncle and some other committee members stayed with him. When it was their turn to leave, it was too late. The French had broken through the obstacles and their armored trucks were racing towards Kim Bai, both on the highway and the dike, taking our village in a pincer movement. My father's group first tried to cross the dike; they could not. They turned back and fled in the direction of the highway. There, they were caught. Strangely enough, the French never went into the village on that operation, so my father and his group would have been safe by just staying back inside Kim Bai's bamboo enclosure. In that cold day of spring, my uncle—the one of my age—was wearing an old heavy coat which years ago my father had used when going duck shooting. By a piece of bad luck, inside a pocket was an old cartridge shell. On searching him and finding the shell, the French took him for a guerrilla fighter. Immediately, they ordered him to be shot. My father, who studied in France in his youth, pleaded with the French lieutenant for his brother's life. He asked him to look closely at the shell; if it was fired recently there must be the smell of gunpowder. The officer checked and agreed that it was fired long ago. That detachment of troops were men from metropolitan France, who did not behave as harshly towards the population as did the colonial troops. My uncle's life was saved. But all in the group were told to follow the troops and carry their ammunition. My father asked whether my uncle could be allowed to go home, as my grandparents were old and needed help. Again the good lieutenant agreed and my uncle was released. Later on, my father told me that in that evening, he and my brother were put in a truck and driven to Hanoi. On the way, he suddenly remembered having in his pocket a paper mentioning that he was president of Kim Bai's evacuation committee. If the French found out, he would be taken as a communist. Quietly, he rolled it into a ball and slipped it into his mouth. All went well until a French soldier in the truck asked what he was chewing. Mumbling a reply, he swallowed.

A month or so after that operation, the French came back. This time, they were colonial troops and went into Kim Bai, pillaging it. Our ancestral home was ransacked. From then on, Kim Bai was at their mercy. They returned at intervals to plunder and terrorize. During the day, the village was abandoned. The villagers took refuge in the nearby Lichee Field. Those who had to still went out to work in the fields, ready however to flee at any moment. Only at night would some people get back to the village to look after their houses. A few months before, Kim Bai had been a hive of activity. Now the people, their buffaloes, cows, pigs and domestic fowl were all gone. There were afternoons in summer when I walked into the village. The sun was shining and everything was looking bright. Yet, I found all paths deserted, all houses empty. No barking dog greeted my passage. The impression was a scary one; it was as if something had happened to take away all living things and only an empty shell of a village was left.

Grandfather was evacuated to the neighboring village of Sao, on the other side of the Hat River. The family followed him. During the last months of his life, we remained gathered around him. But after he died, we began to disperse. It had become too dangerous to stay in our region. "I will remain in Kim Bai to look after his grave and light incense on it," grandmother said. "But all of you will have to go, for your security and to build your lives." Some of my uncles and aunts left for the western highlands, farther away from the front line. My family returned to Sao, to wait for news from my father. Daily, it came under increased surveillance from the communist authorities. We knew that every night spies were posted outside the cottage where we lived to try and overhear any secret conversation that we may have, and which would show that we were in contact with my father in Hanoi. My trips to the far markets to buy latinia leaves for making conical hats were suspect. More and more, I became aware of being followed. One day, just going back to my village from Sao, I crossed an open field and took a fancy on following a zigzag way on the edges of rice fields instead of a more direct route. The next day, a friendly source told me that the spy who was tailing me reported that I was trying to shake him off. It was also alleged that every morning I was making signals to French planes, when in fact I was doing my daily calisthenics at the back garden. The signs were unmistakable. They were preparing to arrest me. I was then seventeen.

Luckily, we finally heard from my father. The situation in Hanoi had settled and he told us to join him there. The problem was to find a guide whom we could trust, and not to arouse the suspicion of the communists while we made preparations to leave. To them, my mother was bringing her children back to her own village, since Kim Bai was not safe anymore. My great-uncle, the former mayor, recently released by the communists, contacted an eastern medicine man who had made several trips to Ha Dong, across the zone of fighting. A fellow villager and member of the old scholar class, he was totally reliable. He would take us with him on his next trip. At Ha Dong, we would be met by my brother. All was arranged. We were only to wait for a signal from him.

The guide's signal came as the lunar year was drawing to a close. We took leave of our hosts in Sao and returned to Kim Bai. With our belongings now reduced to a bag for each person, we crossed the Hat River for the last time. It was a few days before the Tet festival. The mighty river at monsoon time was a peaceful stream running at the edge of a white sand beach. We all forded it, including the youngest ones, for water only came up to our knees. I felt sad to leave the river and its adjoining Lichee Field. As I walked away, images came flooding to my mind. The Field covered in mist, with shapes and colors indistinct, like the delicate shadings of an oil painting. A fine layer of steam rising above the water, warm from the sunshine of the day before, as a cold drizzle came down in the early morning. Autumn was a most beautiful season, perhaps never more so than in evenings when the moon was full and had risen high in the sky. Then the white sand of the beach acquired an unreal brightness and the dark shadows cast by trees were so sharply defined that they looked like being printed over. I was very fond of poetry and was reading all that I could lay my hands on of the "new school" of poets who made their marks in the thirties and forties. From the lyricism of Tan Da and The Lu to the romantism of Xuan Dieu and Huy Can, and the mysticism of Han Mac Tu, that was a flourishing period of Vietnamese poetry. Xuan Dieu, in particular, was the poet of my youth and many of his poems were copied in my schoolboy note book.

> A virginal mist floated in the air trying to follow the moon...
> The sound of a two-stringed violin increased my loneliness,
> It brought no tears, but a feeling of passing sadness.

These verses by Xuan Dieu, every time that I read them, brought back to my memory the image of the Hat River under the autumn moon, so calm and peaceful as to make one forget about war and its misery. I could hear the faint sound of a flute coming from somewhere around the bend of the river, smell the fragrance of ripening paddy, of corn, sugar cane, all the fruit in the Field and feel an inexplicable sadness before the magic beauty of an autumn night. Even as war spread over our native region, that area of the Hat River remained untouched. French troops moved along the dike only a few hundreds meters away, but they never ventured into the Field, still less to the other side of the river. Therefore, once in sight of the Hat, fleeing refugees could slow down their steps. A safe zone had been reached. For them, the river became a symbol of security.

The Tet of 1948 was an austere affair as it followed my grandfather's death and because the war front was so near our village. Several family members had already left our region. Those who remained gathered in the ancestral home for the Tet and to say good-bye to us. We all knew this might be the last get-together for a very long time. In the new year the family would be further dispersed. Some people would, like us, try to reach Hanoi. Others planned to remain in the communist zone and to seek refuge farther into the foothills. As the war dragged on, the future appeared totally uncertain. It was a strange festival. No special food was prepared as offerings to the ancestor's altar except for a few traditional *chung* cakes. Among fellow villagers, no visits were received or made to exchange the season's greetings. There was no card playing and no gambling. Of course, firecrackers were not allowed in the war situation. Even the rite of sweeping the ancestors' graves was observed by few because of the risk of going out into the open fields and being spotted by French planes.

The guide had sent word that we would be leaving very soon after the festival. I thought that he would take advantage of the lull in the fighting which occurred around the Tet. But days went by without news from him. Already, it was the tenth of the month. Communist cadres came to enquire as to when our party was going to leave for my mother's village. Had they found out about our plan to escape? My mother was terrified at the thought that they may arrest me before the family could leave. Indeed, the longer the delay the greater the risk that we might run into a hitch. If the French launched an operation in our area, we would be dispersed and everything must be reorganized before we could try again. That evening however, my great-uncle came to tell us that the date was fixed for the thirteenth. "Everything was fine," he assured us. "The communists knew nothing of our plan." From our village to the town of Ha Dong, the distance was only fifteen kilometers. But the front line had to be crossed and to do so, our party would have to avoid the open fields as much as possible. We would have to skirt villages and take a roundabout route. That way, the guide expected that by leaving at dawn we would be in Ha Dong by mid-afternoon. Once in Ha Dong we would be safe and the next day could go on to Hanoi.

On the eve of our departure, my uncle took leave from his school to come and stay the day with us in Kim Bai. Until then, I had kept the two copies of our family chronicle written in the Chinese script, one by my grandfather and the other by Licentiate Duong. Now that I was leaving, we decided that he was to take one copy to his school, which was located in a still safe area held by the communists, and I was to bring the other copy to Hanoi. I wished to keep grandfather's calligraphy. I believed that my uncle did so too, but before I could say anything, he told me that grandfather's copy should be in my keeping. "You were his student," he gave as a reason, referring to the fact that for several years I had learned Chinese script and the classics from my grandfather.

That afternoon we presented offerings to our ancestors. We prayed for their blessings and their protection to make my family's journey a safe one. All cult instruments in metal and porcelain, including the big gong and all the ceremonial swords, had been buried in the hope that they would be spared by the hostilities. The big pair of elephant tusks in front of the altar had likewise gone underground. The altar room looked bare and already had an abandoned appearance.

Dinner was taken early to allow my uncle to go back to his school. All day, while busy sorting things and packing up for the trip, we did not get around to asking the question that was uppermost in our minds. When were we to meet again? My parents had made their decision; my family was going to Hanoi. What about him? Was he going to stay in the communist zone, or join us one day? It was only as I saw him off at the village gate, when the two of us were alone, that we finally touched on that subject. He said that as long as my grandmother and great-grandmother remained in

Kim Bai, he would stay close to them. After a pause, he added: "The French have committed many atrocities. In time I may join the army to fight them." An expression of anger passed through his eyes. Indeed, French soldiery had descended several times on our village and sacked our ancestral home. Members of our family had suffered under their hands. I watched his bicycle zigzag down the highway, going round numerous trenches dug to prevent its use by French motorized troops, until he disappeared behind the next village. We have not met since.

After saying good-bye to my uncle, I proceeded to the family tomb to pay a last visit to grandfather's grave. It had been four months since he died. The soil looked still new, although grass had grown evenly over the grave. For a long time I sat there. Since he died, I had the impression of being nearer to him and understanding him better. If he were still here to teach me the classics, as in those stable and peaceful summers of yesteryears, there would have been so many questions that I could have asked, so many matters that I could have raised with him. Winter that year was cold and miserable. Grey clouds filled the sky. In the fields all around the tomb, the barren land looked poor and forsaken. My mind turned to harvest times of not so long ago, when the countryside turned into a golden sea of ripening paddy, swinging like waves in the wind, and the air was filled with the sweet scent of the new crop. I remembered the festival-like atmosphere in the fields after the monsoon had broken out, with crowds of villagers busily working the soil to prepare for a new season.

Across the highway, the market of Kim Bai was reduced to a few standing walls. All the roofs had been pulled down. There were no more market meets. The stalls that had sprouted up a year ago had disappeared. As evening approached, I could see one or two lamps lit up. Those few shops that remained open, what could they still sell and to whom? Leaving the tomb, I went along the highway and turned into the brick path leading to the village gate. How many times had I walked on that path, dragging my wooden clogs to make a deafening noise. But now I silently made my way along the tall and proud bamboo enclosure, under the Si gate with its familiar assembly of ghosts, past cottages, ponds and gardens, before coming to the long and straight brick wall of our family compound. As I walked, I tried to etch into my memory all the familiar sights. The new house in our compound had been partially destroyed by order of the authorities while all the other houses were more or less empty not only of occupants but also of furniture. The air of animation and prosperity in grandfather's time had vanished, to be replaced instead by sadness and desolation. Many family members had gone from the ancestral home. Tomorrow was going to be my family's turn. After tomorrow, only two old women would remain in the large compound.

Instead of turning into our gate, I kept on following the narrow path that ran between the Communal Hall and the Nguyen Ancestral Shrine. It led to the old market and from there to the dike. I wanted to climb on its top to once more look towards the beloved Lichee Field and the purple mountains in the horizon where, so we were told, our Viet race had originated. But winter evening spread its veil quickly. All of a sudden, it was dark and I had to trace my steps back to go home.

At dawn tomorrow we would depart. How to avoid communist patrols who were trying to stop people from getting to Ha Dong? How to reach the no man's land of the front line early enough so that French troops had not started their daily operations? And yet not too early, because we could be taken for communist troops and fired upon? How to make the trip a successful one, so that my family could be reunited. My head was full of problems and of plans to deal with contingencies.

That night may be the last spent on the soil of my forebears. But in the optimism of my youth, I refused to think about it. I was confident of going back one day, like my ancestors four centuries ago. Others in the family must have had the same thoughts, but as is always the case with us, we talked about other things and not about what was the innermost of our feelings. When would we see our native place again? When would we be reunited with grandmother? Those who were leaving and those who were staying, no one raised these subjects and so the thoughts of each of us remained silent and secret like prayers. It was the last night and yet, I do not recall feeling the pains of separation, only a feverish expectation to meet the challenge ahead. That night, I wished that dawn would soon break so that we could finally set out on our journey.

Chronological Table

Important dates in Vietnamese history with corresponding generations of the Nguyen family in italics.

Legendary Hong Bang dynasty (2879–258 B.C.). Thuc dynasty (257–207 B.C.). Trieu dynasty (207–111 B.C.). Millennium of Chinese domination (111 B.C.–A.D. 939). Queen Trung (A.D. 40–43). Independence wrested from the Chinese (939). Ngo dynasty (939–965). Dinh dynasty (968–980). Earlier Le dynasty (980–1009) *our ancestors then had the name of Le (?); our village was already called Kim Bai.* Ly dynasty (1010–1225). Tran dynasty (1225–1400) Mongol invasions defeated. Ho dynasty (1400–1407). Later Tran dynasty (1407–1413). Ming domination (1414–1427). Liberation and Le dynasty (1428–1527). Great King Le Thanh Ton (1460–1497). Mac dynasty (1527–1592) *first generation—Nguyen Tue, Count of Hung Giao, minister under the Mac; wife not known.* Country divided between the Northern and Southern courts *second generation— Nguyen Uyen, academician and Mac envoy; second wife, the Phung lady / third generation—Nguyen Hoang, rallied to the Le, deputy minister; wife, Trinh Khiet.* Restored Le dynasty (1592–1788). Rule of the Trinh overlords *fourth generation—Phuc Thien, opposed the Trinh, banished (?); wife, My Hanh.* Country divided between the Trinh and the Nguyen *fifth and sixth generations—Recluse scholars and Zen followers.* Expansion towards the south completed *seventh, eighth and ninth generations—village teachers, impoverished scholars.* Tay Son dynasty (1788–1802) Victory over the Chinese. Nguyen dynasty (1802–1945) Reunification of the country *tenth generation—Nguyen Quang So, the businessman; wife, Tu Thuan / eleventh generation—Nguyen Dinh Dat, the Hermit of the Mountain of the Twins; wife, Chu Thi Uyen.* French conquest (1858–1883). French rule (1883–1945) *twelfth generation—Nguyen Ba Tiep, the governor; wife, Dang Thi Duyet.* Communist revolution 1945. First Indochina war started 1946.

Bibliography

Vietnamese books

Dai Viet Register of High Graduates. Compiled by Nguyen Hoan and others at the end of the eighteenth century.

Duong Quang Ham. *History of Vietnamese Literature*. Hanoi, 1941.

Essays Written in Rainy Days. Pham Dinh Ho born in 1768.

History of Dai Viet. Compiled in the fifteenth century by Ngo Si Lien. Added to in the seventeenth century by later historians.

Le Quy Don (1726–1784). *A General History of Dai Viet*.

Mirror of Vietnam's History. Compiled under the Nguyen dynasty (1844).

Nguyen Hien Le. *Righteous School of the Eastern Capital*. Saigon, 1956.

Pham the Ngu. *A History of Vietnamese Literature*. Saigon, 1963.

Pham Van Son. *A New Vietnamese History*. Saigon, 1961.

Phan Ke Binh. *Vietnamese Customs*. Hanoi, 1913–14.

Phan Khoang. *History of Vietnam Under the French Domination 1884–1945*. Saigon, 1961.

The Revolutionary Life of Cuong De. Saigon, 1957.

Song Bang Be Lang Ngan. *A History of Missions to China*. Hanoi, 1943.

Southern Sky Register of High Graduates. Compiled by Phan Huy On in the second part of the eighteenth century.

Ta Chi Dai Truong. *History of Civil Wars*. Saigon, 1973.

Toan Anh. *Festivals*. Saigon, 1969–74.

Tran Trong Kim. *Confucianism*. Hanoi, 1932–33.

Tran Trong Kim. *Vietnamese History*. Hanoi, 1925.

French books

Buis, G. and C. Daney. *Quand les Français Découvraient L'Indochine*. Paris, 1981.

Maybon, C.B. *Histoire Moderne du Pays d'Annam*. Paris, 1919.

Taboulet, G. *La Geste Française en Indochine*. Paris, 1955–56.

Index